Advances in First Responder Mental Health

Research, Training, and Practice

Volume 1

Series Editors

Vincent Van Hasselt, Nova Southeastern University, Fort Lauderdale, FL, USA

Michael L Bourke, Foundation for First Responder Wellness and Resiliency, Fairfax, VA, USA

This series provides a forum for cutting edge mental health research, training, and clinical/practitioner strategies involving first responders, with implications for researchers, training professionals, and operational personnel. The intent is to overcome the knowledge "silos" that have existed within these arenas. Each volume will focus on intra- and inter-disciplinary sharing of effective policies and procedures, innovative training programs or curricula, evidence-based best practices, and case reviews.

The scope of the series includes all traditional first responders (e.g., police officers, firefighters, paramedics) as well as non-traditional frontline workers (e.g., correctional workers, emergency room professionals, ICU medical personnel, dispatchers). *Advances in First Responder Mental Health: Research, Training, and Practice* is aimed at international researchers and practitioners working in criminology, criminal justice, and psychology as well as law enforcement, fire services, emergency and intensive care medicine, corrections, crime scene investigation, criminal intelligence, investigative analysis, and emergency communications.

Vincent B. Van Hasselt · Michael L. Bourke
Editors

Advances in First Responder Mental Health

Volume 1

Springer

Editors
Vincent B. Van Hasselt
College of Psychology
Nova Southeastern University
Davie, FL, USA

Michael L. Bourke
Foundation for First Responder Wellness and Resiliency
Fairfax, VA, USA

ISSN 3120-5755 ISSN 3120-5763 (electronic)
Advances in First Responder Mental Health
ISBN 978-3-032-27977-4 ISBN 978-3-032-27978-1 (eBook)
https://doi.org/10.1007/978-3-032-27978-1

This Springer imprint is published by the registered company Springer Nature Switzerland AG
The registered company address is: Gewerbestrasse 11, 6330 Cham, Switzerland

Dedicated to Mary Margaret Reilly and the Memory of
Betty Hope Carlson

Preface

The mental health challenges of first responders have been the focus of burgeoning attention from clinicians and researchers over the past few decades. This heightened interest is due, in part, to the growing realization that these individuals are at risk for psychological problems at significantly higher levels than their civilian counterparts. Indeed, anxiety, depression, substance use, and post-traumatic stress disorder in police and firefighters are two to three times greater than national norms. And while completed suicide rates are unclear (due to inconsistent data collection), suicide risk is elevated. Further, research indicates that high levels of stress and mental health disorders extend to other first responder groups as well, including firefighters, correctional officers, emergency communication operators, and crime scene investigators. A common etiologic factor, of course, is continuous trauma exposure; and while the nature of the traumatic events varies across professions, they occur at hazardous levels for all of them.

The majority of books on the topic of mental health in first responders have typically covered a specific aspect of work in this area, such as research or clinical practice/case illustrations. The purpose of this book is to offer broader coverage of relevant topics in both research and clinical work with first responders by subject matter experts in their respective areas. Also incorporated here is a section on training programs relevant to first responders' responses to individuals characterized by mental health and/or physical problems (e.g., dementia, deafness, serious mental illness); strategies and issues related to their own well-being (peer support training, suicide risk assessment) are addressed as well.

Part I, Mental Health Research, contains recent investigations that have been carried out with a variety of first responders. Channer and her associates examine a range of occupational and organization stressors in firefighters from a holistic perspective using the A.M.E.S. (Assemble, Measure, Execute and Systematic Use) organizational health assessment. Their findings underscore the importance of focusing intervention programs on promoting help-seeking behaviors, social support, sleep health, physical fitness, and reducing substance use. Hodges et al., acknowledging the low utilization rates of Employee Assistance Programs (EAPs), consider the role of trust in first responders' awareness, attitudes, and utilization of these programs. Their analysis of transcripts of focus group interviews with police and firefighters yields recommendations for building trust and rapport and improving EAPs for public safety personnel. LaRock and associates present results of the National Wellness Survey for Public Safety Personnel for Crime Scene Investigators. Their findings reveal high levels of both occupational and individual stressors, as well as elevated levels of anxiety, depression, and PTSD symptoms. Implications for prevention and intervention with this historically underserved population are discussed.

Virtual Reality (VR) treatment has, in the past decade, become major areas for clinicians and investigators. Beidel and her colleagues review VR technology and applications to improve first responder mental health. They also critically review current strategies and issues in VR research and treatment and present some of their own work, which is at the forefront of this rapidly evolving field. The impact of first responder stress and trauma exposure has been well documented over the past several years. However, assessment measures specifically designed for these populations are still rare. In response to this need, Schuhmann and her colleagues describe the development and application of the Law Enforcement Officer Stress Survey (LEOSS), a 25-item measure employed to evaluate the unique stressors encountered by police officers. Their investigation examined parametric properties (factor structure, reliability, validity) of the LEOSS, and established cut-off scores to improve the clinical utility of the instrument. Recommendations for the interpretation of scores are also provided.

In Part II, First Responder Training, Livshitz and Martinez cover the rapidly emerging strategy of partnering police officers with mental health professionals to more effectively and humanely respond to persons with a severe mental illness or who are in a mental health crisis. They review these Co-Responder models and describe curricula that have been successfully employed by police departments nationwide. Another program that has been the focus of increased research and application to individuals with a serious mental illness is Crisis Intervention Team (CIT) training. Miller-Anguay and her colleagues describe the CIT model and offer illustrations of its applications. They also present the limited research that is available on this program and its variations.

The next two chapters also deal with the law enforcement response to special populations. Crocker et al. describe their crisis intervention program for law enforcement to assist them in their response to Alzheimer's disease emergencies. Their chapter provides an understanding of why such calls for service are occurring more frequently, as well as how to effectively recognize and react to crises involving individuals with Alzheimer's disease and related dementias. Feldman and his associates acknowledge the differences in culture and communication between police officers and Deaf subjects, and their impact on interactions. They underscore that Deaf individuals are likely to be at a significant disadvantage in law enforcement encounters. Their chapter provides useful training and specific suggestions for law enforcement officers and other first responders in these situations. Bourke et al. describe the Interdiction for the Protection of Children (IPC) program in Indian Country. The goal of IPC is to train law enforcement professionals to recognize indicators that a child might be a victim, at risk of victimization, or missing; as well as identify those who pose a high-risk threat to minors. This highly effective program has been provided in 32 states and territories of the U.S. and several other countries.

The stressors and challenges encountered by correctional officers are reflected by their elevated rates of anxiety, depression, substance abuse, PTSD, and physical health problems. In response to the need for prevention directed toward this population, Rivera-Hartley and her colleagues describe the Peers As Law Enforcement Support program for Correctional personnel (PALS-C). PALS-C teaches peer support volunteers (fellow officers) to: (1) recognize signs and symptoms of stress and related mental health problems (e.g., anxiety, depression), and (2) mitigate risks in their fellow officers by offering support and referring to appropriate resources when necessary.

Noting the frequency with which police officers encounter individuals in suicidal crisis, Taylor et al. underscore the need for training in suicide-risk assessment and intervention. They provide an overview of research in this area as well as considerations in law enforcement encounters with certain high-risk populations. Best practices for assessment, training, and intervention are provided. This part wraps up with Powell's presentation of a mental health training program developed specifically for police officers, but of value to other first responders as well. Included is a highly useful "Primer" of major mental health disorders encountered in the field as well as de-escalation and communication strategies. Case illustrations are included from Powell's many years of experience as a road patrol officer, hostage negotiator, and police academy instructor.

Part IV is titled Clinical Practice and begins with a chapter by Morris and Tumilty that examines trends observed among public safety candidates pre- and post-pandemic. This includes observations by mental health professionals, public safety support/administrative staff, and recruiters. A discussion of the implications of these trends for best practices, as well as recommendations concerning law enforcement officers and candidates, is included. Next, Wallman and Hawkins describe the Clinician's Awareness Program (CAP) designed to provide education to mental health providers on firefighter culture and the complexity and challenges of the firefighting profession. This chapter also offers how CAP provides clinicians opportunities to participate in simulated, scenario-based experiences to facilitate a more realistic understanding of the many tasks and associated risks involved in this profession.

Englert and his associates explore how simulations, games, and mobile applications (apps) can be employed to improve the engagement, performance, and mental health of those who work in emergency settings. Further, they describe ways technology can be utilized to enhance wellness and supplement mental health initiatives. We end with the chapter by Mills that discusses how practitioners can best provide therapy and related services to first responders in an "ethical, appropriate, and successful manner." This chapter is based on the author's years of clinical experience in the area. Mills emphasizes that clinicians are a unique and supportive resource for first responders. He also underscores that clinicians must have the requisite cultural competence, personal qualities, and ethical reasoning to work effectively.

Mental health professionals who work with first responders are well aware of the challenges they historically face in these settings. And while the stigma about seeking outside assistance is gradually decreasing, resistance remains pervasive. We believe an awareness of the strategies and issues in research, training, and practice has considerable utility in our activities with first responders. The editors of this book have many decades of experience as first responders in addition to our work as clinical psychologists. In these dual roles, we have learned that a willingness to expend time and effort to achieve a greater understanding of first responders through academic and (wherever possible) physical immersion in this unique culture is important for acceptance and effectiveness in protecting those who protect us. We are hopeful that our book will be of value in this regard.

Ft. Lauderdale, FL., USA — Vincent B. Van Hasselt
Springfield, VA., USA — Michael L. Bourke

Contents

Contributors

Adrian Alicea Center for the Advancement of Military and Emergency Services Research, Kennesaw State University, Kennesaw, GA, USA;
Department of Psychological Science, Kennesaw State University, Kennesaw, GA, USA

Monty Baker University of Texas Health Science Center at San Antonio, San Antonio, TX, USA;
College of Psychology, Nova Southeastern University, Fort Lauderdale, FL, USA

Deborah C. Beidel UCF RESTORES and Department of Psychology, University of Central Florida, Florida, USA

Ryan A. Black College of Psychology, Nova Southeastern University, Fort Lauderdale, FL, USA

Jessica R. Blalock College of Psychology, Nova Southeastern University, Davie, USA

Michael L. Bourke Raven, Dallas, USA

Clint A. Bowers UCF RESTORES and Department of Psychology, University of Central Florida, Florida, USA

Jake Boyd Texas Department of Public Safety, Austin, Texas, USA

Samuel Browning College of Psychology, Nova Southeastern University, Fort Lauderdale, FL, USA

Teresa Bryant Jupiter Police Department, Jupiter, USA

Bianca Channer Department of Social Work and Human Services, Kennesaw State University, Kennesaw, GA, USA;
Center for the Advancement of Military and Emergency Services (AMES) Research, Kennesaw State University, Kennesaw, GA, USA

Rachel Christopher College of Psychology, Nova Southeastern University, Fort Lauderdale, FL, USA

Tyler L. Collette Center for the Advancement of Military and Emergency Services (AMES) Research, Kennesaw State University, Kennesaw, GA, USA; Department of Psychological Science, Kennesaw State University, Kennesaw, GA, USA

Jillian Crocker College of Psychology, Nova Southeastern University, Fort Lauderdale, FL, USA

Phaina Dubuisson Center for the Advancement of Military and Emergency Services Research, Kennesaw State University, Kennesaw, GA, USA

David Englert USAF Special Operations Command, Hurlburt Field, FL, USA

David M. Feldman College of Psychology, Nova Southeastern University, Fort Lauderdale, FL, USA

Hannah Friedland College of Psychology, Nova Southeastern University, Fort Lauderdale, FL, USA

Dustin Hawkins Indian River County Fire Rescue Department, Vero Beach, FL, USA

Chris Hess Center for the Advancement of Military and Emergency Services (AMES) Research, Kennesaw State University, Kennesaw, GA, USA; Department of Sociology, Kennesaw State University, Kennesaw, GA, USA

Thomas J. Hodges Center for the Advancement of Military and Emergency Services (AMES) Research, Kennesaw State University, Kennesaw, GA, USA

Kristin A. Horan Center for the Advancement of Military and Emergency Services Research, Kennesaw State University, Kennesaw, GA, USA; Department of Psychological Science, Kennesaw State University, Kennesaw, GA, USA

Daniel R. Horning UCF RESTORES and Department of Psychology, University of Central Florida, Florida, USA

Juliette Hubbard College of Psychology, Nova Southeastern University, Fort Lauderdale, FL, USA

Gabrielle L. LaRock College of Psychology, Nova Southeastern University, Fort Lauderdale, FL, USA

Andi Lassiter Minnesota State University, Mankato, MN, USA

Stephanie Livshitz Los Angeles, CA, USA

Carlos Martinez Los Angeles, CA, USA

Marissa Miller-Anguay College of Psychology, Nova Southeastern University, Fort Lauderdale, FL, USA;
Harris County Sheriff's Office, Houston, TX, USA

Colby Mills Mind Balance, LLC, Apex, USA

Brian A. Moore Center for the Advancement of Military and Emergency Services (AMES) Research, Kennesaw State University, Kennesaw, GA, USA;
Department of Psychological Science, Kennesaw State University, Kennesaw, GA, USA

Katherine Moore Center for the Advancement of Military and Emergency Services Research, Kennesaw State University, Kennesaw, GA, USA

Elizabeth Morris The FMRT Group, Winston-Salem, NC, USA

Quina Munson Miami-Dade Corrections and Rehabilitation, Doral, FL, USA

Scott Poland College of Psychology, Nova Southeastern University, Fort Lauderdale, FL, USA

Christopher E. Powell School of Criminal Justice, Nova Southeastern University, Fort Lauderdale, FL, USA

Ryan Reddin College of Psychology, Nova Southeastern University, Fort Lauderdale, FL, USA

Naysha Rivera-Hartley College of Psychology, Nova Southeastern University, Fort Lauderdale, FL, USA

Mac Di Rocco Raven, Dallas, United States

Karla Rodriguez College of Psychology, Nova Southeastern University, Fort Lauderdale, FL, USA

Daniel Sachau Minnesota State University, Mankato, MN, USA

Israel Sanchez-Cardona Center for the Advancement of Military and Emergency Services (AMES) Research, Kennesaw State University, Kennesaw, GA, USA;
Department of Psychological Science, Kennesaw State University, Kennesaw, GA, USA

Samuel Savage College of Psychology, Nova Southeastern University, Fort Lauderdale, FL, USA

Michael Schlenk Center for the Advancement of Military and Emergency Services (AMES) Research, Kennesaw State University, Kennesaw, GA, USA;
Department of Psychology, University of Central Florida, Orlando, USA

Bailee Schuhmann University of Texas Health Science Center at San Antonio, San Antonio, TX, USA;
College of Psychology, Nova Southeastern University, Fort Lauderdale, FL, USA

Tali M. Shir College of Psychology, Nova Southeastern University, Fort Lauderdale, FL, USA

Bridget Spatola College of Psychology, Nova Southeastern University, Fort Lauderdale, FL, USA

Ashley Stripling College of Psychology, Nova Southeastern University, Fort Lauderdale, FL, USA

Taylor Tejera College of Psychology, Nova Southeastern University, Fort Lauderdale, FL, USA

Gregory S. Tony Broward Sheriff's Office, Broward County, FL, USA

Edwin Trejo-Rivera Center for the Advancement of Military and Emergency Services Research, Kennesaw State University, Kennesaw, GA, USA;
Department of Psychological Science, Kennesaw State University, Kennesaw, GA, USA

Victoria Tumilty The FMRT Group, Winston-Salem, NC, USA

Vincent B. Van Hasselt College of Psychology, Nova Southeastern University, Davie, USA;
Broward Sheriff's Office, Fort Lauderdale, USA

Sophie R. Vincent Center for the Advancement of Military and Emergency Services Research, Kennesaw State University, Kennesaw, GA, USA

Olivia Wallman College of Psychology, Nova Southeastern University, Fort Lauderdale, FL, USA

Part I
Mental Health Research

Chapter 1
Mental and Occupational Health of Fire Rescue Personnel: A Model for Conducting Organizational Health Assessments

Bianca Channer, Michael Schlenk, Israel Sanchez-Cardona, Tyler L. Collette, Kristin Horan, Chris Hess, Thomas J. Hodges, and Brian A. Moore

Firefighters comprise a unique portion of the workforce as they are often required to take physical risks and consequently experience traumatic events at a higher rate compared to other occupations. The host of occupational and organizational stressors associated with public safety occupations, such as firefighting, include witnessing deaths and serious injuries, as well as experiencing sleep disturbances due to shift work, each of which can potentiate the risk for subsequent behavioral and mental health issues (Carleton et al., 2019; Doyle et al., 2021; Jahnke et al., 2016; Violanti et al., 2013). Firefighters may also experience degraded job satisfaction, increased trauma symptomology, and psychological strain due to their occupational experiences (Brough, 2004; Igboanugo et al., 2021). As such, there is an urgent need

B. Channer
Department of Social Work and Human Services, Kennesaw State University, Kennesaw, GA, USA

B. Channer · M. Schlenk · I. Sanchez-Cardona · T. L. Collette · K. Horan · C. Hess · T. J. Hodges · B. A. Moore
Center for the Advancement of Military and Emergency Services (AMES) Research, Kennesaw State University, Kennesaw, GA, USA

M. Schlenk
Department of Psychology, University of Central Florida, Orlando, USA

I. Sanchez-Cardona · T. L. Collette · K. Horan · B. A. Moore (✉)
Department of Psychological Science, Kennesaw State University, Kennesaw, GA, USA
e-mail: Brian.Moore@Kennesaw.edu

C. Hess
Department of Sociology, Kennesaw State University, Kennesaw, GA, USA

V. B. Van Hasselt and M. L. Bourke (eds.), *Advances in First Responder Mental Health*, Advances in First Responder Mental Health 1,
https://doi.org/10.1007/978-3-032-27978-1_1

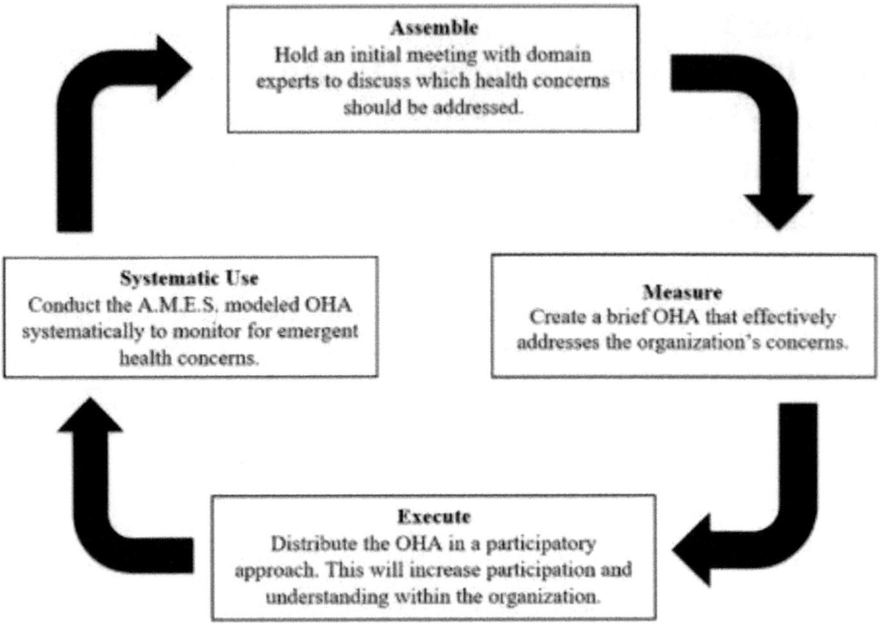

Fig. 1.1 The Four Stages of the A.M.E.S. OHA Model

for culturally informed and organizationally adaptive assessments as a strategy to systematically monitor public safety personnel health and well-being.

Organizational Health Assessments (OHA) are a valuable strategy to conduct systematic evaluations of a department's overall health and the well-being of its workforce, providing current data to inform the development of health promotion interventions. The design and development of evidence-based practices to maintain the health of firefighters, while simultaneously increasing safety and enhancing their resilience to occupational stress, is a significant challenge. Similarly, research to improve firefighters'overall health, resilience, and quality of life presents considerable challenges. Consequently, scientifically valid, evidence-based studies that report on assessing risk factors related to occupational injuries, or on developing and implementing resilience enhancement interventions for firefighters, are lacking. To address this gap in the current research, prospective efficacy research is required to evaluate culturally specific approaches to enhancing health and wellness, while simultaneously optimizing the health of firefighters.

Table 1.1 Demographic characteristics of participants

Characteristic	Category	N	%
Sex	Male	805	96.0
	Female	28	3.4
	Prefer not to answer	5	0.6
Ethnicity	American Indian or Alaska native	3	0.4
	African American or black	64	7.6
	Asian	4	0.5
	Hispanic or Latino	26	3.1
	Native Hawaiian or Pacific islander	5	0.6
	White or Caucasian	702	83.8
	More than one	18	2.2
	Other	12	1.4
Marital status	Cohabiting	18	2.2
	Divorced	49	5.9
	Engaged	21	2.5
	Married	655	78.2
	Single, never married	89	10.6
	Widowed	5	0.6
	Missing	1	0.1
Years in public safety	0–4 years	142	17.0
	5–9 years	152	18.2
	10–14 years	137	16.4
	15–19 years	150	17.9
	20+ years	256	30.6
	Missing	1	0.1
Second job or overtime	0 days per week	203	24.2
	1 or more days per week	182	21.7
	2 or more days per week	183	21.8
	3 or more days per week	181	21.6
	4 or more days per week	87	10.4
	Missing	2	0.2
Age	<20 years old	3	0.4
	20–24 years old	38	4.5
	25–29 years old	105	12.5
	30–34 years old	140	16.7
	35–39 years old	120	14.3
	40+ years old	431	51.4
	Missing	1	0.1

(continued)

Table 1.1 (continued)

Characteristic	Category	N	%
Military service	Air force	23	2.6
	Army	45	5.4
	Marine corps	35	4.2
	Navy	30	3.6
	National Guard/reserves	23	2.8
	I have not previously served in the military	680	81.1
	Missing	2	0.2

Table 1.2 Count data for risk factors and help seeking

	Yes (n)	No (n)	Missing (n)
Psychosocial risk factor			
Mental health challenges	338	481	19
Traumatic brain injuries	31	788	19
Prolonged stress	524	295	19
Recent loss	244	575	19
Legal challenges	113	706	19
Financial challenges	448	371	19
Marital/relationship challenges	420	398	20
Chronic pain	404	420	14
Previous suicide attempts	27	805	6
Suicidal ideation	57	771	10
Family history of suicide	56	778	4
History of abuse, neglect, or trauma	103	720	15
Probable PTSD	105	731	2
Assistance-related questions			
Do you use the employee assistance program (EAP)?	79	658	21
Have you ever sought out mental/behavioral health?	212	607	19

Mental and Occupational Health Concerns

Mental Health Concerns

The unique combination of stressors that firefighters experience places them at increased risk for several mental health concerns, including depression (Chen et al., 2007; Regehr et al., 2000; Wagner et al., 1998), substance abuse (Carey et al., 2011; Haddock et al., 2015; Meyer et al., 2012), burnout (Smith et al., 2018), and psychological strain leading to suicide/suicidal ideation (Savia, 2008; Stanley et al., 2015).

Each of these disorders is commonly precipitated by trauma exposure. In the general population, between 70% and 90% of individuals will be exposed to significant trauma during their lives (Benjet et al., 2016; Kilpatrick et al., 2013). This number is likely closer to 100% for firefighters. As such, trauma-related psychological disorders are likely to be particularly impactful for firefighters.

Potentially traumatic experiences may range from motor vehicle accidents to severe workplace injuries or death (Kilpatrick et al., 2013). Firefighters who are exposed to trauma or high rates of stress are also at risk for developing posttraumatic stress disorder (PTSD), a trauma and stress-related disorder characterized by a range of maladaptive reactions to the experiencing of a catastrophic stressor (American Psychiatric Association, 2013). Currently, reliable estimates of PTSD in firefighters are largely unavailable. Many studies have identified prevalence rates consistent with those among combat veterans (~20%; Corneil et al., 1999; Harvey & Bryant, 1999; Wagner et al., 1998). Yet, other studies have identified prevalence rates ranging from as low as 3.5% (Meyer et al., 2012) to as high as 68% (Regehr et al., 2000). More recently published studies, however, have identified prevalence rates for PTSD, anxiety disorders, and depressive disorders to range between 11%–21.4%, 15%–15.8%, and 14.3%–15%, respectively (Cherry et al., 2021; Petrie et al., 2018). Regardless, the current literature is clear that organizational stress, musculoskeletal injuries, and physical fitness are all associated with the onset and manifestation of PTSD (Mat Salleh et al., 2020).

Occupational Health Concerns

Over the past four decades, firefighter line-of-duty deaths have generally declined (Fahy, 2020), perhaps due to improvements in firefighting techniques and personal protective equipment (Kahn et al., 2017). However, individuals who encounter life-threatening situations and survive must deal with physical and psychological injuries or a combination of both. Physical and mental health are dynamically related, each uniquely contributing to risk factors for injury, illness, and disease. Recent evidence indicates sprains and strains are common among firefighters, with back injuries (32%) being the most commonly reported (Frost et al., 2016). Additionally, firefighters risk developing dysfunctional responses to these experiences when they have poor sleep. Recent research indicates that firefighters average well below the American Academy of Sleep Medicine recommendation of 7–8 hours per day—with just over 5 hours of sleep a night—placing them at increased risk for injuries (Stout et al., 2020). Ensuring adequate, quality sleep in individuals in high-stress environments is paramount for their health and safety and the success of agency operations and community requirements. The current literature is clear that poor sleep is a risk factor for the development of injuries, anxiety, depression, PTSD, suicidal ideation, and poor job performance (Moore et al., 2020; Mysliwiec et al., 2013). Despite this, academic-oriented dissemination efforts often fail to reach the community users most in need. In this case, fire service leadership.

Barriers and Interventions to Health Services

Cultural and structural barriers to firefighters accessing behavioral health services include stigma, fear of a breach of confidentiality, and concerns for future career opportunities (Jones et al., 2020; Kim et al., 2018; Thews et al., 2020). Additional concerns include the low availability of services, a lack of culturally aware providers, and a limited range of delivery capacity (e.g., in-person vs. telehealth). These concerns may also result from previous negative experiences seeking care (Jones et al., 2020). Conversely, firefighters may not know when or where to seek care if their concerns are work-related (Thews et al., 2020). Similarly, firefighters may normalize the stress of working in public safety, furthering barriers to accessing behavioral health services. There is an urgent need for occupational health services aligned with firefighters'culture and adaptable to their work environments. One method that yields brief and effective behavioral health screenings with an actionable plan to address such concerns for firefighters is an Organizational Health Assessment (OHA).

Cox and Castro (2006) developed the mental health needs assessment for the Army to comprehensively evaluate a unit's health while identifying the related service needs during deployment. As indicated, organizational health assessments are designed to be unit-specific and include a variety of health-related factors such as sleep health, PTSD, and substance use (Cox & Castro, 2006). The fire service operates in an organizational structure similar to the U.S. military. Indeed, like military personnel, firefighters are exposed to life-and-death situations and are expected to perform in dynamic contexts, often with little information. Further, firefighters work and live in multi-level organizations where team effectiveness is critical to success yet rarely guaranteed, contributing to high levels of stressors. In turn, these stressors make them susceptible to risks at multiple levels. Enhancing the scientific understanding of the presence and manifestation of known risk factors at various levels in firefighters can improve training experiences and skill retention while reducing occupational health concerns.

Despite their similarities, however, each department operates independently, with little or no national coordination. To our knowledge, dissemination efforts to conduct systematic assessments of behavioral health are limited. The present chapter seeks to extend Cox and Castros' (2006) findings by incorporating a participatory community approach. Herein, we present and propose the Assemble, Measure, Execute, Systematic Use (A.M.E.S.) Model, a four-stage OHA model to assess behavioral and occupational health concerns among firefighters. The A.M.E.S. OHA addresses these barriers by promoting the development of a brief assessment that can comprehensively evaluate a public safety agency's organizational health concerns, be culturally adapted to firefighters, and lead to a collaborative and systematic action plan involving leadership to address the reported concerns. As such, the present study presents the A.M.E.S OHA as a novel tool to assess organizational health concerns in firefighters.

The A.M.E.S. Model

Stage 1: Assemble

Cox and Castro (2006) emphasize the importance of having domain expertise to create an informed OHA. During the *Assemble* stage, an initial meeting should be held with the command staff of the public safety agency and organizational, health, and public safety experts to identify the occupational health concerns to be addressed. This is particularly important as Jones et al. (2020) found that a significant part of previous negative experiences seeking behavioral health services was due to providers' lack of experience and culturally relevant knowledge. Therefore, it is important to include a public safety expert in OHAs and to involve command staff in the process to ensure OHAs are culturally informed about the issues relevant to firefighters and also to allow participation of the agency in decision-making.

Stage 2: Measure

The *Measure* stage entails the creation of a brief OHA tailored to the organization's identified or suspected health concerns. While there are no specific measures or a set number of scales to be used, the OHA should provide a holistic assessment tailored to the agency's needs, while also minimizing the time required to complete the assessment. Based on the information identified with the command staff in the first stage, a literature review is conducted to identify suitable measures relevant to the constructs identified. Broad categories to include in the assessment are occupational resources (e.g., leadership and social support, use of employee assistance programs), occupational and life stressors (e.g., shifts, financial strain, interpersonal conflict); mental health (e.g., posttraumatic stress, anxiety, stress); behavioral health (e.g., alcohol use, sleep quality and quantity, suicidality). All domain experts should then re-evaluate the survey to agree that the created OHA delivers the most relevant assessment for the agency's needs (Cox & Castro, 2006). Additionally, the constructs collaboratively chosen by the organization and domain experts should be time-tested to maximize completion potential.

Stage 3: Execute

Upon mutual agreement by all domain experts, the A.M.E.S. OHA strategy enters the *Execute* stage, in which agencies distribute the assessment via a participatory approach. It is important to work closely with a designated person in the agency to design an implementation strategy that suits the agency's work culture. The execution phase is iterative in nature and often requires multiple complementary recruitment strategies to increase participation. Strategies could include: (1) official notification from the command staff explaining the OHA and providing the hyperlink to complete the anonymous survey; (2) reminders sent through emails; 3) setting a room in the agency to allow participants to complete the survey on tablets or computers before or after their shift. We note that throughout data collection, anonymity must be protected to promote maximum participation and research integrity (Marshall et al., 2021).

Indeed, providing assurances of anonymity helps gain leadership and personnel buy-in during the assessment, increasing participation and contributing to trust in the process and organization. This stage is anticipated to be an interactive process that requires constant engagement for successful completion and implementation.

Stage 4: Systematic Use

During the "*systematic use*" phase, a brief report with the findings should be presented to the command staff after data collection. Aggregated findings should be presented so that command staff can assess or prioritize the needed organizational health services based on the OHA results. Also, the command staff is encouraged to share the findings with other stakeholders in the agency to raise awareness within their personnel or to advocate for resources to implement new health and well-being programs. During a meeting to present the results, the scientific team encourages the command staff to prioritize potential areas of intervention based on the highest need areas and to continue monitoring the progress of any initiative. In congruence with Cox and Castro (2006), the A.M.E.S. OHA is recommended to be systematically enacted annually and adapted to continually identify the most prevalent health concerns to continuously improve individual and organizational health.

Pilot and Presentation of the A.M.E.S. OHA

In this section, we report on the implementation of the OHA A.M.E.S. model among 11 fire departments in the southeastern United States. We implemented this OHA between February, 2024 and May, 2025. Agencies were invited to participate in implementing this organizational assessment as part of a collaboration with the Georgia Department of Public Health through the Center for Disease Control Comprehensive Suicide Prevention Program (the "collaborating agency"). Agency sizes ranged from 27–702 personnel. Of the 11 agencies in our sample, 25% were urban, 62.5% suburban, and 12.5% were rural. To recruit agencies, the research team contacted them through email, outreach events, and referrals. We then met with the command staff to discuss taking part in the organizational health assessment. This study was reviewed by the Institutional Review Board at Kennesaw State University and approved (#IRB-FY23–5). In the following section, we summarized the steps we took to implement the A.M.E.S. O.H.A. with these agencies.

A.M.E.S. Process in Action

Implementing Stage 1: Assemble

To begin the process, a meeting was coordinated with the collaborator agency's command staff, their public safety psychologist, and the research team's health psychologist, licensed clinical social worker, data scientists, and industrial-organizational psychologist. The OHA assessment development meeting's main goals were to: (1) establish the organizational health concerns to evaluate, and (2) discuss the logistics for executing the A.M.E.S. OHA model. During this meeting, the research team discussed current evidence related to occupational stressors, life stressors, mental and behavioral health concerns, and additional resources to guide the conversation. The collaborator agency's command staff provided input on these concerns based on the experiences of their work with fire agencies. The team jointly discusses the most relevant area to assess based on the current literature and fire agencies' work environment and experience. With consensus, the most common organizational health concerns noted by the command staff included social support, alcohol use, and PTSD. Additionally, the meeting covered the following topics: how to engage stakeholders in the agencies and community; the relevance and accuracy of the elements to be assessed; trust and buy-in of personnel; data quality; roll-out of the assessment; and implementation of findings, including capacity building and sustainability.

Implementing Stage 2: Measure

After the initial *Assemble* meeting was conducted with the collaborator agency, the research team identified several well-validated measures to assess the agreed organizational health concerns. Additionally, the A.M.E.S. OHA aimed to provide a comprehensive assessment of other, often comorbid, public safety health conditions in conjunction with the agency's specified concerns (i.e., depression, anxiety, stress, suicidality, PTSD, alcohol use, sleep health, recovery and dysfunctional cognitions, unit cohesion, social support, and employee assistance program [EAP] utilization). The research team designed an initial survey containing the measures of the identified stressors, health concerns, and other comorbid health conditions. With the measures selected, the *Assemble* team held one final meeting to determine if the proposed A.M.E.S OHA was acceptable to assess the discussed concerns. A major concern expressed by the collaborator agency's command staff during this review meeting was the length of the survey, with excessive length being a particular concern for optimal participation. The process only proceeded to the next stage of the model (*Execute*) once all assembled experts agreed on the A.M.E.S. OHA. The final A.M.E.S. OHA contained a demographics section, self-report measures, and a three-item EAP section. Before dissemination to the fire agencies, the research team piloted the survey among research assistants to ensure the OHA was brief and adequately captured variables of interest promptly. The average time to complete the piloted survey was about seven and a half minutes. The measures included in the assessment were the following:

Interpersonal Support Evaluation List—Adapted (ISEL-12)

For this version of the A.M.E.S. OHA, we shortened the ISEL-12 to four items. The ISEL assesses social support using a 4-point Likert scale scored from *Definitely True* to *Definitely False* and indicated suitable internal consistency for a shortened scale ($\omega = 0.69$) in the present study. Questions examine participants' access to close friends or family whom they could turn to for a personal problem, their perceptions about whether or not they often get invited to events, had someone to take care of their chores when sick, and whether they had someone whom they could share their private worries and fears (Cohen et al., 1985; Lambert et al., 2012).

Psychosocial Risk List

This list was created to capture psychosocial challenges that individuals have experienced since starting their public safety careers. Participants respond "*yes*" or "*no*" to list items that include mental health, traumatic brain injury, chronic pain, prolonged stress, recent loss, and legal, financial, and marital or relationship challenges. In addition, participants indicated whether they have experienced a previous suicide attempt, a family history of suicide, or a history of abuse, neglect, or trauma. Last, suicide ideation was measured via the single 4-point Likert-type ($1 =$ not at all to $4 =$ nearly every day) question asking participants if, over the last two weeks, they have been bothered by thoughts that they would be better off dead or thoughts of hurting themselves.

Primary Care PTSD Screen for DSM-5 (PC-PTSD-5)

The PC-PTSD-5 is a 5-item self-report measure that assesses PTSD symptoms using a dichotomous scale scored either *Yes* or *No*. The present study screen indicated strong internal consistency ($\omega = 0.85$). Research suggests that a cut-point of 4 reduced the likelihood of concluding false positives or negatives in large samples of military veterans (Prins et al., 2015; Prins et al., 2016).

Alcohol Use Disorder Identification Test—Consumption (AUDIT-C)

The AUDIT-C is a three-item self-report measure that assesses alcohol use disorder (AUD) using a Likert scale scored from 0 to 4. The AUDIT-C indicated strong internal consistency ($\omega = 0.80$) for the present study. A cut-off score of 4 for men and 3 for women indicates AUD (Bush et al., 1998).

Sleep Health

Sleep health measures were derived from the Naval Behavioral Health Needs Assessment Survey (Booth-Kewley et al., 2013). Participants answered four questions regarding sleep satisfaction on a Likert-type scale ranging from *1 = extremely unsatisfied* to *7 = extremely satisfied* ($\omega = 0.85$) Two additional questions were added to assess the amount of sleep per night (in hours) and if sleep impacts other areas of their life (Likert-type scale ranging from *1 = not at all* to *7 = Extremely;* Booth-Kewley et al., 2013).

Employee Assistance Program (EAP)

Participants also answered questions that examine if they use their agency's EAP, how likely they are to use it, and how effective it is. The item, "How likely are you to use the EAP?" used a Likert scale from *Extremely Unlikely* to *Extremely Likely*. The item, "How effective is the EAP?" used a Likert scale from *Not effective* to *Extremely effective.*

Other Assistance-Related Topics

Two binary (Yes/No) items were added to assess if a participant sought mental health assistance before and if they sought assistance from their EAP before the survey. If participants indicated *No,* then an open-ended free-response question was included to inquire about why.

Implementing Stage 3: Execute

Once the survey was finalized, the research team along with the sponsor's command staff designed an implementation strategy to collect data. We determined the most appropriate strategy was to use an anonymous link to the survey, which was hosted online on the *Qualtrics* platform. A major concern expressed by command staff was a lack of participation of the agencies' personnel due to worries about privacy and anonymity. To address these concerns, the research team created a template letter for fire departments to inform personnel about the assessment's purpose and their participation. We sent the template email with the link to the leadership or contact person in each agency. They distributed the A.M.E.S. OHA directly to participants' work emails. The emails instructed potential participants to complete the A.M.E.S. OHA at their discretion using personal or work devices. The research team also created a QR code with the link to the survey and distributed flyers to be posted in the fire stations. Participating agencies were advised to give their personnel two weeks to complete the assessment. An additional 2 weeks were allocated for anticipated follow-ups (as needed). In one case, a fire captain personally visited each station to ensure personnel who did not engage with email systems knew of the QR code to complete the assessment. The total agency time commitment was expected to be one month. A member of the research team monitored the response rate of each fire agency and provided feedback to the specific department's command staff to send reminders to their personnel. What we found was that on average, it took the fire department forty-three days to complete the OHA.

During the data collection across 11 agencies, a total of 838 responses were collected, which represented roughly 61% of personnel. This participation rate is better than the reported average employee participation rate in workplace screening-focused wellness initiatives (48%) and exceeds the predicted participation rates for workplace screening-focused programs without incentives (22%; Huang et al., 2016). An important consideration to note is that while many firefighters finished the survey quickly, without interruption (Median time to completion = 6.14 minutes), many took an exceptionally long time to finish once initiating the survey. This may be due to factors such as interruptions, poor internet connection, and/or the context in which the OHA was completed. Future OHAs should implement strategies such as providing a designated area outside the work environment to reduce cognitive load. Additionally, occupational stressors associated with being on duty and working emergency calls versus being off duty during data collection may have influenced responses. In the following section, we present the major findings of the OHA from the 11 agencies.

Demographics

Firefighters in the present sample were primarily male (96.1%), married (78.3%), had 10 or more years of experience (64.9%), and/or reported no prior military experience

(81.3%). The present sample was primarily white (83.8%) and worked overtime or a second job one (21.8%), two (21.9%), or three (21.7%) days a week. In terms of age, the sample had just over half (51.5%) being over 40 years old. Table 1.1 provides the full range of data for demographics.

Social Support

Overall, approximately a quarter of participants reported scores associated with moderate to low levels (<2.5) of social support (n = 199; 23.7%). While only a small proportion of personnel believed that they did not have someone to turn to when faced with a personal problem (8.3%), a larger proportion did not feel they had anyone to share their most private worries and fears with (20.5%). Many participants also felt that they did not often get invited to do things with others (28.6%) nor did they have someone to turn to for help if they were sick (13.7%).

Historical and Psychosocial Factors

Prolonged stress (62.5%), financial (53.5%), marital or relationship (50.12%), and mental health (40.3%) challenges emerged as the most common concerns participants indicated having since beginning their public safety career. While not as prevalent, challenges such as recent loss (29.1%), legal challenges (13.48%), and traumatic brain injury (3.7%) were also reported. Moreover, 27 (3.2%) of participants had experienced a suicide attempt, 56 (6.7%) participants had a family history of suicide, and 103 (12.3%) had a history of abuse, neglect, or trauma. Four hundred and four participants (48.6%) reported chronic pain (largely in the back, upper body, and knees). Notably, most participants ($n = 265$; 65.8%) who indicated they experienced chronic pain indicated they had pain in multiple areas of their body.

PTSD and Suicidal Ideation

A substantial proportion of participants (12.5%) reported clinical levels of probable PTSD (>4). Most participants (92.0%) reported no suicidal ideation over the past 2 weeks; however, 54 (6.4%) participants experienced such thoughts for several days, and three (0.4%) participants held such thoughts over half of the days. Count data for psychosocial risk factors, probable PTSD, and suicidal ideation can be found in Table 1.2.

Alcohol Use Disorder

Three hundred twenty-six participants (38.9%) met the cut-off score indicating alcohol use disorder. This includes 315 male participants (39.1%), and 34.38% of female (n = 11) participants. It is important to note only 32 females were in the OHA (see Table 1.1). Most participants indicated they had had more than six drinks at least once in the last month (56.9%).

Sleep Health

Many participants reported obtaining 5 hours or fewer of sleep per day (61.7%). Three hundred eighty-nine participants (46.4%) reported mild to extreme dissatisfaction with their ability to fall asleep, 551 participants (65.8%) were mildly to extremely dissatisfied with their quality of sleep, and 589 participants (70.9%) reported that they were mildly to extremely dissatisfied with their quantity of sleep. Moreover, 272 participants (32.5%) indicated mild to extreme dissatisfaction with their daytime functioning as it relates to sleep. When asked how much sleep impacts other areas of their life, 457 participants (54.5%) indicated moderate to extreme impact.

EAP and Assistance-Related Topics

A vital component of managing psychosocial health is the utilization of resources. As such, we were interested in the utilization of mental health and EAP resources available to participants. Approximately a quarter of participants (25.3%) reported previously seeking professional assistance for mental healthcare. Most participants (78.5%) indicated that they do not use their EAP. Another 9.5% of participants indicated that they do not know what EAP is. Most participants (75.7%) were indifferent or indicated they were unlikely to use the EAP. Unsurprisingly, 76.13% of respondents indicated that the EAP was not at all to moderately effective, with only 9.8% providing a strong endorsement for the service.

Implementing Stage 4: Systematic Use

After the survey closed, the research team cleaned and analyzed the data. Although in this chapter we present the aggregated data from 11 departments, for our implementation, we generated an individualized brief report for each agency that detailed the A.M.E.S. OHA's findings and provided recommendations to develop a plan of action that addresses the indicated concerns. We provided each agency with a digital copy of the report. The research team scheduled a meeting with each agency to briefly present the key findings and recommendations based on the results of the OHA. We used this meeting to reiterate to the command staff the importance of systematically conducting these assessments and to discuss action plans based on the results. Some of the key recommendations were quarterly training workshops to provide personnel awareness on the four major identified organizational health concerns: sleep health, alcohol use, chronic pain, and history of abuse, neglect, and trauma. We also provided insight on how to leverage their existing resources to continue promoting health and well-being in the agency. Most agencies expressed that budget constraints are a major challenge to implementing new health promotion practices and programs. We used the meeting to empower the command staff to use the report to advocate for more internal or external funding. Also, the research team recommended an annual A.M.E.S OHA to determine how health concerns change due to the implemented interventions.

Discussion

This chapter's objective was to present an organizational health assessment model (OHA) adapted to the fire service. Based on the work of Cox and Castro (2006), we proposed the A.M.E.S. model to identify organizational health concerns among fire service personnel. The four-stage A.M.E.S. modeled OHA offers a novel and collaborative baseline organizational health assessment to identify mental and occupational health concerns of firefighters and inform agency-specific preventative wellness programming. The A.M.E.S. OHA model follows a series of participatory steps to design and implement contextualized assessment based on the needs of the fire service. The model offers a heuristic process that can be adapted to other fire service and public safety agencies. Additionally, working with a public safety agency that was actively engaged in wellness initiatives may enhance firefighter's participation.

A major strength of this approach is the participatory approach used in the organizational health assessment's design and implementation. From the beginning, command staff is involved in the discussion of the constructs to assess and in the decision-making process concerning the implementation of the assessment. Leadership engagement in these organizational health initiatives is crucial for their effectiveness. Engaging command staff and subject matter experts in the process ensures not only buy in but also developing processes relevant and customizable to the department's needs and challenges. Although this participatory approach provides advantages, it presents some challenges. Engaging partners is time-consuming and requires developing trustful and equal relationships between partners and the research team to allow open communication and discussion in the *Assemble* and *Measure* steps of the model. Also, ensuring continuous engagement of partners in all stages of the process could be challenging. For example, in the *Execute* stage command staff engagement is necessary to send out the survey, reminders or engage in continuous reflection to change the data collection strategy if necessary. Likewise, empowering command staff to use the results to promote health and well-being initiatives is crucial to sustain changes in the department. In summary, the Organizational Health Assessment is a first step to understand and address health issues in fire service and public safety agencies.

Identifying Health Concerns

As an organizational health strategy, the A.M.E.S. OHA model is a stakeholder, informed community-based participatory research model that provides a systematic way to identify key stressors and organizational health concerns in the fire service. We provided a summary of the implementation of the model across 11 departments. We found that sleep dysfunction and AUD to be the most prevalent concerns. Many of the participants (61.7%) indicated a sleep deficit, warranting intervention. Most personnel reported 10 or more years of experience and were 40 years of age or older, which may inform these findings due to prolonged stress and increased experiences with occupational hazards. These findings are aligned with the current literature (Dyal et al., 2022) and highlight the importance of workplace stressors on firefighters. This is particularly concerning as Stout et al. (2020) reported that firefighters sleeping fewer than six hours per night exhibited worsened performance and increased risk for injuries. This has direct implications for community and individual safety.

The majority of participants were reasonably satisfied with their ability to fall asleep. It is also worth noting that most participants indicated that sleep impacts other areas of their life. A preponderance of participants reported moderate to high levels of social support, which may be protective for organizational health and explain lower rates of PTSD and suicidality and increased drinking rates. Concurrently, most firefighters did not report using the EAP, reported being somewhat unlikely to use it, and deemed it ineffective (see supporting Table 2). This is interesting as Thews et al. (2020) indicated that firefighters experience difficulties with scheduling appointments, filing workers' compensation claims, and insurance. Additional research should examine the process for firefighters to use the EAP and identify target points of action.

The finding that 56.9% of participants reported binge drinking is surprising. Although the majority were males, 34.38% of the females in the OHA met the AUD cut-off. There is currently a lack of literature that independently investigates female health and substance use in the fire service. One study found greater tobacco use among female firefighters than among males, but lower alcohol use compared to the general population (Jahnke et al., 2012). Conversely, Gulliver et al. (2019) indicated female fire recruits binge drinking rates became comparable to men after only one year. This warrants additional consideration as it is also known that females are at an increased risk for PTSD and suicidality compared to males (Noor et al., 2019). The increased AUD rates among females may be attributed to "fitting in" with the masculine culture of the fire service. Future research would benefit from targeted interventions including gender differences in alcohol use behaviors.

Although firefighters display higher rates of suicidality than the general population, the heterogeneity of sampling and measured suicidality constructs creates variation with reported suicidality rates being between 3.1% and 46.8% (Park et al., 2019; Stanley et al., 2015, 2016; Vigil et al., 2019, 2021). A total of 12.5% of participants met the cut-off score for PTSD, which is on the lower end of existing literature examining firefighters (Cherry et al., 2021; Petrie et al., 2018; Noor et al., 2019). This could also be explained by the high levels of reported cohesion and social support, which may be protective against occupational stress.

Future Considerations

Organizational health assessments are an initial step in developing and sustaining health initiatives in the agencies. Systematic data collection of health concerns is crucial to strategically design health promotion practices and programs. For example, to the participating agencies, we recommended quarterly psychoeducational training discussing improvements in sleep health and/or the difference between alcohol use and misuse. However, we recognized that additional multilevel approaches and primary, secondary, and tertiary interventions are necessary to promote healthy behaviors. An important element of the model is to educate the command staff to use the results to strategically implement and advocate for health promotion programs in their agencies. Leadership support in high-stress environments is associated with higher mental health outcomes (Adler et al., 2014). Additionally, our study found that the majority (76.13%) of firefighters found their EAP not at all to moderately effective, and further research is needed to explore this finding in more detail. Researchers and practitioners implementing this model must understand that transparency, communication, and leadership support with health initiatives are key to success.

Conclusion

Overall, the A.M.E.S. OHA model offers a brief, yet effective four-stage collaborative model to assess organizational health in firefighters. Future research should extend the use of OHAs to other emergency service occupations such as police, 911, and incarceration units. Additionally, multicultural differences among firefighters should be considered to better inform future training and program development. Organizational health assessments provide firefighters with a preventative assessment to better guide necessary organizational health services specific to the agencies that implement them, improving first responder wellness and the communities they serve.

Author Note The opinions of the authors are those of the authors alone and do not reflect or represent the opinions or standing of Kennesaw State University, the Georgia Department of Public Health, or the Centers for Disease Control. Funding provided to the Georgia Department of Public

Health through the Center for Disease Control Comprehensive Suicide Prevention Program. Group Authorship includes Will Ownbey, Edwin Trejo Rivera, DeAndre Cain, Elizabeth Head, and Lisa Dawson. We thank Dr. Carla Moore and Chief Chad Jones for their expertise in early conversations surrounding this topic. We would also like to thank the Georgia Office of Public Safety Support for their extensive cultural contributions and partnership in identifying participating agencies.

Declarations Data Availability
The data are available upon request to the corresponding author.

Conflict of Interest: The authors have no conflicts of interest to report.

Ethics Approval Statement: This study was deemed human subjects research and approved by the Institutional Review Board at Kennesaw State University IRB-FY23-5.

Informed Consent: All participants in the present study provided informed consent.

References

Adler, A. B., Saboe, K. N., Anderson, J., Sipos, M. L., & Thomas, J. L. (2014). Behavioral health leadership: New directions in occupational mental health. *Current Psychiatry Reports, 16*(10), 484–491. https://doi.org/10.1007/s11920-014-0484-6

American Psychiatric Association. (2013). *Diagnostic and statistical manual of mental disorders* (5th edition). https://dsm.psychiatryonline.org/doi/book/10.1176/appi.books.9780890425596

Benjet, C., Bromet, E., Karam, E. G., Kessler, R. C., McLaughlin, K. A., Ruscio, A. M., Shahly, V., Stein, D. J., Petukhova, M., Hill, E., Alonso, J., Atwoli, L., Bunting, B., Bruffaerts, R., Caldas-de-Almeida, J. M., de, G.,. G., Florescu, S., Gureje, O., Huang, Y., & Koenen, K. C. (2016). The epidemiology of traumatic event exposure worldwide: Results from the world mental health survey consortium. *Psychological Medicine, 46*(2), 327–343. https://doi.org/10.1017/S0033291715001981

Booth-Kewley, S., Beckerley, S., Hilton, S., & Taylor, M. (2013). *Behavioral health needs assessment survey (BHNAS): Overview of survey items and measures.* Defense Technical Information Center. https://apps.dtic.mil/sti/citations/ADA621661

Brough, P. (2004). Comparing the influence of traumatic and organizational stressors on the psychological health of police, fire, and ambulance officers. *International Journal of Stress Management, 11*(3), 227–244. https://doi.org/10.1037/1072-5245.11.3.227

Bush, K., Kivlahan, D. R., McDonell, M. B., Fihn, S. D., & Bradley, K. A. (1998). The AUDIT alcohol consumption questions (AUDIT-C). An effective brief screening test for problem drinking. *Archives of Internal Medicine, 158*(16), 1789–1795. https://doi.org/10.1001/archinte.158.16.1789

Carey, M. G., Al-Zaiti, S. S., Dean, G. E., Sessanna, L., & Finnell, D. S. (2011). Sleep problems, depression, substance use, social bonding, and quality of life in professional firefighters. *Journal of Occupational & Environmental Medicine, 53*(8), 928–933. https://doi.org/10.1097/JOM.0b013e318225898f

Carleton, R. N., Afifi, T. O., Taillieu, T., Turner, S., Krakauer, R., Anderson, G. S., MacPhee, R. S., Ricciardelli Cramm, H. A., Groll, D., & McCreary, D. R. (2019). Exposure to potentially traumatic events among public safety personnel in Canada. *Canadian Journal of Behavioral Science/Revue Canadienne des sciences du comportement, 51*(1), 37–52. https://doi.org/10.1037/cbs0000115

Chen, Y.-S., Chen, M.-C., Chou, F. H.-C., Sun, F.-C., Chen, P.-C., Tsai, K.-Y., & Chao, S.-S. (2007). The relationship between quality of life and posttraumatic stress disorder or major depression for firefighters in Kaohsiung, Taiwan. *Quality of Life Research, 16*(8), 1289–1297.

Cherry, N., Galarneau, J. M., Melynk, A., & Patten, S. (2021). Prevalence of mental ill-health in a cohort of first responders attending the fort mcmurray fire. *Canadian Journal of Psychiatry, 66*(8), 719725. https://doi.org/10.1177/0706743720974824

Cohen, S., Mermelstein, R., Kamarck, T., & Hoberman, H. M. (1985). Measuring the functional components of social support. In I. G. Sarason & B. R. Sarason (Eds.), *Social support: Theory, research, and applications*. Springer.

Corneil, W., Beaton, R., Murphy, S., Johnson, C., & Pike, K. (1999). Exposure to traumatic incidents and prevalence of posttraumatic stress symptomatology in urban firefighters in two countries. *Journal of Occupational Health Psychology, 4*(2), 131–141. https://doi.org/10.1037/1076-8998.4.2.131

Cox, A. L. & Castro, C. A. (2006). The mental health needs assessment. In *Human Dimensions in Military Operations–Military 'Leader's strategies for Addressing Stress and Psychological Support,* 7–1–7-8. http://www.rto.nato.int/abstracts.asp

Doyle, J. N., Campbell, M. A., & Gryshchuk, L. (2021). Occupational stress and anger: Mediating effects of resiliency in first responders. *Journal of Police and Criminal Psychology, 36*(3), 463–472. https://doi.org/10.1007%2Fs11896-021-09429-y

Dyal, M. A., Smith, T. D., DeJoy, D. M., & Moore, B. A. (2022). Occupational stress and burnout in the fire service: Examining the complex role and impact of sleep health. *Behavior Modification, 46*(2), 374–394. https://doi.org/10.1177/01454455211040049

Frost, D. M., Beach, T. A. C., Crosby, I., & McGill, S. M. (2016). The cost and distribution of firefighter injuries in a large Canadian fire department. *Work, 55*(3), 497–504. https://doi.org/10.3233/WOR-162420

Gulliver, S. B., Zimering, R. T., Dobani, F., Pennington, M. L., Morissette, S. B., Kamholz, B. W., Knight, J. A., Keane, T. M., Kimbrel, N. A., Carpenter, T. P., & Meyer, E. C. (2019). Alcohol use and mental health symptoms in female firefighter recruits. *Occupational Medicine, 69*(8–9), 625–631. https://doi.org/10.1093/occmed/kqaa015

Haddock, C. K., Day, R. S., Poston, W. S., Jahnke, S. A., & Jitnarin, N. (2015). Alcohol use and caloric intake from alcohol in a national cohort of U.S. career firefighters. *Journal of Studies on Alcohol and Drugs, 76*, 360–366.

Harvey, A. G., & Bryant, R. A. (1999). The relationship between acute stress disorder and posttraumatic stress disorder: A 2-year prospective evaluation. *Journal of Consulting and Clinical Psychology, 67*(6), 985–988. https://doi.org/10.1037/0022-006X.67.6.985

Huang, H., Mattke, S., Batorsky, B., Miles, J., Liu, H., & Taylor, E. (2016). Incentives, program configuration, and employee uptake of workplace wellness programs. *Journal of Occupational and Environmental Medicine, 58*(1), 30–34.

Igboanugo, S., Bigelow, P., & Mielke, J. (2021). Health outcomes of psychosocial stress within firefighters: A systematic review of the research landscape. *Journal of Occupational Health, 63*(1). https://doi.org/10.1002/1348-9585.12219

Jahnke, S. A., Carlos Poston, W. S., Haddock, C. K., Jitnarin, N., Hyder, M. L., & Horvath, C. (2012). The health of women in the US fire service. *BMC Women's Health, 12*(39), 1–12. https://doi.org/10.1186/1472-6874-12-39

Jahnke, S. A., Carlos Poston, W. S., Haddock, C. K., & Murphy, B. (2016). Firefighting and mental health: Experiences of repeated exposure to trauma. *Work, 53*(4), 737–744. https://doi.org/10.3233/wor-162255

Jones, S., Agud, K., & McSweeney, J. (2020). Barriers and facilitators to seeking mental health care among first responders: Removing the darkness. *Journal of the American Psychiatric Nurses Association, 26*(1), 43–54. https://doi.org/10.1177/1078390319871997

Kahn, S. A., Palmieri, T. L., Sen, S., Woods, J., & Gunter, O. L. (2017). Factors implicated in safety-related firefighter fatalities. *Journal of Burn Care & Research, 38*(1), e83–e88. https://doi.org/10.1097/BCR.0000000000000434

Kilpatrick, D. G., Resnick, H. S., Milanak, M. E., Miller, M. W., Keyes, K. M., & Friedman, M. J. (2013). National estimates of exposure to traumatic events and PTSD prevalence using DSM-IV and DSM-5 criteria. *Journal of Traumatic Stress, 26*(5), 537–547. https://doi.org/10.1002/jts.21848

Kim, J. E., Dager, S. R., Jeong, H. S., Ma, J., Park, S., Kim, J., Choi, Y., Lee, S. J., Kang, I., Ha, E., Cho, H. B., Lee, S., Kim, E. J., Yoon, S., & Lyoo, I. K. (2018). Firefighters, posttraumatic stress disorder, and barriers to treatment: Results from a nationwide total population survey. *PLoS One, 13*(1), 1–14. https://doi.org/10.1371/journal.pone.0190630

Lambert, J. E., Benight, C. C., Harrison, E., & Cieslak, R. (2012). The firefighter coping self-efficacy scale: Measure development and validation. *Anxiety, Stress & Coping, 25*(1), 79–91.

Marshal, R. E., Milligan-Saville, J., Petrie, K., Bryant, R. A., Mitchell, P. B., & Harvey, S. B. (2021). Mental health screening amongst police officers: Factors associated with under-reporting symptoms. *BMC Psychiatry, 21*(135), 1–8. https://doi.org/10.1186/s12888-021-03125-1

Mat Salleh, M. N. B., Ismail, D. H. B., & Mohd Yusoff, D. H. B. (2020). Prevalence and predictors for PTSD among firefighters. *A Systematic Review. International Journal of Public Health Research, 10*(1), Article 1. https://spaj.ukm.my/ijphr/index.php/ijphr/article/view/259

Meyer, E. C., Zimering, R., Daly, E., Knight, J., Kamholz, B. W., & Gulliver, S. B. (2012). Predictors of posttraumatic stress disorder and other psychological symptoms in trauma-exposed firefighters. *Psychological Services, 9*(1), 1–15. https://doi.org/10.1037/a0026414

Mysliwiec, V., McGraw, L., Pierce, R., Smith, P., Trapp, B., & Roth, B. J. (2013). Sleep disorders and associated medical comorbidities in active duty military personnel. *Sleep, 36*(2), 167–174. https://doi.org/10.5665/sleep.2364

Noor, N., Pao, C., Dragomir-Davis, M., Tran, J., & Arbona, C. (2019). PTSD symptoms and suicidal ideation in US female firefighters. *Occupational Medicine, 69*(8–9), 577–585. https://doi.org/10.1093/occmed/kqz057

Park, H., Kim, J. I., Min, B., Oh, B., & Kim, J. H. (2019). Prevalence and correlates of suicidal ideation in Korean firefighters: A nationwide study. *BMC Psychiatry, 19*(1), 1–9. https://doi.org/10.1186/s12888-019-2388-9

Petrie, K., Miligan-Saville, J., Gayed, A., Deady, M., Phelps, A., Dell, L., Forbes, D., Bryant, R. A., Calvo, R. A., Glozier, N., & Harvey, S. B. (2018). Prevalence of PTSD and common mental disorders amongst ambulance personnel: A systematic review. *Social Psychiatry and Psychiatric Epidemiology, 53*(9), 897–909. https://doi.org/10.1007/s00127-018-1539-5

Prins, A., Bovin, M. J., Kimerling, R., Kaloupek, D. G., Marx, B. P., Pless Kaiser, A., & Schnurr, P. P. (2015). *The primary care PTSD screen for DSM-5 (PC-PTSD-5).* [Measurement instrument].

Prins, A., Bovin, M. J., Smolenski, D. J., Mark, B. P., Kimerling, R., Jenkins-Guarnieri, M. A., Kaloupek, D. G., Schnurr, P. P., Pless Kaiser, A., Leyva, Y. E., & Tiet, Q. Q. (2016). The primary care PTSD screen for DSM-5 (PC-PTSD-5): Development and evaluation within a veteran primary care sample. *Journal of General Internal Medicine, 31*, 1206–1211. https://doi.org/10.1007/s11606-016-3703-5

Regehr, C., Hill, J., & Glancy, G. D. (2000). Individual predictors of traumatic reactions in firefighters. *The Journal of Nervous and Mental Disease, 188*(6), 333.

Savia, J. S. (2008). *Suicide among North Carolina professional firefighters: 1984–1999* (UMI Number: 3305393) [Doctoral dissertation, Regent University]. https://www.proquest.com/openview/244669405929f9c340cddd98459d3578/1?pq-origsite=gscholar&cbl=18750

Smith, T. D., Hughes, K., DeJoy, D. M., & Dyal, M.-A. (2018). Assessment of relationships between work stress, work-family conflict, burnout and firefighter safety behavior outcomes. *Safety Science, 103*, 287–292. https://doi.org/10.1016/j.ssci.2017.12.005

Stanley, I. H., Hom, M. A., Hagan, C. R., & Joiner, T. E. (2015). Career prevalence and correlates of suicidal thoughts and behaviors among firefighters. *Journal of Affective Disorders, 187*, 163–171. https://doi.org/10.1016/j.jad.2015.08.007

Stanley, I. H., Hom, M. A., & Joiner, T. E. (2016). A systematic review of suicidal thoughts and behaviors among police officers, firefighters, EMTs, and paramedics. *Clinical Psychology Review, 44*, 25–44. https://doi.org/10.1016/j.cpr.2015.12.002

Stout, J. W., Beidel, D. C., Brush, D., & Bowers, C. (2020). Sleep disturbance and cognitive functioning among firefighters. *Journal of Health Psychology, 26*(12), 2248–2259. https://doi.org/10.1177/1359105320909861

Thews, K. N., Winkelmann, Z. K., Eberman, L. E., Potts, K. A., & Games, K. E. (2020). Perceived barriers to reporting mental and behavioral illness in the fire service. *International Journal of Athletic Therapy and Training, 25*, 31–36. https://doi.org/10.1123/ijatt.2019-0035

Vigil, N. H., Beger, S., Gochenour, K. S., Frazier, W. H., Vadeboncoeur, T. F., & Bobrow, B. J. (2021). Suicide among the emergency medical systems occupation in the United States. *Western Journal of Emergency Medicine, 22*(2), 326–332. https://doi.org/10.5811%2Fwestjem.2020.10.48742

Vigil, N. H., Grant, A. R., Perez, O., Blust, R. N., Chikani, V., Vadeboncoeur, T. F., Spaite, D. W., & Bobrow, B. J. (2019). Death by suicide–the EMS profession compared to the general public. *Prehospital Emergency Care, 23*(3), 340–345. https://doi.org/10.1080/10903127.2018.1514090

Violanti, J. M., Fekedulegn, D., Andrew, M. E., Charles, L. E., Hartley, T. A., Vila, B., & Burchfiel, C. M. (2013). Shift work and long-term injury among police officers. *Scandinavian Journal of Work, Environment, & Health, 39*(4), 361–368. https://doi.org/10.5271/sjweh.3342

Wagner, D., Heinrichs, M., & Ehlert, U. (1998). Prevalence of symptoms of posttraumatic stress disorder in German professional firefighters. *American Journal of Psychiatry, 155*(12), 1727–1732. https://doi.org/10.1176/ajp.155.12.1727

Chapter 2
Building Trust in Employee Assistance Programs for Public Safety Personnel: Trust in Employee Assistance Programs for Police and Firefighters

Thomas J. Hodges, Kristin Horan, Adrian Alicea, Edwin Trejo-Rivera, Sophie R. Vincent, Phaina Dubuisson, Katherine Moore, Bianca Channer, Chris Hess, and Brian A. Moore

Emergency services employees such as law enforcement officers and fire rescue personnel experience high levels of occupational and traumatic stress and a high prevalence of mental and behavioral health concerns (Haugen et al., 2017) are present in public safety employees such as law enforcement officers and fire rescue personnel. Reported utilization rates of EAPs in public safety workplaces are low (Bowers et al., 2019) even though public safety personnel can access resources and treatments at no or low cost through employer-provided Employee Assistance Programs (EAPs). Major barriers to accessing EAP services among public safety personnel include stigma toward mental health and emotional expression, as well as fears about confidentiality (Jones et al., 2020; Newell et al., 2022). However, while research has

T. J. Hodges (✉) · K. Horan · A. Alicea · E. Trejo-Rivera · S. R. Vincent · P. Dubuisson · K. Moore · C. Hess · B. A. Moore
Center for the Advancement of Military and Emergency Services Research, Kennesaw State University, Kennesaw, GA, USA
e-mail: Thomas.Hodges@kennesaw.edu

K. Horan
e-mail: khoran1@kennesaw.edu

A. Alicea
e-mail: aalicea@students.kennesaw.edu

E. Trejo-Rivera
e-mail: etrejori@students.kennesaw.edu

S. R. Vincent
e-mail: svince15@kennesaw.edu

V. B. Van Hasselt and M. L. Bourke (eds.), *Advances in First Responder Mental Health*, Advances in First Responder Mental Health 1,
https://doi.org/10.1007/978-3-032-27978-1_2

uncovered these barriers in first responder populations, less is known about how human resources managers can increase the usage of EAPs among public safety personnel (Drew & Martin, 2023). Leveraging the Healthy and Resilience Organizations model (Acosta et al., 2012; Salanova et al., 2012), this study explores trust in EAPs in public safety workplaces through focus groups conducted with public safety personnel.

EAPs are services offered through workplaces to support employees and their families through various life stressors, including legal, marital, and health-related issues. EAPs refer employees to resource providers and provide free, confidential, and short-term counseling (Taranowski & Mahieu, 2013). For example, EAPs may offer general counseling or specialized financial or substance use counseling services. Employers may be keen to provide their employees with an EAP as they may improve productivity when tailored to manage life stressors, which motivates workplaces to include EAPs in employee benefits packages (Attridge, 2009). Indeed, EAPs have effectively improved absenteeism, presenteeism, distress, engagement, and life satisfaction (Attridge, 2009). Despite these benefits, utilization remains low among the general workforce (Weiss, 2010).

In public safety workplaces or adjacent high-risk work settings, published evaluations of EAPs show that treatments and services offered through EAPs are generally effective when used (Clavelle, 2009; Clavelle et al., 2012; Shakespeare-Finch & Scully, 2005; Thoen et al., 2020), but several barriers to utilization exist. First, multiple studies show that employee awareness of the presence of an EAP, awareness of services offered, and knowledge about the utilization process tend to be low (Drew & Martin, 2023). Second, public safety personnel may carry negative attitudes toward counseling and asking for help due to the stigma surrounding mental health and fears about confidentiality (Newell et al., 2022). Additionally, public safety personnel may feel they will lose their job if they report any trouble with their

P. Dubuisson
e-mail: rdubuiss@kennesaw.edu

K. Moore
e-mail: kmoor219@kennesaw.edu

C. Hess
e-mail: chess11@kennesaw.edu

B. A. Moore
e-mail: bmoore50@kennesaw.edu

B. Channer
Department of Social Work and Human Services, Kennesaw State University, Kennesaw, GA, USA
e-mail: bchanner@kennesaw.edu

C. Hess
Department of Sociology and Criminal Justice, Kennesaw State University, Kennesaw, GA, USA

K. Horan · A. Alicea · E. Trejo-Rivera · B. A. Moore
Department of Psychological Science, Kennesaw State University, Kennesaw, GA, USA

mental health (Haugen et al., 2017). For example, police may worry they will be deemed unfit for duty if they tell someone they are struggling with suicidality.

Organizations may be able to address low levels of awareness and perceived stigma through leadership training or promotion of the EAP through programs that employees already trust, such as peer support or chaplain services (Clavelle, 2009; Shakespeare-Finch & Scully, 2005). Additionally, managers can vet EAP counselors, clinicians, and service providers for competency in working with public safety personnel. For instance, having counselors with prior public safety experience, exposure, or training can foster positive attitudes toward the EAP (Newell et al., 2022). While previous research has identified these specific barriers, a more general theme running through them is trust: trust that EAP usage will remain confidential, trust that EAP counselors will understand the experiences of public safety professionals, and ultimately trust that EAPS are in the best interest of personnel.

Trust and Healthy Emergency Services Organizations

The current study explores the role of trust in first responders'awareness, attitudes, and usage of EAPs. *Trust* refers to a willingness to be vulnerable with another party, such as your organization, and the expectation that this party will act in your best interest (Mayer & Davis, 1999). When an individual believes that a party possesses adequate ability, cares about their welfare, and acts with justice and fairness, a perception of trust is fostered (Mayer et al., 1995). Trust is important for organizational health outcomes, as trust is linked to positive employee attitudes (Cho & Park, 2011) and performance outcomes (Brown et al., 2015). Trust can describe "vertical" relationships, meaning how frontline employees trust up through the organizational hierarchy, starting with their immediate managers and moving to the top levels of leadership (Acosta et al., 2012; Dirks & Ferrin, 2001). Vertical trust in the organization can be distinguished from employees' trust in their coworkers and immediate work teams (Acosta et al., 2012; Tan & Lim, 2009). By this logic, trust can also extend to the personnel of auxiliary services, such as the counselors of an EAP that a third party provides. Moreover, personnel's trust in leaders may influence the effectiveness of leadership initiatives to promote EAPs or other services.

Trust may be especially important for public safety organizations, such as police and fire departments, which face unique risks to employees' health. Public safety personnel regularly deal with traumatic events and stressors in their work, including responding to assaults, car accidents, and house fires that can result in severe injury and death. Owing to these stressful experiences, public safety personnel are at increased risk for mental health challenges, including burnout (Alexander, 1999; Smith et al., 2018), depression (Chen et al., 2007; Regehr et al., 2000; Santa Maria et al., 2018; Wagner et al., 1998), substance misuse (Carey et al., 2011; Meyer et al., 2012), and suicide (Savia, 2008; Stanley et al., 2015; Violanti et al., 2009). Additionally, many public safety personnel work long shifts at irregular hours—routinely 24 hours at a time or more for fire services and 12 hours for law enforcement—which can disrupt sleep and lead to fatigue and other negative health outcomes (Riedy et al., 2021; Senjo, 2011). Moreover, these shift work arrangements can interfere with family obligations, leading to increased stress at home (Cox et al., 2022). In addition to these risks, the modest salaries of public safety personnel contribute to financial stressors or prompt individuals to work overtime or second jobs (Riedy et al., 2021).

Trust in public safety organizations may help public safety personnel be resilient to the adverse outcomes associated with their occupation. Ironically, public safety is known for stigma against mental health (Haugen et al., 2017). Thus, trust in coworkers may facilitate mutual support among employees, for example, by making coworkers more likely to help each other and talk about stressors and traumas experienced on the job and at home (Horan et al., 2021). Trust in managers and leadership may encourage communication that improves protocols and management related to health and well-being. Indeed, there may be a reciprocal relationship between an organization's health and individuals' trust in their organization. According to the Healthy and Resilient Organizations (HERO) model, organizations can enact healthy practices such as improving communication, redesigning tasks, and implementing policies that encourage work-life balance (Acosta et al., 2012). In turn, these healthy and resilient organizations are more worthy of the trust of their employees. With increased trust, employees are more likely to be engaged in their work and subsequently perform better at their jobs (Salanova et al., 2012).

Despite the benefits that trust may have on organizational health of public safety personnel, most research on organizational trust focuses on other sectors, such as manufacturing (Jain & Sinha, 2005; Lin, 2010; Mayer & Gavin, 2005) or non-emergency public services (Kiffin-Petersen & Cordery, 2003; Suárez et al., 2009). Moreover, studies of EAPs more often focus on other public sector workers such as educators (Elson et al., 2020), employees of universities (Roberts-DeGennaro, 1989; Silberman et al., 2007; Yamatani et al., 1999), and government bureaucrats (Csiernik et al., 2012; Hsu et al., 2020; Nord & Littrell, 1990). Indeed, EAPs have primarily been developed to address the needs of these conventional employees, meaning they may not be optimized for the needs and culture of public safety personnel, including how the unique factors (i.e., trauma exposure, stressful environments) of public safety work relate to trust. Therefore, the current study sought to explore and describe the role of trust in how public safety employees relate to their EAP. Following the framework of awareness, attitudes, and usage laid out by Trice et al. (1978), we asked the following research question: What factors influence EAP awareness, attitudes, and utilization among public safety employees?

Materials and Methods

Procedure

The current study relied on qualitative data from focus group interviews with first responders. To recruit participants, the investigators provided the leaders of partnered agencies with email templates and recruitment flyers to distribute to their employees. The recruitment materials reiterated that participation in the study is not a requirement of their employment, and that no employee would be penalized for choosing to participate or not participate in the research study. Employees interested in participating completed an initial screener. The screener informed the participants of the study's procedure, risks, benefits, and compensation and then asked for their consent to participate. For individuals who consented to participate, the screener progressed to collect basic demographic and contact information.

The focus groups took place in Spring 2024. They were held on-site at agency headquarters and satellite stations, except for the individual interview, which took place online. The focus groups were scheduled to last approximately one hour, ranging from 30 minutes to 1 hour and 15 minutes. A semi-structured interview protocol guided the focus groups, with questions focused on awareness, attitudes, and usage of EAPs. Questions were worded to avoid bias by asking about positives (e.g., what does your agency do well to promote EAP usage?) and negatives (e.g., what does your agency not do well when promoting the EAP?). The protocol includes instructions, content questions, probing questions, and timing cues.

The focus groups were facilitated by the first author, a male post-doctoral researcher, with formal training in qualitative methods and prior experience working with first responders (but no prior interactions with the participating groups). A research assistant accompanied the facilitator to take field notes and provide the facilitator with feedback. After each focus group, the interviewer and assistant briefly discussed major themes to assess saturation, and the investigators also shared views of saturation with the rest of the team. Audio of the focus groups was recorded, transcribed automatically with Microsoft Word software, and then checked for accuracy by the investigators. Investigators then removed any personally identifiable information from the transcripts, including participant names, names of other personnel, names of service providers, and references to the agency's location. We did not perform any member checking of the transcripts. In the following results, respondents' names were replaced with epithets. The study and its materials received approval from the Institutional Review Board of Kennesaw State University (#IRB-FY24–360).

We followed the Consolidated criteria for reporting qualitative research (COREQ) guidelines to report our research methods (Tong et al., 2007).

Participants

In total, the research team conducted eight focus group interviews and one individual interview across four different agencies in the state of Georgia. Most focus groups had four participants, although they ranged in size from three to six participants. The study relied on purposive sampling by seeking both police and fire personnel. The participants were all first responder personnel (e.g., police or fire) working for agencies that have previously partnered with the research team on a long-term program to reduce suicidality. We chose the agencies using a convenience sampling approach. The investigators informed the agencies' leadership of an opportunity for their personnel to participate in a research study. The leaders then informed their personnel via email and face-to-face meetings. We are unsure of the number of agency personnel who were informed of the opportunity and decided not to participate. However, given the total number of personnel across these agencies, we estimate our participation rate to be 18.7%.

There were three municipal agencies from different jurisdictions (two police and one fire department) and one college police agency. Details on the agencies and their participation are provided in Table 2.1. In addition to conducting focus groups, we reviewed publicly available information on each agency's EAP, including the services provided and any available policy documents. The agencies ranged in the services offered, from mental health and substance misuse counseling only to a longer list of services that included tax preparation, legal consultation, employee discounts, and identity theft protection.

To be included in the study, individuals must have been 18 years of age or older and employed as a first responder in an agency offering an EAP as a benefit of employment. A total of 36 first responders participated in the interviews. 20 participants were fire personnel (55.6%) and 16 were police personnel (44.4%). Over half (58.3%) of the participants were not supervisors. A third of the participants were female, although notably 100% of the fire personnel were male. The majority of participants were white (86.0%) and between the ages of 25 and 54 (94.4%). Additional demographic information is reported in Table 2.2.

Table 2.1 Profile of participating agencies

	Service	Type	Location	Number of focus group/ interviews	Total number of participants
1	Fire/ rescue	Municipal	Rural	4	20
2	Police	Municipal	Metro	2	8
3	Police	College	Rural	1	1
4	Police	Municipal	Rural	2	7

Data Analysis

Using NVivo (QSR International Pty Ltd., 2018), qualitative data analysis was conducted on the interview transcripts. To analyze the data, two of the co-authors who were then unfamiliar with the data were tasked with coding the interview transcripts. They completed a Frame of Reference Training prior to coding (e.g. Galura et al., 2022; Roch et al., 2012). The coding scheme involved four parent codes (awareness, attitudes, usage, change) informed by theoretical and empirical research related to EAP utilization (e.g. Trice et al., 1978). Under each parent theme, the coders were allowed to identify child codes. After the initial round of coding, the investigators reviewed the child codes and created working definitions. Discrepancies between the coders were resolved by referencing relevant literature (Sturmer & Gerstein, 1999; Pryor & Reeder, 2011; Britt & McFadden, 2012). The coders then iterated through the transcripts again, updating codes to reflect the refined framework. In the final round of coding, the coders flagged additional areas of disagreement, which were resolved by the team collectively. With these codes established, the investigators derived major themes and subthemes from codes that were most frequent and appeared across most of the focus groups. We did not perform any participant checking.

Results

The overarching theme is trust: trust in peers, trust in the EAP counselors, and organizational considerations, which covers issues of policy and leadership. These issues manifest across the study's three focus areas of awareness, attitudes, and utilization. Below, we discuss these three focus areas, going through each of the subthemes in each area. Table 2.3 shows the themes in each area.

Awareness

Overall, awareness of EAP programs was mixed. Some focus groups confidently stated that they knew about the EAP program, what services were offered, and how to contact EAP providers. Other groups had a cursory awareness: they had heard of the EAP program but were less familiar with its services and how to contact it. Finally, several groups demonstrated confusion about what the EAP was, mixing up EAP with other programs, such as peer support, non-employer-sponsored support groups, and even the research team's engagement. Within focus groups, awareness was not always evenly distributed, with some participants having very little knowledge of the EAP because they were new hires. Other participants told us that they had used the EAP before and as a result were acquainted with contacting, scheduling, and using EAP services. Some participants were also familiar with the EAP because of their job

Table 2.2 Demographics of focus group interview participants

Variable	Category	n	%
Age	18–24 years old	1	2.8
	25–34 years old	10	27.8
	35–44 years old	15	41.6
	45–54 years old	9	25.0
	55+ years old	1	2.8
Gender	Male	24	66.7
	Female	12	33.3
Race/ethnicity	White	31	86.0
	Black or African American	1	2.8
	Multiple	2	5.6
	Hispanic, Latino, or Spanish origin	0	0.0
	Some other race, ethnicity, or origin	2	5.6
	Asian	0	0.0
	American Indian or Alaska native	0	0.0
Occupation	Fire/EMS	20	55.6
	Police/law enforcement	15	41.6
	Other	1	2.8
Supervisor	No	21	58.3
	Yes	13	36.1
	Not specified	2	5.6

$N = 36$

Table 2.3 Themes present among participants

	Awareness	Attitudes	Utilization
Trust: Peers		Stoicism/stigma	Confidentiality
Trust: EAP	Showing face	Insiders/outsiders	Rapport
Organization	Plain sight	Cost benefits	Mandated use

as administrators or supervisors. Several of the supervisors told us that they learned about the EAP as a part of their supervisory training and felt it was their duty to be informed of the EAP so they could pass the information on to subordinates in need.

Two consistent subthemes related to trust in the EAP and organizational considerations are that EAP providers need to build awareness through site visits and "showing face." Second, organizations frequently promote the EAP through regular channels, but these channels are often ignored (i.e., emails).

Trust in EAP Providers: Showing Face

A subtheme of awareness was trust in providers. As discussed with the other themes, many of the participants told us they were more likely to trust their peers rather than outside counselors from the EAP. Building trust in EAP providers starts well before personnel schedule a counseling session. While agencies promote awareness of the EAP through orientation and by posting information on bulletin boards, participants emphasized that EAP providers need to actively build rapport by "showing face"—coming to the department and making themselves familiar to the public safety personnel they serve:

> Show your face more. Like you said, when was the last time that we've seen anyone? I can't even remember the program [when] they came out and talked to us. And that was two years ago. Like if she came in right here, I'd been like [sic], "I don't know who she is." That was two years ago. Well, it's not good enough.
>
> Firefighter

For several organizations, the EAP provider was introduced to personnel at a meeting marking the start of the EAP program (or the onboarding of a new EAP provider). However, participants told us they had not seen the EAP representative at their department since that initial meeting. For two departments, several years had passed since the meeting. The other two departments had never seen the EAP provider on the premises. This lack of face time not only contributed to a lack of awareness but also impacted the participants' trust in the EAP program.

> Even if it's just coming in, dropping off goodies for the officers just to let them know, "Hey, we're here and we're available for you." Something that pours into the officers will definitely help build more of that trust. We'll go, "Okay, they're trying."
>
> Police Officer

Organizational Considerations: Plain Sight

All the groups we spoke to told us their organizations promoted the EAP. However, the level of promotion varied by department, and it was generally "hidden in plain sight." The information was available, but it was often lost in a sea of other information, making the EAP something people have heard of but have little knowledge of. The most common example participants gave was hearing about the EAP during orientation, a day when new hires are already inundated with other information. This exchange between two police personnel exemplifies the problem:

> *Police Officer #1:* There is so much stuff in their orientation.
>
> *Police Officer #2:* It's a lot.
>
> *Police Officer #1:* Their brain is just 90 to nothing. Like I even give [sic] my new hires, "After your orientation, take a nap. Just go somewhere," because it's a lot of information. So I could see it getting lost.

> *Police Officer #2:* Especially for officers because they have to go to HR. And then they go to the training, and then training is like, "OK, we're going to do this, this, and this." IT sets them up on the computer, shows them how to use the computer. They come to me, I go over policies. I put them in the computer. They go to [the Records Department]. They get fingerprints. So it's a lot.

Besides new hire orientation, many departments promoted their EAP via emails or newsletters, a mode of communication that participants told us they routinely ignored. Participants told us that even physical media, such as flyers posted on bulletin boards, tended to get drowned in a sea of information. These communication efforts may be essential: the alternative would be to not communicate about the EAP. However, our data suggest that these routine communications must be supplemented by efforts to "show face" and build rapport. Being present would be an additional means of communicating about the EAP. It would also allow for EAP providers to begin to build trust with the public safety professionals they serve.

Attitudes

Much of the focus group discussions entailed describing attitudes common among public safety personnel. On one hand, this included frequent references to a stoic attitude held by many public safety personnel, and relatedly a stigma against seeking help or talking about mental health. A second subtheme within attitudes concerned a sense of identity, with public safety personnel often describing a difference between people inside the profession and outside of it. In this respect, they tended to describe EAP counselors as outsiders. These two subthemes, stoicism/stigma and insider/outsider were largely related to negative attitudes toward the EAP. A third subtheme was less frequent but nevertheless important: some participants were encouraged by the cost-benefits of using an EAP instead of going through their insurance to pay for counseling.

Trust in Peers: Stoicism/Stigma

The focus groups consistently portrayed public safety as a profession where stoicism is expected: public safety personnel see themselves as the helpers, not people who need help.

> I'm not gonna talk to a professional. Cause I think I am the professional.
>
> Firefighter

Stoicism has a corollary in stigma. The focus groups frequently referred to a stigma against discussing mental health problems.

> When you're in a room full of first responders, the last thing you want to do is show any type of weakness… It's a stigma, it's a stereotype, it's a whatever. It's the truth.
>
> Police Officer

In some instances, participants told us this stigma resulted from fearing reprisals. For example, some participants said they thought asking for help would mark them as weak, holding them back from promotions. Others expressed that they would be placed on administrative leave and required to work at the front desk in plain clothes rather than be allowed to patrol in uniform. These concerns seemed to be more prevalent with police officers, as participants who were police personnel told us there was a concern that someone could be deemed unfit for duty:

> With law enforcement, a lot of people think that if they seek mental health treatment, they're going to take your gun away.
>
> Police Officer

Several participants mentioned that they thought mental health stigma was lessened today compared to years past. Indeed, they saw the new generation as more willing to seek help and were optimistic that newer generations could be taught to seek help instead of trying to hide their problems. Conversely, some worried that the "old school" mentality could easily transfer from tenured personnel to new personnel:

> [When] you're speaking that type of lingo to a rookie officer that's young and just got in a car, now that rookie officer might feel like they have to live up to what that senior vet just said, "I'm old school, I'm a big boy, I can handle it." So now they've adopted that same mindset in their career.
>
> Police Officer

Trust in EAP Providers: Insiders/Outsiders

All of the focus groups expressed that outsiders—people who were not police and fire personnel—had a hard time relating to the work of public safety professionals. Outsiders, they told us, could not understand the types of stressors and traumas that public safety personnel face on a daily basis. This lack of understanding sometimes extended to the basics of working as a first responder. For example, one participant told us their human resources administrator did not understand that fire personnel worked 24-hour shifts. More frequently, the concern about outsiders is that they cannot manage to hear about the traumas of public safety, such as seeing dead bodies. More than once, our participants told us stories of people going to counselors to discuss their problems only to have the counselors become upset:

> If I go to a counselor for dealing with a bad call, and then the next thing you know, you start explaining to those people, that counselor, about the call that you're on. People have dealt with where that counselor breaks down and starts crying. Well, then you're sitting here counseling the counselor.
>
> Firefighter

While the participants believed that outsiders could not understand them, they frequently said that speaking about their problems with peers was easier. This might seem to contradict the earlier theme of stoicism, in which many participants told us they were not supposed to talk about their problems. However, several discussions showed that the stoic culture of first responders was not absolute. Most individuals would be willing to talk to a trusted group of peers. For example, fire personnel told us they regularly held an informal debriefing with each other after returning from a difficult call. Police personnel told us they had a small circle of confidants to turn to with issues. Crucially, this circle of trust did not extend to everyone in their department. For people outside the circle of trust, it seems the personnel are worried about stigma and appearing stoic.

Beyond turning to trusted peers, participants frequently praised non-EAP services such as chaplains with prior public safety experience. They told us that these services knew how to relate to them better than "college-educated" counselors and people who never worked in public safety.

Organizational Considerations: Cost Benefits

Free counseling was a reason that public safety professionals might go to the EAP. Some cited the relatively low salaries of public safety professionals. Nevertheless, some still told us they would be more likely to use outside counselors despite the cost benefits of the EAP, pointing to concerns about confidentiality and trust.

Utilization

A final area of findings concerns how public safety personnel utilize EAPs. We did not ask participants directly if they have ever used the EAP. However, much of the focus group discussions revolved around issues related to usage, including what it would take for personnel to consider using the EAP; how the limited number of counseling sessions discouraged personnel from wanting to use the EAP in the first place; and how mandated EAP usage under certain circumstances might contribute to the notion that EAPs are a last resort.

Trust in Peers: Confidentiality

The most prevalent concern we heard about EAPs was that they lack confidentiality. Concerns of confidentiality took several forms. First, participants told us that if they inquired about the contact information for the EAP, then their colleagues would recognize they were using the EAP:

And at that point, you're, not only are you struggling, but now you're embarrassed, too. Yeah. Because now everybody in the department knows you got a problem.

Firefighter

Many lauded efforts to post the contact information on bulletin boards and computer systems as helping to reduce this concern. Nevertheless, some told us that they still thought their use of the EAP would "get around." One participant told us that rumors are quick to spread in a small town. Another participant provided an elaborate theory of how someone's EAP use could be leaked, even though the system is supposed to be confidential:

Well, when that company has to go to the city and say, "Okay, well, this person's came to see me. They've billed me for this many sessions. Well, they know you're there." Okay, well, does this person, are they a counselor in substance abuse? Are they, you know, marriage counseling? So, at the end of the day, they do know that you're there for one reason or another.

Firefighter

Coincidentally, another participant debunked this theory in a separate focus group, telling us that she had worked as a city administrator and seen that the paperwork used anonymous codes rather than the names of personnel. Participants who used the EAP also told us they trusted it was confidential. Still, the common perception across our focus groups was that using the EAP was not as confidential as promised. A final source of confidentiality concerns was mandated referrals to the EAP, discussed below.

Trust in EAP Providers: Rapport

Regarding utilization, only a few of our participants told us they had ever used the EAP. Indeed, they volunteered this information, as we did not ask out of respect for their privacy. Those who told us they used the EAP generally had positive things to say about it.

I would have no problem with saying that I went to the EAP. I think it's a great program. My kids think it's a great program. It actually helped them a lot. Nobody knows any of this.

Police Officer

However, a consistent complaint about the EAP related to its role as a temporary service: participants felt they did not have enough sessions with counselors to build rapport. Once they could express themselves to their counselor, their allotted number of sessions would end, and they would have to find an outside counselor to continue with. At this point, they would not only have to pay out of pocket, but they would also have to start over with the counselor, recounting the same difficulties again:

You only get "x" number of sessions. And by the time I finally develop a rapport and feel comfortable talking to this other person, my sessions are up.

Police Officer

This concern over the limited number of sessions dovetails with the previous theme of lacking trust for outsiders. Public safety personnel may not immediately trust counselors and require multiple sessions to feel comfortable discussing deeper issues. Without adequate sessions to build rapport, some participants told us they would rather avoid the EAP altogether, instead paying out of pocket for a counselor they found independently of the EAP. This essentially undermines the recognized cost benefits of using EAPs. On a positive note, participants implied that they could come to trust EAP counselors, only that this trust was squandered when the allotted number of counseling sessions ran out.

Organizational Considerations: Mandated Use

Almost all the groups noted that an employee could be mandated to use EAP services if they were facing termination. In these cases, they told us, employees who failed a drug test or were having behavioral issues would be asked to see the EAP to save their jobs. In these cases, EAP usage is not entirely confidential, with the EAP representative reporting to the agency if a specific individual has started and completed a required course of services. Still, none of the participants expressed that the EAP provided the agency with particular details beyond starting and finishing services. Nevertheless, these mandatory usage policies seemed to drive a perception that EAP usage was not normal and only for remediation rather than prevention and maintenance. In turn, these mandated use policies drove the concerns of mistrust that we have already discussed that EAPs lack confidentiality and that the use of EAPs was stigmatized:

> [If] Command [has] anything to do with any sort of counseling, mandated or not, your guys are automatically going to shut down. And they're not going to want to have anything to do with it.
>
> Police Officer

Discussion

The current study's findings show how important the different dimensions of trust are to EAP awareness, attitudes, and utilization related to EAPs. Previous research has distinguished between the focal points of trust within organizations, differentiating between trust in leadership, managers, coworkers, and within teams (Acosta et al., 2012; Andersen, 2005; Tan & Lim, 2009). Interestingly, vertical trust (i.e., trust in managers and leadership) has been suggested to help foster trust between coworkers and within teams (Acosta et al., 2012). However, whereas previous research distinguishes between the foci of trust based mainly on a role within an organization (i.e., teams, managers, leadership), the current study showed the value of rapport and shared experience in shaping circles of trust for public safety personnel. The focus groups expressed that they would trust other public safety personnel more than individuals outside that profession. This extended to EAP counselors and other mental health resources, such as chaplains or local church groups. Crucially, these outsiders could gain trust in two ways. First, they could have previous experience working in public safety. For example, one group told us of a non-EAP counseling service comprised of counselors with prior experience in public safety. The second way they could gain trust is by showing their face more, including visiting departments and stations simply to socialize.

The data also suggested that trust is not evenly shared within organizations despite the preference for outsiders over insiders. The primary source of this lack of trust seemed to be a perceived stigma around mental health. Despite the stigma, many of the participants told us that they trusted some of their coworkers to discuss mental health. For fire personnel, their station and the team they "run calls" with are their most trusted. For police, close friends or partners are trusted most.

Additionally, one group expressed a substantial lack of trust in leadership specifically. The same group said they would not trust their peer support program because the people in it lack tenure. The difference between what qualifies as an insider and an outsider may not be clear-cut, and the distinction between the two lies in the level of trust in service providers. If a service provider can familiarize themselves with the population, then the providers can make themselves more trustable, qualifying them as more of an insider.

Organizational policies and leadership influenced the trust that employees had in EAPs. The Healthy and Resilient Organizations model highlights the importance of trust in fostering healthy workplaces and increasing performance (Acosta et al., 2012; Salanova et al., 2012). With greater trust in organizations, human resource policies and initiatives such as EAP programs are more likely to impact organizational outcomes and performance because employees' trust in the initiative facilitates their usage. While this model generally suggests that trust mediates policies on outcomes, the current data suggest a more dynamic relationship where trust, policies, and outcomes may be reciprocal. While we framed our study around the idea that awareness would lead to attitudes and, ultimately, utilization, trust in EAPs may also work in the opposite direction, with experiences of EAP usage influencing other personnel. Indeed, many of the attitudes toward EAPs expressed by the public safety personnel in the current study were not first-hand experiences of the EAP. Instead, many participants told us about attitudes developed through word of mouth. This suggests that positive experiences with using EAPs can improve attitudes and awareness of EAPs, which may drive EAP usage. Initiatives wanting to enhance the EAP should leverage individuals with high levels of trust in the organization, such as "champions" who utilize programming similar to the EAP. Evaluations of these efforts could even employ network analysis techniques to determine key personnel to champion change initiatives.

Recommendations for Increasing Trust in EAPs

Previous research identified barriers to EAP utilization in public safety workplaces and suggested recommendations for managers to overcome these barriers (Clavelle, 2009; Drew & Martin, 2023; Newell et al., 2022; Shakespeare-Finch & Scully, 2005). Drawing on focus groups conducted with public safety personnel, the current study's findings suggest several ways that trust can be increased and leveraged to improve awareness, attitudes, and utilization of EAPs among public safety personnel.

Confidentiality of EAPs is vital to building more trust among first responders. However, most of the agencies surveyed expressed privacy concerns. One problem is that employees may need to ask their supervisor, human resources manager, or a colleague for the EAP contact information. This creates a potential for gossip, limiting the proper confidentiality of the EAP. Two participating agencies had a solution to this problem: post the EAP contact information in various places around the station. Flyers with information and QR codes were easy for employees to access without involving another person. Still, police agencies expressed a need for this promotion to also occur outside of the office, as they worried their co-workers would be suspicious if they showed up at the station while on patrol duty. One participant suggested adding a QR code for the EAP to the police computer system used in patrol cars. We expect agencies that put this recommendation in place will have greater EAP awareness and usage, although it is only part of what it takes to build more trust.

In addition to concerns about how EAP information is accessed, there is a clear need to establish a "bill of rights" for employees referred to the EAP. Suppose agencies insist on using EAPs as a "last resort" for employees facing termination. In that case, they must be transparent with all employees about what information can and cannot be reported to them under referral and non-referral use. They should be clear about the circumstances under which voluntary use may be reported to an employer. When employees are mandated to use the EAP, they should be informed of what information is kept confidential and by what metrics their participation in the EAP will be judged. Being transparent about what data employers can receive under mandatory use can help personnel trust that voluntary use is confidential. One of the agencies we interviewed shared their policy on EAP referrals, but it was not very detailed and contained no information about confidentiality.

Moreover, the policy was written in legalese rather than layman's terms. Additionally, EAP policies are typically only communicated to employees during new hire orientations, buried in other information, benefits, and policies. Agencies must dedicate time aside from orientation to inform personnel of EAPs, perhaps at "meet and greet" sessions where EAP providers are invited to the agency.

For our focus group participants, EAPs are synonymous with therapy or counseling. This is despite many EAPs offering multiple benefits, including tax preparation and employee discounts. Several groups expressed surprise to hear about these other benefits, and many said they were interested in using these services that could save them money. Agencies—and EAP providers themselves—need to promote all services offered by EAPs, not only counseling. Moreover, they may benefit from putting non-counseling services at the forefront of awareness campaigns. If employees get used to using the EAP for tax preparation, for example, then they may begin to normalize using the EAP for other services.

Focus group participants routinely expressed mistrust of EAP providers. Part of the mistrust stemmed from not knowing the providers personally. Many did not trust talking to a stranger over the phone. Other participants lamented that they had never seen their EAP representative or had only met the representative once at a city-wide meeting. Meanwhile, community groups offering counseling frequently visited one of the participating agencies. Personnel at that agency knew these community group representatives by name, and they told us they were more likely to contact these familiar faces before going to their EAP. In short, EAP providers need to show their face more, and agencies need to encourage these face-to-face interactions. We recommend scheduling regular visits for the EAP representatives to be on-site, provide information, or simply drop by to say hello. This puts more work on EAP providers, but that is the point. If usage is low, then the benefit is not benefiting employees.

As several focus groups expressed confusion between EAPs and other services, it would be helpful for agencies to communicate the similarities and differences in the various support programs available. These overviews could help employees understand the entire support landscape available to them. It would also help them decide which services to use at what points. In particular, noting that EAP is a short-term solution could help curtail some of the disappointment that EAP users felt when their allotted counseling sessions ran out. Specifying the number of sessions and the downside of transferring from the EAP to another provider would be a good start. For their part, EAPs and benefit providers could attempt to build systems that ensure continuity of care between EAP referrals and counseling received after allotted sessions run out. For example, EAPs could work to source counselors covered under an agency's insurance policy, allowing personnel to continue seeing the same provider.

Limitations

Rigorous qualitative research should be credible, dependable, confirmable, and transferable (Ahmed, 2024). The study's documentation and reporting of its methodology help to make it dependable, and the multi-stage team effort to code data contributes to its confirmability. However, the current study is limited in its credibility insofar as participants may have censored themselves. Given that interviews were conducted at participants' workplaces, stigma around mental health and concerns about coworker perceptions may have caused some participants to censor themselves or otherwise temper their responses. However, the research team has had a prolonged engagement with these departments, collaborating on organizational health assessments and training (Channer et al., in press). This familiarity likely contributed to trust in the research team and improved the research team's ability to understand the participant's worldviews (Johnson et al., 2020). This prolonged engagement, however, may make the findings less transferable than other sampling strategies. That is, we relied on existing relationships with organizations to recruit participants, which means the sample may have certain characteristics that make it different than other public safety agencies. Namely, given these organizations have long-standing partnerships with our team of health researchers, this may signify that the organizations already have a strong commitment to health. Alternatively, they may be organizations whose leadership who believe their organizations have a problem with mental health. Future research could address these concerns through anonymous research, such as surveys, or by recruiting research participants outside of workplaces.

Conclusion

The current study investigated awareness, attitudes, and usage of EAPs in public safety workplaces. While workplace health initiatives such as EAPs depend on trust of personnel, barriers to trust may exist in public safety workplaces that limit the effectiveness of EAPs. Focus group interviews with police and fire personnel suggested that mistrust may stem from low awareness of EAP resources as well as a lack of personally knowing EAP providers. Stoic attitudes and stigma may also contribute to a mistrust of EAPs, as do concerns about confidentiality, limited EAP sessions, and mandatory referrals. However, on a positive note, participants recognized that EAPs are cheaper than paying out of pocket for counseling. Campaigns to increase awareness of EAPs should center around building trust in EAPs providers, clarifying the role of EAPs within a larger system of resources, and describing in plain language the steps taken to ensure confidentiality under voluntary and mandatory use. Future research could also focus on EAP providers to learn more about their attitudes toward public safety personnel and their preparedness to counsel individuals in this sector. Such findings could help inform accreditation programs for EAP providers, perhaps by assisting them to create unique curricula for working with occupations that experience high rates of trauma and stress. Additionally, research could investigate the impact of trust-building activities on awareness and attitudes toward EAPs.

Acknowledgments We acknowledge Dr. Israel Sánchez-Cardona for timely comments and advice. We also acknowledge Will Ownbey for efforts related to scheduling data collection, as well as all the staff of the Center for the Advancement of Military and Emergency Services Research for continued support.

The current study was conducted as part of a project funded by the Centers for Disease Control and Prevention, a comprehensive suicide prevention program, as a partnership between the Center for the Advancement of Military and Emergency Services (AMES) Research and the Georgia Department of Public Health's Injury Prevention Program (DeAndre Cain, Elizabeth Head, Lisa Dawson, Jinny Jang, and Philip Hudson). Finally, we also would like to thank the first responders and their command teams for the time they provided to ensure this work is completed.

Funding Funding for this research was provided by the Center for Disease Control Comprehensive Suicide Prevention Program to the Georgia Department of Public Health's Injury Prevention Program.

Statements and Declarations

Competing Interests The authors have no conflicts of interest to disclose with respect to the research, authorship, and/or publication of this article.

Compliance with Ethical Standards The study and its materials received approval from the Institutional Review Board of Kennesaw State University (#IRB-FY24–360). All participants provided written informed consent prior to enrollment.

References

Acosta, H., Salanova, M., & Llorens, S. (2012). How organizational practices predict team work engagement: The role of organizational trust. *Ciencia & Trabajo, 14*, 7–15.

Ahmed, S. K. (2024). The pillars of trustworthiness in qualitative research. *Journal of Medicine, Surgery, and Public Health, 2*, 100051. https://doi.org/10.1016/j.glmedi.2024.100051

Alexander, C. (1999). Police psychosocial burnout and trauma. In J. M. Violanti & D. Paton (Eds.), *Police trauma: Psychological aftermath of civilian combat* (pp. 54–64). Charles C. Thomas Publisher.

Andersen, J. A. (2005). Trust in managers: A study of why Swedish subordinates trust their managers. *Business Ethics: A European Review, 14*(4), 392–404. https://doi.org/10.1111/j.1467-8608.2005.00420.x

Attridge, M. (2009). Employee assistance programs: A research-based primer. *International Handbook of Work and Health Psychology*, 383–407.

Bowers, C. A., Beidel, D. C., & Marks, M. R. (2019). *Mental health intervention and treatment of first responders and emergency workers*. IGI Global.

Britt, T. W., & McFadden, A. C. (2012). Understanding mental health treatment-seeking in high stress occupations. In J. Houdmont, S. Leka, & R. Sinclar (Eds.), *Contemporary occupational Health Psychology: Global perspectives on research and practice* (Vol. 2, pp. 57–73).

Brown, S., Gray, D., McHardy, J., & Taylor, K. (2015). Employee trust and workplace performance. *Journal of Economic Behavior & Organization, 116*, 361–378.

Carey, M. G., Al-Zaiti, S. S., Dean, G. E., Sessanna, L., & Finnell, D. S. (2011). Sleep problems, depression, substance use, social bonding, and quality of life in professional firefighters. *Journal of Occupational & Environmental Medicine, 53*(8), 928–933. https://doi.org/10.1097/JOM.0b013e318225898f

Channer, B., Schlenk, M., Sanchez-Cardona, I., Collette, T. L., Horan, K., Hess, C., Hodges, T., & Moore, B. A. (in press). Mental and occupational health of fire rescue personnel: A model for conducting organizational health assessments. In V. Van Hasselt *(Ed.), Advances in first responder mental health: Research, training, and practice.*

Chen, Y.-S., Chen, M.-C., Chou, F. H.-C., Sun, F.-C., Chen, P.-C., Tsai, K.-Y., & Chao, S.-S. (2007). The relationship between quality of life and posttraumatic stress disorder or major depression for firefighters in Kaohsiung. *Taiwan. Quality of Life Research, 16*(8), 1289–1297.

Cho, Y. J., & Park, H. (2011). Exploring the relationships among trust, employee satisfaction, and organizational commitment. *Public Management Review, 13*(4), 551–573.

Clavelle, P. R. (2009). Consulting to the intelligence community: An employee assistance program model. *Consulting Psychology Journal: Practice and Research, 61*(1), 14.

Clavelle, P. R., Dickerson, S. J., & Murphy, M. W. (2012). Counseling outcomes at a US Department of defense employee assistance program. *Journal of Workplace Behavioral Health, 27*(3), 127–138.

Cox, M., Norris, D., Cramm, H., Richmond, R., & Anderson, G. S. (2022). Public safety personnel family resilience: A narrative review. *International Journal of Environmental Research and Public Health, 19*(9), 5224. https://doi.org/10.3390/ijerph19095224

Csiernik, R., Chaulk, P., & McQuaid, S. (2012). A process evaluation of a Canadian public sector employee assistance program. *Journal of Workplace Behavioral Health, 27*(3), 160–180. https://doi.org/10.1080/15555240.2012.701169

Dirks, K. T., & Ferrin, D. L. (2001). The role of trust in organizational settings. *Organization Science, 12*(4), 450–467.

Drew, J. M., & Martin, S. (2023). Mental health and wellness initiatives supporting United States law enforcement personnel: The current state-of-play. *Journal of Community Safety and Well-Being, 8*(Suppl_1), S12–S22.

Elson, T. D., Heinrich, S. R., Richards, J. F., Wirawan, R. Y., & Shepard, D. S. (2020). Cost-benefit analysis of an employee assistance program for a geographically dispersed workforce in South Australia. *Journal of Workplace Behavioral Health, 35*(1), 37–54. https://doi.org/10.1080/15555240.2019.1676161

Galura, S. J., Horan, K. A., Parchment, J., Penoyer, D., Schlotzhauer, A., Dye, K., & Hill, E. (2022). Frame of reference training for content analysis with structured teams (FORT-CAST): A framework for content analysis of open-ended survey questions using multidisciplinary coders. *Research in Nursing & Health, 45*(4), 477–487.

Haugen, P. T., McCrillis, A. M., Smid, G. E., & Nijdam, M. J. (2017). Mental health stigma and barriers to mental health care for first responders: A systematic review and meta-analysis. *Journal of Psychiatric Research, 94*, 218–229.

Horan, K. A., Marks, M., Ruiz, J., Bowers, C., & Cunningham, A. (2021). Here for my peer: The future of first responder mental health. *International Journal of Environmental Research and Public Health, 18*(21), Article 21. https://doi.org/10.3390/ijerph182111097

Hsu, Y., Wang, C., & Lan, J. (2020). Evaluating the performance of employee assistance programs (EAP): A checklist developed from a large sample of public agencies. *Asia Pacific Journal of Management, 37*(3), 935–955. https://doi.org/10.1007/s10490-019-09659-z

Jain, A. K., & Sinha, A. K. (2005). General health in organizations: Relative relevance of emotional intelligence, trust, and organizational support. *International Journal of Stress Management, 12*(3), 257–273. https://doi.org/10.1037/1072-5245.12.3.257

Johnson, J. L., Adkins, D., & Chauvin, S. (2020). A review of the quality indicators of rigor in qualitative research. *American Journal of Pharmaceutical Education, 84*(1), 7120. https://doi.org/10.5688/ajpe7120

Jones, S., Agud, K., & McSweeney, J. (2020). Barriers and facilitators to seeking mental health care among first responders: Removing the darkness. *Journal of the American Psychiatric Nurses Association, 26*(1), 43–54.

Kiffin-Petersen, S., & Cordery, J. (2003). Trust, individualism and job characteristics as predictors of employee preference for teamwork. *The International Journal of Human Resource Management, 14*(1), 93–116. https://doi.org/10.1080/09585190210158538

Lin, C.-P. (2010). Modeling corporate citizenship, organizational trust, and work engagement based on attachment theory. *Journal of Business Ethics, 94*(4), 517–531.

Mayer, R. C., & Davis, J. H. (1999). The effect of the performance appraisal system on trust for management: A field quasi-experiment. *Journal of Applied Psychology, 84*(1), 123–126.

Mayer, R. C., Davis, J. H., & Schoorman, F. D. (1995). An integrative model of organizational trust. *Academy of Management Review, 20*(3), 709–734. https://doi.org/10.2307/258792

Mayer, R. C., & Gavin, M. B. (2005). Trust in management and performance: Who minds the shop while the employees watch the boss? *Academy of Management Journal, 48*(5), 874–888. https://doi.org/10.5465/amj.2005.18803928

Meyer, E. C., Zimering, R., Daly, E., Knight, J., Kamholz, B. W., & Gulliver, S. B. (2012). Predictors of posttraumatic stress disorder and other psychological symptoms in trauma-exposed firefighters. *Psychological Services, 9*(1), 1–15. https://doi.org/10.1037/a0026414

Newell, C. J., Ricciardelli, R., Czarnuch, S. M., & Martin, K. (2022). Police staff and mental health: Barriers and recommendations for improving help-seeking. *Police Practice and Research, 23*(1), 111–124.

Nord, J., & Littrell, J. M. (1990). Predictors of supervisors' referrals of employees to an employee assistance program. *Employee Assistance Quarterly, 5*(2), 21–40. https://doi.org/10.1300/J022v05n02_02

Pryor, J. B., & Reeder, G. D. (2011). HIV-related stigma. In *HIV/AIDS in the post-HAART era: Manifestations, treatment and epidemiology* (pp. 790–806). PMPH-USA, Ltd.

QSR International Pty Ltd. [software]. (2018). *NVivo qualitative data analysis* (Version 12). https://support.qsrinternational.com/nvivo/s/

Regehr, C., Hill, J., & Glancy, G. D. (2000). Individual predictors of traumatic reactions in firefighters. *The Journal of Nervous and Mental Disease, 188*(6), 333.

Riedy, S. M., Fekedulegn, D., Vila, B., Andrew, M., & Violanti, J. M. (2021). Shift work and overtime across a career in law enforcement: A 15-year study. *Policing: An. International Journal, 44*(2), 200–212. https://doi.org/10.1108/PIJPSM-08-2020-0134

Roberts-DeGennaro, M. (1989). Needs assessment for a university-based employee assistance program. *Employee Assistance Quarterly, 4*(3), 11–25. https://doi.org/10.1300/J022v04n03_02

Roch, S. G., Woehr, D. J., Mishra, V., & Kieszczynska, U. (2012). Rater training revisited: An updated meta-analytic review of frame-of-reference training. *Journal of Occupational and Organizational Psychology, 85*(2), 370–395. https://doi.org/10.1111/j.2044-8325.2011.02045.x

Salanova, M., Llorens, S., Cifre, E., & Martínez, I. M. (2012). We need a hero! Toward a validation of the HEalthy and Resilient Organization (HERO) Model. *Group & Organization Management, 37*(6), 785–822. https://doi.org/10.1177/1059601112470405

Santa Maria, A., Wörfel, F., Wolter, C., Gusy, B., Rotter, M., Stark, S., Kleiber, D., & Renneberg, B. (2018). The role of job demands and job resources in the development of emotional exhaustion, depression, and anxiety among police officers. *Police Quarterly, 21*(1), 109–134. https://doi.org/10.1177/1098611117743957

Savia, J. S. (2008). *Suicide among North Carolina professional firefighters: 1984–1999* (Publication No. 3305393) [Doctoral dissertation, Regent University]. Pro Quest LLC. https://www.proquest.com/openview/244669405929f9c340cddd98459d3578/1?pq-origsite=gscholar&cbl=18750

Senjo, S. R. (2011). Dangerous fatigue conditions: A study of police work and law enforcement administration. *Police Practice and Research, 12*(3), 235–252.

Shakespeare-Finch, J., & Scully, P. (2005). A multi-method evaluation of an Australian public safety employee assistance program. *Employee Assistance Quarterly, 19*(4), 71–91.

Silberman, A., Kendall, J. W., Price, A. L., & Rice, T. A. (2007). University employee assistance program response to traumas on campus. *Journal of Workplace Behavioral Health, 22*(2–3), 91–109. https://doi.org/10.1300/J490v22n02_07

Smith, T. D., Hughes, K., DeJoy, D. M., & Dyal, M.-A. (2018). Assessment of relationships between work stress, work-family conflict, burnout and firefighter safety behavior outcomes. *Safety Science, 103*, 287–292. https://doi.org/10.1016/j.ssci.2017.12.005

Stanley, I. H., Hom, M. A., Hagan, C. R., & Joiner, T. E. (2015). Career prevalence and correlates of suicidal thoughts and behaviors among firefighters. *Journal of Affective Disorders, 187*, 163–171. https://doi.org/10.1016/j.jad.2015.08.007

Sturmer, P. J., & Gerstein, L. H. (1999). Message source characteristics and employee assistance program advertising. Beliefs in program effectiveness and intentions to self-refer. *Employee Assistance Quarterly, 15*(1), 77–105.

Suárez, T., Caballero, A., & Sánchez, F. (2009). Incidencia de la mentira en la confianza y la cooperación en el ámbito laboral. *Revista Latinoamericana de Psicología, 41*(2), 224.

Tan, H. H., & Lim, A. K. H. (2009). Trust in coworkers and trust in organizations. *The Journal of Psychology, 143*(1), 45–66. https://doi.org/10.3200/JRLP.143.1.45-66

Taranowski, C. J., & Mahieu, K. M. (2013). Trends in employee assistance program implementation, structure, and utilization, 2009 to 2010. *Journal of Workplace Behavioral Health, 28*(3), 172–191.

Thoen, M. A., Dodson, L. E., Manzo, G., Piña-Watson, B., & Trejos-Castillo, E. (2020). Agency-offered and officer-utilized suicide prevention and wellness programs: A national study. *Psychological Services, 17*(2), 129.

Tong, A., Sainsbury, P., & Craig, J. (2007). Consolidated criteria for reporting qualitative research (COREQ): A 32-item checklist for interviews and focus groups. *International Journal for Quality in Health Care, 19*(6), 349–357. https://doi.org/10.1093/intqhc/mzm042

Trice, H. M., Beyer, J. M., & Hunt, R. E. (1978). Evaluating implementation of a job-based alcoholism policy. *Journal of Studies on Alcohol, 39*(3), 448–465.

Violanti, J. M., Fekedulegn, D., Charles, L. E., Andrew, M. E., Hartley, T. A., Mnatsakanova, A., & Burchfiel, C. M. (2009). Suicide in police work: Exploring potential contributing influences. *American Journal of Criminal Justice, 34*(1), 41–53. https://doi.org/10.1007/s12103-008-9049-8

Wagner, D., Heinrichs, M., & Ehlert, U. (1998). Prevalence of symptoms of posttraumatic stress disorder in German professional firefighters. *American Journal of Psychiatry, 155*(12), 1727–1732. https://doi.org/10.1176/ajp.155.12.1727

Weiss, R. M. (2010). Employee assistance program (EAP) referral agents' conceptions of the causes and treatment of alcohol dependence. *Journal of Workplace Behavioral Health, 25*(3), 195–200.

Yamatani, H., Santangelo, L. K., Maue, C., & Heath, M. C. (1999). A comparative analysis and evaluation of a university employee assistance program. *Employee Assistance Quarterly, 15*(1), 107–118. https://doi.org/10.1300/J022v15n01_05

Chapter 3
Crime Scene Investigators: Findings from the National Wellness Survey for Public Safety Personnel

Gabrielle L. LaRock, Ryan A. Black, Michael L. Bourke, Vincent B. Van Hasselt, Teresa Bryant, and Jessica R. Blalock

Crime scene investigators (CSIs) have the role of examining, evaluating, documenting, processing, and collecting evidence at crime scenes (International Crime Scene Investigators Association, n.d.). They play a crucial role in the criminal justice system, often working under highly stressful and demanding conditions. Unlike other first responders, CSIs face distinct occupational stressors, since they are not directly exposed to traumatic events as they occur, but rather, are deeply immersed in their aftermath. They often spend extended periods of time at crime scenes and engage more intimately with various aspects of the event than other first responders involved in the incident (Leone & Keel, 2016). The mental health of CSIs is a growing concern, as repeated exposure to traumatic environments and high-stress working conditions have been shown to heighten stress levels, contribute to the onset of mental health symptoms and disorders, increase job burnout, and diminish cognitive functioning.

The psychological impact on CSIs can be substantial, with many reporting instances in which "the stress had become too much for them to cope" (Sollie et al., 2017). These professionals encounter a wide range of occupational stressors. Key demands associated with CSI work-related activities include: exposure to human suffering (Sollie et al., 2017), the pressure to balance conflicting goals and

G. L. LaRock (✉) · R. A. Black · V. B. Van Hasselt · J. R. Blalock
College of Psychology, Nova Southeastern University, Davie, USA
e-mail: gl840@mynsu.nova.edu

M. L. Bourke
Raven, Dallas, USA

V. B. Van Hasselt
Broward Sheriff's Office, Fort Lauderdale, USA

T. Bryant
Jupiter Police Department, Jupiter, USA

V. B. Van Hasselt and M. L. Bourke (eds.), *Advances in First Responder Mental Health*, Advances in First Responder Mental Health 1,
https://doi.org/10.1007/978-3-032-27978-1_3

deadlines imposed by other on-scene personnel while ensuring their work remains meticulous and error-free (van de Eeden et al., 2017), administrative burdens (Sollie et al., 2017), high caseloads (Levin et al., 2021), long and irregular work hours (Kelty & Gordon, 2014), frequent on-call responsibilities (Sollie et al., 2017), and the physically demanding and often hazardous conditions of crime scenes (Sollie et al., 2017).

Evidence suggests that one of the most significant factors influencing stress levels of CSIs is their exposure to traumatic stimuli (Van Patten & Burke, 2001). The number of traumatic death events processed does not appear to be a major contributing factor; however, stress levels have been shown to vary based on the specific components of the crime scene under investigation (Waugh, 2013). For example, crime scenes that show higher levels of violence and morbidity are associated with more symptoms of post-incident stress. The most significant increases in post-incident stress are rooted in incidents that remind CSI's of their loved ones (Clark et al., 2015), involve an individual with whom they have a personal connection (Ferraro, 2024), a child victim (Ferraro, 2024), multiple deaths (Clark et al., 2015), and a line of duty officer fatality (Leone & Keel, 2016). Further, the presence of a victim's loved ones at the scene can further challenge a CSI's ability to remain detached, significantly adding to their stress (Kelty & Gordon, 2014).

The CSI's organization also plays a role in their post-incident stress experience. Agencies with in-house crime labs, peer support programs, and stress mitigation training (Leone & Keel, 2016), as well as those perceived by CSIs as supportive and appreciative of their work (Clark et al., 2015), are associated with lower stress levels. Agencies requiring CSIs to be sworn officers were found to have a significant impact on stress mitigation, as sworn CSIs demonstrated greater awareness of stress reduction programs, and were more likely to be required to participate in these following exposure to critical incident stress (Leone & Keel, 2016). Some CSIs have reported that certain team colleagues may display certain negative attitudes or lower quality work that create conflict. This may prove to be a greater source of stress than the actual work itself (Sollie et al., 2017). Finally, circumstances within a CSI's personal life (e.g., relationship conflict, financial burden) may affect their ability to manage stress at work (Plombon et al., 2020).

While not directly involved in traumatic incidents, CSIs often experience negative psychological impacts due to repeated exposure to the aftermath of crimes. These high rates of exposures to critical incidents have been associated with elevated levels of post-incident stress symptoms. Illustrative are the findings of Clark et al. (2015), who studied 51 CSIs from 14 agencies across a large Midwestern state. They found that 63% reported moderate to high levels of post-incident stress following exposure to critical incidents. Further, Adderley et al. (2012) examined 12 CSIs from a United Kingdom police force and observed that they exhibited increased heart rate, not due to physical activity, but as a result of stress when conducting the crime scene investigation. Additionally, Levin et al. (2021) noted that among the 419 CSIs from seven crime laboratories and medical examiner offices in the United States that were included in his study, feelings of burnout were common, highlighting the emotional strain associated with their work.

Moreover, this repeated exposure increases CSIs risk of developing posttraumatic stress disorder (PTSD) compared to the general population. Indeed, studies conducted to date have estimated prevalence rates for PTSD in CSIs to range between 9.3% and 19.9% (Mrevlje, 2018; Nho & Kim, 2017; Rosansky et al., 2019), compared to general U.S. population lifetime rates of 6.1% (Goldstein et al., 2016). Even for those who do not meet full criteria for PTSD, subthreshold symptomatology may be present. For example, Mrevlje (2018) observed that among the 64 male Slovene CSIs, 12.5% exhibited elevated PTSD symptomatology, despite not meeting criteria for a PTSD diagnosis. Traumatic functioning was also prevalent and included cognitive avoidance, traumatically induced perceptual problems, moderately impaired reality testing, and failure to modify their behavior in accordance with contextual demands. Rosansky et al. (2019) found that commonly elevated PTSD symptoms of hypervigilance and strong negative beliefs about oneself, others, or the world were present in over half of the 225 CSIs sampled across geographic regions of the U.S.

The National Wellness Survey for Public Safety Personnel

The Fairfax County (Virginia) Police Department (FCPD) has endured 15 suicides of active and retired law enforcement officers in the past 30 years, five of which occurred within the last eight years (Bourke et al., 2024). In 2017, an officer died by suicide in the parking lot of the police station. The resulting grief propelled the agency to make unprecedented efforts to (1) de-stigmatize the effects of trauma, and (2) underscore the benefits of asking for help. In 2018, FCPD approved the 2018–2019 Fairfax County Public Safety Mental Health Pilot Survey, the goals of which were to "raise awareness and reduce stigma about psychological health, trauma, and suicide" (Mills et al., 2020, p. 2). During this time, the Behavioral Analysis Unit of the United States Marshals Service provided analytical support for the pilot survey and, in collaboration with FCPD and Nova Southeastern University, developed a survey instrument to broaden the internal agency-specific evaluation for administration of a national survey of public safety professionals (Bourke et al., 2024).

The primary aim of the National Wellness Survey for Public Safety Personnel was to identify personal and occupational stressors as well as access to mental health services in public safety professionals. The present investigation was part of a more comprehensive evaluation of mental health in a wide range of first responder populations. Guided by previous research, the study objectives were to determine: (a) the prevalence and severity of anxiety, depression, PTSD, alcohol use, and suicidal ideation in a national sample of CSIs, (b) access to mental health resources, and (c) barriers to seeking treatment.

Participants

Agencies at the federal, state, local, and tribal levels and private entities were identified to collect a national representative sample of 301 CSIs. Inclusion criteria included being 18 years of age or older and having been in the role of a CSI sometime throughout their public safety career.

A total of 301 participants indicated that they had served the role of a CSI. Demographic characteristics of the sample are presented in Table 3.1. A higher number of men than women were represented, with most participants falling between the ages of 36 and 55. The majority of participants (90.0%) identified as White. Additionally, a large portion of the participants (72.7%) indicated they were a parent or guardian to a child or children and 90.3% reported being in a committed relationship. Further, of the participants 45.1% indicated working between 41 and 49 hours a week (including overtime).

Departmental demographics, including work environment, and agency size are listed in Table 3.2. Majority of the participants indicated they worked in an urban environment. Of the participants 28.7% identified working with agencies that had over 1000 employees. Departmental locations with the most participants included Virginia (40.4%), Ohio (14.7%), and California (9.9%).

Procedure

The National Wellness Survey for Public Safety Personnel obtained information in five areas: (a) life experiences, aimed at understanding participants' exposure to stressful events; (b) personal and professional history of trauma exposure focused on traumatic experiences, including various specific scenarios; (c) individual and departmental demographics gathered data related to time spent on the job, agency size, and type of community served; (d) stress and stress management inquired about personal and occupational stressors, coping mechanisms, and behaviors the CSIs engaged in to manage stress; and (e) health and wellness elicited information about previous mental health history, including diagnosis, access to services, and barriers to seeking treatment. Also included was an assessment battery (see Measures below) to assess current symptomatology.

Participants were provided with information explaining the purpose and anticipated benefits of the research, the identification of the researchers conducting the study, the expected duration of participation, and a statement of voluntary participation. Additionally, participants were provided with a notice that refusing or discontinuing at any time would incur no penalty, and a statement that the data obtained will remain strictly confidential and anonymous. Further, they received clear and thorough directions on how to complete the assessment measures via the online survey. The investigation was approved by the participating university's Institutional Review Board.

Table 3.1 Demographic characteristics

Characteristics	*n*	%
Sex		
Male	228	76.3
Female	71	23.7
Age range		
18 to 20	0	0
21 to 25	4	1.3
26 to 35	49	16.3
36 to 45	111	37.0
46 to 55	119	39.7
56 or older	17	5.7
Race		
White	271	90.0
Black or African American	10	3.3
Asian	7	2.3
American Indian or Alaska native	8	2.7
Other	8	2.7
Native Hawaiian or other Pacific islander	3	1.0
Ethnicity		
Hispanic, Latino, or Spanish origin	20	6.6
Sexual orientation		
Heterosexual or straight	289	97.3
Gay or lesbian	3	1.0
Bisexual	3	1.0
Other	2	0.7
Education		
Bachelor's degree	139	46.3
Some college (no degree)	67	22.3
Associate's degree	43	14.3
Master's degree	38	12.7
High school diploma/ GED	11	3.7
Trade or technical certification	1	0.3
Doctoral/ professional degree	1	0.3
U.S. military veteran	62	20.7
Supervisory status	91	30.4
Committed relationship	270	90.3
Parent or Guardian	218	72.7
Weekly hours		
Less than 40 hours	4	1.3

(continued)

Table 3.1 (continued)

Characteristics	*n*	%
40 hours	65	21.9
41 to 49 hours	134	45.1
50 to 59 hours	60	20.2
60 to 69 hours	24	8.1
70 to 79 hours	5	1.7
80 hours or more	5	1.7

Note $N = 301$. Weekly hours included overtime hours

Table 3.2 Departmental demographics

Characteristics	*n*	%
Agency size		
1 to 4 employees	5	1.7
5 to 9 employees	5	1.7
10 to 24 employees	20	6.7
25 to 49 employees	24	8.0
50 to 99 employees	41	13.7
100 to 249 employees	52	17.3
250 to 499 employees	31	10.3
500 to 999 employees	36	12.0
1000 or more employees	86	28.7
Work environment		
Urban	214	71.1
Rural	141	46.8
Specific facility, camp, or grounds	31	10.3
Cyber crimes	14	4.7
Home	6	2.0

Note $N = 301$

Participants received an email from the United States Marshals Service's Behavioral Analysis Unit containing a brief description of the study and a link to access the survey. Upon clicking the link, they were directed to the informed consent page where the study goals, potential harms and benefits were discussed. Once the participant consented to participate, they were directed to complete the online questionnaires. Those who did not consent to the study, or wished to cease participation, were prompted to close the webpage. Participants were allowed to skip any question. If the subject responded with "Yes" or "Maybe" to a question asking if they had experienced recent (within the past month) stress-related symptoms, they were asked to also complete the Posttraumatic Stress Disorder Checklist for DSM-5 (PCL-5; Weathers et al., 2013). Otherwise, the survey concluded by allowing an open text response for the participant to provide feedback on anything they chose to disclose. Anonymity was reiterated, and due to the sensitive nature of certain questions, respondents were provided with the contact information for Safe Call Now, a nationwide confidential, comprehensive, 24-hour crisis referral service for all public safety employees, emergency services personnel, and their family members.

The survey was sent out in three separate waves. The first email included an initial introduction with relevant information related to the survey and an accessible, individual link. Approximately one week later, a reminder email was sent with a new individualized and accessible link. The subject was asked to disregard the email if they had already completed the survey. The reminder was sent in this manner because participants' email addresses were not being tracked; consequently, researchers could not send it to only those who had not yet opened or completed the survey. With the goal of reaching those individuals who perhaps intended to complete the survey but were away from work or simply had become busy with other tasks, a third and final reminder email was sent one week later with the same aforementioned content.

This research was conducted using the online survey platform Qualtrics (https://www.qualtrics.com), where the data were directly input by the participants. Qualtrics is a web-based tool to conduct survey research, evaluations, and other data collection activities. Although the software can identify a computer's Internet Protocol (IP) address, this information was not collected or stored by the researchers. Further, participants were allowed to access the survey from any electronic device, both public and private, which further reduced the ability to identify an individual based on their IP address. Information collected was kept strictly confidential and was only viewed by researchers conducting the study on password-protected computers. No identifying information was collected from the online survey. Upon the study's completion, all emails from distribution lists were permanently deleted.

Measures

The measures below were included in Sect. 5 (Health and Wellness) to obtain specific information about symptoms experienced by CSIs.

Generalized Anxiety Disorder (GAD-7)

The GAD-7 (Spitzer et al., 2006) is a 7-item (α=0.937) self-report screening measure for the presence of clinically significant anxiety symptoms. Respondents are asked to rank items on a four-point Likert scale (0 = Not at all; 3 = Nearly every day) to assess the severity of anxiety symptoms that have occurred over the past two weeks. Total scores range between 0 and 21, with higher scores indicative of greater symptom severity. This instrument has been validated as a diagnostic tool for generalized anxiety disorder (GAD) with a cut off score of 10 (sensitivity 89%, specificity 82%) (Spitzer et al., 2006). Within the U.S. general population, prevalence of GAD ranges between 1.6 and 5% (Spitzer et al., 2006), with the *Diagnostic and Statistical Manual of Mental Disorders fifth edition, Text Revision* (*DSM-5-TR*) estimating 2.9% (American Psychiatric Association [APA], 2022).

Patient Health Questionnaire (PHQ-9)

The PHQ-9 (Kroenke & Spitzer, 2002) is a 9-item ($\alpha = 0.894$) self-report measure quantifying the symptoms and severity of depression. Respondents are asked to rate each item on a four-point Likert scale (0 = Not at all; 3 = Nearly every day) to assess the presence and severity of depressive symptoms within the past two weeks. Total scores range from 0 to 27; higher scores are associated with decreased functionality and increased symptom-related difficulty (Kroenke & Spitzer, 2002). A recent meta-analysis concluded the PHQ-9 cutoff score of 10 or more maximized combined sensitivity (83%–92%) and specificity (82%–88%) in 29 studies using a semi-structured interview to detect major depression (Levis et al., 2019). Within the U.S. general population, prevalence of Major Depressive Disorder (MDD) has been found to be 7% among adults (APA, 2022).

Posttraumatic Stress Disorder Checklist for DSM-5 (PCL-5)

The PCL-5 (Weathers et al., 2013) is a 20-item ($\alpha = 0.929$) self-report measure assessing the DSM-5 symptoms of PTSD. Respondents are asked to rate each item on a 5-point scale (0 = Not at all; 4 = Extremely) to assess symptom severity within the past month. Total symptom severity scores range from 0 to 80, with higher scores indicative of greater symptom severity. Initial research suggests that a PCL-5 cutoff score between 31 and 33 represents clinical significance and indicates the individual may benefit from PTSD treatment (Weathers et al., 2013). The PCL-5 has demonstrated good internal consistency, test-retest reliability, and convergent and discriminant validity (Blevins et al., 2015). Between 6.1 and 8.3% of U.S. adults meet criteria for PTSD in the general population (APA, 2022).

Cut, Annoyed, Guilty, and Eye (CAGE)

The Cut, Annoyed, Guilty, and Eye (CAGE; Ewing, 1984) is a 4-item ($\alpha = 0.787$) self-report screener for excessive drinking and alcoholism. Respondents are asked to rate each item on a dichotomous scale (Yes/No) for items related to personally feeling the need to reduce their alcohol consumption, annoyed by others' criticism related to their drinking, personal guilt associated with their drinking, and the need for a drink first thing in the morning. Total scores that meet or exceed the cutoff score of two result in a "positive screening" for excessive alcohol consumption. This measure was chosen due to the ease of administration, established efficacy, and considerable potential for screening high-risk groups (Ewing, 1984). Compared to other alcohol screening measures (e.g., Alcohol Use Disorder Identification Test [AUDIT]; Babor et al., 1992), CAGE questions have proven superior for detecting alcohol abuse and dependence, with sensitivity ranging between 43% and 94% and specificity between 70% and 97% (Fiellin et al., 2000). Within the U.S. general population, 8.6% have difficulty with alcohol abuse (APA, 2022).

Columbia Suicide Severity Rating Scale (C-SSRS)

The C-SSRS (Posner et al., 2011) is a brief suicide screening assessment ($\alpha = 0.8$) used to identify individuals at risk for suicide, assess the severity an immediacy of risk, and gauge the level of support needed (Posner et al., 2011). Participants are asked to endorse binary responses (Yes/No) to identify potential risk for passive and active suicidal ideation, as well as suicidal behavior. In the general U.S. population, passive suicidal ideation prevalence ranges from 5.8% for one-year prevalence to 10.6% for lifetime prevalence. Active suicidal ideation prevalence ranges from 2% (one year) to 9% (lifetime) (Liu et al., 2020).

Results

Past Professional Roles

CSIs served in the following other public safety roles during their career: Sworn Law Enforcement (86%; $n = 259$); Internet Crimes Against Children (ICAC) Investigators (13.6%; $n = 41$); Military—Active Duty (12.6%; $n = 38$); Emergency Medical Services—Professional (12.3%; $n = 37$); Fire and Rescue - Professional (11.6%; $n = 35$); Fire and Rescue—Volunteer (11.3%; $n = 34$); Corrections (11%; $n = 33$); Public Safety Communications (10.6%; $n = 32$); Other Public Safety Role (10.6%, $n = 32$); Emergency Medical Services—Volunteer (10.3%; $n = 31$); Wildland Firefighter (9.6%; $n = 29$); Military—Reserve or National Guard (8%; $n = 24$); Reserve/Auxiliary Law Enforcement (7.6%; $n = 23$); Tribal Law Enforcement (1.7%; $n = 5$).

Trauma Exposure

CSIs endorsed exposure to the following traumatic incidents at work: accidental death that did not result from your actions (95.4%; $n = 286$); serious assault, non-accidental injury, and/or severe human suffering caused by another person (93.7%; $n = 279$); suicide (89.9%; $n = 268$); non-accidental death (88%; $n = 264$); life threatening illness, or severe human suffering due to natural causes (82%; $n = 246$);

Table 3.3 Prevalence of previous mental health history

Mental health diagnoses	Past 30 days (%)	Past year (%)	More than one year ago (%)	Childhood or Adolescence (%)
Depressive disorder	0.4	1.8	10.2	1.8
Panic disorder	0.4	0.7	4.9	1.1
PTSD	1.4	2.8	9.1	0
Anxiety disorder	1	2.1	5.6	1.7
ADHD	0.7	0.3	2.8	4.9
Substance abuse	0.7	0.7	1	0
Sleep disorder	1	4.2	13.2	1.4

Note $N = 301$

sexual assault or other unwanted sexual experiences that caused distress (73.3%; $n = 219$); situations involving civil mass disorder (65.7%; $n = 197$); kidnapping or a hostage situation (63.3%; $n = 190$); serious injury or harm that resulted from your actions (22.4%; $n = 67$); death that resulted from your actions (12.4%; $n = 37$).

Mental Health Information

Previous Diagnoses

Table 3.3 highlights previous mental health diagnoses respondents received ranging from childhood/adolescence to the past 30 days from when they took the survey. These include a depressive disorder (e.g., dysthymia, major depressive disorder), panic disorder (e.g., panic attacks), posttraumatic stress disorder (PTSD) or another trauma-related disorder, anxiety disorder (e.g., phobia, generalized anxiety disorder), attention deficit hyperactivity disorder (ADHD), sleep disorder, and substance use disorder. Per participants, a mental health diagnosis more than one year ago was the most prevalent and included depressive disorder, PTSD, and sleep disorder.

Anxiety

Almost 50.7% of respondents endorsed experiencing anxiety symptoms beyond the minimal severity threshold. Specifically, 26.4% endorsed mild anxiety, 12.7% endorsed moderate anxiety, and 11.6% endorsed severe anxiety levels. In combination, 24.5% of respondents that endorsed anxiety symptoms met or exceeded the diagnostic cutoff (10) for Generalized Anxiety Disorder. Mean, standard deviations, and ranges are listed in Table 3.4.

Depression and Suicidality

Slightly more than 51.7% of respondents endorsed experiencing depressive symptoms beyond the minimal severity threshold. More specifically, 28.6% endorsed mild depressive symptoms, 13.4% endorsed moderate depressive symptoms, 5.9% endorsed moderately severe depressive symptoms, and 3.8% endorsed severe depressive symptoms. Together, 23.1% of respondents endorsed depressive symptoms that met or exceeded the diagnostic cutoff score ($\geq$10) for major depressive disorder. Means, standard deviations, and range are listed in Table 3.4.

The C-SSRS highlighted that 7.8% of participants reported experiencing thoughts of passive suicidal ideation (i.e., thoughts of wishing they were dead or wishing they could go to sleep and not wake up). Passive ideation represents the presence of thoughts of suicide or self-harm, but no plan to carry it out. Further, 4.1% reported experiencing thoughts of active suicidal ideation, which represents thoughts of suicide and a plan to carry it out. Of the respondents who endorsed having a suicidal plan (n = 12), 11 respondents thought about how they would die by suicide, two respondents had an intention of acting on the suicidal thoughts, and one respondent attempted to die by suicide, started to do something to end their life before something or someone stopped them, or took steps toward preparing to end their life.

Alcohol Use

Based on the results from the CAGE, 21.5% endorsed consuming alcohol to the extent that met or exceeded the cutoff score for "positive screening," representing a potential problem with alcohol abuse. Mean, standard deviations, and range are listed in Table 3.4.

Posttraumatic Stress Symptoms

Finally, 38.5% ($n = 116$) of respondents did not complete the PCL-5. This decrease in responses is likely due to the survey design as the PCL-5 was prompted only if the CSI endorsed stress-related symptoms. However, of the 185 participants who did complete this measure, 25.4% ($n = 47$) received scores above the threshold representing clinical significance, which suggests that PTSD treatment may be beneficial in symptom reduction. Mean, standard deviations, and range are listed in Table 3.4.

Table 3.4 Current mental health symptomatology

Measure	N	M	SD	Range
GAD-7	292	1.74	1.18	0–21
PHQ-9	290	6.12	5.78	0–27
CAGE	292	0.60	0.89	0–4
PCL-5	185	1.25	0.44	0–80

Note. Score Interpretations: GAD-7 (0–4 minimal; 5–9 mild; 10–14 moderate; 15–21 severe); PHQ-9 (0–4 minimal; 5–9 mild; 10–14 moderate; 15–19 moderately severe; 20–27 severe); CAGE (score of 2 or more is indicative of excessive alcohol consumption); PCL-5 (31–33 indicative of probable PTSD)

Stress

For this section, when at least 30% of participants endorsed a stressor, it is reported below.

Professional Stressors

Participants were asked to indicate stressors they experienced in their professional life during the past year. The following were commonly endorsed professional stressors by CSIs: negative media about the profession (84.1%; $n = 253$); concerns about exposure to COVID-19 (80.7%; $n = 243$); responding to critical incidents (78.1%; $n = 235$); negative attitudes from the general public about the profession (73.8%; $n = 222$); low morale in the workforce (68.8%; $n = 207$); government officials outside the organization do not understand what they deal with (64.8%; $n = 195$); being directly involved in critical incidents (59.5%; $n = 179$); higher-level leadership does not understand the challenges they deal with (57.5%; $n = 173$); higher-level leadership does not run the organization effectively (50.8%; $n = 153$); concerns about sleep disruption while on call (48.5%; $n = 146$); overworked (47.8%; $n = 144$); threats made toward them or their co-workers because of their profession (47.8%; $n = 144$); co-workers do not pull their own weight (46.8%; $n = 141$); lack of community support (43.2%; $n = 130$); being involved in critical incidents involving a child or children (42.9%; $n = 129$); micromanagement from their supervisor (37.2%; $n = 112$); higher-level leadership does not enable them to do their job effectively (35.9%; $n = 108$); inadequate equipment/ resources (31.2%; $n = 94$).

Personal Stressors

Participants were asked to indicate stressors in their personal life they experienced within the past year. The following were commonly endorsed personal stressors: lack of sleep/ sleep issues (61.8%; $n = 186$); lack of time for recreational activities

(54.5%; $n = 164$); lack of time for personal life tasks (52.2%; $n = 157$); lack of time with significant other (47.2%; $n = 142$); lack of time with friends (46.8%; $n = 141$); financial worries (44.2%; $n = 133$); someone close to you contracted COVID-19 (40.2%; $n = 121$); health problems—family member (39.5%; $n = 119$); lack of time with children (38.2%; $n = 115$); lack of time with family other than their significant other or children (36.2%; $n = 109$); health problems—self (34.9%; $n = 105$); grief or loss (32.6%; $n = 98$); care of a child or children (30.9%; $n = 93$).

Additional Stressors Specific to Women

Female CSIs were asked an additional series of questions related to stressors. Respondents identified the following as stressors they have encountered as a female in a public safety role within the past year: feeling the need to prove themselves because they are female (11.6%; $n = 35$); lack of respect from colleagues (9%; $n = 27$); familial responsibilities interfering with job duties (6%; $n = 18$); having to tolerate unwanted sexist or sexual language (5%; $n = 15$); limited promotion potential (4.7%; $n = 14$); lack of respect from the public (4.3%; $n = 13$); career impacts due to pregnancy (2.7%; $n = 8$); pay differential (1.3%; $n = 4$).

Coping Strategies

Respondents were asked about activities to counteract the effects of stress; they endorsed the following: spend time with family (86.4%; $n = 260$); use humor (64.1%; $n = 193$); exercise to reduce stress (61.5%; $n = 185$); escape through television or streaming services (58.5%; $n = 176$); recreational activities (56.8%; $n = 171$); spend time with pets (53.5%; $n = 161$); engage with nature (52.8%; $n = 159$); spend time in-person with friends (52.5%; $n = 158$); drink socially (47.2%; $n = 142$); comfort/ stress eating (38.2%; $n = 115$); healthy sexual behavior (29.6%; $n = 89$); escape in social media for entertainment purposes (28.2%; $n = 85$); find comfort through praying or meditation (26.9%; $n = 81$); escape through video games (19.9%; $n = 60$); involvement in church groups/ activities (15.9%; $n = 48$); drink to numb the pain/ stress (14.3%; $n = 43$). CSIs also endorsed the use of various forms of humor as a method to counteract the effects of stress. Table 3.5 illustrates the frequency and subjects of the humor over a two-week period.

Table 3.5 Use of humor

Humor subject	Several days (%)	More than half of the days (%)	Nearly everyday (%)
Self-deprecating	44.3	7.6	12.7
Workplace interactions	44.3	16.6	25.3
Sexual innuendos	26.9	5.2	10.3
Offender	39.5	11.7	9.3
Victim	17.8	3.1	2.8
Family life	45.7	15.1	12.4
Society/human	38.1	22.8	29.9

Note $N = 301$

Support and Treatment

Utilization of Behavioral Health Resources

In the Health and Wellness section of the survey, participants were asked to report their accessibility to, and interest in, engaging with behavioral health resources offered by either their department or elsewhere in the community. CSIs accessed various services within or through their department, including a doctoral-level-psychologist or non-doctoral-level counselor (24.8%; $n = 73$); peer support team member (19.3%; $n = 57$); psychiatrist (7.5%; $n = 22$); and chaplain, clergy, or other spiritual services (7.1%; $n = 21$). Outside resources utilized for professional reasons included a primary care physician or practitioner for mental health care (12.3%; $n = 35$), doctoral-level psychologist or non-doctoral-level counselor (13.7%; $n = 39$), clergy or other spiritual services (9.2%; $n = 26$), and psychiatrist (8.3%; $n = 24$).

Barriers to Seeking Treatment

The survey also attempted to determine reasons for not seeking treatment. Participants were asked about their reluctance to seek mental health resources in the past. The respondents who expressed an interest in seeking assistance but had not acted on their interest endorsed reasons for not doing so: they wanted to handle it on their own (38.2%; $n = 115$); fears it would impact their career, future employment, or security clearance (37.2%; $n = 112$); concerns about confidentiality (35.5%; $n = 107$); "It's the way I am – I don't ask for help" (33.6%; $n = 101$); stigma—concerns they would appear weak (29.9%; $n = 90$); stigma—concerns they would appear unstable or "crazy" (28.2%; $n = 85$); "I just keep putting it off" (24.6%; $n = 74$); "I didn't think it was a big deal" (23.9%; $n = 72$); they wanted to handle it within their family (14.3%; $n = 43$); financial concerns about coverage (14.6%; $n = 44$).

In response to being asked if they believed a co-worker seeking counseling or mental health treatment for stress-related problems may hurt their career, 19.8%

responded "Yes," 36.2% responded "Not sure," and the remaining 44% responded "No."

Discussion

The aim of this study was to shed light on the mental health challenges faced by crime scene investigators (CSIs), a population that frequently encounters traumatic events, yet remains underrepresented in mental health research. Specifically, this study sought to examine: (1) the prevalence and severity of stress, anxiety, depression, PTSD, and suicidal ideation among CSIs, (2) their access to mental health resources, and (3) the barriers they face in seeking treatment.

CSIs are regularly exposed to highly distressing scenes, including suicides, homicides, fatal accidents, and human remains-situations that most individuals never encounter. Consistent with previous research, this study found that such exposure is linked to heightened rates of anxiety, depression, PTSD symptoms, and suicidal ideation. Alarmingly, 23.1% of the participants reported depressive symptoms meeting the clinical threshold for major depressive disorder, 24.5% screened positive for Generalized Anxiety Disorder, 25.4% reported clinically significant PTSD symptoms, and 21.5% screened positive for alcohol abuse. Additionally, 7.8% of CSIs reported passive suicidal ideation and 4.1% reported active suicidal ideation. These findings underscore the psychological toll of cumulative trauma exposure and the urgent need for targeted mental health interventions in this population.

The study revealed that CSIs face a multitude of stressors, both job-related and personal. The most notable occupational stressors included: negative media and public perception, concerns about exposure to COVID-19, exposure and involvement in critical incidents, and low morale. Additionally, many CSIs reported frustration with government officials' and higher-level administrators' lack of understanding concerning their work. On a personal level, common stressors were: insufficient sleep, financial concerns, and limited time for personal tasks and spending time with family and friends—highlighting the job's impact beyond the workplace. Notably, female CSIs reported additional challenges related to gender biases, including the need to prove themselves and a lack of respect from colleagues, suggesting a need for further research on gender disparities within the field.

CSIs employed various coping strategies, most commonly spending time with family, using humor, exercising, watching television or streaming services, and engaging in recreational activities. Humor plays a significant role in the coping methods of first responders as a whole (Craun & Bourke, 2014). However, for CSIs, it has been shown to play a crucial role in emotion regulation, strengthening group cohesion, and managing the psychological toll of their work (Vivona, 2014). CSIs use humor as an informal gauge to assess their colleagues' well-being. Those actively engaging in humor are often perceived as emotionally resilient, whereas withdrawal from humor may signal distress (Vivona, 2014). The use of humor, therefore, not only aids in emotional resilience, but also facilitates peer support, which is crucial in this high-stress profession. While adaptive coping mechanisms were predominant, some CSIs reported engaging in maladaptive strategies such as alcohol use (socially: 47.2%; to numb pain/stress: 14.3%) and stress eating (38.2%). Notably, results from the CAGE self-report screener indicated that 21.5% of the CSIs exceeded the threshold for excessive alcohol consumption. Other studies, such as Rosansky et al. (2019), have observed even higher prevalence rates, with over one-third of their sample of 225 CSIs reporting alcohol use as a means of coping with work-related trauma. These results emphasize the need to promote positive coping strategies, while addressing the presence of maladaptive behaviors.

Barriers to mental health treatment were a significant concern. Many CSIs preferred to manage stress independently and feared potential career repercussions or breaches of confidentiality. Interestingly, difficulty accessing services was not a major barrier, suggesting that deterrents to treatment are more cultural and organizational rather than logistical. Addressing these barriers requires normalizing mental health care within the profession and reinforcing confidentiality protections. For those CSIs who were able to overcome these cultural barriers and utilized mental health resources, the majority reported positive and beneficial experiences.

While our study has limitations, including variations in job descriptions among CSIs and the impact of geographic and agency differences (e.g., allocated resources, training requirements, size), future research is needed regarding specific job-related variables (e.g., shift schedule, caseload, geographic crime trends) that contribute to mental health stressors. Additionally, the survey's timing during the COVID-19 pandemic may have influenced responses, warranting a follow-up investigation to assess patterns of post-pandemic responding. Another limitation of note is the large number of missing responses ($n = 116$) from respondents on the PCL-5. This is likely the result of the survey design in which respondents who did not endorse a stressor, were not prompted to answer the PCL-5 questions. Moreover, the number of participants identifying as a person of color, female, or other minority was limited. Additional research should study stressors and mental health concerns of CSIs who identify with a minority group. This is important in light of additional stressors such as discrimination and the impact of the hypermasculine culture. Finally, the use of self-report measures among first responders poses a risk of under-reporting mental health symptoms due to professional culture and stigma surrounding mental health (Henderson et al., 2016; Rodriguez et al., 2023).

CSIs play a vital role in the criminal justice system, but often at a significant psychological cost. However, despite the intense stressors and demands of the job, the majority report high levels of job satisfaction. In fact, when compared to colleagues in other law enforcement units (e.g., traffic, homicide, and public order units), CSIs were found to be the most satisfied and least dissatisfied with their jobs (Arin, 2015). Further, Clark et al. (2015) reported that out of the 51 CSIs included in their study, 70% indicated they would choose the same career path again without hesitation. However, despite encouraging evidence of job satisfaction, our findings underscore the need for: (1) increased awareness of the psychological impact of CSI work and (2) enhanced mental health resources tailored to their unique challenges. The data further suggest that CSIs feel nearly as comfortable seeking support from peers as from mental health professionals, highlighting the potential value of peer support programs (e.g., Van Hasselt et al., 2019). Such strategies could provide an important outlet for CSIs, fostering shared understanding and reduced stigma often associated with mental health challenges.

To cultivate a culture of openness and support, agencies must ensure confidentiality and eliminate fears of administrative repercussions for seeking help. Establishing policies sensitive to the mental health needs inherent in this profession is essential. Early intervention approaches, such as behavioral health training and peer support programs specifically designed for CSIs (e.g., Bryant et al., 2022; Plombon et al., 2020; Van Hasselt & Bryant, 2024), can promote emotional well-being, encourage help-seeking behavior, and provide crucial support for those in crisis. Additionally, there is evidence suggesting that CSIs who believe their organizations prioritize stress management and employee well-being experience lower burnout and secondary traumatic stress (Levin et al., 2021). This highlights the importance of agency-led initiatives aimed at fostering psychological resilience. By prioritizing mental health initiatives, strengthening peer support networks, and promoting a supportive organizational culture, law enforcement agencies can better safeguard CSIs'well-being and effectiveness in their demanding and essential roles.

References

Adderley, R., Smith, L. L., Bond, J. W., & Smith, M. (2012). Physiological measurement of crime scene investigator stress. *International Journal of Police Science & Management, 14*(2), 166–176. https://doi.org/10.1350/ijps.2012.14.2.274

American Psychiatric Association. (2022). *Diagnostic and statistical manual of mental disorders* (5th ed., text rev.). https://doi.org/10.1176/appi.books.9780890425787

Arin, S. (2015). *Understanding the factors influencing job satisfaction of crime scene investigators in Turkey* (Order No. 3702521). ProQuest One Academic. (1685390305). https://ezproxylocal.library.nova.edu/login?url=https://www.proquest.com/dissertations-theses/understanding-factors-influencing-job/docview/1685390305/se-2

Babor, T. F., La Fuente, J. R., Saunders, J., & Grant, M. (1992). AUDIT, the alcohol use disorders identification test: Guidelines for use in primary health care. Geneva: *Substance Abuse Department*. World Health Organization, WHO/PSA, 4, 1–29.

Blevins, C. A., Weathers, F. W., Davis, M. T., Witte, T. K., & Domino, J. L. (2015). The posttraumatic stress disorder checklist for DSM-5 (PCL-5): Development and initial psychometric evaluation. *Journal Trauma Stress, 28*(6), 489–498. https://doi.org/10.1002/jts.22059

Bourke, M., Bradley, S. T., & Van Hasselt, V. B. (2024). *The National Wellness Survey for public safety personnel*. The Police Chief. https://www.policechiefmagazine.org/research-in-brief-national-wellness-survey-public-safety-personnel/

Bryant T., Van Hasselt, V.B., & Miller, M.V. (September, 2022). Mental health awareness for the crime scene investigator: Considerations for stress management and investigator burnout. *Presentation to the Medicolegal Death Investigators Conference*. International Forensic Medicine Association, Daytona Beach.

Clark, R., Distelrath, C., Vaquera, G., Whiterich, D., & DeZolt, E. (2015). Critical-incident trauma and crime scene investigation: A review of police organizational challenges and interventions. *Journal of Forensic Identification, 65*(6), 2015. https://collected.jcu.edu/soc-facpub/32

Craun, S. W., & Bourke, M. L. (2014). The use of humor to cope with secondary traumatic stress. *Journal of Child Sexual Abuse, 23*(7), 840–852. https://doi.org/10.1080/10538712.2014.949395

Ewing, J. A. (1984). Detecting alcoholism. *JAMA*, 252(14), 1905. https://jamanetwork.com/journals/jama/article-abstract/394693

Ferraro, A. (2024). *The Correlation and Distinguishment of Vicarious Trauma in Crime Scenes and the Psychological Effects it has on Crime Scene Investigators* [Thesis, Stevenson University]. Crime Scene Investigator Network.

Fiellin, D. A., Reid, M. C., & O'Connor, P. G. (2000). Screening for alcohol problems in primary care: A systematic review. *Archives of Internal Medicine, 160*(13), 1977–1989. https://doi.org/10.1001/archinte.160.13.1977

Goldstein, R. B., Smith, S. M., Chou, S. P., Saha, T. D., Jung, J., Zhang, H., Pickering, R. P., Ruan, W. J., Huang, B., & Grant, B. F. (2016). The epidemiology of DSM-5 posttraumatic stress disorder in the United States: Results from the National Epidemiologic Survey on alcohol and related conditions-III. *Social Psychiatry and Psychiatric Epidemiology, 51*(8), 1137–1148. https://doi.org/10.1007/s00127-016-1208-5

Henderson, S. N., Van Hasselt, V. B., LeDuc, T. J., & Couwels, J. (2016). Firefighter suicide: Understanding challenges for mental health professionals. *Professional Psychology: Research and Practice, 47*, 224–230.

International Crime Scene Investigators Association. (n.d.). What is ICSIA? https://www.icsia.org/what-is-icsia/

Kelty, S. F., & Gordon, H. (2014). No burnout at this coal-face: Managing occupational stress in forensic personnel and the implications for forensic and criminal justice agencies. *Psychiatry, Psychology and Law, 22*(2), 273–290. https://doi.org/10.1080/13218719.2014.941092

Kroenke, K., & Spitzer, R. L. (2002). The PHQ-9: A new depression diagnostic and severity measure. *Psychiatric Annals, 32*(9), 509–515. https://doi.org/10.3928/0048-5713-20020901-06

Leone, M. C., & Keel, R. A. (2016). Occupational stress and the crime scene investigator. *Journal of Law and Criminal Justice, 4*(1), 63–74. https://doi.org/10.15640/jlcj.v4n1a4

Levin, A. P., Putney, H., Crimmins, D., & McGrath, J. G. (2021). Secondary traumatic stress, burnout, compassion satisfaction, and perceived organizational trauma readiness in forensic science professionals. *Journal of Forensic Sciences, 66*(5), 1758–1769. https://doi.org/10.1111/1556-4029.14747

Levis, B., Benedetti, A., & Thombs, B. D. (2019). Accuracy of patient health Questionnaire-9 (PHQ-9) for screening to detect major depression: Individual participant data meta-analysis. *BMJ, l1476*. https://doi.org/10.1136/bmj.l1476

Liu, R. T., Bettis, A. H., & Burke, T. A. (2020). Characterizing the phenomenology of passive suicidal ideation: A systematic review and meta-analysis of its prevalence, psychiatric comorbidity, correlates, and comparisons with active suicidal ideation. *Psychological Medicine, 50*(3), 367–383. https://doi.org/10.1017/S003329171900391X

Mills, C., Milloy, J., & Carson, J. (2020). Assessing needs: Using a wellness survey to guide interventions. In C. Bowers, D. Beidel, & M. Marks (Eds.), *Mental health intervention and treatment of first responders and emergency workers* (pp. 1–15). IGI Global. https://doi.org/10.4018/978-1-5225-9803-9.ch001

Mrevlje, T. P. (2018). Police trauma and Rorschach indicators. *Rorchachiana, 39*(1), 1–19. https://doi.org/10.1027/1192-5604/a000097

Nho, S. M., & Kim, E. A. (2017). *Journal of Korean Academy of Nursing, 47*(1), 39–48. https://doi.org/10.4040/jkan.2017.47.1.39

Plombon, B. A., Bryant, T., & Van Hasselt, V. B. (2020). Behavioral health training for crime scene investigators. *Florida Division of the International Association for Identification News*, January–March 30–35.

Posner, K., Brown, G. K., Stanley, B., Brent, D. A., Yershova, K. V., Oquendo, M. A., Currier, G. W., Melvin, G. A., Greenhill, L., Shen, S., & Mann, J. J. (2011). The Columbia-suicide severity rating scale: Initial validity and internal consistency findings from three multisite studies with adolescents and adults. *The American Journal of Psychiatry, 168*(12), 1266–1277. https://doi.org/10.1176/appi.ajp.2011.10111704

Rodriguez, S., Ferrell, B., Cipriano, R. J., Van Hasselt, V. B., Falzone, L., Kuhlman, K., Acosta, W., & Miller, M. V. (2023). Law enforcement mental health: Strategies and issues in prevention and treatment. *Practice Innovations, 9*(1), 52–64.

Rosansky, J. A., Cook, J., Rosenberg, H., & Sprague, J. E. (2019). PTSD symptoms experienced and coping tactics used by crime scene investigators in the United States. *Journal of Forensic Sciences, 64*(5), 1444–1450. https://doi.org/10.1111/1556-4029.14044

Sollie, H., Kop, N., & Euwema, M. C. (2017). Mental resilience of crime scene investigators: How police officers perceive and cope with the impact of demanding work situations. *Criminal Justice and Behavior, 44*(12), 1580–1603. https://doi.org/10.1177/0093854817716959

Spitzer, R. L., Kroenke, K., Williams, J. B., & Löwe, B. (2006). A brief measure for assessing generalized anxiety disorder: The GAD-7. *Archives of Internal Medicine, 166*(10), 1092–1097. https://doi.org/10.1001/archinte.166.10.1092

Van Hasselt, V.B., & Bryant, T. (2024, April). Behavioral health training for crime scene investigators. *Presentation to the Gold Coast Forensic Association.* West Palm Beach.

Van Hasselt, V. B., Klimley, K. E., Rodriguez, S., Themis-Fernandez, M., Henderson, S. N., & Schneider, B. A. (2019). Peers as law enforcement support (PALS): An early prevention program. *Aggression and Violent Behavior, 48*, 1–5. https://doi.org/10.1016/j.avb.2019.05.004

Van Patten, I. T., & Burke, T. W. (2001). Critical incident stress and the child homicide investigator. *Homicide Studies: An Interdisciplinary & International Journal, 5*(2), 131–152. https://doi.org/10.1177/1088767901005002003

Vivona, B. D. (2014). Humor functions within crime scene investigations: Group dynamics, stress, and the negotiation of emotions. *Police Quarterly, 17*(2), 127–149. https://psycnet.apa.org/doi/10.1177/1098611114531418

Waugh, J. R. (2013). *Exposure to traumatic death events and traumatic event-related stress in crime scene investigators: A multiple regression analysis* (Publication No. 3559912) [Doctoral dissertation, Capella University]. ProQuest One Academic.

Weathers, F. W., Litz, B. T., Keane, T. M., Palmieri, P. A., Marx, B. P., & Schnurr, P. P. (2013). The PTSD checklist for DSM-5 (PCL-5). *Scale available from the National Center for PTSD.*. www.ptsd.va.gov

Chapter 4
Virtual Reality Treatment and Training: An Evaluative View of the Research

Deborah C. Beidel, Clint A. Bowers, and Daniel R. Horning

The exponential growth of virtual reality in recent years has resulted in a now multi-billion-dollar industry capturing the attention of every field looking to achieve immersion, presence, and interactivity within their practice. But what exactly is virtual reality, and how is this technology being used to improve first responder mental health? In this chapter, we will first present an overview of virtual reality, its methods of delivery, and how this modality has been integrated into treatment and training with first responders. The extant literature on the incorporation of VR into first responder training and treatment is small, but we will provide a critique of what is available. Finally, we will provide some suggestions for the future.

What Is Virtual Reality?

Virtual reality is one component of the umbrella term *extended reality*, which refers to "all real-and-virtual combined environments and human–machine interactions generated by computer technology and wearables" (Fast-Berglund et al., 2018). In addition to virtual reality (VR), extended reality also encompasses augmented reality (AR), augmented virtuality (AV), and mixed reality (MR). VR creates an entirely artificial virtual environment offering full virtualization while AR and AV augment the real world with virtual information. MR is a broader term that combines or merges the virtual and real worlds (Buhl & Winter, 2008). Augmented reality (AR) overlays real-world objects with a layer of virtual objects or information. Think backup cameras on modern vehicles, the lines guiding you into a straight line are digital overlays on real-world objects. AR users have more control over the physical

D. C. Beidel (✉) · C. A. Bowers · D. R. Horning
UCF RESTORES and Department of Psychology, University of Central Florida, Florida, USA
e-mail: Deborah.Beidel@ucf.edu

V. B. Van Hasselt and M. L. Bourke (eds.), *Advances in First Responder Mental Health*, Advances in First Responder Mental Health 1,
https://doi.org/10.1007/978-3-032-27978-1_4

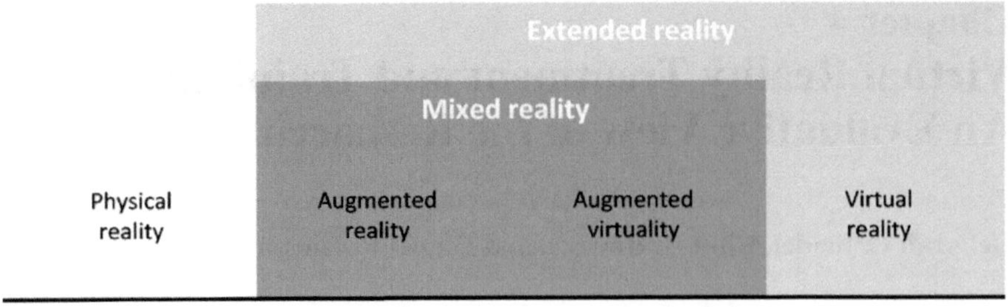

Fig. 4.1 *Note* Drascic and Milgram's (1996) version of the reality virtuality continuum and positions the terms AR, AV, MR, VR, and XR between the physical and virtual realities. Image courtesy of Wohlgenannt et al. (2020)

world than users of VR which requires full immersion (Xie et al., 2021). AV refers to a "virtual world augmented with the mapping of an image or video from the real world in virtual objects" (Valente et al., 2016). Think the use of a Zoom background during a video call to display a generic office space instead of the actual background. Both AR and AV are located between the physical and virtual realities, and both are mixed reality which is defined as "a particular subset of Virtual Reality (VR) related technologies that involve the merging of real and virtual worlds" (Milgram & Kishino, 1994). The diagram below visually depicts these various modalities. In this chapter we focus on virtual reality for the treatment of first responders; however, we will also address how these other modalities are used in the training of first responders (Fig. 4.1).

Returning to the main topic of this chapter, virtual reality is the use of computer technology to facilitate immersion, presence, and interactivity within an artificially created virtual world. If you were to remove the use of computer technology from the equation you would see that immersion, presence, interactivity, and virtual worlds are something we experience on a daily basis. In fact, the use of virtual worlds to achieve immersion, presence, and interactivity is already common practice among first responders without assistance from computer technology. Think first-aid or triage training. A virtual world is created via scenarios drawing from the experience and imagination of those organizing the event. Manikins with artificial wounds and sounds of sirens or injured victims are used to achieve immersion and presence for those participating. The ability to perform first-aid to these manikins as well as collaborate with teammates encourages interactivity among the trainees. Although this is effective in achieving immersion, presence, and interactivity these virtual worlds are limited by physical reality. Computer assisted virtual reality, however, does not share the same limitations and can create scenarios not possible in the physical world. The artificial trauma victims in VR could have injuries that increase in severity based on interactivity from the user, or there could be hazardous components added to evaluate the trainee's ability to respond to environmental stressors. VR provides a medium to achieve immersion, presence, interactivity, and virtual worlds that increase the efficacy of the scenario to serve its intended purpose while reducing the risk of danger from physical reality.

Methods of Delivering Virtual Reality

The growth in VR popularity among consumers has allowed for more affordable and available VR devices among those engaging in both personal and professional applications of the technology. Thus, VR's ability to augment immersion, presence, interactivity, and virtual world construction to improve mental health conditions has resulted in innovative strategies to evaluate its potential. The availability of VR allows for clinicians and researchers to evaluate the bounds of its clinical capabilities and apply this to the prevention, understanding, and treatment of mental health conditions. But how is this technology delivered? The two most widely used methods of delivering the VR experience are through head-mounted displays (HMD) and world-fixed displays (WFD). HMDs are a computer-based visual display attached to the head that allows users to immerse themselves into a virtual world by blocking out physical reality (Brooks, 1999). A pair of screens projects images onto each eye within the HMD that reacts to a tracking sensor on the HMD that tells the computer where the user is looking. The computer uses this to quickly display a visual image from the vantage point of the user's position allowing the user to explore the virtual world as if it was physical reality (Sherman & Craig, 2003). Speakers attached to the HMD offer sounds associated with the immersive environment and haptics, to simulate touch and motion, can be delivered using controllers to improve the immersive experience (Mach et al., 2019). WFDs, by contrast, project visuals onto physical surfaces and administer sounds via speakers that are not affixed to the user directly. WFD's are usually a room or fishtank-like space to immerse the user by projecting graphic imagery onto the screens surrounding them (Sherman & Craig, 2003). The CAVE system from the Electronic Visualization Lab at the University of Illinois at Chicago is a popular example of a WFD (Cruz-Neira et al., 1992). Although both methods are successful in achieving the necessary components of virtual reality, HMDs are most used in practical applications of this technology within healthcare settings (Fig. 4.2).

Why Is VR Mental Health Treatment Relevant to First Responders?

First responders in the United States respond to more than 50 million emergency calls a year increasing their susceptibility to injury, death, and traumatic exposure (McCallion, 2012; National Fire Protection Association, 2014). In a sample of 359 police officers from the Buffalo, New York police department, 60% reported being

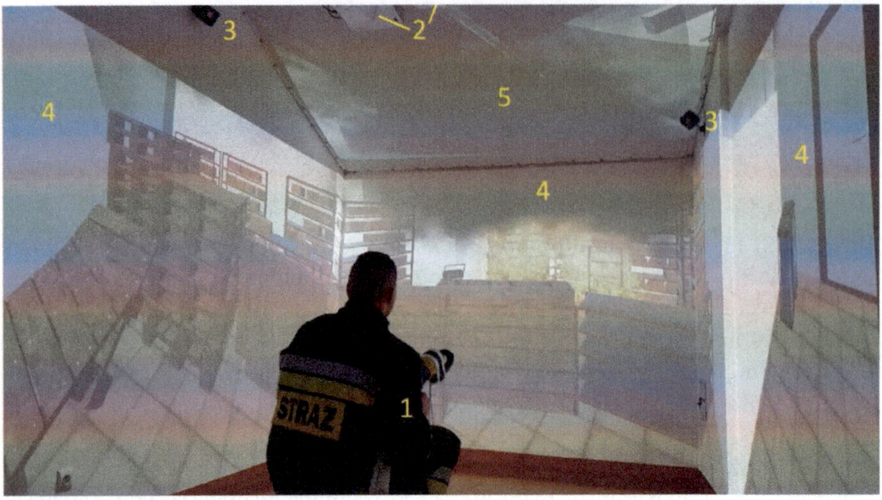

Fig. 4.2 *Note* CAVE simulator. The virtual environment surrounds the cadet using a nozzle integrated with a training simulation. Virtual environment: storage room (warehouse). 1—trainee with nozzle; 2—short throw projectors; 3—motion capture system (HTC Vive's base stations); 4—image projected on the walls; 5—image projected on the screen located above the trainee. Practical skills training in enclosure fires: An experimental study with cadets and firefighters using CAVE and HMD-based virtual training simulators. *Fire Safety Journal*, *125*, 103,440. Image courtesy of Grabowski (2021)

involved in or witnessing five or more critical incidents within the line of duty, with 75% reporting a critical incident that occurred within the past month (Hartley, 2013). Another study with a sample of approximately 160 firefighters found that 90% reported at least one critical incident within the past year and an average of over six exposures to critical incidents on a yearly basis (Corneil et al., 1999). As a result of the increased exposure to traumatic events, first responders are at heightened risk for developing mental health disorders. In fact, the prevalence rates for PTSD diagnosis among first responders range from 8% to 32% compared to lifetime prevalence rate of PTSD which is 6.8% to 7.8% among U.S. Americans (American Psychiatric Association, 2013; Kleim & Westphal, 2011; National Institute of Mental Health, 2017). Another study conducted in 2012 noted that at least one-quarter million first responders were suffering from full-or partial-PTSD (Haugen et al., 2012). Although PTSD prevalence rates among first responders are a common theme among literature, existing data also suggest that first responders are also at risk for depression (Darensburg et al., 2006; Fullerton et al., 2006), substance abuse (Kimbrel et al., 2011; Murphy et al., 1999), and suicide (Violanti, 2004). Similar to equipping first responders with lifesaving personal protective equipment, the implementation of evidence-based interventions that moderate exposure to occupational trauma, are crucial for ensuring public health, safety, and the longevity of first responders (O'Dare, 2024). The increased exposure to critical incidents, high prevalence of mental health conditions, and unique nature of trauma-based psychological treatment suggest that immersion, presence, interactivity, and virtual world construction have the capability to innovate novel and efficacious interventions for first responders.

The Relationship Between Exposure and Avoidance

Knowing that frequent exposure to potentially traumatic events and hazardous situations results in a higher prevalence of PTSD among first responders, we now must examine what psychological mechanisms are behind the onset of trauma-based symptoms. The Diagnostic and Statistical Manual of Mental Disorders (fifth ed.; DSM–5; American Psychiatric Association, 2013) identifies the types of events capable of producing PTSD, which are either directly experienced, witnessed, experienced by a close family member or friend, or experienced through actual or threatened death, serious injury or sexual violence, repeated or extreme exposure to aversive details of the traumatic event, and categorizes PTSD symptoms as: re-experiencing, avoidance, negative alterations in mood and cognition, and alterations in arousal and reactivity. The extent to which first responders are exposed to these events warrant increased attention to the treatment of trauma-related psychological disorders among this population. The myriad of symptoms that may characterize PTSD presents challenges for clinicians when selecting an appropriate treatment target. Examining the clinical presentation of PTSD in first responders, the literature suggests that intrusive symptoms (unwanted memories, unpleasant dreams or nightmares, and flashbacks) result in avoidance behaviors that reinforce symptoms of arousal (e.g., anger, sleep dysregulation, hypervigilance, and anxiety) which have the potential to cause significant distress in the lives of those affected (Beidel et al., 2019). Thus, focusing on the avoidance symptoms related to PTSD and traumatic stress became a focal point for research in this area. Consequently, exposure therapy is regarded as a first-line treatment due to its ability to effectively reduce PTSD symptoms (APA, 2017; International Society for Traumatic Stress Studies [ISTSS], 2018).

The mechanisms associated with exposure therapy can be explained via the Emotional Processing Theory (Foa & Kozak, 1986), which states that a phobic fear structure is activated upon confrontation with trauma-relevant information. Specifically, within exposure therapy the fear structure is activated by repeated confrontation with a feared stimulus (imaginal or in vivo) with the goal of achieving habituation and extinguishing the anxious reaction (Foa et al., 2006). Effective exposure therapy requires the client to confront the stressors related to the traumatic event in extensive detail to engage as many sensory modalities as possible (Lang, 1968). However, the level of immersion and presence needed for efficacious delivery of exposure therapy is particularly difficult to achieve in the context of imaginal exposure, as many patients show problems with visualizing the traumatic event or related details (Rizzo & Shilling, 2017). During imaginal exposure, the therapist has limited ability to ensure that the patient is imaging the scene as described which can result in within-session distraction and avoidance, with the potential to diminish treatment outcomes. Additionally, imaginal exposure lacks the ability to provide direct contact with sensory stimuli shown to be effective in achieving presence and immersion (sounds, smell, sights, and touch) (Beidel et al., 2019). In contrast, in-vivo exposure has a challenge in providing real-life stimuli that are suitable for efficacious exposure while considering safety precautions (Bohil et al. 2011). In fact, the events that create combat-related PTSD are unable to be reproduced within a clinic environment rendering the use of in-vivo exposure therapy infeasible (Beidel et al., 2019). This can be applied to the use of exposure therapy to treat first responders as they too are exposed to critical incidents unable to be re-created in real-life settings.

Despite the shortcomings associated with imaginal and in-vivo exposure therapy, its clinical efficacy remains well documented (Foa et al., 1999, 2003; Powers et al., 2010). However, treatment often resulted in symptom reduction, not necessarily symptom remission. Further, until recently, treatment outcome was limited to assessment of primary PTSD symptoms and did not assess change in related behaviors such as sleep, anger, and depression. The virtual reality option can deliver exposure therapy through a medium that can effectively deliver immersion, presence, and interactivity, and virtual world scene construction to treat PTSD symptoms more effectively for those with repeated occupational exposure to extreme stressors.

Virtual Reality Exposure Therapy

Virtual reality's ability to achieve immersion, presence, interactivity, through the use of a computer-generated virtual world and exposure therapy's intention to reduce avoidance behaviors via repeated exposure to feared stimuli gave way to a novel intervention called virtual reality exposure therapy (VRET). VRET allows clients to experience sensory cues associated with feared stimuli in a way that is not possible through imaginal or in-vivo exposure (Beidel et al., 2019). VRET provides the ability to engage with immersive and interactive imagery to effectively present the specific cues (sometimes called triggers) that produce emotional distress, autonomic arousal, and behavioral avoidance (Beidel et al., 2014). VRET has the potential to address barriers associated with traditional treatments such as inability to fully immerse in the traumatic scene and provide direct contact with a traumatic cue (Canadian Agency for Drugs and Technologies in Health, 2014). For example, it is difficult to imagine a smell, even though smells are common triggers of distress for clients with PTSD. Further, dropout rates for traditional exposure-based treatments are as high as 48% (Cottraux et al., 2008; McDonagh et al., 2005). Using head-mounted display, VRET can simulate sights, sounds, vibrations, and smells tailored to the client's individual trauma by integrating real time computer graphics and sensory cues (Gerardi et al., 2010, 2008) (Fig. 4.3).

VRET is an ecologically valid and emotionally engaging modality that has the advantage of increased control over stimuli, infinite ability to repeat exposure, and the distinctive possibility to simulate environments unable or unsafe to be reproduced within physical reality (Difede et al., 2007; Gamito et al., 2010; Miloff et al., 2016). All of this suggests that VRET would be a highly effective intervention for reducing

Fig. 4.3 *Note* Virtual reality, used as part of exposure therapy, within the UCF RESTORES clinic at the University of Central Florida in Orlando, Florida. Image courtesy of UCF RESTORES

PTSD and, in fact, would have an efficacy that ranks it higher than other empirically supported PTSD treatments such as prolonged exposure, cognitive processing therapy (CPT), and eye movement desensitization and reprocessing (EMDR). But does the literature support this claim? The International Society for Traumatic Stress Studies (ISTSS) includes VRET in its 2018 guidelines as a treatment for PTSD but states that although promising, VRET lacks sufficient evidence to support it as a gold standard treatment. A qualitative review concluded that VRET has the potential to be useful in the treatment of different types of trauma (Gonçalves et al., 2012) and other studies reported that early research on VRET in veterans with chronic, treatment-resistant PTSD yielded promising outcomes for VR-based exposure (Rothbaum et al., 1999, 2001).

Beyond promise and potential, studies have recently emerged that evaluate the efficacy of VRET as a treatment for PTSD compared to traditional interventions. Two recently published meta-analyses on the use of VRET to treat anxiety disorders found small (Fodor et al., 2018) and medium (Carl et al., 2019) effect sizes in favor of VRET versus control comparisons in terms of reducing PTSD symptom severity. However, the literature on VRET efficacy for PTSD remains mixed with some studies suggesting VRET significantly reduces the severity of PTSD compared to other interventions (Difede et al., 2007; Gamito et al., 2010; McLay et al., 2011; Miyahira et al., 2012; Ready et al., 2010; Roy et al., 2010), while other studies suggest that the efficacy of VRET is no better than some traditional treatments (McLay et al., 2017; Reger et al., 2016).

Overall, VRET is found to be effective in treating PTSD although whether it is better than traditional therapies is still unclear (Deng, 2019). Additionally, it is important to note that virtual reality is not the basis for treatment change—VR is a powerful tool with the potential to increase the efficacy of standard exposure therapy. In other words, VR may save time and money in the exposure process with positive results in the treatment of various anxiety disorders to include specific phobias, acrophobia, social phobia, generalized anxiety disorders, panic disorder, and PTSD (Botella et al., 1998; Carlin et al., 1997; Rothbaum & Hodges, 1999; Wolitzky-Taylor et al., 2008). Additionally, a 46-study meta-analysis found that the dropout rate for VRET was estimated at 16% which is lower than the attrition rates of CBT and traditional therapy (Benbow & Anderson, 2019). Although the literature is mixed on whether the efficacy of VRET surpasses that of traditional therapy, it is important to note that the VR industry is exponentially growing in popularity, technological advancement, affordability, and accessibility. As a result, the ability of this technology to positively impact first responder mental health is undoubtedly worthy of continued exploration. Considering that VRET has already demonstrated the ability to provide immersive and relevant sensory stimuli, low attrition rates, and unique scene construction not attainable through traditional means, highlights the importance of maximizing the potential of VR to influence the future of PTSD treatment. The affordability and availability of HMD-based VR technology has been increasing over the last decade (Rizzo & Shilling, 2017) which will inspire clinical researchers to evaluate the bounds of this technology to determine the efficacy of computer-based immersion, presence, interactivity, and virtual worlds as it relates to first responder psychopathology.

Quantitative and Qualitative Measurement

Attempts to measure the efficacy of psychological interventions traditionally orient qualitatively through the use of surveys. Whether the client completes the surveys themselves, the clinician, or a third party with knowledge of the client's psychopathological functioning, the main goals are usually to assess the efficacy of the intervention administered or to innovate new methods of treating similar conditions. In the treatment of first responders, common qualitative measurements are:

- Clinician-Administered PTSD Scale for DSM-5 (CAPS-5)
- Posttraumatic Stress Disorder Checklist for DSM-5 (PCL-5)
- Traumatic Life Events Questionnaire (TLEQ)
- Trauma-Related Guilt Inventory (TRGI)
- World Health Organization Disability Assessment Schedule 2.0 (WHODAS 2.0)
- Quality of Life Scale (QOLS)
- Structured Clinical Interview for DSM-5, Clinician Version (SCID-5-CV)
- Patient Health Questionnaire-9 (PHQ-9)
- Generalized Anxiety Disorder-7 (GAD-7)
- Life Events Checklist (LEC-5 (LEC-5)
- Subjective Units of Distress Scale (SUDS)

Beyond qualitative measurement, the nature of first responder psychopathology and intent of exposure therapy to create a physiological reaction to feared stimuli has brought attention to the use of biometrics to facilitate quantitative measurement. Biometrics is the use of distinctive physical attributes to achieve quantitative measurement. This includes the psychophysical measurement of human behavior and psychological state (Jain et al., 2007). Examples of biometrics that are currently in use among psychological research are:

- Eye-tracking, which measures the fixation and duration of an eye movement behavior by analyzing the distance between the pupil center and the reflection of the cornea (Bergstrom & Schall, 2014).
- Facial expression analysis (fEMG), which measures emotional response by recording facial muscle activities via electrodes placed on two major facial skin regions (Yoo et al., 2017; McGhee et al., 2018).
- Galvanic skin response (GSR), which measures the variation of skin conductance caused by changes of sweat glands (Tarnowski et al., 2018).
- Heart rate variability (HRV), which indicates an individual's variance of heart rate speed (Williams et al., 2015).

Including biometrics in VR-assisted interventions allows researchers to collect and analyze physiological feedback from the client as they undergo repeated exposure to fear stimuli. The combined use of qualitative and quantitative measurement in psychological treatment and research allows for the analysis of physiological responses beyond conscious control while also assessing the psychological effect reported by the individual. Through this process we can determine discrepancies, identify habituation, and assess the overall functioning of clients as they undergo trauma-related interventions (Xie et al., 2021). VR has the potential to aid in both qualitative and quantitative measurement by providing eye-tracking and attentional data to the clinician as well as allowing the client to explore the bounds of a computer-generated virtual world to provide a more meaningful qualitative assessment of how they were feeling in that moment vs. how they are feeling now.

VRET with First Responders

There are numerous studies affirming the efficacy of VRET for the treatment of combat-veterans with PTSD. Yet, despite the similar traumatic events to which military personnel and first responders are exposed, the incorporation of VR for the treatment of PTSD in first responders has not been realized. In their cogent review of its potential, Rizzo et al. (2021) note the evolution of therapeutic VR systems. Their first and groundbreaking BRAVEMIND system focused on treating combat trauma. The second iteration included scenarios to address traumas experienced by military medics and military sexual assault survivors, whereas the newest iteration includes scenarios for civilian first responders. Yet, despite its promise to enhance treatment outcomes for first responders with PTSD, in addition to our own work (discussed below), we identified only one other study where VRET was used. In a randomized controlled trial (Difede et al., 2007), rescue workers who were directly exposed to the World Trade Center attack were randomly assigned to VRET ($n = 13$) or to a waitlist control ($n = 8$). Five firefighters were included in the study, but it was unclear how many were in each condition. At post-treatment, there was a statistically and clinically significant difference in scores on the CAPS only for the VRET group, with a very large between group effect size (Cohen's $d = 1.54$). In clinical terms, scores for the VR group fell from the severe range at pretreatment to the upper end of the mild range at post-treatment, and 7 out of the 10 treatment completers no longer had a PTSD diagnosis at post-treatment. Treatment gains were maintained at 6-month follow-up. Importantly, all of the participants in this trial had not responded to a prior trial of traditional imaginal exposure therapy. The authors suggest that the enhanced treatment outcomes were due to VR's ability to enhance immersion. Specifically, all of the participants in the VRET condition reported high engagement in VR, whereas they had low engagement in imaginal exposure therapy. The authors noted that VR's ability to engage multiple sensory stimuli may increase engagement and provided emotional resonance for the therapeutic process. The authors also noted that the phenomenology of trauma memories are usually more fragmented and rely on more than visual stimuli, when compared to non-traumatic memories (e.g., Hackmann et al., 2004). As noted, VR allows more intensive engagement with these senses, providing more powerful involvement with the traumatic cues.

We agree with Difede et al.'s (2007) observations about how VR may enhance treatment outcomes. Below we present our work developing a more effective treatment for PTSD and its application to first responders. After that, we will discuss the state of affairs with respect to dissemination and implementation of incorporating VR into the treatment for PTSD with this population.

Trauma Management Therapy

Trauma Management Therapy (TMT) is a multi-component behavioral treatment for PTSD designed for first responders, military service members, and veterans that uses the following to achieve optimal treatment outcomes:

- Individual exposure therapy treatment augmented by virtual reality.
- Biometric measurement
- Group treatment that includes skills training in the following:
  - Sleep hygiene
  - Social reintegration
  - Anger management/Problem solving
  - Brief behavioral activation

First developed about 30 years ago to solve the challenge of effective treatment for Vietnam-era veterans, TMT has been developed further and refined for people in high-risk professions, including first responders (Beidel et al., 2019). TMT deviates from the prolonged exposure treatment model by continuing exposure treatment until within-session habituation is achieved via self-reported distress and biometric feedback. Consistent with basic learning principles, the repeated presentation of the stimulus (trigger) in the absence of the traumatic event, allows for habituation to occur i.e., the patient returns to a psychological and physiological state resemblant of routine functioning before treatment is discontinued. This change occurs because the repeated, but unreinforced, presentation of the anxiety-producing stimuli results in learning (or over-learning) that the presentation of the fear cues (gun shots, sirens, etc.) does not signal the occurrence of the original negative outcome. Consistent with the models of within-session and between-session habituation, initial exposure therapy as incorporated into TMT, could last 90–120 minutes in order for within-session habituation to occur. Later sessions may last only 15–20 minutes as between-session habituation is achieved.

Although early studies of TMT did not include VR (Beidel et al., 2011), research with PTSD treatment for veterans of the Iraq and Afghanistan conflicts incorporated use of the BRAVEMIND system, which included an HMD display, earphones/speakers, scent machine, and haptics. Using an intensive outpatient format, TMT, augmented by VR, significantly reduced symptoms of PTSD as indicated by CAPS scores dropping by 52.4 points, with 65.9% of participants no longer meeting diagnostic criteria for PTSD at post-treatment. This study also found significant decreases in depression, anger, and social isolation and had a dropout rate of 2% (Beidel et al., 2017). A second study, which consisted of a randomized controlled trial of TMT vs exposure therapy alone (both conditions using VR) found that both TMT and exposure therapy alone resulted in decreased symptoms of PTSD, depression, and anxiety among Iraq and Afghanistan veterans; however, social interactions increased and social functioning improved only in the TMT group. Treatment gains were maintained at three and six-month follow-up (Beidel et al., 2019).

As clinical services expanded to include first responders and survivors of mass shootings and natural disasters, it became evident that there was a need for a system that could create any disaster/traumatic event. We created a system that would allow a clinician to construct unique traumatic events without the need to rely on pre-existing scenarios. The first iteration of this system was evaluated with 14 first responders in a feasibility trial (Beidel et al., 2024). All first responders had a diagnosis of PTSD when they entered the trial. Using a two-week intensive outpatient program (IOP) format consistent of daily exposure treatment augmented by VR, the results indicate that the new VR system was feasible to use and did not produce iatrogenic treatment effects. Furthermore, the treatment significantly reduced symptoms of PTSD and related emotional distress, reduced disability, and improved daily functioning. None of the 14 first responders met criteria for PTSD at post-treatment. Treatment efficacy was maintained at three-month follow-up. Given the promise of adding VR to traditional exposure therapy, it is important to examine why there has been only minimal uptake of incorporating VR as a modality for the treatment of PTSD in first responders. Below we identify several factors which could be attenuating the adoption of this modality.

The first issue could be *financial*. Current off-the-shelf systems require a "gaming" computer, head-mounted display, dual monitors, and other hardware. Although prices are decreasing, it still represents a significant investment and may not be cost-effective if a therapist does not have a practice that consists solely of patients with trauma and PTSD. Along this line, unlike the Veteran's Administration (VA), there is *no large health care administration that is federally funded and provides treatment for the behavioral health of first responders*. When faced with the crisis of PTSD among veterans, the VA invested in personnel training and equipment (i.e., the Bravemind system) so that VA therapists could provide exposure therapy, and in some cases VRET, to veterans in need. In some instances, the uptake and delivery of this treatment did not occur; however, the point is that the finances necessary to introduce, train, and implement this treatment were shouldered by the federal government, not the individual therapist. This government opportunity does not exist for first responders. An alternative may be the large insurance companies who cover a significant number of fire and police departments and could invest in such resources.

Another potential barrier is *therapist training and comfort*. Much of the delivery of mental health treatment in the United States is provided by masters level clinicians, but they are the least likely to have had *training* in exposure therapy. As we noted previously, VR is a powerful tool that allows more immersion into the re-created traumatic event and the accompanying cues (when compared to imagination alone). However, using VR without the requisite training in exposure therapy is unlikely to result in a positive treatment outcome. Additionally, the therapist must have a level of *comfort* in using, maintaining, and troubleshooting the VR hardware system. Although there is some training involved, it does not take an extensive period of time (1–2 months) to feel comfortable using the system and its components. What is above the level of most clinicians is the need to program in order to develop specific scenarios and cues for which their patients may be seeking treatment.

One final barrier is that most systems reside on a desktop in the clinician's office. Since the COVID-19 pandemic, an increasingly larger share of people are receiving behavioral health services via *telehealth*. Until now, the use of VR was not conducive to delivery via telehealth as it resided on a stand-alone computer in the therapists office. Therefore, those who preferred to receive therapy via telehealth or did not live within range of a brick and mortar clinic were not able to avail themselves of this treatment modality.

VR and Occupational Stress

During disaster situations, first responders and emergency medical personnel experience high levels of occupational stress; yet, there is no opportunity to take time off and relax. Telecommunicators working during one Category 4 hurricane were deployed to the emergency management center, where they worked for 72–96 hours with minimal breaks and rest periods, generating high levels of stress. One successful stress mitigation strategy is walking in a natural environment. As little as 15 minutes of walking in nature can decrease stress and improve cognitive functioning (Ohly et al., 2016). Since taking a physical nature walk is not possible during emergency situations, our clinic has been studying whether a "virtual 15 minute" walk through nature, via VR, could decrease occupational stress. The results of our preliminary study with 33 helicopter flight nurses and telecommunicators indicate this may be a viable approach to decrease "in the moment stress" for first responders.

One specific requirement for this intervention is that the headset would have to be durable, not require internet access during system use, and have an extended battery life. The latter two are critical as first responders often work in areas where there is no internet or electrical power. Feasibility testing indicated that both pediatric flight nurses and EMS/telecommunicators reported that the VR headsets (which allowed a virtual walk along a beach, in a forest, etc.) were: (a) helpful following a traumatic emergency call, (b) feasible to use on a break, and (c) relaxing. Further, assessment of state anxiety before and after using the headset significantly decreased the user's stress level following a traumatic/stressful call ($t(66) = 10.14, p < 0.001$). These data require further replication and have not yet been evaluated in a disaster setting, but the results are promising and represent a minimally invasive strategy to reduce stress "in the moment" (or shortly thereafter).

Prevention and Training

In conjunction with the growing research on the applications of VR technology to *treat* mental health conditions, another application is VR-assisted *prevention and training* for first responders. Just as VR can customize the therapeutic environment, VR-assisted training setups can be customized to train first responders to deal with critical events more effectively. In fact, many entities have already adopted this technology to optimize prevention and training:

- New York Police Department (NYPD) uses VR for active shooter training.
- Transportation Deutsche Bahn plans to conduct VR trainings for scenarios that cannot be taught on real trains (e.g., handling fire).
- PwC conducts diversity and inclusion trainings in VR.
- Columbia University and Harvard Medical School use VR to train surgeons.
- Shell uses VR for safety training in deep-water oil projects.
- Verizon uses VR to train their store clerks to manage hostage and robbery situations (Fig. 4.4).

Considering that a first responder's ability to deal with critical events increases with the extent of training received (Xie et al., 2021), innovative strategies that optimize immersion into these scenarios as anticipatory stressors has the potential to improve both their ability to conduct their job functions as well as maintain effective mental health following real-world traumatic exposure. First responder training in the real world can be expensive and time consuming (Karabiyik et al., 2019), whereas

Fig. 4.4 *Note* Images of virtual environments used in presented simulators. Limitations concerning simplified fire simulations and simplified water distribution simulation are discussed in sect. 2.8. The level of smoke was decreased, and the brightness was increased to increase the readability of images. Practical skills training in enclosure fires: An experimental study with cadets and firefighters using CAVE and HMD-based virtual training simulators. *Fire Safety Journal*, *125*, 103,440. Image courtesy of Grabowski (2021)

first responder training in virtual reality can significantly reduce training costs and improve performances (Koutitas et al., 2021). In fact, VR training is already being increasingly used to train military and law enforcement professionals to practice de-escalating critical situations, administer safety trainings, and media dissemination (Wohlgenannt et al., 2020).

The ability of VR to increase the customizability training scenarios could make prevention and training appealing, intuitive, and safe as opposed to traditional measures that are limited by what is physically available (Xie et al., 2021). For example, with VR, an instructor can control a virtual fire (position, intensity, and damage caused) in which a firefighter is being trained to evacuate a building. This allows first responders to easily train in an environment that mimics real-world challenges with minimal exposure to dangerous situations. But how does this affect first responder mental health? Much like how exposure therapy intends to use repeated exposure to feared stimuli to reduce the stress response, training and prevention models aim to equip first responders with the psychological tools necessary to successfully navigate critical incidents by exposing them to computer-generated scenarios. This exposure to an artificial critical incident is intended to improve occupational effectiveness and reduce psychopathological symptoms following exposure to a potentially traumatic event in the line of duty. For example, stress inoculation training (originally developed by Donald Meichenbaum in 1979) aims to train effective coping strategies for mentally processing unique critical incident scenarios by preemptively identifying maladaptive coping mechanisms and replacing them with adaptive coping mechanisms to reduce the likelihood of adverse reactions following exposure to real-life potentially traumatic events. VR-SIT enhances this experience by enabling controlled exposure to meaningful and interactive scenarios representative to real-world exposures without risking the safety of those in high-risk professions (Serino et al., 2013).

VR-SIT has proven to be impactful in improving relaxation, improving performance outcomes, increasing heart rate variability (to demonstrate the ability of this technology to achieve immersion and presence), and reducing arousal among military service members (Hourani et al., 2011; Kosinska et al., 2013; Lewis et al., 2015), suggesting its applicability to develop and improve adaptive coping mechanisms among first responders when exposed to critical incidents. In a different preventative/training application, Conges et al. (2020) used a VR scenario where a first responder team rescued an injured man lying on a subway station platform that was on fire. This training system, known as the EGCERSIS project, provides a framework for training a crisis management team on critical sites, is delivered with VR technology and useful when the responder agencies were not co-located during the training. Other researchers have demonstrated the efficacy of VR platforms to:

- Train squad leaders to respond appropriately to an emergency situation (Mossel et al., 2017)
- Safely train on specialized bomb demolition tasks (Haskins et al., 2020)
- Train ambulance crews of proper use and location of equipment on an ambulance bus (Koutitas et al., 2019). This study used augmented reality (AR) in addition to VR.

Summary and Future Directions

In summary, the potential of virtual reality technology to augment exposure therapy and effectively treat the unique mental health needs of first responders shows great promise in enhancing PTSD treatment efficacy. Although to date, few studies have applied VR to the treatment of first responders with PTSD, the growing affordability, accessibility, and applicability of extended reality technology suggest that its integration into first responder mental health should be seriously considered. The demonstrated ability of VR to achieve immersion, presence, interactivity, and virtual world construction for first responder training and prevention supports its applicability to mitigation and treatment. First responders experience multiple unpredictable critical incidents and traumatic events throughout their careers, putting them at high risk for the development of mental health symptoms, PTSD, and suicide. Thus, efficacious treatments are essential, as prevention and resiliency training cannot guarantee psychopathological immunity. Ongoing innovations which are designed specifically with first responders in mind, can provide insights into both the promise and limitations of VR for the treatment of PTSD in the first responder community.

References

American Psychiatric Association. (2013). *Diagnostic and statistical manual of mental disorders* (5th ed.). https://doi.org/10.1176/appi.books.9780890425596

American Psychological Association. (2017). *Clinical practice guideline for the treatment of post-traumatic stress disorder (PTSD) in adults.* [Data set]. PsycEXTRA. https://doi.org/10.1037/e501872017-001

Beidel, D. C., Bowers, C. A., R., N.,. A., Seaver, C., Rozek, D., McDaniel, C., & Horning, D. R. (2024). Virtual-reality exposure treatment for first responder PTSD: A pilot investigation. *Frontiers in Virtual Reality, 5.* https://doi.org/10.3389/frvir.2024.1336523

Beidel, D. C., Frueh, B. C., Neer, S. M., Bowers, C., & Rizzo, A. (2014). Using virtual reality as part of an intensive treatment program for PTSD. *Interservice/Industry Training, Simulation, and Education Conference (I/ITSEC).*

Beidel, D. C., Frueh, B. C., Neer, S. M., Bowers, C. A., Trachik, B., Uhde, T. W., & Grubaugh, A. (2019). Trauma management therapy with virtual-reality augmented exposure therapy for combat-related PTSD: A randomized controlled trial. *Journal of Anxiety Disorders, 61*, 64–74. https://doi.org/10.1016/j.janxdis.2017.08.005

Beidel, D. C., Frueh, B. C., Neer, S. M., & Lejuez, C. W. (2017). The efficacy of trauma management therapy: A controlled pilot investigation of a three-week intensive outpatient program for combat-related PTSD. *Journal of Anxiety Disorders, 50*, 23–32. https://doi.org/10.1016/j.janxdis.2017.05.001

Beidel, D. C., Frueh, B. C., Uhde, T. W., Wong, N., & Mentrikoski, J. M. (2011). Multicomponent behavioral treatment for chronic combat-related posttraumatic stress disorder: A randomized controlled trial. *Journal of Anxiety Disorders, 25*(2), 224–231. https://doi.org/10.1016/j.janxdis.2010.09.006

Benbow, A. A., & Anderson, P. L. (2019). A meta-analytic examination of attrition in virtual reality exposure therapy for anxiety disorders. *Journal of Anxiety Disorders, 61*, 18–26. https://doi.org/10.1016/j.janxdis.2018.06.006

Bergstrom, J. R., & Schall, A. (Eds.). (2014). *Eye tracking in user experience design.* Elsevier.

Bohil, C. J., Alicea, B., & Biocca, F. A. (2011). Virtual reality in neuroscience research and therapy. *Nature Reviews Neuroscience, 12*(12), 752–762. https://doi.org/10.1038/nrn3122

Botella, C., Baños, R., Perpiñá, C., Villa, H., Alcañiz, M., & Rey, A. (1998). Virtual reality treatment of claustrophobia: A case report. *Behaviour Research and Therapy, 36*(2), 239–246. https://doi.org/10.1016/s0005-7967(97)10006-7

Brooks, F. (1999). What's real about virtual reality? *IEEE Computer Graphics and Applications, 19*(6), 16–27. https://doi.org/10.1109/38.799723

Buhl, H. U., & Winter, R. (2008). Full virtualization—BISE's contribution to a vision. *Business & Information Systems Engineering, 1*(2), 133–136. https://doi.org/10.1007/s12599-008-0023-2

Canadian Agency for Drugs and Technologies in Health. (2014). Virtual reality exposure therapy for adults with post-traumatic stress disorder: A review of the clinical effectiveness. https://www.ncbi.nlm.nih.gov/books/NBK253832/

Carl, E., Stein, A. T., Levihn-Coon, A., Pogue, J. R., Rothbaum, B., Emmelkamp, P., Asmundson, G. J., Carlbring, P., & Powers, M. B. (2019). Virtual reality exposure therapy for anxiety and related disorders: A meta-analysis of randomized controlled trials. *Journal of Anxiety Disorders, 61*, 27–36. https://doi.org/10.1016/j.janxdis.2018.08.003

Carlin, A. S., Hoffman, H. G., & Weghorst, S. (1997). Virtual reality and tactile augmentation in the treatment of spider phobia: A case report. *Behaviour Research and Therapy, 35*(2), 153–158. https://doi.org/10.1016/s0005-7967(96)00085-x

Conges, A., Evain, A., Benaben, F., Chabiron, O., & Rebiere, S. (2020). Crisis management exercises in virtual reality. In *2020 IEEE conference on virtual reality and 3D user interfaces abstracts and workshops (VRW)* (pp. 87–92). IEEE. https://doi.org/10.1109/VRW50115.2020.00022

Corneil, W., Beaton, R., Murphy, S., Johnson, C., & Pike, K. (1999). Exposure to traumatic incidents and prevalence of posttraumatic stress symptomatology in urban firefighters in two countries.

Journal of Occupational Health Psychology, 4(2), 131–141. https://doi.org/10.1037/1076-8998.4.2.131

Cottraux, J., Note, I., Yao, S. N., De Mey-Guillard, C., Bonasse, F., Djamoussian, D., Mollard, E., Note, B., & Chen, Y. (2008). Randomized controlled comparison of cognitive behavior therapy with Rogerian supportive therapy in chronic post-traumatic stress disorder: A 2-year follow-up. *Psychotherapy and Psychosomatics, 77*(2), 101–110. https://doi.org/10.1159/000112887

Cruz-Neira, C., Sandin, D. J., DeFanti, T. A., Kenyon, R. V., & Hart, J. C. (1992). The CAVE: audio visual experience automatic virtual environment. *Communications of the ACM, 35*(6), 64–72. https://doi.org/10.1145/129888.129892

Darensburg, T., Andrew, M. E., Hartley, T. A., Burchfiel, C. M., Fekedulegn, D., & Violanti, J. M. (2006). Gender and age differences in posttraumatic stress disorder and depression among Buffalo police officers. *Traumatology, 12*(3), 220–228. https://doi.org/10.1177/1534765606296271

Deng, W., Hu, D., Xu, S., Liu, X., Zhao, J., Chen, Q., Liu, J., Zhang, Z., Jiang, W., Ma, L., Hong, X., Cheng, S., Liu, B., & Li, X. (2019). The efficacy of virtual reality exposure therapy for PTSD symptoms: A systematic review and meta-analysis. *Journal of Affective Disorders, 257*, 698–709. https://doi.org/10.1016/j.jad.2019.07.086

Difede, J., Cukor, J., Jayasinghe, N., Patt, I., Jedel, S., Spielman, L., Giosan, C., & Hoffman, H. G. (2007). Virtual reality exposure therapy for the treatment of posttraumatic stress disorder following September 11, 2001. *Journal of Clinical Psychiatry, 68*(11), 1682–1689. https://doi.org/10.4088/jcp.v68n1102

Drascic, D., & Milgram, P. (1996). Perceptual issues in augmented reality. In Proceedings of SPIE: Stereoscopic displays and virtual reality systems III (Vol. 2653, pp. 123–134). SPIE.

Fast-Berglund, Å., Gong, L., & Li, D. (2018). Testing and validating extended reality (xR) technologies in manufacturing. *Procedia Manufacturing, 25*, 31–38. https://doi.org/10.1016/j.promfg.2018.06.054

Foa, E. B., Davidson, R. T., & Frances, A. (1999). The expert consensus guideline series. Treatment of posttraumatic stress disorder. The expert consensus panels for PTSD. *Journal of Clinical Psychiatry*, 3–76. http://ci.nii.ac.jp/ncid/BA4247510X

Foa, E. B., Huppert, J. D., & Cahill, S. (2006). Emotional processing theory: An update. In B. O. Rothbaum (Ed.), *Pathological anxiety: Emotional processing in etiology and treatment* (pp. 3–24). The Guilford Press.

Foa, E. B., & Kozak, M. J. (1986). Emotional processing of fear: Exposure to corrective information. *Psychological Bulletin, 99*(1), 20–35. https://doi.org/10.1037/0033-2909.99.1.20

Foa, E. B., Rothbaum, B. O., & Furr, J. M. (2003). Augmenting exposure therapy with other CBT procedures. *Psychiatric Annals, 33*(1), 47–53. https://doi.org/10.3928/0048-5713-20030101-08

Fodor, L. A., Coteț, C. D., Cuijpers, P., Szamoskozi, Ș., David, D., & Cristea, I. A. (2018). The effectiveness of virtual reality based interventions for symptoms of anxiety and depression: A meta-analysis. *Scientific Reports, 8*(1). https://doi.org/10.1038/s41598-018-28113-6

Fullerton, C. S., Ursano, R. J., Reeves, J., Shigemura, J., & Grieger, T. (2006). Perceived safety in disaster workers following 9/11. *Journal of Nervous and Mental Disease, 194*(1), 61–63. https://doi.org/10.1097/01.nmd.0000195307.28743.b2

Gamito, P., Oliveira, J., Rosa, P., Morais, D., Duarte, N., Oliveira, S., & Saraiva, T. (2010). PTSD elderly war veterans: A clinical controlled pilot study. *Cyberpsychology, Behavior and Social Networking, 13*(1), 43–48. https://doi.org/10.1089/cyber.2009.0237

Gerardi, M., Cukor, J., Difede, J., Rizzo, A., & Rothbaum, B. O. (2010). Virtual reality exposure therapy for post-traumatic stress disorder and other anxiety disorders. *Current Psychiatry Reports, 12*, 298–305. https://doi.org/10.1007/s11920-010-0128-4

Gerardi, M., Rothbaum, B. O., Ressler, K., Heekin, M., & Rizzo, A. (2008). Virtual reality exposure therapy using a virtual Iraq: Case report. *Journal of Traumatic Stress, 21*(2), 209–213. https://doi.org/10.1002/jts.20331

Gonçalves, R., Pedrozo, A. L., Coutinho, E. S. F., Figueira, I., & Ventura, P. (2012). Efficacy of virtual reality exposure therapy in the treatment of PTSD: A systematic review. *PLoS One, 7*(12), e48469. https://doi.org/10.1371/journal.pone.0048469

Grabowski, A. (2021). Practical skills training in enclosure fires: An experimental study with cadets and firefighters using CAVE and HMD-based virtual training simulators. *Fire Safety Journal, 125*, 103440. https://doi.org/10.1016/j.firesaf.2021.103440

Hackmann, A., Ehlers, A., Speckens, A., & Clark, D. M. (2004). Characteristics and content of ntrusive memories in PTSD and their changes with treatment. *Journal of Traumatic Stress, 17*(3), 231–240. https://doi.org/10.1023/b:jots.0000029266.88369.fd

Hartley, T. A., Violanti, J. M., Sarkisian, K., Andrew, M. E., & Burchfiel, C. M. (2013). PTSD symptoms among police officers: Associations with frequency, recency, and types of traumatic events. *PubMed*. https://pubmed.ncbi.nlm.nih.gov/24707587

Haskins, J., Zhu, B., Gainer, S., Huse, W., Eadara, S., Boyd, B., Laird, C., Farantatos, J., & Jerald, J. (2020). Exploring VR training for first responders. In *2020 IEEE conference on virtual reality and 3D user interfaces abstracts and workshops (VRW)*. IEEE. https://doi.org/10.1109/VRW50115.2020.00018

Haugen, P. T., Evces, M., & Weiss, D. S. (2012). Treating posttraumatic stress disorder in first responders: A systematic review. *Clinical Psychology Review, 32*(5), 370–380. https://doi.org/10.1016/j.cpr.2012.04.001

Hourani, L. L., Kizakevich, P. N., Hubal, R., Spira, J., Strange, L. B., Holiday, D. B., & McLean, A. N. (2011). Predeployment stress inoculation training for primary prevention of combat-related stress disorders. Journal of CyberTherapy & Rehabilitation, 4(1), 101–116. https://www.rvht.net/pubs/JCR%204(1).pdf#page=103

International Society for Traumatic Stress Studies. (2018). *Posttraumatic stress disorder prevention and treatment guidelines: Methodology and recommendations*. http://www.istss.org/treating-trauma/new-istss-prevention-and-treatment-guidelines.aspx

Jain, S., Shapiro, S. L., Swanick, S., Roesch, S. C., Mills, P. J., Bell, I., & Schwartz, G. E. R. (2007). A randomized controlled trial of mindfulness meditation versus relaxation training: Effects on distress, positive states of mind, rumination, and distraction. *Annals of Behavioral Medicine, 33*(1), 11–21. https://doi.org/10.1207/s15324796abm3301_2

Karabiyik, U., Mousas, C., Sirota, D., Iwai, T., & Akdere, M. (2019). A virtual reality framework for training incident first responders and digital forensic investigators. In *International symposium on visual computing* (pp. 469–480). Springer. https://doi.org/10.1007/978-3-030-33723-0_38

Kimbrel, N. A., Steffen, L. E., Meyer, E. C., Kruse, M. I., Knight, J. A., Zimering, R. T., & Gulliver, S. B. (2011). A revised measure of occupational stress for firefighters: Psychometric properties and relationship to posttraumatic stress disorder, depression, and substance abuse. *Psychological Services, 8*(4), 294–306. https://doi.org/10.1037/a0025845

Kleim, B., & Westphal, M. (2011). Mental health in first responders: A review and recommendation for prevention and intervention strategies. *Traumatology, 17*(4), 17–24. https://doi.org/10.1177/1534765611429079

Kosinska, L., Ilnicki, S., Wiederhold, B. K., Maciolek, J., Szymanska, S., Opalko-Piotrkiewicz, E., Siatkowska, A., Ilnicki, P., Zbyszewski, M., & Glibowska, A. (2013). *VR stress inoculation training results for polish ISAF soldiers–a study of 4 cases. In new tools to enhance posttraumatic stress disorder diagnosis and treatment* (Vol. 108, pp. 149–160).

Koutitas, G., Smith, K. S., & Lawrence, G. (2021). Performance evaluation of AR/VR training technologies for EMS first responders. *Virtual Reality, 25*(1), 83–94. https://doi.org/10.1007/s10055-020-00436-8

Koutitas, G., Smith, K. S., Lawrence, G., Metsis, V., Stamper, C., Trahan, M., & Lehr, T. (2019, June). *A virtual and augmented reality platform for the training of first responders of the ambulance bus. In proceedings of the 12th ACM international conference on pervasive technologies related to assistive environments* (pp. 299–302). https://doi.org/10.1145/3316782.3321542

Lang, P. J. (1968). Fear reduction and fear behavior: Problems in treating a construct. In J. M. Schlien (Ed.), *Research in psychotherapy* (pp. 90–103). American Psychological Association. https://doi.org/10.1037/10546-004

Lewis, G. F., Hourani, L., Tueller, S., Kizakevich, P., Bryant, S., Weimer, B., & Strange, L. (2015). Relaxation training assisted by heart rate variability biofeedback: Implication for a military predeployment stress inoculation protocol. *Psychophysiology, 52*(9), 1167–1174. https://doi.org/10.1111/psyp.12455

Mach, V., Valouch, J., Adámek, M., & Ševčík, J. (2019). Virtual reality—Level of immersion within the crime investigation. *MATEC Web of Conferences, 292*, 01031. https://doi.org/10.1051/matecconf/201929201031

McCallion, T. (2012). And the survey says: NASEMSO analysis provides snapshot of EMS industry. *PubMed, 37*(1), 34–35. https://doi.org/10.1016/s0197-2510(12)70015-3

McDonagh, A., Friedman, M., McHugo, G., Ford, J., Sengupta, A., Mueser, K., Demment, C. C., Fournier, D., Schnurr, P. P., & Descamps, M. (2005). Randomized trial of cognitive-behavioral therapy for chronic posttraumatic stress disorder in adult female survivors of childhood sexual abuse. *Journal of Consulting and Clinical Psychology, 73*(3), 515–524. https://doi.org/10.1037/0022-006x.73.3.515

McGhee, J. T., Hamedi, M., Fatoorechi, M., Roggen, D., Cleal, A., Prance, R., & Nduka, C. (2018). Towards a novel biometric facial input for emotion recognition and assistive technology for virtual reality. *International Journal of Child Health and Human Development, 11*(2), 243. https://www.questia.com/library/journal/1P4-2136876881/towards-a-novel-biometric-facial-input-for-emotion

McLay, R. N., Baird, A., Webb-Murphy, J., Deal, W., Tran, L., Anson, H., Klam, W., & Johnston, S. (2017). A randomized, head-to-head study of virtual reality exposure therapy for posttraumatic stress disorder. *Cyberpsychology, Behavior, and Social Networking, 20*(4), 218–224. https://doi.org/10.1089/cyber.2016.0554

McLay, R. N., Wood, D. P., Webb-Murphy, J. A., Spira, J. L., Wiederhold, M. D., Pyne, J. M., & Wiederhold, B. K. (2011). A randomized, controlled trial of virtual reality-graded exposure therapy for post-traumatic stress disorder in active duty service members with combat-related post-traumatic stress disorder. *Cyberpsychology, Behavior, and Social Networking, 14*(4), 223–229. https://doi.org/10.1089/cyber.2011.0003

Milgram, P., & Kishino, F. (1994). A taxonomy of mixed reality visual displays. *IEICE Transactions on Information and Systems, 77*(12), 1321–1329. https://cs.gmu.edu/~zduric/cs499/Readings/r76JBo-Milgram_IEICE_1994.pdf

Miloff, A., Lindner, P., Hamilton, W., Reuterskiöld, L., Andersson, G., & Carlbring, P. (2016). Single session gamified virtual reality exposure therapy for spider phobia vs. traditional exposure therapy: Study protocol for a randomized controlled non-inferiority trial. *Trials, 17*(1). https://doi.org/10.1186/s13063-016-1171-1

Miyahira, S. D., Folen, R. A., Hoffman, H. G., Garcia-Palacios, A., Spira, J. L., & Kawasaki, M. (2012). The effectiveness of VR exposure therapy for PTSD in returning warfighters. *Annual Review of Cybertherapy and Telemedicine, 181*, 128–132. https://pubmed.ncbi.nlm.nih.gov/22954842

Mossel, A., Froeschl, M., Schoenauer, C., Peer, A., Goellner, J., & Kaufmann, H. (2017, March). VROnSite: Towards immersive training of first responder squad leaders in untethered virtual reality. In *2017 IEEE virtual reality (VR)* (pp. 357–358). IEEE. https://doi.org/10.1109/VR.2017.7892324

Murphy, S. A., Beaton, R. D., Pike, K. C., & Johnson, L. C. (1999). Occupational stressors, stress responses, and alcohol consumption among professional firefighters: A prospective, longitudinal analysis. *International Journal of Stress Management, 6*, 179–196.

National Fire Protection Association. (2014). *Fire department calls*. http://www.nfpa.org/news-and-research/fire-statistics-and-reports/fire-statistics/the-fire-service/fire-department-calls/fire-department-calls

National Institute of Mental Health. (2017). *Post-traumatic stress disorder (PTSD).* https://www.nimh.nih.gov/health/statistics/post-traumatic-stress-disorder-ptsd.shtml

O'Dare, K., Mathis, A., Tawk, R., Atwell, L., & Jackson, D. (2024). State level policies on first responder mental health in the US: A scoping review. *Administration and Policy in Mental Health and Mental Health Services Research, 1-18.* https://doi.org/10.1007/s10488-024-01352-8

Ohly, H., White, M. P., Wheeler, B. W., Bethel, A., Ukoumunne, O. C., Nikolaou, V., & Garside, R. (2016). Attention restoration theory: A systematic review of the attention restoration potential of exposure to natural environments. *Journal of Toxicology and Environmental Health, Part B, 19*(7), 305–343. https://doi.org/10.1080/10937404.2016.1196155

Powers, M. B., Halpern, J. M., Ferenschak, M. P., Gillihan, S. J., & Foa, E. B. (2010). A meta-analytic review of prolonged exposure for posttraumatic stress disorder. *Clinical Psychology Review, 30*(6), 635–641. https://doi.org/10.1176/appi.focus.11.3.428

Ready, D. J., Gerardi, R. J., Backscheider, A. G., Mascaro, N., & Rothbaum, B. O. (2010). Comparing virtual reality exposure therapy to present-centered therapy with 11 US Vietnam veterans with PTSD. *Cyberpsychology, Behavior, and Social Networking, 13*(1), 49–54. https://doi.org/10.1089/cyber.2009.0239

Reger, G. M., Koenen-Woods, P., Zetocha, K., Smolenski, D. J., Holloway, K. M., Rothbaum, B. O., Difede, J., Rizzo, A. A., Edwards-Stewart, A., Skopp, N. A., Mishkind, M., Reger, M. A., & Gahm, G. A. (2016). Randomized controlled trial of prolonged exposure using imaginal exposure vs. virtual reality exposure in active duty soldiers with deployment-related posttraumatic stress disorder (PTSD). *Journal of Consulting and Clinical Psychology, 84*(11), 946–959. https://doi.org/10.1037/ccp0000134

Rizzo, A., Hartholt, A., & Mozgai, S. (2021). From combat to COVID-19—Managing the impact of trauma using virtual reality. *Journal of Technology in Human Services, 39*(3), 314–347. https://doi.org/10.1080/15228835.2021.1915931

Rizzo, A., & Shilling, R. (2017). Clinical virtual reality tools to advance the prevention, assessment, and treatment of PTSD. *European Journal of Psychotraumatology, 8*(sup5). https://doi.org/10.1080/20008198.2017.1414560

Rothbaum, B. O., & Hodges, L. F. (1999). The use of virtual reality exposure in the treatment of anxiety disorders. *Behavior Modification, 23*(4), 507–525. https://doi.org/10.1177/0145445599234001

Rothbaum, B. O., Hodges, L. F., Ready, D., Graap, K., & Alarcon, R. D. (2001). Virtual reality exposure therapy for Vietnam veterans with posttraumatic stress disorder. *Journal of Clinical Psychiatry, 62*(8), 617–622. https://doi.org/10.4088/jcp.v62n0808

Roy, M. J., Francis, J., Friedlander, J., Banks-Williams, L., Lande, R. G., Taylor, P., Blair, J., McLellan, J., Law, W., Tarpley, V., Patt, I., Yu, H., Mallinger, A., Difede, J., Rizzo, A., & Rothbaum, B. (2010). Improvement in cerebral function with treatment of posttraumatic stress disorders. *Annals of the New York Academy of Sciences, 1208*(1), 142–149. https://doi.org/10.1111/j.1749-6632.2010.05689.x

Serino, S., Tibesti, S., Villani, D., Cypress, P., Faggioli, A., & Riva, G. (2013). Toward a validation of cyber-interventions for stress disorders based on stress inoculation training: A systematic review. *Virtual Reality, 18*(1), 73–87. https://doi.org/10.1007/s10055-013-0237-6

Sherman, W. R., & Craig, A. B. (2003). Understanding virtual reality—Interface, application, and design. *Presence, 12*(4), 441–442. https://doi.org/10.1162/105474603322391668

Tarnowski, P., Koozie, M., Majkowski, A., & Rak, R. J. (2018). Combined analysis of GSR and EEG signals for emotion recognition. In *In 2018 international interdisciplinary PhD workshop (IIPhDW)* (pp. 137–141). IEEE. https://doi.org/10.1109/iiphdw.2018.8388342

Valente, L., Feijó, B., Ribeiro, A., & Clua, E. (2016). The concept of pervasive virtuality and its application in digital entertainment systems. *Lecture Notes in Computer Science, 187–198.* https://doi.org/10.1007/978-3-319-46100-7_16

Violanti, J. M. (2004). Predictors of police suicide ideation. *Suicide & Life-threatening Behavior/ Suicide and Life-threatening Behavior, 34*(3), 277–283. https://doi.org/10.1521/suli.34.3.277.42775

Williams, D. P., Cash, C., Rankin, C., Bernardi, A., Koenig, J., & Thayer, J. F. (2015). Resting heart rate variability predicts self-reported difficulties in emotion regulation: A focus on different facets of emotion regulation. *Frontiers in Psychology, 6*. https://doi.org/10.3389/fpsyg.2015.00261

Wohlgenannt, I., Simons, A., & Stieglitz, S. (2020). Virtual reality. *Business & Information Systems Engineering, 62*, 455–461. https://doi.org/10.1007/s12599-020-00658-9

Wolitzky-Taylor, K. B., Horowitz, J. D., Powers, M. B., & Telch, M. J. (2008). Psychological approaches in the treatment of specific phobias: A meta-analysis. *Clinical Psychology Review, 28*(6), 1021–1037. https://doi.org/10.1016/j.cpr.2008.02.007

Xie, B., Liu, H., Alghofaili, R., Zhang, Y., Jiang, Y., Lobo, F. D., Li, C., Li, W., Huang, H., Akdere, M., Mousas, C., & Yu, L. F. (2021). A review on virtual reality skill training applications. *Frontiers in Virtual Reality, 2*, 645153. https://doi.org/10.3389/frvir.2021.645153

Yoo, J. W., Lee, D. R., Cha, Y. J., & You, S. H. (2017). Augmented effects of EMG biofeedback interfaced with virtual reality on neuromuscular control and movement coordination during reaching in children with cerebral palsy. *NeuroRehabilitation, 40*(2), 175–185. https://doi.org/10.3233/nre-161402

Chapter 5
Law Enforcement Stress Survey (LEOSS): Validation and Clinical Utility

Bailee Schuhmann, Monty Baker, Ryan A. Black, Rachel Christopher, Vincent B. Van Hasselt, Samuel Browning, and Ryan Reddin

Law Enforcement Stress Survey (LEOSS): Validation and Clinical Utility

Law enforcement officers (LEOs) encounter a wide range of stressors while serving their communities and dealing with recent events (i.e., COVID-19 pandemic, social unrest). Policing has been identified as one of the top five most stressful occupations (Dantzer, 1987; Sekar et al., 2013). Consequently, stress in this population has garnered research interest for nearly half a century (Richard & Feil, 1976; Steinberg & McEvoy, 1974). Moreover, a burgeoning body of evidence suggests that stress in LEOs can lead to a variety of negative mental and physical health outcomes (Gershon et al., 2009; Mumford et al., 2021). Since early investigation into law enforcement stress, researchers have identified several sources and risk factors associated with negative stress reactions in LEOs. Specifically, such research highlights the impact of organizational stressors, family stressors, law enforcement subculture, and potentially traumatic events in the development of negative stress reactions.

Author Note: Correspondence concerning this article should be addressed to Bailee Schuhmann, PhD, Department of Psychiatry and Behavioral Sciences, The University of Texas Health Science Center at San Antonio, 7703 Floyd Curl Dr., San Antonio, TX 78229, United States. Email: schuhmann@uthscsa.edu.

B. Schuhmann (✉) · M. Baker
University of Texas Health Science Center at San Antonio, San Antonio, TX, USA
e-mail: schuhmann@uthscsa.edu

B. Schuhmann · M. Baker · R. A. Black · R. Christopher · V. B. Van Hasselt · S. Browning · R. Reddin
College of Psychology, Nova Southeastern University, Fort Lauderdale, FL, USA

V. B. Van Hasselt
Broward Sheriff's Office, Broward County, FL, USA

V. B. Van Hasselt and M. L. Bourke (eds.), *Advances in First Responder Mental Health*, Advances in First Responder Mental Health 1,
https://doi.org/10.1007/978-3-032-27978-1_5

Previous research has identified organizational stressors as particularly impactful for police officers (Bishopp et al., 2019; Newman & Rucker-Reed, 2004). For example, Liberman et al. (2002) found that routine occupational stress was a better predictor of general psychological distress than cumulative exposure to critical incidents in the field for a sample of 733 police officers in New York City, Oakland, and San Jose. Additionally, Ermasova et al. (2020) reported poor personal relationships with supervisor(s), and unfair promotional opportunities as the leading causes of stress in 427 police officers in Illinois. McCarty and Skogan (2012) noted organizational stressors, including lack of social support, agency size, and perceived unfairness, significantly predicted burnout in 2,078 sworn personnel across 12 police agencies in the U.S.

Varied work schedules, extended hours, and time spent away from the home can contribute to family stress by having a negative effect on relationships and family activities for LEOs (Ma et al., 2015; Sheehan & Van Hasselt, 2003). It has also been cautioned that LEOs' change in behavior following critical incident exposure can impact their family system (Violanti, 1999). Law enforcement subculture reinforces self-reliance, which often keeps LEOs from reaching out to their loved ones for support, and has been found to exacerbate negative stress reactions (Miller, 2006; Violanti, 1999). As a result, LEOs perceive and, in fact, receive less social support in times of crisis (Prati & Pietrantoni, 2010). Additionally, divorce is common among LEOs, with some studies indicating divorce rates as high as 70% (Wetherington, 2021), which can be attributed to, as well as add to, an officer's stress level.

LEOs are frequently exposed to traumatic events as a part of their job. Commonly referred to as critical incidents, these include officer-involved shootings, failed rescue attempts, witnessing a fatality, murder/suicides, injury or death of a partner in the line of duty, and incidents in which the victim is a child (Ermasova et al., 2020; Sheehan & Van Hasselt, 2003). LEOs who are exposed to frequent and significant critical incidents are more likely to have negative stress reactions which may overwhelm coping abilities putting them at greater risk of experiencing negative sequelae (Baldwin et al., 2019; Miller, 2008). Moreover, harmful stress-related physical health problems characterize an estimated 14% of officers (Mumford et al., 2021). Some of these include high blood pressure, coronary heart disease, and gastrointestinal disorders (Brown & Campbell, 1994; Lord et al., 1991; Terry, 1981). Further, as Blum (2000) contends, many of these issues can compromise an officer's decision-making as well as the accuracy and speed of their mental activity.

Unrecognized negative stress has been demonstrated to have deleterious effects among LEOs including, but not limited to, increase risk of cardiovascular-related illness (Magnavita et al., 2018; Zimmerman, 2012), gastrointestinal disorders (Huerta-Franco et al., 2013), high blood pressure (Sörensen et al., 2000), posttraumatic stress disorder (PTSD; Klimley et al., 2018), substance abuse (Cross & Ashley, 2004; Irizar et al., 2021), interpersonal violence (Neidig et al., 1992), and marital discord (Sheehan, 2000; Sheehan & Van Hasselt, 2003). In the most extreme form, the negative sequale of stress may culminate in suicide, arguably the most maladaptive response to stress. Violanti and Steege (2021) illustrate the magnitude of this problem in their recent findings suggesting that LEOs are 54% more likely to die by suicide than decedents that held general occupations. In addition, Miller (2006) noted LEOs are three times more likely to die by suicide than be killed in the line of duty. These data could suggest that officers are fairly well trained to physically survive dangerous encounters, however are significantly less prepared to manage their reactions to them.

The aforementioned findings point to the importance of comprehensive stress prevention and treatment efforts for law enforcement. Despite evidence that early detection and intervention substantially reduce the likelihood of symptom development in trauma-exposed police officers (Sheehan & Van Hasselt, 2003), few measures have been developed to evaluate the severity of exposure to their unique stressors.

The Law Enforcement Officer Stress Survey (LEOSS)

In an effort to address this void, Van Hasselt et al. (2003) developed a brief stress screening tool, the Law Enforcement Officer Stress Survey (LEOSS), that assesses stress levels based on stressors unique to law enforcement. This measure consists of 25 scenarios which the officer rates on two dimensions: (1) the "Likelihood" of the officer experiencing the scenario, and (2) the "Difficulty Level" of the scenario for the officer. The Likelihood and Difficulty subscales are then combined to provide a Full-Scale score. Two studies have already been conducted by Van Hasselt et al., (2003, 2008) to examine psychometric properties of the LEOSS.

Development

The LEOSS was developed utilizing the behavioral-analytic method of test construction, which places emphasis on a functional analysis of the target demographic with respect to the behavior-environment interactions (D'Zurilla & Goldfried, 1971; Van Hasselt et al., 2003). This approach ensures greater social validity, as members of the actual target group provide input throughout the test development process. The five steps outlined in the behavioral-analytic model used to construct the LEOSS are: (1) situational analysis, (2) item development, (3) response enumeration, (4) response evaluation, and (5) construction of the instrument. First, LEOs submitted an item pool of situations they found stressful. The inclusion of items submitted by LEOs themselves increases the "social validity" (i.e., relevant, important, applicable to the consumer) of the measure (Schwartz & Baer, 1991). This pool was narrowed to 89 items and re-worded into situational items. These items were evaluated based on two factors: the "Likelihood" that an officer would encounter the scenario, and the "Difficulty" of the situation for that officer. The 89 initial item pool was decreased to 25 based on these ratings, and the current LEOSS was constructed. (See Van Hasselt et al., 2003, for a more detailed description of the test development procedures.)

Psychometric Properties

Psychometric properties of the LEOSS were evaluated by Van Hasselt et al. (2008). Internal reliability was examined through item-total correlations, which ranged from 0.287 to 0.674 for the difficulty scale. Further, test–retest reliability for all three of the scales (Likelihood, Difficulty, and Full Scale) were $r = 0.578$, $r = 0.621$, and $r = 0.672$, respectively. Validity was assessed by determining the relationship between LEOSS scores and the Police Stress Survey (PSS; Spielberger et al., 1981), a 60-item self-report measure. Scores on the LEOSS were significantly correlated with PSS scores, suggesting that the scales measure similar constructs. Further, a major validity concern addressed in this study was that of social desirability. Officers are unlikely to endorse stigma-causing admissions about their emotional well-being. Van Hasselt et al. (2008) found that the LEOSS Full Scale scores were not significantly related to a measure of social desirability, the Reynolds Short Form A (Reynolds, 1982), suggesting that social desirability had minimal impact on officers' responses.

The purpose of the present study is twofold: (1) to combine modern test theory (i.e., Item Response Theory) and classical test theory approaches to assessing reliability and validity of the LEOSS, and (2) to establish psychometric cut-off scores to improve the clinical utility of the instrument. By grouping score ranges into severity categories, clinicians will be able to better understand the level of stress an officer may be experiencing based on their score obtained using the LEOSS. As McCreary et al. (2017) point out, this provides clinicians a method to evaluate treatment outcome. It also has value in giving organizations a better understanding of stress levels in their officers.

Method

Participants

The present study utilized archival data collected from 247 active-duty police officers employed in the U.S. at the time of original data collection. The majority of participants were between 30–39 years old (42.5%), followed by 20–29 (26.3%). Sixty-four percent of the sample were married, 20.6% single, 6.1% engaged, and 7.7% either separated or divorced. Sixty-one percent of participants had children. Most of the sample was male (93.5%) and Caucasian (82.2%), consistent with national demographics of law enforcement professionals (Data USA, 2019). Seventy-five percent of the sample had less than 15 years of law enforcement experience. The sample represented police officers from a wide range of agencies, population areas, geographic regions, and level of jurisdiction (i.e., municipal, county, state, college). (See Table 5.1 for Demographic Characteristics of participants.) Further, officer demographics were not significantly associated with LEOSS Difficulty scores or subscale scores.

Table 5.1 Demographic characteristics of participants ($N = 247$)

Characteristic	*n*	%
Gender		
Male	125	93.3
Female	9	6.7
Age		
20–29	65	26.3
30–39	105	42.5
40–49	46	18.6
50–59	15	6.1
60–69	4	1.6
Ethnicity		
White/Caucasian	203	82.2
Hispanic or Latino	25	10.1
Black/African American	9	3.6
Other	3	1.2
Region of work		
Northeast	213	86.2
Southeast	22	8.9
Southwest	11	4.5
Midwest	–	–
Northwest	–	–
Years of service		
0–5	72	29.1
6–10	48	19.4
11–15	39	15.8
16–20	10	7.5
21–25	18	7.3
26+	9	3.6
Department type		
Municipal	142	57.5
County	55	22.3
State	43	17.4
College	6	2.4
Marital status		
Married	157	63.6
Engaged	15	6.1
Single	51	20.6
Divorced	13	5.3
Separated	6	2.4

(continued)

Table 5.1 (continued)

Characteristic	*n*	%
Other	2	0.8
Highest education level completed		
Some high school	1	0.4
GED	5	2.0
High school	30	12.1
Some college	82	33.2
Associates degree	36	14.6
4-year college degree (Bachelor's)	73	29.6
Master's degree	16	6.5
Doctorate degree	–	–
History of Military Service	61	24.7
Attended Job Counseling	22	8.9

Note Dashes indicate no participant endorsed the demographic criterion; Percentages may not equal 100% due to missing data

Procedure

Data were obtained from approximately 247 law enforcement officers prior to the present study. These archival data contain officer scores on measures of stress, resilience, affect, and social desirability. Law enforcement personnel were recruited from both rural and urban agencies across the Central and Eastern United States from 2011–2012. Participants were provided a letter detailing the purpose of the study, study requirements, and instructions for submitting survey responses upon completion. Respondents consented to participation by voluntarily completing a survey related to stress, coping, and resilience. Inclusion criteria included being a law enforcement officer and between the ages of 18 and 65. No incentive or compensation was provided for participation.

Measures

Demographic Questionnaire

A demographic questionnaire asked about participants' sociodemographic characteristics (age, gender, ethnicity, marital status, children, education level), service in law enforcement (region, years of service, department type, work environment, receipt of job counseling), and history of military service.

Law Enforcement Officer Stress Survey (LEOSS)

The Law Enforcement Officer Stress Survey (LEOSS) is composed of 25 items that address unique challenges and stresses encountered by officers (e.g., executing an arrest warrant, responding to a silent alarm) and was developed as an early warning stress screening measure for police officers (Van Hasselt et al., 2003). The items are rated on two separate seven-point Likert scales: "Likelihood" that the event will occur (1 = *Not at All Common;* 7 = *Extremely Common*), and "Difficulty" (or stress) of the situation would cause (1 = *Not at All Difficult/Problematic*; 7 = *Extremely Difficult/ Problematic*). Van Hasselt et al. (2008) reported that the LEOSS has good levels of internal consistency, validity, and test–retest reliability. Test–retest correlation coefficients were calculated for the Likelihood ($r = 0.578, p < 0.01$) and Difficulty ($r = 0.621, p < 0.01$) subscales, as well as the Full Scale ($r = 0.672, p < 0.01$). The alpha coefficients for Likelihood and Difficulty subscales, as well as the Full Scale, were 0.874, 0.908, and 0.874, respectively. The Full Scale of the LEOSS was also moderately, but significantly, related to the Police Stress Survey (PSS; Spielberger et al., 1981) ($r = 0.407, p < 0.001$).

Operational and Organizational Police Stress Questionnaire (PSQ-Op and PSQ-Org)

The PSQ-Op and PSQ-Org (McCreary & Thompson, 2006) each consist of 20 items that assess perceived levels of operational (e.g., working alone at night, risk of being injured) and organizational (e.g., dealing with co-workers and supervisors) stress in police officers. Participants rate how much stress each item has caused them in the past six months using a seven-point scale (*1 = no stress at all* to *7 = a lot of stress*). Cronbach's alpha was .93 for the PSQ-Op, and .92 for the PSQ-Org (McCreary & Thompson, 2006). Both measures were positively correlated with other general stress measures, such as the short version of the Police Daily Hassles Scale (Hart et al., 1993) and negatively correlated with measures of negative life events (McCreary & Sadava, 1998), among others.

Additionally, scores of both the PSQ-Op and PSQ-Org were shown to be negatively correlated with self-ratings of the Job Satisfaction Survey (JSS; Spector, 1997) (−0.19 to −0.56) and the positive-work related emotions subscale of the Job-related Affective Well-Being Scale (JAWS; Van Katwyk et al., 2000) (−0.20 to −0.25), and positively correlated with scores from the negative work-related emotions subscale from the JAWS (0.27 to 0.34) (McCreary & Thompson, 2006).

Posttraumatic Stress Disorder Symptom Checklist (PCL)

The PCL (Weathers et al., 1991) is a 17-item questionnaire that provides a correspondence between individual items and the DSM-IV diagnostic symptom criteria for PTSD (Weathers et al., 1991). Participants are asked to think of the worst experience they had in life and to indicate the extent to which they experienced PTSD symptoms (e.g., "repeated, disturbing memories of the event") because of it. Responses are rated on a 5-point scale (1 = *not at all*; 5 = *extremely*). Weathers et al. (1991) reported that the PCL has strong internal consistency (alpha = 0.94) and temporal stability (retest $r = 0.88$, 1-week interval), and it has a significant correlation (i.e., r >0 .75) with other measures of PTSD symptomatology (Ruggiero et al., 2003).

Patient Health Questionnaire, 9-Item (PHQ-9)

The PHQ-9 (Kroenke et al., 2001) is a 9-item self-report measure designed to screen and measure levels of depressive symptoms. Participants are asked to report how often, in the past four weeks, they were affected by the items listed (e.g., "Feeling tired or having little energy"). PHQ-9 items correspond directly to diagnostic criteria for a Major Depressive Episode, as set forth in the *DSM-IV* (4th ed.; *DSM-IV*; APA, 1994). Kroenke et al. (2001) note that the PHQ is a useful clinical and research tool that serves as a reliable and valid measure of depression severity.

Short Form of the Taylor Manifest Anxiety Scale (TMAS)

The short form of the TMAS consists of 20 true/false items drawn from the Minnesota Multiphasic Inventory (MMPI) that attempts to assess behavioral manifestations of anxiety (Bendig, 1956; Hicks et al., 1980). The original TMAS was composed of 50 such true/false items (Taylor, 1953). A study of 59 undergraduates indicated a high three-week test–retest reliability, ($r = 0.89$; Taylor, 1953), and a study of 64 neuropsychiatric patients showed good correspondence between TMAS scores and clinician ratings of behavioral manifestations of anxiety ($r = 0$ .60; Buss, 1955). Development of the short form involved psychometric scrutiny of individual questions, leading to deletion of items with questionable validity (Buss, 1955; Hoyt & Magoon, 1954). Despite its brevity, the internal consistency reliability of the short form is not significantly lower than the original TMAS ($r = 0.76$ versus $r = 0.82$).

Marlowe-Crowne Social Desirability Scale

The Marlowe-Crowne Social Desirability Scale (MCSDS; Crowne & Marlowe, 1960) is a 33-item measure examining the tendency to present oneself in a favorable light (i.e., "defensiveness") (Crowne & Marlowe, 1960). This instrument was included because it has been found that first responder populations often under-report difficulties (Coman & Evans, 1991; Sewell, 1983). Therefore, they are susceptible to a social desirability bias when answering self-report measures in research. Higher scores reflect a tendency toward greater social desirability. Crowne and Marlowe (1960) reported a Kuder–Richardson internal consistency coefficient of 0.88 on 39 undergraduates, and a test–retest reliability of 0.89 for 31 of these students who completed the questionnaire one month later. Validation data for 39 undergraduates include correlations of 0.40 and 0.54 with the MMPI Correction and Lie scales, respectively (Crowne & Marlowe, 1960).

Data Analytic Plan

A comprehensive psychometric analysis of all retained items was conducted to establish reliability and validity of the LEOSS, including examining (1) item response functioning via Rasch modeling (i.e., partial credit model; Masters, 1982), (2) internal structure via Exploratory Factor analysis (EFA), (3) convergent and discriminant validity via correlations with criterion variables, and (4) reliability via Cronbach's alpha. All statistical analyses were conducted using SPSS version 26.

Results

Item Functioning

We estimated item-specific discrimination values utilizing Winsteps software; the item-specific discrimination values ranged from 0.8 to 1.2, supporting utilization of the Rasch model (Linacre & Wright, 2000). We fit a partial credit model to examine response styles on the LEOSS Difficulty scale. Results revealed response options were not functioning as intended as evidenced by disordered averages and Andrich thresholds in the majority of items. Of note, disordered averages and thresholds indicate that those who endorse lower/higher response options may not correspond with lower/higher levels of the attribute (e.g., stress). This is not surprising as the middle response options (2–6) were not labeled thus these were likely not interpreted consistently (Bergkvist, 2021). To address this issue, response options were collapsed as follows (*1 = 1, 2–6 = 2, and 7 = 3*). All analysis proceeded using the collapsed response options.

Internal Structure

To determine the internal structure (i.e., dimensionality) of the Difficulty Scale of the LEOSS, an exploratory factor analysis (EFA) using an oblique rotation (promax) was performed. Since the factor loading for items 6 and 9 were considerably lower than all other items, they were removed from the analysis. With these exclusions,[1] a parallel

[1] Of note, items 6 and 9 were removed from the scale due to relatively low factor loadings (0.38 and 0.25, respectively). This is consistent with previous literature indicating a standardized loading

analysis using EFA methodology (i.e., Monte Carlo simulation) was employed to determine the number of statistically significant factors to retain (Hayton et al., 2004). Results revealed four significant factors accounting for 54.21% of the common variance. The six items that comprise the first factor reflect difficulties associated with responding to calls that may cause physical harm. The seven items that comprise the second factor reflect difficulties related to lack of perceived integrity/loyalty within the department. The five items that comprise the third factor reflect difficulties attributable to lack of control and uncertainty on the job. Finally, the five items that comprise the fourth factor reflect difficulties attributable to work-life conflict (see Table 5.2 for specific factor loadings and eigenvalues). As expected, there was a correlation between the factors (see Table 5.3), suggesting presence of a second order factor of Overall Difficulty. These findings suggest there are 4 subscale scores (i.e., difficulty attributable to physically threatening calls, lack of perceived integrity, lack of control, and work-life conflict), and a full difficulty scale score that can be measured by the LEOSS.

Reliability

The internal consistency reliability of the LEOSS Difficulty Scale was good ($\alpha = 0.90$). Similar findings were observed for each of the identified Difficulty subscales and were within the acceptable range ($\alpha = 0.70$ to 0.83; see Table 5.3 for further details).

Convergent and Discriminant Validity

To establish convergent and discriminant validity of the LEOSS Difficulty scale, the associations between the LEOSS Difficulty score and the criterion variables were examined using Pearson correlations. It was hypothesized that LEOSS Difficulty scores would be more strongly correlated with other measures of stress (i.e., PSQ-ORG, PSQ-OPS, PCL) than measures of depression and anxiety (i.e., PHQ-9, TMAS). This hypothesis was formally tested using a "Pattern Hypothesis Test" as described in Steiger (2005). The LEOSS Difficulty scale was more strongly associated with the PSQ-OPS, PSQ-ORG, and PCL ($\bar{r} = 0.346$) than the PHQ-9 and the TMAS ($\bar{r} = 0.184$), $z = 3.241$, $p < 0.002$, providing evidence of convergent and discriminant validity. According to Cohen's (1992) guidelines, medium correlations were observed between the LEOSS Difficulty scale and the PSQ-OPS ($r = 0.30$, p

of less than .4 is not a reliable indicator of construct (Brown, 2015). The parallel analysis was rerun without these items, yielding the same number of dimensions. The results of the factor analysis excluding items 6 and 9 are provided in the text. Items were then renumbered based on these exclusions.

Table 5.2 Factor loadings for exploratory analysis with promax rotation of LEOSS items using the difficulty scale

	Factor loading			
Item	Physically threatening calls	Lack of perceived integrity	Lack of control	Work-life conflict
1. Burglary in progress with armed assailant	**0.82**	−0.02	−0.05	−0.01
2. Alarm at bank with history of break ins	**0.86**	−0.02	−0.07	−0.12
3. Executing search and arrest warrant for violent criminal	**0.72**	−0.20	0.04	0.19
4. Barricaded subject with potential hostage	**0.56**	0.23	−0.04	0.05
5. Motor vehicle accident with injuries and possible fatalities	**0.51**	−0.00	0.18	0.01
6. Unfounded civilian rights violation	0.05	**0.51**	−0.05	0.09
7. Work demands interfere with family plans	0.01	0.18	−0.27	**0.67**
8. Containment of public demonstration	**0.45**	0.29	0.04	−0.04
9. Investigating fellow officer for illegal activity	0.08	**0.50**	0.11	−0.07
10. Subordinates not completing assigned tasks	0.01	**0.77**	0.10	−0.19
11. Relying on untrustworthy/incompetent employee	−0.28	**0.43**	0.17	0.17

(continued)

Table 5.2 (continued)

	Factor loading			
Item	Physically threatening calls	Lack of perceived integrity	Lack of control	Work-life conflict
12. Solving high profile case with high media attention	0.13	**0.56**	−0.02	0.21
13. Lose data on your computer	−0.02	−0.13	0.22	**0.53**
14. Demands from work leaves little energy for family	0.01	0.01	−0.04	**0.67**
15. Inability to complete project due to changing direction of supervisor	−0.03	**0.43**	−0.10	0.33
16. Code 3 call and radio dies	0.10	−0.02	**0.39**	0.31
17. Shiftwork disrupting sleep	0.01	0.13	0.15	**0.32**
18. Unresolved marital conflict due to interfering work schedule	0.04	−0.10	0.15	**0.51**
19. Pulled off case for political reasons	−0.06	**0.50**	0.22	0.05
20. High speed chase in unsafe weather conditions	−0.02	−0.04	**0.62**	0.23
21. Investigating suspected suicide of officer	−0.03	0.15	**0.75**	−0.07

(continued)

Table 5.2 (continued)

	Factor loading			
Item	Physically threatening calls	Lack of perceived integrity	Lack of control	Work-life conflict
22. Injured from assault and back-up is late	−0.04	0.09	**0.73**	−0.08
23. Respond to shooting in progress	0.29	0.07	**0.50**	−0.09
Eigenvalues	7.47	2.15	1.58	1.27
% of variance	32.46	9.35	6.86	5.53

Note Factor loadings in bold type were considered for subscale interpretation

Table 5.3 Factor correlations and reliability of LEOSS

Factor	1	2	3	4	5
1. Physically threatening calls	(0.834)	0.492	0.452	0.376	0.737
2. Lack of perceived integrity		(0.801)	0.602	0.560	0.840
3. Lack of control			(0.811)	0.458	0.842
4. Work-life conflict				(0.695)	0.712
5. LEOSS difficulty score					(0.902)
M(SD)	1.855 (0.334)	1.844 (0.363)	1.931 (0.462)	1.932 (0.329)	1.876 (0.299)

Note Reliability coefficients (α) are included along the principal diagonal

< 0.001), PSQ-ORG ($r = 0.40, p < 0.001$), and PCL ($r = 0.24, p = 0.001$), whereas there were small correlations observed with the PHQ-9 ($r = 0.19, p = 0.008$) and the TMAS ($r = 0.17, p = 0.02$; see Table 5.4 for further details). The LEOSS Difficulty scale was not significantly associated with MCSDS scores ($r = -0.06, p = 0.43$), suggesting responses to the LEOSS Difficulty scale were not explained by social desirability.

Scoring and Interpretation Recommendations

Based on the psychometric evaluation, it is recommended to calculate average subscale scores and an average Difficulty scale score (i.e., sum items that comprise respective scale and divide by number of scale items). Higher scores on the first

Table 5.4 Convergent and discriminant validity correlations with the LEOSS

Variable	1	2	3	4	5	6
1. PSQ-ORG	(0.932)	0.792**	0.426**	0.428**	0.325**	0.400**
2. PSQ-OPS		(0.930)	0.451**	0.525**	0.404**	0.394**
3. PCL			(0.904)	0.667**	0.452**	0.243**
4. PHQ-9				(0.857)	0.535**	0.194*
5. TMAS					(0.660)	0.17*
6. LEOSS difficulty score						(0.902)
M(SD)	52.96 (22.01)	52.70 (20.82)	25.51 (9.42)	13.80 (4.23)	5.39 (2.80)	1.88 (.30)

Note PSQ-ORG = Police Stress Questionnaire-Organizational; PSQ-OPS = Police Stress Questionnaire-Operational; PCL = Posttraumatic Stress Disorder Symptom Checklist; PHQ-9 = Patient Health Questionnaire; TMAS = Short Form of the Taylor Manifest Anxiety Scale; LEOSS = Law Enforcement Officer Stress Survey. Reliability coefficients (α) are included along the principal diagonal. * $p < 0\ .05$, ** $p < 0.01$

subscale suggest an individual is experiencing greater difficulties/problems with calls that may cause physical harm. Additionally, higher scores on second subscale would suggest that an individual is experiencing greater difficulties related to lack of perceived integrity within the department. Higher scores on the third would imply the individual is experiencing greater difficulty attributable to a lack of control. Higher scores on the fourth subscale indicate the individual is experiencing greater difficulties with work-life conflicts. Finally, a total Difficulty score would indicate greater difficulties with occupational stressors.

A guide for interpreting Difficulty subscales and total scale scores is provided in Table 5.5. This guide was based on careful evaluation of the distribution of mean scores relative to the response categories. For example, individuals with raw scores that correspond with an average rating of 1 (*not at all difficult/problematic*) across the items were described as experiencing little to no difficulty.

Subscale scores can provide additional information regarding the area in which the law enforcement officer is experiencing the most difficulty. Additionally, examination of the Likelihood scale can provide supplementary information regarding the frequency of specific stressors.

These are general guidelines and therefore are not intended to be diagnostic in nature. Regardless of the score, officers are encouraged to seek mental health services when stress is a problem in their life. The interpretations provided are intended to aid police officers in understanding their current levels of stress.

Table 5.5 Interpretive guide and scoring recommendations of LEOSS total and subscale difficulty scores

Average score on LEOSS	Interpretation	PSQ-OPS	PSQ-ORG	PCL
		M(SD)		
1 to less than 1.5	Little to no difficulty	30.11	40.00	22.75
1.5 to less than 6.5	Some level of difficulty	53.62	53.60	25.73
6.5 to 7.0[a]	Extreme levels of difficulty	–	–	–

Note Average scores range from 1–7, with higher scores indicating greater levels of difficulty with stress. On average, participants scored a 1.88 on the total LEOSS Difficulty Scale, 1.86 on the physical threat subscale, 1.84 on the lack of perceived integrity subscale, and 1.93 on the lack of control and work-life conflict subscales. PSQ-ORG = Police Stress Questionnaire-Organizational; PSQ-OPS = Police Stress Questionnaire-Operational; PCL = Posttraumatic Stress Disorder Symptom Checklist; PHQ-9 = Patient Health Questionnaire; TMAS = Short Form of the Taylor Manifest Anxiety Scale; LEOSS = Law Enforcement Officer Stress Survey

[a] No one in the sample scored, on average, 6.5 or higher across all items (highest average was 6.43). However, this category was retained as it is certainty possible for such an extreme score to occur

Discussion

The purpose of the present study was to combine modern and classical test theories to evaluate reliability and validity as well as establish psychometric cut-off scores to improve the clinical utility of the Law Enforcement Officer Stress Survey (LEOSS). This was accomplished by assessing item scale functioning, examining internal structure, and adding to the current literature regarding the LEOSS reliability and validity. After evaluating item response functioning, response options were collapsed into three options due to the disordered nature of the Andrich thresholds. Using this response scale, results indicated the LEOSS Difficulty Scale has good internal reliability as well as convergent and discriminant validity, which is consistent with previous studies (Van Hasselt et al., 2008). Also, the factor structure of the LEOSS Overall Difficulty Scale revealed four significant subscales reflecting an officer's level of difficulty with Physically Threatening Calls, Lack of Perceived Integrity, Lack of Control, and Work-Life Conflict. Scoring and interpretation guidelines were established to provide clinical guidance to suggest when further assessment is warranted.

By grouping score ranges into severity categories, users will be able to better understand the level of stress an officers may be experiencing. The LEOSS was developed to address unique challenges and stresses encountered by officers (e.g., executing an arrest warrant, responding to a silent alarm), and be used as an early warning stress screening measure for law enforcement officers (Van Hasselt et al., 2003). Although this instrument has been validated in prior research, development of psychometric cut-off scores had not been previously established (Browning, 2013; Van Hasselt et al., 2003, 2008).

This study provides an important contribution to the area of law enforcement research stress evaluations. First, there is a paucity of research focused on rapid screening of law enforcement stress, especially as it relates to self-assessment. Second, although some law enforcement stress measures exist, the use of the behavioral analytic model of test construction allows for the development of a socially valid assessment, making the applicability of items particularly relevant to the consumer group of police officers. Additionally, extant measures, such as the Police Stress Survey (PSS; Spielberger et al., 1981) and the Police Stress Questionnaire (PSQ; McCreary & Thompson, 2006), have limitations to their utility. Both measures are lengthier than the LEOSS and the PSS, potentially making administration difficult and relevance diminished given the changes and challenges in police work since their development. Further, the PSQ was developed and validated using a sample of Canadian police officers, and may not be generalizable to the stressors faced by US law enforcement given the cultural differences and context of stress (e.g., less violent crime and gun usage in Canada; United Nations, n.d.). Finally, research has illuminated disturbingly high levels of mental health problems (e.g., in law enforcement personnel). A brief, practical stress screening measure should have value in the development of heuristic prevention and intervention strategies.

Historically, mental health problems have been viewed as a sign of weakness due to the cynicism, lack of empathy, masculine role associated with law enforcement culture (Bell & Eski, 2016). This cultural stigma makes officers reluctant to disclose mental illness and seek mental health services or assessment (Edwards & Kotera, 2020). With consideration of these traditional barriers, the brevity and simplicity of the LEOSS offers self-assessment, allowing police officers to complete the measure independently and confidentially. LEOSS scoring and interpretation guidelines can facilitate the personal evaluation of an officer's current stress level. While continued efforts are needed to address the issues of attitudinal and cultural change surrounding the well-being and mental health of police officers, development of the LEOSS is a step in this direction. Future research should examine the acceptance and utilization of the LEOSS to demonstrate the efficacy of self-administered assessments despite the historic cultural stigma.

There are several advantages to employing a systematic model of test construction that incorporates stressful situations identified by the relevant target group. By allowing the target population (i.e., police officers) direct involvement in the process, content validity is increased. This improves the accuracy of the interpretations drawn from the results of this measure (Furr, 2018). In addition to providing data regarding the current levels of law enforcement stress, the LEOSS identified the four above mentioned subfactors of stress experienced by police officers. Subscales point to which specific aspects of the job a police officer finds particularly stressful. With this information, mental health providers can better identify prevention and intervention strategies to improve the LEO's coping abilities for such situations.

There are several limitations of this study that warrant mention. One major limitation is that only self-report instruments were used to collect data. The absence of non-self-report measures limits the ability to validate the LEOSS against external criteria (e.g., performance indicators, clinical diagnosis, behavioral measures). Additionally, the absence prohibits us from establishing the LEOSS classification accuracy (i.e., specificity and sensitivity) that would be helpful. This would be of particular importance given the previously mentioned cultural stigma of mental health in this population, since participants may have under-reported the severity of their problems. While administration of interview-based instruments is often preferred to address social desirability, we attempted to assess for effects of social desirability on participant responses using the Marlowe-Crowne Social Desirability Scale. Future research should look to incorporate behavioral measures and external criteria to strengthen the validation of the LEOSS. Secondly, there were several demographic categories that few or no participants endorsed. Item categories that were not endorsed by any participants were removed from analysis (e.g., employment with a Federal law enforcement agency, doctoral-level education, Asian ethnicity). Therefore, the impact of these predictors remains unknown, and limits generalizability of findings to groups that were not included. Further, while the demographics of our sample are representative of policing across the nation, more inclusive efforts in sampling diverse populations should be included in future research. Third, the present study only included a single sample to evaluate psychometric properties of the LEOSS. Consequently, we were unable to conduct a confirmatory factor analysis to confirm the presence of a higher order factor, justifying the use of a total score. Nevertheless, the relatively strong correlations between the four factors provide evidence of a second-order factor representing Overall Difficulty.

The LEOSS is a practical self-assessment tool that is easily accessible and relevant to the experiences of law enforcement officers. Further, the LEOSS has potential utility as a prevention measure. Officers would complete the measure on a regular basis to assess their current stress level and self-monitor changes. This would allow them to be better informed regarding the possible need for further mental health follow-up.

While the LEOSS may be used as a self-screening tool, it may be used in other settings. For example, it may have value as a useful and valid device for clinicians working with officers to: (1) assess changes in stress over time, and (2) determine factors contributing to their current symptom presentation. Information obtained from the LEOSS (i.e., overall difficulty level with occupational stress and specific domains) has the potential to facilitate more immediate identification and recognition of stress in police officers than what has been possible to date.

Future research should assess a clinical sample of LEOs utilizing the LEOSS psychometric cut-off scores to determine ease of use and clinical guidelines. In addition, further investigation is suggested to evaluate LEOSS utility in primary prevention, resiliency enhancement, or hardiness interventions targeting the unique stressors experienced by law enforcement personnel. Given the burgeoning body of evidence showing that LEOs are at risk for stress-related disorders, such instruments are urgently needed. Moreover, it is hoped that heightened awareness of stress and its effects will culminate in expanded efforts directed toward stress reduction and intervention for police officers and their families.

References

Baldwin, S., Bennell, C., Andersen, J. P., Semple, T., & Jenkins, B. (2019). Stress-activity mapping: Physiological responses during general duty police encounters. *Frontiers in Psychology, 10*, 2216.

Bell, S., & Eski, Y. (2016). 'Break a leg—it's all in the mind': Police officers' attitudes towards colleagues with mental health issues. *Policing: A Journal of Policy and Practice, 10*(2), 95–101. https://doi.org/10.1093/police/pav041

Bendig, A. W. (1956). The development of a short form of the Manifest Anxiety Scale. *Journal of Consulting Psychology, 20*(5), 384. https://doi.org/10.1037/h0045580

Bergkvist, L. (2021). Negative effects of unlabeled response scales. *International Journal of Market Research, 63*(6), 772–785. https://doi.org/10.1177/1470785320981815

Bishopp, S. A., Piquero, N. L., Worrall, J. L., & Piquero, A. R. (2019). Negative affective responses to stress among urban police officers: A general strain theory approach. *Deviant Behavior, 40*(6), 1–20. https://doi.org/10.1080/01639625.2018.1438069

Blum, L. N. (2000). *Force under pressure: How cops live and why they die*. Lantern Books.

Brown, J. M., & Campbell, E. A. (1994). *Stress and policing: Sources and strategies*. Wiley.

Brown, T. A. (2015). *Confirmatory factor analysis for applied research*. Guilford.

Browning, S. L. (2013). *Risk and resilience in law enforcement stress: Contributions of the Law Enforcement Officer Stress Survey (LEOSS)* (Unpublished doctoral dissertation). Nova Southeastern University.

Buss, A. H. (1955). Stimulus generalization as a function of clinical anxiety and direction of generalization. *The Journal of Abnormal and Social Psychology, 50*(2), 271–273. https://doi.org/10.1037/h0039950

Cohen, J. (1992). Quantitative methods in psychology: A power primer. *Psychological Bulletin, 112*(1), 155–159.

Coman, G., & Evans, B. (1991). Stressors facing Australian police in the 1990s. *Police Studies: The International Review of Police Development, 14*, 153.

Cross, C. L., & Ashley, L. (2004). Police trauma and addiction: Coping with the dangers of the job. *FBI Law Enforcement Bulletin, 73*, 24.

Crowne, D. P., & Marlowe, D. (1960). A new scale of social desirability independent of psychopathology. *Journal of Consulting Psychology, 24*, 349–354.

Dantzer, M. L. (1987). Police-related stress: A critique for future research. *Journal of Police and Criminal Psychology, 3*(1), 43–48.

Data USA. (2019). *Police officers*. https://datausa.io/profile/soc/police-officers

D'Zurilla, T. J., & Goldfried, M. R. (1971). Problem solving and behavior modification. *Journal of Abnormal Psychology, 78*(1), 107–126. https://doi.org/10.1037/h0031360

Edwards, A. M., & Kotera, Y. (2020). Mental health in the UK police force: A qualitative investigation into the stigma with mental illness. *International Journal of Mental Health and Addiction*, 1–19. Advance online publication. https://doi.org/10.1007/s11469-019-00214-x

Ermasova, N., Cross, A., & Ermasova, E. (2020). Perceived stress and coping among law enforcement officers: An empirical analysis of patrol versus non-patrol officers in Illinois, USA. *Journal of Police and Criminal Psychology, 35*, 48–63. https://doi.org/10.1007/s11896-019-09356-z

Furr, R. M. (2018). *Psychometrics: An introduction*. SAGE Publications.

Gershon, R. M., Barocas, B., Canton, A. N., Li, X., & Vlahov, D. (2009). Mental, physical, and behavioral outcomes associated with perceived work stress in police officers. *Criminal Justice and Behavior, 36*, 275–289. https://doi.org/10.1177/0093854808330015

Hart, P. M., Wearing, A. J., & Headey, B. (1993). Assessing police work experiences: Development of the Police Daily Hassles and Uplifts Scales. *Journal of Criminal Justice, 21*, 553–572.

Hayton, J. C., Allen, D. G., & Scarpello, V. (2004). Factor retention decisions in exploratory factor analysis: A tutorial on parallel analysis. *Organizational Research Methods, 7*(2), 191–205. https://doi.org/10.1177/1094428104263675

Hicks, R. A., Ostle, J. R., & Pellegrini, R. J. (1980). A unidimensional short form of the TMAS. *Bulletin of the Psychonomic Society, 16*(6), 447–448.

Hoyt, D. P., & Magoon, T. M. (1954). A validation study of the Taylor Manifest Anxiety Scale. *Journal of Clinical Psychology, 10*, 357–361. https://doi.org/10.1002/1097-4679(195410)10:4%3c357::AID-JCLP2270100411%3e3.0.CO;2-0

Huerta-Franco, M. R., Vargas-Luna, M., Tienda, P., Delgadillo-Holtfort, I., Balleza-Ordaz, M., & Flores-Hernandez, C. (2013). Effects of occupational stress on the gastrointestinal tract. *World Journal of Gastrointestinal Pathophysiology, 4*(4), 108–118. https://doi.org/10.4291/wjgp.v4.i4.108

Irizar, P., Puddephatt, J. A., Gage, S. H., Fallon, V., & Goodwin, L. (2021). The prevalence of hazardous and harmful alcohol use across trauma-exposed occupations: A meta-analysis and meta-regression. *Drug and Alcohol Dependence, 226*. https://doi.org/10.1016/j.drugalcdep.2021.108858

Klimley, K. E., Van Hasselt, V. B., & Stripling, A. M. (2018). Posttraumatic stress disorder in police, firefighters, and emergency dispatchers. *Aggression and Violent Behavior, 43*, 33–44. https://doi.org/10.1016/j.avb.2018.08.005

Kroenke, K., Spitzer, R., & Williams, J. (2001). The PHQ-9: Validity of a brief depression severity measure. *Journal of General Internal Medicine, 16*(9). https://doi.org/10.1046/j.1525-1497.2001.016009606.x

Liberman, A., Best, S., Metzler, T., Fagan, J., & Marmar, C. (2002). Routine occupational stress and psychological distress in police. *Policing: An International Journal, 25*(2), 429–436.

Linacre, J. M., & Wright, B. D. (2000). *Winsteps*. http://www.winsteps.com/index

Lord, V. B., Gray, D. O., & Pond, S. B. (1991). The police stress survey: Does it measure stress? *Journal of Criminal Justice, 19*, 139–150

Ma, C. C., Andrew, M. E., Fekedulegn, D., Gu, J. K., Hartley, T. A., Charles, L. E., Violanti, J. M., & Burchfiel, C. M. (2015). Shift work and occupational stress in police officers. *Safety and Health at Work, 6*(1), 25–29.

Magnavita, N., Capitanelli, I., & Garbarino, S. (2018). Work-related stress as a cardiovascular risk factor in police officers: A systematic review of evidence. *International Archives of Occupational and Environmental Health, 91*, 377–389.https://doi.org/10.1007/s00420-018-1290-y

Masters, G. N. (1982). A Rasch model for partial credit scoring. *Psychometrika, 47*, 149–174.

McCarty, W., & Skogan, W. (2012). Job-related burnout among civilian and sworn police personnel. *Police Quarterly, 16*(1), 66–84. https://doi.org/10.1177/1098611112457357

McCreary, D. R., Fong, I., & Groll, D. (2017). Measuring police stress meaningfully: Establishing norms and cut-off values for the Operational and Organizational Police Stress Questionnaires. *Police Practice and Research, 18*(6). https://doi.org/10.1080/15614263.2017.1363965

McCreary, D. R., & Sadava, S. W. (1998). Stress, drinking, and the adverse consequences of drinking in two samples of young adults. *Psychology of Addictive Behaviors, 12*(4), 247–261. https://doi.org/10.1037/0893-164X.12.4.247

McCreary, D. R., & Thompson, M. M. (2006). Development of two reliable and valid measures of stressors in policing: The operational and organizational police stress questionnaires. *International Journal of Stress Management, 13*(4), 494. https://doi.org/10.1037/1072-5245.13.4.494

Miller, L. (2006). *Practical police psychology: Stress management and crisis intervention for law enforcement.* Charles C. Thomas.

Miller, L. (2008). Military and police psychology: Mutual contributions to crisis intervention and stress management. *International Journal of Emergency Mental Health, 10*, 9–26.

Mumford, E. A., Liu, W., & Taylor, B. G. (2021). Profiles of US law enforcement officers' physical, psychological, and behavioral health: Results from a nationally representative survey of officers. *Police Quarterly, 24*(3), 357–381.

Neidig, P., Russel, H., & Seng, A. (1992). Interspousal aggression in law enforcement families: A preliminary investigation. *International Review of Police Development, 30*, 30–38.

Newman, D. W., & Rucker-Reed, M. L. (2004). Police stress, state-trait anxiety, and stressors among US marshals. *Journal of Criminal Justice, 32*(6), 631–641.https://doi.org/10.1016/j.jcrimjus.2004.08.003
Prati, G., & Pietrantoni, L. (2010). An application of the social support deterioration deterrence model to rescue workers. *Journal of Community Psychology, 38*, 901–917. https://doi.org/10.1002/jcop.20404
Reynolds, W. M. (1982). Development of a reliable and valid short form of the Marlowe-Crowne social desirability scale. *Journal of Clinical Psychology, 38*, 119–125.
Richard, W. C., & Feil, R. D. (1976). Health factors in police job stress. In W. H. Kroes & J. J. Hurrell (Eds.), *Job stress and the police officer.* HEW Publications, U.S. Government Printing Office.
Ruggiero, K. J., Del Ben, K., Scotti, J. R., & Rabalais, A. E. (2003). Psychometric properties of the PTSD checklist-civilian version. *Journal of Traumatic Stress, 16*(5), 495–502. https://doi.org/10.1023/A:1025714729117
Schwartz, I. S., & Baer, D. M. (1991). Social validity assessments: Is current practice state of the art? *Journal of Applied Behavior Analysis, 24*(2), 189–204.
Sekar, M., Subburaj, A., & Sundaram, M. S. (2013). Policing the most stressful occupation: A study on Tamil Nadu Head Constables. *International Journal of Business Management & Economic Research, 4*(5), 814–822.
Sewell, J. D. (1983). The development of a critical life events scale for law enforcement. *Journal of Police Science and Administration, 11*, 109–116.
Sheehan, D. C. (Ed.). (2000). *Domestic violence by police officers.* U.S. Government Printing Office.
Sheehan, D. C., & Van Hasselt, V. B. (2003). Identifying law enforcement stress reactions early. *FBI Law Enforcement Bulletin, 72*, 12–17.
Sörensen, L., Smolander, J., Louhevaara, V., Korhonen, O., & Oja, P. (2000). Physical activity, fitness and body composition of Finnish police officers: A 15-year follow-up study. *Occupational Medicine, 50*(1), 3–10.
Spector, P. E. (1997). *Job satisfaction: Application, assessment, causes, and consequences* (Vol. 3). SAGE Publications.
Spielberger, C. D., Westberry, L. G., Grier, K. S., & Greenfield, G. (1981). *The police stress survey: Sources of stress in law enforcement.* Human Resources Institute (Monograph Series Three, No. 6). University of South Florida, College of Social and Behavioral Sciences.
Steiger, J. H. (2005). Comparing correlations: Pattern hypothesis tests between and/or within independent samples. Contemporary Psychometrics: A festschrift for Roderick P. McDonald. Mahwah, NJ, US: Lawrence Erlbaum Associates, Inc, 377–414.
Steinberg, J. L., & McEvoy, D. W. (1974). *The police and the behavioral sciences.* Charles C. Thomas.
Taylor, J. A. (1953). A personality scale of manifest anxiety. *The Journal of Abnormal and Social Psychology, 48*(2), 285.
Terry, W. (1981). Police stress: The empirical evidence. *Journal of Police Science and Administration, 9*, 61–75.
United Nations. (n.d.) Data UNODC. https://dataunodc.un.org/content/country-list
Van Hasselt, V. B., Sheehan, D. C., Malcolm, A. S., Sellers, A. H., Baker, M. T., & Couwels, J. (2008). The Law Enforcement Officer Stress Survey (LEOSS):Evaluation of psychometric properties. *Behavior Modification, 32*, 133–151.https://doi.org/10.1177/0145445507308571
Van Hasselt, V. B., Sheehan, D. C., Sellers, A. H., Baker, M. T., & Feiner, C. (2003). A behavioral-analytic model for assessing stress in police officers: Development of the Law Enforcement Officer Stress Survey (LEOSS). *International Journal of Emergency Mental Health, 5*, 77–84.
Van Katwyk, P. T., Fox, S., Spector, P. E., & Kelloway, E. K. (2000). Using the job-related affective well-being scale (JAWS) to investigate affective responses to work stressors. *Journal of Occupational Health Psychology, 5*(2), 219–230.https://doi.org/10.1037/1076-8998.5.2.219

Violanti, J. M. (1999). Trauma in police work: A psychosocial model. In J. M. Violanti and D. Paton (Eds.), *Police trauma: Psychological aftermath of civilian combat* (pp. 88–98). Charles C. Thomas.

Violanti, J. M., & Steege, A. (2021). Law enforcement worker suicide: An updated national assessment. *Policing, 44*(1), 18–31. https://doi.org/10.1108/PIJPSM-09-2019-0157

Weathers, F. W., Huska, J. A., & Keane, T. M. (1991). *PCL-C for DSM-IV*. National Center for PTSD—Behavioral Science Division. http://library.niwap.org/wp-content/uploads/2015/PTSDChecklist.pdf

Wetherington, J. (2021). Officer wellness spotlight: The law enforcement family. *FBI Law Enforcement Bulletin*. https://leb.fbi.gov/spotlights/officer-wellness-spotlight-the-law-enforcement-family#:~:text=Where%20the%20national%20average%20of%20marriages%20ending%20in,there%20is%20no%20difference%20between%20the%20two%20groups

Zimmerman, F. H. (2012). Cardiovascular disease and risk factors in law enforcement personnel: A comprehensive review. *Cardiology in Review, 20*(4), 159–166.

Part II
First Responder Training

Chapter 6
Co-Responder Training for Law Enforcement

Stephanie Livshitz and Carlos Martinez

The role of law enforcement officers as first responders in mental health emergencies has come under criticism with increasing demand for alternative options, especially in the wake of high-profile cases with tragic and arguably avoidable consequences. Communities, individuals in crisis, and police agencies have been significantly impacted by these negative outcomes, resulting in calls for change within the structure of law enforcement and their responses to individuals with mental illness (Congressional Research Service, 2022; Kamin et al., 2022). While law enforcement entities are predicated on a paramilitary environment (Fortenbery, 2018), with police officers enforcing the law while ensuring public safety, mental health professionals are tasked with client care, which may include rapport building, assessment and evaluation, and therapeutic intervention. Criminal and mental health-related police calls require different approaches, and there is a likelihood of escalation when an individual in crisis is criminalized (Morabito et al., 2012). This finding demonstrates the importance of training and collaboration between law enforcement and mental health agencies in properly assessing and addressing crisis situations.

Background: CIT and Co-Responding

In 1988, the Crisis Intervention Team (CIT) model was developed through a collaborative effort between the Memphis Police Department, The National Alliance on Mental Illness (NAMI), mental health professionals, church administrators, and the

S. Livshitz (✉) · C. Martinez
Los Angeles, CA, USA
e-mail: StephanieLivshitz@proton.me

C. Martinez
e-mail: Dr.carlos.martinez@outlook.com

V. B. Van Hasselt and M. L. Bourke (eds.), *Advances in First Responder Mental Health*, Advances in First Responder Mental Health 1,
https://doi.org/10.1007/978-3-032-27978-1_6

Universities of Memphis and Tennessee. CIT training is meant to prepare volunteer officers to handle mental health-related crisis calls by equipping them with the skill set necessary when addressing these unique situations (*Crisis Intervention Team*, n.d.; *Overview*, n.d.). Although conflicting data exists (Morabito et al., 2012), there have been some favorable outcomes when comparing CIT-trained to untrained officers in their responses to individuals with mental illness. Compton et al. (2009) determined that CIT officers are likely to utilize less physical force, viewing alternative responses as more effective when handling crisis calls. Furthermore, evidence suggests that CIT training decreases the likelihood that officers will physically engage an uncooperative individual, possibly due to their ability to identify signs of mental illness (Morabito et al., 2012). Officers with CIT training have shown higher effectiveness in de-escalating and resolving crisis calls through referrals (Compton et al., 2014) and increasing knowledge and understanding of mental health conditions (Compton et al., 2014; Ellis, 2014). With research suggesting that CIT training contributes to a more effective response from law enforcement in addressing a mental health crisis in the field, it is reasonable to hypothesize that combining a police officer and a professional with specialized mental health training could yield additional benefits. Moreover, If CIT programs are effective, they could pave the way for a partnership between law enforcement and mental health professionals (Compton et al., 2009). Combining these two entities' knowledge and skill sets may lead to a more well-rounded approach, revolutionizing how mental health-related police call-outs are handled.

There is an increasing call nationwide for co-responder teams, and the development and implementation of such programs are underway, although research on their efficacy remains limited. A type of Police-Mental Health Collaboration (PMHC) program, the co-response model generally pairs an officer with a mental health professional and assigns them the task of responding to crisis calls that involve mental illness (*Learning about police—Mental health collaboration programs*, n.d.). Helfgott et al.'s (2016) review of the Seattle Police Department's crisis response team revealed the benefits of pairing an officer with a mental health professional. Findings indicate that patrol officers were provided with assistance and relief, in turn freeing up their resources and presumably increasing their availability to respond to other radio calls In addition, several cases resulted in referrals for mental health and/or substance use treatment, further lessening the burden on police officers and the criminal justice system (Helfgott et al., 2016; Shapiro et al., 2014). Another important statistic to consider, and one that has not been widely studied, is the effect co-responder models have on police use of force. Data have suggested that co-responder models have the potential to decrease force and provide opportunities for effective alternatives to involuntary hospitalizations (Blais et al., 2020); however, additional research is needed. These findings echo the sentiment that there is the prospect of improved community-police relations and favorable results for individuals suffering from a mental health crisis (Balfour et al., 2021) through the implementation of co-responder models. Furthermore, data indicate that this type of collaborative response to police call-outs has the ability to provide those in crisis with alternatives to justice system involvement, at least in the short term (Shapiro et al., 2014), with service consumers reporting they felt more understood and less criminalized when contacted by a co-responder team (Lamanna et al., 2017).

Case Vignette: Below is a real-life scenario where all identifying information, including agencies involved, has been removed.

> A 911 call was generated for a male inside a vehicle with boarded-up windows parked in the middle of the train tracks. Patrol officers arrived on the scene and requested a co-responder team report for assistance due to a possible mental health-related crisis. The individual inside of the vehicle was identified via license plate through the use of law enforcement resources. A clinician, officer, and supervisor responded to the scene, and additional information was gathered using a mental health database accessed by the clinician. Upon the co-responder team's arrival, multiple police officers were in formation and preparing for a tactical approach towards the vehicle. The clinician notified patrol officers of the propensity for escalation after a review of clinical documents revealed a history of violence, including the use of weapons and impulsivity. Due to the concerning nature of these reports and patrol officers' inability to see inside the vehicle to assess whether or not there were any weapons present, the tactical approach was halted. At that time, the clinician initiated verbal contact with the client at a safe distance using the radio in a police vehicle. After multiple attempts and continued verbal engagement, announcing oneself as a mental health professional and reassuring the individual that the role of the team is to assist in a crisis, the client exited the vehicle. He was observed to be fully nude with a syringe in one hand and a knife in the other while rambling incoherently. Through the employment of verbal de-escalation techniques and negotiations, the client dropped both sharp objects. At that time, it became safe for patrol officers to approach and detain for purposes of further assessment and hospital transport. The co-responder team met the officers and client at the hospital, at which time an involuntary hospitalization was initiated. Due to the concerns regarding propensity for violence based on historical information, the hospital staff was advised and agreed to house the client in a separate room to avoid endangering others at the hospital. Although anecdotal, this collaboration between law enforcement and mental health could have prevented an injury to officers and client. If officers approached and the individual emerged with a knife in hand, the result could have been deadly force. Furthermore, while the individual who was experiencing a mental health crisis would be receiving necessary stabilization and treatment through hospitalization, other clients could be kept safe by the sharing of pertinent information with hospital staff. In this specific scenario, neither public safety nor client care was sacrificed.

Crisis response work is often unpredictable and requires a wide range of skills, including recognizing a mental health crisis, engaging in effective de-escalation techniques, and appropriately utilizing available resources. A focus group composed of Philadelphia police officers voiced a valid concern, stating that crisis calls come with a risk of becoming violent. The associated dangers were believed to interfere with the plausibility of limiting police responses to mental health crisis calls while also recognizing that the mere presence of law enforcement could serve to escalate the individual (Shefner et al., 2023). To address the safety risks associated with these cases, while acknowledging the need for an alternative to the standard patrol response, an argument can be made for the importance of a mental health professional responding in partnership with a police officer. Through a collaborative relationship between the two entities, it is possible to deploy a supportive client-centered approach and engage in de-escalation techniques while also recognizing the potential for escalation and the importance of public safety. A collaboration can further assist in appropriately identifying needs such as community referrals versus involuntary placement (Balfour et al., 2021; Blais et al., 2020).

Conflicting reports regarding the frequency of hospitalizations exist (Shapiro et al., 2014), with Lamanna et al. (2017) suggesting that co-responding led to an increase in such dispositions while a decrease in rates of hospital transports has also been found (Blais et al., 2020). Although additional research is needed, hospital transports performed by co-responder teams, whether at a higher or lower rate, may be considered a successful outcome if the client's presentation requires such a referral (Shapiro et al., 2014).

Case Vignette: Below is a real-life scenario where all identifying information, including agencies involved, has been removed.

> A police response was initiated for an individual reporting suicidal thoughts. Once patrol officers arrived at the scene, a co-responder team was called to conduct an evaluation. Upon speaking with the client, he reiterated suicidal thoughts and endorsed a refusal to return to his living situation. There are several ways this scenario could have played out without a thorough assessment of the client's needs. For example, patrol officers may have simply initiated an involuntary hospitalization due to the client's suicidal statement and transported him to an emergency department. The client may have been held for up to 72 hours; however, in a more likely scenario, he would have been released within 24 hours or less once seen by the psychiatrist and no longer considered an "imminent" risk. The client's immediate stressor regarding housing would not be resolved, possibly causing another police call out and thus, perpetuating the cycle of repeated 911 calls and hospitalizations. Another possible outcome would have been for police officers to determine that the client does not pose an imminent threat, as his statements could have been interpreted as conditional to his living situation. This could have led to the client becoming desperate and following up with risky behavior in order to gain the support he was requesting. With the assistance of a co-response team, there was an opportunity for a thorough assessment. The clinician gathered that the client had a recent trauma and receives outpatient services; however, he missed an appointment the same day as the police call due to transportation issues. It was determined by the co-responder team that this client would be better served by meeting with his existing therapist, who had an already established relationship with the client, and who may provide assistance with alternative housing. As a result, voluntary transport to the client's outpatient clinic was agreed upon. Once at the clinic, the team accompanied the client inside, and the mental health co-responder met with the client's therapist to relay pertinent information for continuity of care purposes. The client's therapist was aware of the recent trauma that the client had experienced and indicated that she would work with the client in addressing his immediate needs as well as engaging him in longer-term grief counseling. While new housing generally cannot be obtained in one day, making the therapist aware of the crisis call and the client's concerns appeared to bring comfort. As the co-responder team was leaving the clinic, the client approached to express his gratitude to both the clinician and officer. This scenario resulted in a positive outcome for the client and may have helped build trust between a community member and law enforcement officer, taking a step towards bridging the existing gap.

The call for law enforcement agencies to implement co-responder programs continues to gain traction as the concept of effective and appropriate policing in response to crises is evolving. In Krider et al.'s (2020) review of several existing co-responder models, various program designs and approaches to a collaboration between law enforcement, mental health, and additional relevant entities were found. Co-response models may include an officer and mental health professional going together to a call or alternatively, a request for mental health follow-up can be made after patrol response. A partnership with law enforcement and community members who receive specialized training and have first-hand experience related to mental health or substance use is also a recognized practice. An additional multifaceted design that has been implemented includes a team made up of police, mental health, and the fire department. Further, Krider et al. (2020) noted a program taking the form of outreach with high-risk populations through the use of a co-response team. Their goal is to provide individuals in need with appropriate referrals, presumably lowering the risk of future crises.

Collaborative Training

This section delves into the significance of mental health training within the law enforcement context, exploring key learning concepts that can enhance its effectiveness. The approach to such training—whether attendance should be mandated or voluntary—presents a challenge. While mandated training ensures a baseline level of competency across the board, volunteer participation often signals a higher level of engagement and intrinsic motivation, potentially leading to more profound learning outcomes (Martinez, 2021). This section further outlines the development of specialized curricula for sworn officers and civilian clinicians, aiming to foster a synergistic approach to crisis intervention. Through a blend of interdisciplinary training strategies, practical examples, and best practices, this discussion not only highlights the current landscape of law enforcement mental health training, but also charts a path forward, emphasizing innovation, assessment, and the pivotal role of ongoing education in adapting to the evolving demands of public safety and mental health care

Key Learning Concepts

Andragogy, or Adult Learning Theory, proposes distinct characteristics and needs in adult learners, diverging significantly from child learning paradigms. This theory, extensively developed by Malcolm Knowles (1980), outlines principles integral to designing and implementing effective adult training. Its application is particularly relevant in structuring training programs for law enforcement officers and clinicians within co-responder models. This approach emphasizes practical, problem-centered learning directly applicable to their work, such as role-playing real-life scenarios to improve communication and investigative skills. It leverages the existing experience of trainees, fostering peer learning where officers and clinicians share successful and unsuccessful techniques and insights when interacting with persons suspected of a mental health or cognitive crisis. Andragogy also supports self-directed learning, allowing trainees to choose modules relevant to their community needs, such as substance abuse response. Immediate application of learned skills ensures retention and practicality, while scenario-based learning using detailed case studies enhances problem-solving and adaptability. Additionally, a collaborative learning environment in interdisciplinary modules promotes mutual respect and teamwork, which are essential for an effective co-response.

Self-Concept

The self-concept is a concept within the theory of Andragogy. Adult learners transition from dependence to a self-directed state, necessitating training environments that foster autonomy and self-regulation (Knowles et al., 2015). The real-life application of self-concept occurs when training programs enable participants to engage actively in their learning process, promoting self-assessment and setting personal learning objectives. Examples of setting personal learning objectives would be allowing the participants to set their expectations or takeaways from the training at the start of the class, regularly reviewing their progress toward the goals throughout the course, and verifying if the targets were reached after the training.

Experience

Adults contribute their diverse personal and professional experiences to the formal learning environment, an experience that is a vital learning resource (Merriam & Bierema, 2013). Both clinicians' and officers' experiences play a significant role as educational tools such as simulations, role-plays, and case study analyses. Experience and knowledge allow the integration of new knowledge with existing experiences to enhance learning efficacy. For example, when conducting a suicide risk assessment, a clinician may be more apt to complete a safety plan due to their clinical training and experience. In contrast, a police officer may be quicker to involuntarily hospitalize the individual without considering a safety plan with other stakeholders.

Extraneous Cognitive Load Theory

The motivation for adult learning is often linked to real-life challenges and tasks (Knowles, 1980). Training content must be directly relevant and applicable, addressing the immediate and practical challenges law enforcement and mental health professionals encounter. For example, the Extraneous Cognitive Load Theory states that how information is presented can significantly impact learning efficiency. The phenomenon known as "death by PowerPoint," characterized by slides overloaded with text and unnecessary details, exemplifies a common instructional pitfall that can hinder learning by unnecessarily burdening cognitive processing (Sweller et al., 1998). For example, training materials should be designed with clarity and conciseness, using visual aids strategically to focus attention on key concepts and reduce cognitive load and mental fatigue. Aside from "death by PowerPoint," knowing the audience for the specific training is also important. If the audience were patrol officers and field clinicians, it would positively impact the participants if the training modules replicated a typical call for service. The training would end with scenarios where the students collaborate and decide if they need to safety plan or begin the process for an involuntary mental evaluation hold. The flow of the training would change if the audience for the training were custody officers or forensic clinicians who were tasked with caring for individuals in a custodial setting.

Need to Know

Adults engage more effectively in learning when they understand the reasons behind the need for new knowledge or skills (Knowles et al., 2015). Clarifying the objectives and outcomes of the training from the outset can help align the learning process with personal and professional growth goals and broader community benefits. Anecdotally, the majority of officers and clinicians properly complete their job assignments; however, through personal experience, it has been known that many of the calls for services were resolved by a "that's how I was trained to do it" or "that's how it has always been done" mentality. Validating the field personnel's positive actions can help to empower the employee. Drawing a parallel between field practices and agency protocols may help personnel feel that their decisions to manage risk were the right call and further add to their agency's best practices.

Social Learning Theory

Articulated by Albert Bandura in the 1970s, this theory posits that learning occurs within a social context and can result from observing others and modeling their behaviors. It underscores the importance of observational learning, imitation, and modeling in acquiring new behaviors, skills, and attitudes, emphasizing that individuals can learn by observing the actions and outcomes of others' behaviors (Bandura, 1977). In the context of co-responder training for law enforcement and clinicians, Social Learning Theory offers valuable insights into designing training programs that leverage the social environment to enhance learning and skill acquisition. For example, when feasible, small group seating should be used rather than stadium-style arrangements. In addition, the participants should be seated purposely based on work assignments (not sitting with their friends) and, if possible, "time on the job" (have senior officers sit with less senior officers or clinician students). This will help foster observational learning and imitation based on experience level and personal and professional culture. For larger police departments or regional training centers, participants can learn from employees from other geographical areas.

Training Curriculum for Sworn Officers

The training curriculum for sworn officers in a co-responder model is designed to equip law enforcement personnel with the knowledge, skills, and attitudes necessary to collaborate effectively with mental health professionals in crisis situations. This section outlines the required competencies, the importance of scenario-based training methodologies, and the legal and ethical considerations underpinning effective and respectful crisis intervention.

Essential Competencies

Sworn officers must possess a broad range of competencies to navigate the complexities of mental health crises effectively. These include, but are not limited to, understanding mental health conditions, de-escalation techniques, communication skills, empathy, legal responsibilities, and cultural competence. Mastery of these competencies presumably allows officers to recognize signs of mental illness, engage individuals in crisis safely and respectfully, and work collaboratively with mental health clinicians to achieve the best outcomes for the person in crisis and concerned stakeholders.

Scenario-Based Training

Scenario-based training plays a crucial role in preparing officers for the realities of co-response interventions. This approach involves realistic, simulated encounters with individuals experiencing mental health crises, providing officers with opportunities to apply their skills in controlled yet dynamic environments. Scenario-based exercises should cover a wide range of situations, from non-violent crises to situations requiring immediate intervention, and include debriefing sessions to reflect on actions taken, decisions made, and areas for improvement. In the scenario-based training and debriefing portion, legal and ethical considerations are foundational to the overall outcome, ensuring officers understand the rights of individuals with mental illnesses and the legal frameworks governing their intervention. Ethical considerations, including respect for individuals' dignity, autonomy, and the importance of informed consent, are equally critical. Officers should be trained to navigate these complex legal and ethical landscapes confidently, ensuring their actions are lawful and morally sound (Watson et al., 2010).

Training Curriculum for Clinicians

Integrating civilian clinicians into law enforcement operations through co-responder models necessitates a comprehensive training curriculum tailored to their unique roles. The curriculum should provide clinicians with an understanding of law enforcement operations, ensure their safety in various environments, and foster effective collaboration between themselves and sworn officers. Below, we dive into the essential components of an effective curriculum.

Insights into Law Enforcement Operations

Civilian clinicians should understand law enforcement operations, including the legal and procedural frameworks governing police work. Familiarity with the structure of law enforcement agencies, the roles and responsibilities of officers, and the decision-making processes in crisis interventions is crucial (Reuland et al., 2021). This knowledge enables clinicians to align their mental health expertise with the operational realities of police work, ensuring interventions are clinically effective, ethically sound, and operationally feasible. Anecdotal information obtained pre and post-training shows that co-response clinicians find value and greater respect when they understand the nature of law enforcement operations and legal requirements when responding to mental health crisis calls for service (Martinez, 2024).

Safety Protocols

Safety is paramount in co-responder models. Clinicians venturing into the field with law enforcement officers must be versed in safety protocols and situational awareness. Training should cover personal safety measures, radio communication skills, de-escalation techniques, and the use of protective equipment. Clinicians should also be trained to recognize and respond to signs of escalating risk during interventions, working closely with law enforcement partners to ensure the safety of all involved (Watson & Fulambarker, 2012).

Collaboration

Effective collaboration between civilian clinicians and law enforcement officers is the cornerstone of successful co-responder models. Training should emphasize team-building, communication skills, and conflict-resolution strategies. Clinicians should learn how to integrate their mental health expertise with law enforcement strategies seamlessly, ensuring that interventions are therapeutically sound and tactically safe.

Joint training sessions that simulate real-life scenarios can enhance mutual understanding and respect, laying the groundwork for effective teamwork in the field (Wood et al., 2017). One example is integrating clinicians in mental health training instruction and curriculum design.

Assessment and Evaluation

The continuous assessment and evaluation of training programs and intervention outcomes are critical to the success and improvement of co-responder models. This process ensures that the training provided to law enforcement and mental health professionals meets the intended objectives and that interventions effectively address the needs of individuals in crisis. This section explores methodologies for evaluating training effectiveness and intervention outcomes, highlighting the importance of quantitative and qualitative measures.

Training Effectiveness

Evaluating the effectiveness of training programs involves assessing participants' acquisition of knowledge and skills and their ability to apply these in practice. Kirkpatrick's Four-Level Training Evaluation Model provides a framework for this assessment, encompassing reaction, learning, behavior, and results (Kirkpatrick & Kirkpatrick, 2006). Surveys and feedback forms can gauge participants' responses and the perceived value of the training. Pre- and post-tests and skills demonstrations offer insights into participants' learning. Feedback from instructors can assess observed behavior changes throughout the course. For example, at the start of the course, students can verbally (qualitative) provide information on their level of comfort and attitudes toward the mentally ill before training. In contrast, at the end of the course, students can verbally share their experiences and key takeaways while completing a standardized survey or course evaluation.

Continuous Improvement

The ultimate goal of assessment and evaluation is to measure effectiveness and identify areas for improvement. This involves a continuous cycle of data collection, analysis, and feedback integration into training programs and operational protocols. Engaging frontline officers, clinicians, and community stakeholders in the evaluation process ensures that diverse perspectives inform the ongoing development and refinement of co-responder models (Draine et al., 2011).

Synthesizing key learning theories and concepts provides a robust framework for designing effective mental health training programs within law enforcement. By understanding adult learners' unique characteristics and needs, incorporating observational learning and modeling techniques, managing cognitive load, and fostering active, contextualized learning experiences, training programs can better prepare both sworn officers and civilian clinicians for the complexities of co-responder models. The significance of interdisciplinary training cannot be overstated, as it promotes mutual respect, shared goals, effective communication, and collaborative problem-solving between law enforcement and mental health professionals. Through joint training sessions that simulate real-life scenarios, teams can develop the skills and strategies necessary for coordinated crisis interventions, ultimately enhancing community safety and well-being.

Further, the continuous assessment and evaluation of training effectiveness and intervention outcomes are essential for driving continuous improvement in co-responder models. By employing methodologies, such as Kirkpatrick's Four-Level Training Evaluation Model and measuring immediate impacts and long-term consequences, agencies can identify areas for refinement and ensure that their responses to mental health crises remain effective and responsive to evolving community needs.

Existing Co-Responder Programs

Specific program structures, practices, and implementation vary depending on many factors including available funding and resources, departmental structure, mental health programming, and community dynamics (Krider et al., 2020). The Los Angeles Police Department (LAPD), recognized as a national law enforcement-mental health training site since 2010, has embedded in it the Mental Evaluation Unit (MEU). As part of MEU, the Systemwide Mental Assessment Response Team (SMART), which was developed in 1993, pairs an LAPD officer with a Los Angeles County Department of Mental Health (LACDMH) employee. This unit has grown and been modified over the last 31 years to include multiple components and a shift in approach from secondary responding to "co-responding" with the patrol officers. Additional components of MEU are the Case Assessment Management Program (CAMP) which partners a detective with a mental health professional to conduct follow-ups in an effort to mitigate risk, provide referrals, and connect clients to relevant care. To further collaborate with mental health and deliver a high standard of training to first responders, a 40-h POST-certified course known as Mental Health Intervention Training (MHIT) was developed and implemented. In addition, this unit employs the Senior Lead Program, composed of officers tasked with building relationships between themselves and community members, first responders, and additional professional entities that come into contact with clients the SMART team responds to. The MEU also consists of a triage desk operating 24 h a day, 7 days a week, which serves to further assist patrol officers and other agencies that call in through coordination and dispatching of co-response teams. The triage desk is tasked with recording incidents by generating reports and storing them in a secure database, which can serve to assist the co-responder teams in the case that a future incident occurs by providing valuable information regarding client history (*Los Angeles Police Department Mental Evaluation Unit*, 2021).

The Los Angeles County Sheriff's Department (LASD) formed the Mental Evaluation Team (MET) in 1991, making it the first co-responder program in the United States (Bille, 2023). MET pairs a Sheriff's Deputy with a Los Angeles County Department of Mental Health (LACDMH) employee to assist individuals in crisis. MET teams co-respond to the scene of a call for service with patrol deputies to provide evaluation and intervention services which may include the deployment of verbal de-escalation strategies, referrals for services, or transport to psychiatric facilities (*MET*, n.d.). The LASD's co-response model components include a triage desk, the Risk Assessment and Management Program (RAMP), and the Veterans Mental Evaluation Team (VMET). The triage desk, which operates 24 h a day, 7 days a week, serves to assist patrol units through the screening of calls for service, dispatching of MET, and coordination between officers and receiving facilities if the client is to be transferred to the hospital by a patrol unit. RAMP pairs a clinician with a deputy who is assigned high-acuity cases with the goal of providing intensive case management to reduce crises and link individuals to the appropriate level of care. VMET is a collaborative effort between MET, Department of Veterans Affairs, and federal police geared toward intervening with veterans in crisis, engaging in outreach to decrease the risk of suicide, and providing support to and advocacy for veterans at risk for crisis (Luna et al., 2023).

The Bexar County Sheriff's Office, identified as a national law enforcement-mental health learning site, deploys a co-responder team for mental health crisis calls, a post-crisis follow-up team, and an evaluation team inside of their county jail facility (*Bexar County Sheriff's Office*, n.d.). The Commissioners Court in Bexar County, Texas developed their co-responder program in 2020, named the Specialized Multidisciplinary Alternate Response Team (S.M.A.R.T.). Through the Southwest Texas Regional Advisory Council (STRAC), in collaboration with the Bexar County Sheriff's Office, Bexar County Office of Criminal Justice, Center for Health Care Services, and Acadian Ambulance Service, S.M.A.R.T. can respond to mental health-related calls for service and provide the appropriate follow-up. The goal of this newly formed multidisciplinary co-response program is to intervene in a mental health crisis, de-escalate, provide resources, and avoid involvement in the criminal justice system when such an outcome is feasible (*About S.M.A.R.T.*, n.d.).

The Vancouver Police Department (VPD) created a co-response model in 1978, referred to as "Car 87." This program pairs law enforcement with psychiatric nurses who are deployed to emergency calls and perform evaluations, provide outpatient resources, and accelerate referrals for their regional healthcare facility. Further, these teams, operational seven days a week, engage in outreach efforts, provide support to those with mental health conditions and their family members, and administer medication. The VPD, in partnership with Vancouver Coastal Health, coordinates efforts to provide appropriate services to clients through the department's Mental Health Unit. The VPD has officers working as part of the Assertive Community

Treatment (ACT) and Assertive Outreach Teams (AOT). ACT teams work with high-acuity clients requiring intensive support and care services and are composed of mental health, medical, and law enforcement personnel. The AOT, on the other hand, is a transitional program that works toward connecting clients with appropriate community services (Mental Health Initiatives, 2024).

An alternate form of co-responding can be seen through a review of the teams deployed throughout areas of Queensland, Australia. The teams include police officers and staff from the Department of Youth Justice; they are focused on addressing juvenile offenders or those at-risk for offending through active outreach of identified youth. While patrolling areas frequented by the target population, the team can attempt to build rapport and intervene on the youth's behalf by taking them from high-risk settings to a more appropriate location such as a treatment facility or their home. Further description of this initiative indicates that these teams assist with locating missing children, address crises with family members, and assist in adherence to conditions set forth for justice-involved juveniles on bail (*First of five new 24/7 co-responder teams rolled out,* 2023).

A long-standing collaboration formed between the Yale Child Study Center and the New Haven Police Department, the Child Development-Community Policing (CD-CP) program, is another example of a multidisciplinary partnership changing the way law enforcement interacts with individuals in need. The CD-CP program, originating in 1991, serves minors and families affected by violence and trauma. This co-responder team includes police officers, mental health clinicians, child protective services staff, and the Yale Center for Traumatic Stress and Recovery (YCTSR) faculty and trainees. Their partnership allows for early intervention with vulnerable children, disrupting their path toward violence and criminal behavior by offering support with the use of a co-responder model. Through the CD-CP program, law enforcement responds with appropriate clinical staff to crisis callouts where a minor is either victimized or witnesses a violent or distressing event, engages in post-event follow-ups at their homes, and provides outreach services in affected neighborhoods. In addition, the co-responder teams deliver death notifications; and, they refer affected families to the YCTSR Trauma Clinic for treatment-focused intervention (The Child Development-Community Policing Program, 2022).

A program created by The Office of Deputy Commissioner Collaborative Policing (DCCP) in 2016 partners the New York Police Department (NYPD) with the Department of Health and Mental Hygiene (DOHMH). Two police officers are partnered with one clinician from the DOHMH and are tasked with responding to those in a mental health-related crisis. They aim to engage with the individual, assess for mental health needs, and provide emergency services if necessary. Additional partnerships can be seen throughout cities in New York, such as the Heroin Overdose Prevention and Education program (Project HOPE) in Staten Island, Manhattan, and areas of the Bronx. In addition, The Collaborative Legal Engagement Assistance Response (Project CLEAR) was established in Brooklyn in 2018. These projects aim to offer diversion in the form of treatment versus prosecution for certain narcotics-related charges (*Collaborative Policing—NYPD*, n.d.).

The Portland Police Department, also recognized as a law enforcement mental health learning site, has within it the Behavioral Response Program. Through this program, a co-responder model deploys non-law enforcement personnel with officers to mental health-related crisis calls. In addition, there are alternate response teams composed of two clinical staff members who respond without police officers to calls that do not reach the level of acuity requiring law enforcement presence. Further, the Behavioral Intervention Unit (BHU) coordinates and provides crisis intervention training to its police officers (Special Services, 2023).

Wellington, New Zealand's police agency, deployed a co-response team (CRT) as a trial throughout 2020 and 2021 to measure its effectiveness in the region. The CRT pilot program took a multi-agency approach, partnering a paramedic, police officer, and mental health professional. An evaluation of this pilot program, conducted by Otago University, revealed a decrease in hospital transports and wait times once in the emergency room during CRT response days. Also, there was a decrease in emergency room recidivism in the following month (Brook, 2022). A co-responder model can also be found operating in areas of Queensland, Australia. As described by Fisher et al.'s (2024) qualitative study, the partnership between the Queensland Police Service and Metro South Addiction and Mental Health Service forms their Metro South Mental Health Co-responder Program. A clinician and police officer are paired in an unmarked car and serve as secondary responders to police callouts with a mental health component. The study's participants, composed of mental health and law enforcement personnel, found the co-responder program to be a favorable practice. Further, improved outcomes in mental health-related police call-outs, such as alternatives to hospitalizations through the use of proper assessment, interventions, and referrals for relevant services, were also noted. With that said, barriers to implementation and differences in policies between mental health and law enforcement were also discovered. It was noted that a co-responder model, while beneficial in many ways, can affect police coverage in other areas due to this particular program's practice of rotating police officers from their patrol stations. Researchers noted a possible solution by providing funding and assigning staff directly to the co-responder unit, which is already a known practice in other agencies nationwide.

Conclusion

As the above text demonstrates, a collaborative relationship between law enforcement and outside entities can take many forms. Co-responder programs will vary based on resources, funding, department size, service areas, and staffing. There are many agencies nationwide that have implemented their version of a co-response team, with only a small portion briefly reviewed above. Readers are encouraged to visit each department's website for a detailed description of their programs and review additional agencies to better understand what it looks like when co-responding is taken from theory to practice. Due to the differences in the types of co-responder programs and regions served, it would be difficult to compare and contrast various models regarding program efficacy. Through data collection within each department, however, specific program successes may be measured when comparing calls for service outcomes, such as uses of force, arrests, and hospitalization statistics, before and after program implementation.

Innovation, assessment, and ongoing education are key pillars in adapting to the evolving demands of public safety and mental health care. As we navigate the complexities of the societal landscape, the integration of law enforcement and mental health services through co-responder models holds immense promise in fostering safer, more compassionate communities. By embracing interdisciplinary collaboration, leveraging cutting-edge or classic learning theories, and prioritizing continuous improvement, we can chart a path toward more effective crisis intervention and support for those in need.

References

About S.M.A.R.T. (n.d.) Bexar County, TX—Official Website. https://www.bexar.org/3459/About-SMART

Balfour, M. E., Hahn Stephenson, A., Delany-Brumsey, A., Winsky, J., & Goldman, M. L. (2021). Cops, clinicians, or both? Collaborative approaches to responding to behavioral health emergencies. *Psychiatric Services, 73*(6). https://doi.org/10.1176/appi.ps.202000721

Bandura, A. (1977). *Social learning theory*. Prentice Hall.

Bexar County Sheriff's Office. (n.d.). CSG Justice Center. Retrieved May 3, 2024, from https://csgjusticecenter.org/projects/law-enforcement-mental-health-learning-sites/bexar-county-tx-sheriffs-department/

Bille, E. (2023, September 5). *Co-response models in policing*. FBI: Law Enforcement Bulletin. https://leb.fbi.gov/articles/featured-articles/co-response-models-in-policing

Blais, E., Landry, M., Elazhary, N., Carrier, S., & Savard, A.-M. (2020). Assessing the capability of a co-responding police-mental health program to connect emotionally disturbed people with community resources and decrease police use-of-force. *Journal of Experimental Criminology, 18*,. https://doi.org/10.1007/s11292-020-09434-x

Brook, E. (2022, March 1). *The power of "three brains."*. https://www.policeassn.org.nz/news/the-power-of-three-brains/

The Child Development-Community Policing Program. (2022). Medicine.yale.edu. Retrieved May 23, 2024, from https://medicine.yale.edu/childstudy/services/community-and-schools-programs/yctsr/community-policing/#page-container

Collaborative Policing—NYPD. (n.d.). Retrieved March 16, 2024, from https://www.nyc.gov/site/nypd/bureaus/administrative/collaborative-policing.page

Compton, M. T., Bakeman, R., Broussard, B., Hankerson-Dyson, D., Husbands, L., Krishan, S., Stewart-Hutto, T., D'Orio, B. M., Oliva, J. R., Thompson, N. J., & Watson, A. C. (2014). The police-based crisis intervention team (CIT) model: I. Effects on officers' knowledge, attitudes, and skills. *Psychiatric Services, 65*(4), 517–522. https://doi.org/10.1176/appi.ps.201300107

Compton, M. T., Demir Neubert, B. N., Broussard, B., McGriff, J. A., Morgan, R., & Oliva, J. R. (2009). Use of force preferences and perceived effectiveness of actions among crisis intervention team (CIT) police officers and non-CIT officers in an escalating psychiatric crisis involving a subject with schizophrenia. *Schizophrenia Bulletin, 37*(4), 737–745. https://doi.org/10.1093/schbul/sbp146

Congressional Research Service. (2022, October 17). *Issues in law enforcement reform: Responding to mental health crises*. Congress.gov. https://crsreports.congress.gov/product/pdf/R/R47285

Crisis Intervention Team. (n.d.). Memphis Police Department. Retrieved March 16, 2024, from https://www.memphispolice.org/about/partnerships-initiatives/crisis-intervention-team/

Draine, J., Wolff, N., Jacoby, J. E., Hartwell, S., & Duclos, C. W. (2011). *Understanding community mental health: Theory and practice in engaging with complex problems.* Columbia University Press.

Ellis, H. A. (2014). Effects of a crisis intervention team (CIT) training program upon police officers before and after crisis intervention team training. *Archives of Psychiatric Nursing, 28*(1), 10–16. https://doi.org/10.1016/j.apnu.2013.10.003

First of five new 24/7 co-responder teams rolled out. (2023, May 20). Ministerial media statements. https://statements.qld.gov.au/statements/97762

Fisher, O. J., Donahoo, C., Bosley, E., du Cloux, R., Garner, S., Powell, S., Pickard, J., Grevis-James, N., & Wyder, M. (2024). Barriers and enablers to implementing police mental health co-responder programs: A qualitative study using the consolidated framework for implementation research. *Implementation Research and Practice, 5*, 26334895231220260. https://doi.org/10.1177/26334895231220259

Fortenbery, J. (2018, June 13). *Police militarization in a democratic society.* FBI: Law Enforcement Bulletin. https://leb.fbi.gov/articles/featured-articles/police-militarization-in-a-democratic-society

Helfgott, J. B., Hickman, M. J., & Labossiere, A. P. (2016). A Descriptive evaluation of the Seattle Police Department's crisis response team officer/mental health professional partnership pilot program. *International Journal of Law and Psychiatry, 44*, 109–122. https://doi.org/10.1016/j.ijlp.2015.08.038

Kamin, D., Weisman, R. L., & Lamberti, J. S. (2022). Promoting mental health and criminal justice collaboration through system-level partnerships. *Frontiers in Psychiatry, 13*,. https://doi.org/10.3389/fpsyt.2022.805649

Kirkpatrick, D. L., & Kirkpatrick, J. D. (2006). *Evaluating training programs: The four levels* (3rd ed.). Berrett-Koehler Publishers.

Knowles, M. S. (1980). *The modern practice of adult education: From pedagogy to andragogy.* Cambridge Adult Education.

Knowles, M. S., Holton III, E. F., & Swanson, R. A. (2015). *The adult learner: The definitive classic in adult education and human resource development* (8th ed.). Routledge.

Krider, A., Huerter, R., Gaherty, K., & Moore, A. (2020). *Responding to individuals in behavioral health crisis via co-responder models: The roles of cities, counties, law enforcement, and providers.* Policy Research, Inc. National League of Cities. https://www.theiacp.org/sites/default/files/SJCResponding%20to%20Individuals.pdf

Lamanna, D., Shapiro, G. K., Kirst, M., Matheson, F. I., Nakhost, A., & Stergiopoulos, V. (2017). Co-responding police-mental health programmes: Service user experiences and outcomes in a large urban centre. *International Journal of Mental Health Nursing, 27*(2), 891–900. https://doi.org/10.1111/inm.12384

Learning about police—Mental health collaboration programs (n.d.). Bureau of Justice Assistance. Retrieved March 4, 2024, from https://bja.ojp.gov/program/pmhc/learning#3-0

Los Angeles Police Department Mental Evaluation Unit. (2021). https://csgjusticecenter.org/wp-content/uploads/2020/02/MEU-Program-Outline-June-2021.pdf

Luna, R. G., Mills, A., Doherty, A., Kennard, J., Green, B., Wilcox, A., Schnakenberg, D., Bojorquez, R., Barnes, S., Briz, A., & Medrano, R. (2023). *Report to the Sheriff civilian oversight commission regarding the mental evaluation team program of the Los Angeles County Sheriff's Department.* Los Angeles County Sheriff's Department.

Martinez, C. (2021). Los Angeles Police Department's mental health intervention training: A quantitative study (29261604) [Doctoral dissertation, Touro University Worldwide]. Proquest.

Martinez, C. (2024). *Qualitative post course feedback from in-service mental health crisis training for co-responders* [Unpublished raw data]. Los Angeles Police Department's Mental Health Intervention Training.

Mental Health Initiatives. (2024). Vancouver Police Department. Retrieved March 13, 2024, from https://vpd.ca/policies-strategies/mental-health-initiatives/

Merriam, S. B., & Bierema, L. L. (2013). *Adult learning: Linking theory and practice.* Jossey-Bass.

MET. (n.d.). Los Angeles County Sheriff's Department. Retrieved March 13, 2024, from https://lasd.org/transparency/met/

Morabito, M. S., Kerr, A. N., Watson, A., Draine, J., Ottati, V., & Angell, B. (2012). Crisis intervention teams and people with mental illness: Exploring the factors that influence the use of force. *Crime & Delinquency, 58*(1), 57–77. https://doi.org/10.1177/0011128710372456

Overview. (n.d.). University of Memphis CIT Center. Retrieved March 16, 2024, from http://www.cit.memphis.edu/overview.php?page=1

Reuland, M., Schwarzfeld, M., & Draper, L. (2021). Law enforcement responses to people with mental illnesses: A guide to research-informed policy and practice. *Psychiatry, Psychology, and Law.*

Shapiro, G. K., Cusi, A., Kirst, M., O'Campo, P., Nakhost, A., & Stergiopoulos, V. (2014). Co-responding police-mental health programs: A review. *Administration and Policy in Mental Health and Mental Health Services Research, 42*(5), 606–620. https://doi.org/10.1007/s10488-014-0594-9

Shefner, R. T., Koppel, R., Wood, J., & Anderson, E. D. (2023). Co-deployment is an answer, but what are the questions? Insights from officer focus groups in Philadelphia. *Police Practice and Research, 24*(6), 728–734. https://doi.org/10.1080/15614263.2023.2180360

Special Services. (2023). Portland, ME—Official website. Retrieved March 16, 2024, from https://www.portlandmaine.gov/1205/Special-Services

Sweller, J. (1988). Cognitive load during problem-solving: Effects on learning. *Cognitive Science, 12*(2), 257–285. https://doi.org/10.1207/s15516709cog1202_4

Sweller, J., Van Merrienboer, J. J. G., & Paas, F. G. W. C. (1998). Cognitive architecture and instructional design. *Educational Psychology Review, 10*(3), 251–296. https://doi.org/10.1023/A:1022193728205

Watson, A. C., & Fulambarker, A. J. (2012). The Crisis intervention team model of police response to mental health crises: A primer for mental health practitioners. *Best Practices in Mental Health, 8*(2), 71–81.

Watson, A. C., Morabito, M. S., Draine, J., & Ottati, V. (2010). A consensus approach to improving police interactions with persons with mental illness. *American Journal of Public Health.*

Wood, J. D., Watson, A. C., & Fulambarker, A. J. (2017). The "gray zone" of police work during mental health encounters: Findings from an observational study in Chicago. *Police Quarterly.*

Chapter 7
Crisis Intervention Team (CIT) Training for First Responders

Marissa Miller-Anguay, Bridget Spatola, Karla Rodriguez, and Samuel Savage

In response to communities and agencies across the country demanding effective and humane responses from law enforcement, Crisis Intervention Team (CIT) training was developed. This is a police-based specialized response that was developed collaboratively with community mental health professionals. CIT is designed to train law enforcement personnel in de-escalation strategies, including recognizing mental illnesses, utilizing active listening skills, and having knowledge of community resources for mental health support. Many agencies are now using CIT training for law enforcement as well as correctional officers. Despite the utilization and longevity of this training, limited research evaluating the efficacy and implementation of acquired skills outside of training exists as well as the applications across other first responder groups.

Mental Illness Stigma and The Criminal Justice System

The World Health Organization (2022) estimates that 1 in 8 people worldwide experience mental illness; however, it remains a highly stigmatized condition. The stigma surrounding mental illness manifests in various ways, including perpetuating misconceptions, fear, and prejudice. This manifestation leads to the marginalization and exclusion of individuals with mental health conditions from society. This stigma can be seen in societal attitudes, institutional practices, and even within healthcare

M. Miller-Anguay · B. Spatola · K. Rodriguez · S. Savage
College of Psychology, Nova Southeastern University, Fort Lauderdale, FL, USA

M. Miller-Anguay (✉)
Harris County Sheriff's Office, Houston, TX, USA
e-mail: m.milleranguay@outlook.com

V. B. Van Hasselt and M. L. Bourke (eds.), *Advances in First Responder Mental Health*, Advances in First Responder Mental Health 1,
https://doi.org/10.1007/978-3-032-27978-1_7

systems, where individuals may be met with skepticism, judgment, or inadequate support when seeking services.

The stigmatization of mental illness is further evident in its criminalization by society. There are two primary beliefs that connect mental illness to the criminal justice system: (1) deinstitutionalization, and (2) the action that individuals with mental illnesses are inherently dangerous and have an increased likelihood of engaging in criminal behavior, particularly acts of violence (Hiday & Burns, 2010). The notion that deinstitutionalization has contributed to the criminalization of mental illness stems from the observation that as mental health facilities were downsized or closed, individuals with mental illnesses were left without adequate community-based support systems. This lack of sufficient resources, including mental health services and housing, has led many individuals with mental illnesses to become involved in the criminal justice system. They may be arrested for offenses related to their mental health condition or engage in behaviors that result in interactions with law enforcement (Hiday & Burns, 2010). Additionally, the second belief, that individuals with mental illness are dangerous and prone to committing crimes, specifically violent ones, is a prevailing stereotype deeply ingrained in society (Hiday & Burns, 2010). This perception has been perpetuated by media portrayals, stigmatizing language, and a limited understanding of mental health issues (Benbow, 2007). Although some individuals with mental illnesses may exhibit behaviors that pose a risk to themselves or others, most individuals with mental illnesses are not violent.

Perception and Bias Among Criminal Justice Personnel

Due to the prevalent misunderstanding of mental illness, coupled with the historically perpetuated perception of violence and the associated stigma, it comes as no surprise that a significant proportion of individuals with mental illness find themselves incarcerated within the correctional system in the United States. According to the American Psychological Association (2014), about 64% of jail inmates, 54% of state prisoners, and 45% of federal prisoners have mental health concerns. Lowder et al. (2019) highlighted that professionals who had higher levels of exposure and interactions with individuals with serious mental illnesses (SMIs) tended to hold fewer positive attitudes and exhibited less tolerance when in close proximity to them, compared to those with fewer interactions. It is reasonable to conclude that the frequency and nature of professionals' contact with individuals with SMIs can shape their perceptions and attitudes toward mental illness. This finding can be extended to other professions within the criminal justice system, such as law enforcement. Time spent on scenes involving individuals with mental illness could potentially contribute to law enforcement officer (LEO) burnout and, consequently, foster negative attitudes toward this population. Therefore, the crucial need for enhanced psychoeducation and training initiatives aimed at promoting understanding and empathy among all professionals working within the criminal justice system must be emphasized. By providing comprehensive education and training on mental health issues, professionals can develop the necessary knowledge and skills to effectively respond to and support individuals with mental illness.

Frequent Law Enforcement Encounters

LEOs in the U.S. are facing an unprecedented increase in their response to incidents involving someone with a mental health problem, surpassing any previous period in the history of policing (Puntis et al., 2018). Between 7% and 31% of police calls involve individuals with mental illness (Shapiro et al., 2015). While this increase is occurring worldwide, the impact may vary in certain areas and could account for the variation in data. For example, mental health critical incidents (MHCI) constitute more than 20% of dispatches in New York City, while for some agencies MHCI account for only 10% (Abramson, 2021; Watson et al., 2008). As the first line of defense, LEOs often become de facto mental health providers responding to a broad spectrum of situations involving individuals with mental illness. These incidents may include crises triggered by mental health symptoms, suicidal ideation, homelessness, or erratic behavior that leads to disturbances in public spaces (Council of State Governments Justice Center, 2021). The range of responses required by law enforcement can vary from providing support and connecting individuals with appropriate mental health services, to encountering and managing potentially dangerous situations (Shapiro et al., 2015).

As the primary line of defense in communities, LEOs often find themselves responding to challenging and complex situations involving individuals with mental health conditions; yet, they frequently express a sense of inadequacy in their training to handle such scenarios. Many officers feel that they lack the necessary skills in crisis de-escalation and a fundamental understanding of psychological conditions (Park, 2019). This deficiency in training can have significant repercussions on how law enforcement responds to MHCIs, often resulting in unnecessary arrests, hospitalizations, and placing added strain on both law enforcement agencies and the communities they are entrusted to protect (Constantine et al., 2010; Cooper et al., 2004; Puntis et al., 2018).

Development of Crisis Intervention Team (CIT) Training

During the 1960s, there were significant efforts to deinstitutionalize mental illness. In the 1980s, legislation shifted mental health care away from hospitals, limiting where an individual could receive treatment if experiencing a mental health crisis. As a result, emergency services were called, and police frequently became involved. Moreover, at this time, LEOs had little to no training or knowledge about individuals experiencing mental illness. A catalyst event occurred in 1988 when Memphis police officers responded to a call that involved an individual with schizophrenia and demonstrating suicidality. Officers were unsuccessful in de-escalating the situation, and when the individual suddenly moved toward them with a knife, they discharged their firearms, killing the man (Browning et al., 2011). Although officers were trained to use deadly force when they perceive their own or someone else's life to be in grave danger, this incident was criticized as the perception of the call was that the only life in danger was that of the man demonstrating suicidality and self-harm. This incident also added to the racial tension in Memphis at the time as the man was identified as black and the officers were white. As a result, communities and agencies across the country demanded effective and humane responses from law enforcement. In response, the Memphis Police Department partnered with the National Alliance for the Mentally Ill (NAMI), mental health professionals, and local universities to develop training and implement a specialized unit; thus, the Memphis CIT program, otherwise known as the "Memphis Model", was created. Since then, thousands of agencies have adopted the Memphis model, and over time, other models that include the partnership of mental health and law enforcement have been developed.

CIT Training Models

Memphis Model

This model aimed to reduce the lethality between police encounters and individuals diagnosed with mental health disorders, and provide adequate assistance through the civil treatment system instead of submitting these individuals to the criminal justice system (Rogers et al., 2019). The Memphis model consists of a 40-hour training instructed by community mental health workers, people diagnosed with mental health disorders, families, and advocates (see Fig. 1; Rogers et al., 2019). An additional component of the Memphis model is specialized training for dispatch operators to recognize calls requiring CIT-trained officers to respond (Rogers et al., 2019). As part of the Memphis model, there is an identified mental health facility that police officers routinely use to direct individuals experiencing a mental health crisis when necessary (Rogers et al., 2019). Overall, the Memphis model can be viewed as a "community partnership" where there is a standard of care regarding police encounters and individuals with mental health and substance use issues (Rogers et al., 2019). The emphasis on collaboration with the community regarding psychiatric emergency receiving facilities and social services agencies is crucial to improve interactions between police officers and individuals with a mental health diagnosis or crisis (Watson et al., 2017). Thus, the training also involves engaging with advocacy groups, families, and individuals with psychological diagnoses, which allows for firsthand experiences to reduce mental health stigma (Watson et al., 2017).

Supporting evidence for the Memphis model suggests more officer satisfaction and a reduction in the use of force (Rogers et al., 2019). The Memphis model has

CRISIS INTERVENTION TEAM (CIT)

TIME	Monday	Tuesday	Wednesday	Thursday	Friday
8:00	Introduction and CIT Overview	Crisis Communication	Domestic Violence Crisis Intervention	PTSD	Officer Self-Care and Wellness Officer Carringington Davie Police Department
8:30					
9:00	Introduction and CIT Overview with NAMI				
9:30	BREAK (9:30-9:45 am)	BREAK (9:30-9:45 am)	BREAK (9:30-9:45 am)	BREAK (9:30-9:45 am)	BREAK 9:30-9:45 am
10:00	Baker Act	Crisis Communication Practical	Personality Disorders	LGBTQ+	Autism
10:30					
11:00					
11:30					
12:00	LUNCH	LUNCH	LUNCH	LUNCH	LUNCH
12:30					
1:00	Substance Use	Crisis Intervention	SITE VISITS	SCENARIO BASED TRAINING	Consumer/Family Panel Families
1:30					
2:00					
	BREAK (2:30-2:45 PM)	BREAK (2:30-2:45 PM)			BREAK (2:30-2:45 PM)
2:30	Substance Use	Crisis Intervention			Mental Fitness
3:00					
3:30					
4:00	Adult Mental Health	Youth Mental Health and Suicide Prevention			Evaluations
4:30					Graduation
5:00					

Fig. 1 Sample CIT training schedule, Memphis model. *Note* This schedule is a CIT training mocked after the Memphis Model

also been found to effectively prevent individuals with mental health disorders or in a mental health crisis from being incarcerated. Instead, they are given access to appropriate mental health care based on their level of distress (Rogers et al., 2019). Compton et al. (2008) found Memphis CIT-trained officers were more likely to report being well-prepared in police encounters involving mental health illnesses while also rating the mental health system and emergency rooms as helpful. Stigma and stereotyping have also decreased as CIT-trained officers are better at approaching such encounters (Rogers et al., 2019). Specifically, stigma related to schizophrenia, depression, alcohol and cocaine dependence decreased as a result of training (Bahora et al., 2008). Verbal negotiations have also been found to increase with CIT-trained officers (Compton et al., 2014). However, it must be noted that it is difficult to measure the reduction of lethality due to environmental confounding variables that can influence CIT training effects (Compton et al., 2014).

Crisis Intervention Team for Youth (CIT-Y)

The purpose of the youth version of the CIT model is to prevent them from encountering the juvenile justice system (Kubiak et al., 2019). CIT-Y ensures that youths are also provided with the appropriate assessment and treatment services as adults when needed (Doulas & Lurigio, 2010). CIT-Y follows the CIT model for adults with adaptations (e.g., adolescent development, adolescent psychiatric disorders and treatments, family experiences) for youth development and mental health (Kubiak et al., 2019). This training is an eight-hour supplemental course that is offered for officers who have completed the CIT 40-hour training (Kubiak et al., 2019). Research has shown that CIT-Y trained officers changed their behaviors toward youth experiencing a mental health crisis (Doulas & Lurigio, 2010; Kubiak et al., 2019). CIT-Y also provides the opportunity for officers to understand youth mental health disorders as more than "acting out" behaviors (Kubiak et al., 2019).

R-Model

The R-Model (Research–Respond–Refer) was developed in 2018 with Minnesota law enforcement due to the demand for an updated crisis intervention response by police officers and to conduct research regarding mental health disorders, crisis, and trauma (Peterson et al., 2020). The model was established to build on the foundation of the current crisis intervention training (e.g., Memphis model; Kutylowski, 2020). The creators of the R-model conducted interviews and participated in ride-alongs with the Minnesota Police Department to develop this model (Kutylowski, 2020). The R-Model training consists of a one-day training that includes a review of the current state of law enforcement's involvement with mental health, and how to recognize a mental health crisis and respond to the crisis. It also offers guest speakers who present on trauma, treatment and resources, as well as agency initiatives (Peterson et al., 2020). This model can be adapted, customized, and found beneficial for various police agency sizes and demographics (Kutylowski, 2020; Peterson et al., 2020).

Research has determined that the R-model has decreased stigma and increased officers' self-reported knowledge of mental health resources with this eight-hour training model compared to the typical 40-hour training (Peterson et al., 2020). This was evident in a study by Peterson et al. (2020) which found decreased mental health crisis calls at a one-year follow-up. Additionally, after the R-model implementation, officers indicated changes in the agency environment, crisis call response, and reduced emergency department visits (Peterson et al., 2020).

Crisis Outreach and Support Team (COAST)

The Crisis Outreach and Support Team (COAST) was piloted by the city of Hamilton, Ontario, in 1997 and instituted in 2001 (Wood et al., 2011). COAST included plain-clothed police officers, mental health workers, social workers, as well as child and youth crisis workers to be on call, ready to work at any time of the day or night (Wood et al., 2011). The need for the outreach mobile unit is determined by the nature of the call and the mental health worker who is part of the team. Teams dispatched to the scene arrive in an unmarked police car to decrease the intimidation of police presence. By phone support or a dispatched call, a management plan is developed to assess the immediate situation and provide follow-up plans as well as referrals if warranted. Additionally, COAST attends not only to police calls, but also mental health agencies' concerns and provides crisis intervention when needed (Wood et al., 2011). In 2006, COAST introduced CIT training to members of this team in order to provide information on more effective interaction strategies between LEOs and civilians (Wood et al., 2011).

COAST has been found to allow for more inpatient admissions after a crisis, as police and mental health providers on these teams can learn which individuals are better suited for hospitalization (Ghelani et al., 2023). This program is a useful development within police services to educate officers on the accurate treatment of individuals with mental health diagnoses. Further, based on the research conducted by Ghelani et al. (2023), the connections made between the community and the COAST team have become stronger since implementation.

Co-Responder

The Co-responder model involves the collaboration of law enforcement and mental healthcare workers to provide community services, either in person or remotely (Puntis et al., 2018; Shapiro et al., 2015). The purpose of this collaboration is to permit police and mental healthcare workers to provide accurate services related to their specialty (i.e., police can prevent potential injury, and mental health workers can provide crisis intervention) (Shapiro et al., 2015). This framework has been implemented in British Columbia, Ontario, Nova Scotia, Tennessee, Georgia, California, Victoria, and Florida (Shapiro et al., 2015). These programs strive for accountability and allow for cost-effective solutions to law enforcement‘s current response to mental health (Shapiro et al., 2015).

The Co-responder model aims to provide crisis intervention to those in need, prevent injury to all parties, and provide accurate referrals for the community while also reducing pressures on the justice and health care systems (Shapiro et al., 2015). Having a mental health professional at the scene decreases the chance of police detainment of someone who is experiencing a mental health crisis, within safety limits. Although, it should be noted that there is limited research on the utilization and efficacy of the Co-responder model (Puntis et al., 2018). However, this approach appears to improve care for individuals in mental health crises and reduces the liability for police officers, thereby increasing the safety for both civilians and officers (Puntis et al., 2018).

Mental Health Response Training

Specific mental health training is available for those outside of the mental health field, including police officers, teachers, caseworkers, and parents. In a systematic review, Booth et al. (2017) found that many programs focus on raising awareness, methods to enact change, and various training deliveries (e.g., short or long in length, mental health professionals as trainers, face to face). These trainings provide a broad understanding of mental health and how to work with those who have a mental health diagnosis (Booth et al., 2017). Scenario-based training, where individuals interact with actors demonstrating different mental health diagnoses, are also utilized to assist learning (Booth et al., 2017). A primary concern in mental health response training pertains to who provided the training, and the specific content covered, since most training is limited to a specific mental health focus, making it difficult to generalize to all mental health crises (Booth et al., 2017).

Natural disasters and the crises experienced afterwards are often seen as a community response, which includes contacting, assessing, educating, supporting, and providing interventions within the community (Gard & Ruzek, 2006). These elements are also known as psychological first aid and consists of four phases (the pre-impact or preparatory phase, the impact phase, the response phase, and the recovery phase) (Gard & Ruzek, 2006). This mental health response training can be taught and provided by non-mental health professionals, allowing for a more community-based action in light of natural disasters and mental health crises.

Impact of CIT Training

As mental health crisis calls have increased in frequency over the years, the popularity of CIT training among law enforcement agencies has also increased. However, sending LEOs to mental health training for five days may not be practical due to insufficient workforce or budgetary limitations for some police departments. Therefore, assessing CIT's efficacy and feasibility and fostering support for implementing this training across various police departments is paramount. This section examines the effect CIT training has on personnels' ability to utilize diversion and de-escalation tactics with individuals with mental illness in the available empirical research. LEOs' overall perception of their encounters was also explored. A total of 54 articles published from 2006 to 2022 were reviewed. Empirical studies and meta-analyses of empirical studies were included. Articles were sorted by recency and relevancy, leaving a final total of 44 articles.

Attitudes, Perceptions, and Knowledge of Mental Illness

Approximately 20% of emergency calls are related to a mental health crisis, leading to increased law enforcement involvement instead of immediate treatment (Abramson, 2021). These calls create additional stress for individuals with psychological disorders and LEOs alike. LEOs who experience adverse interactions with those in crisis can develop negative attitudes and perceptions of mental health conditions. One component of CIT is dedicated to reducing police stigma surrounding mental health by increasing the knowledge of psychological disorders and familiarity with symptoms. LEOs can then effectively resolve situations by referring to the appropriate care rather than incarceration. Research suggests that CIT training effectively targets and changes attitudes and perceptions of LEOs while also adding to their knowledge of the signs and symptoms of mental illness (Bahora et al., 2008; Booty et al., 2020; Bratina et al., 2020; Compton et al., 2008, 2014, 2017; Cross et al., 2014; Mulay et al., 2016; Rogers et al., 2019). The reduction of mental health stigma provides opportunities for increased public safety for LEOs and those in mental health crises.

Beliefs regarding serious mental illness can positively or negatively impact interactions between those with mental illness and LEOs. Ellis (2014) found officer knowledge, perception, and attitude toward mental illness to statistically improve following participation in CIT training. Another study surveyed officers post-training who believed that they could increase their knowledge of the symptoms of mental illness as well as increase empathy and patience, and decrease stigmatizing attitudes (Hanafi et al., 2008). This increase in empathy and decrease in social distance (behavioral manifestation of stigma) among CIT officers was also found in other studies (Compton et al., 2014; Ritter et al., 2010). Even when assessing CIT efficacy between volunteers and assigned officers, knowledge regarding mental illnesses appeared to be equally effective (Compton et al., 2017). This finding suggests that even though an officer may not have the motivation to attend CIT, they complete the training with more knowledge.

Although many studies seem to evaluate general mental health, some researchers focused on disorders that LEOs may frequently encounter. Demir et al. (2009) examined LEOs' perceptions related to a schizophrenia diagnosis after CIT training. Researchers found that after the training, officers were less likely to endorse myths regarding the cause of schizophrenia and instead presented attitudes that reduced stigma. Assessing attitudes and perceptions toward schizophrenia was also studied by Compton et al. (2006), similarly reported that post-CIT officers showed improvements in attitudes and knowledge toward individuals with schizophrenia while also displaying reduced levels of social distance. Officers also indicated increased support for programs that treat schizophrenia and substance use disorders (Compton et al., 2006). Similar results were observed by Bahora et al. (2008) who found that CIT-trained officers decreased social distance among those with depression, cocaine dependence, schizophrenia, and alcohol dependence. This research provides evidence that CIT successfully changes the attitudes, perceptions, and overall knowledge of LEOs.

However, there are conflicting results. For example, one study found no significant differences in levels of mental illness stigma between CIT-trained officers and non-CIT-trained officers (Haigh et al., 2018). Researchers attributed this finding to the anxiety surrounding mental health crisis incidents rather than poor CIT outcomes. Nick et al. (2022) reported a decrease in the stigma of mental illness among CIT officers; however, they also noted a reduction in stigma among those assigned to road patrol. These results indicate that the level of exposure to mental illness may decrease stigma without direct intervention.

Based on these studies, there is clear support for CIT's impact on reducing negative attitudes and perceptions while increasing knowledge of the various psychological disorders' signs and symptoms. CIT techniques, such as de-escalation and communication skills, facilitate LEOs' ability to correct myths and reduce mental health stigma, which can lead to increased rapport-building. Ultimately, CIT can increase public safety for officers and individuals suffering from psychological distress.

Diversion Versus Arrests

Since the deinstitutionalization of psychiatric hospitals, there seems to be an increase in pressure placed on officers, who are neither familiar with the signs and symptoms of mental disorders nor the resources available to those suffering from psychological distress (Ellis, 2014). Officers' ability to recognize the signs and symptoms of psychological disorders protects the community and connects these people to services. There have been data to suggest positive outcomes associated with a diversion to mental health services through CIT (Cowell et al., 2004). Results demonstrated clinically meaningful and statistically significant reductions in psychiatric symptoms (Cowell et al., 2004). These findings suggest that CIT officers not only accurately identify individuals in need of psychiatric care; they are likely to reduce psychiatric morbidity by referring individuals with severe mental illness to treatment earlier than might occur otherwise (Strauss et al., 2005). However, LEOs are left to make quick and difficult decisions based on community and officer safety.

Several investigative efforts have examined CIT's impact on diversion rates. These have shown that officers are less likely to make an arrest, and instead, increase referrals to psychiatric services (Compton et al., 2008, 2017; Lattimore et al., 2003; Rogers et al., 2019). A meta-analysis revealed that Special Weapons And Tactics (SWAT) callouts, use of force, and arrests of individuals with mental illness decreased post-CIT training (Browning et al., 2011). This study also found that public confidence and support increased after implementing CIT. Taheri (2016) observed that CIT-trained officers were less likely to arrest individuals with mental illness when compared to non-CIT-trained officers. Further, officers reported making fewer emergency detentions due to the utilization of CIT techniques and persuaded those in crisis to seek and be transported to voluntary treatment (Hassell, 2020). When comparing two departments, the one with more CIT officers reported significantly higher Baker Act (involuntary commitment) rates, which can be attributed to CIT training goals (Klimley et al., 2021). Mulay et al. (2016) compared two studies that added to the evidence of CIT's impact on arrest rates. Both demonstrated that CIT officers are more likely than their non-trained counterparts to transport and connect those in a mental health crisis to services (Mulay et al., 2016). Teller et al. (2006) reviewed police dispatch logs before and after CIT training; they found that CIT-trained officers were more likely to transport persons to a treatment facility during a mental health crisis. This difference is highlighted by Compton et al. (2014), who found a 40% referral rate of CIT officers compared to a 29% referral rate of non-CIT officers. Another study indicated that 85% of mental health cases were diverted rather than resulting in an arrest (Bratina et al., 2020). Franz and Borum (2010) monitored CIT encounters from multiple police agencies in central Florida over five years. Data from approximately 1,500 crisis incidents were analyzed and sorted into two categories: cases that resulted in arrests versus prevented arrests. Prior to CIT training, approximately 19% of mental health calls would have resulted in arrests; however, after CIT training, only 3% of calls resulted in arrests (Franz & Borum, 2010). These results highlight a significant reduction in the arrest rate of those with mental illness, which adds support to the contention that CIT impacts arrest rates.

The literature also distinguishes the referral rates to psychiatric treatment facilities from emergency departments (EDs). This difference is an important consideration as psychiatric facilities are focused on long-term care compared to EDs, which focus on stabilization and acute care. Comartin et al. (2019) noted a sustained increase in monthly transports to a crisis center rather than an ED post-CIT training. Prior to training, 9% of mental health incidents were taken to crisis centers, while post-training, 31% were taken to the crisis center (Comartin et al., 2019). A longitudinal study also examined the effect of CIT diversion compared to arrest rates over six years. Results indicated that of approximately 10,000 mental health crisis calls, 25% were referred to psychiatric emergency services, 31% were transported to the local hospitals, and about 3% resulted in an arrest (Teller et al., 2006). Even when crisis centers were farther away from the scene, CIT officers traveled the extra distance to connect the individual to appropriate care (Comartin et al., 2019). Although these results seem promising, the important factor to consider is accessibility to treatment facilities. Watson et al. (2011) found that areas with more access to mental health services reported increased transport of those in a mental health crisis. However, those with fewer resources did not report statistically significant differences. Based on these results, CIT is deemed effective in increasing officers' understanding of available psychiatric services that may offer long-term care, compared to EDs that focus on short-term stabilization.

De-Escalation

De-escalation can be referred to as the strategic slowing down of events to allow LEOs the time, distance, space, and tactical flexibility required during high-intensity situations (US Department of Justice, 2015). CIT's approach to de-escalation incorporates techniques that assist LEOs' communication with those experiencing psychological distress. Such techniques include being empathetic, non-judgmental, and actively listening to the individual. In order to measure CIT-trained officers' utilization of these skills, Morabito et al. (2012) examined the use of force during mental health crises. They found that LEOs who received CIT training endorsed less physical force when confronted with resistance from those with mental illness compared to officers without CIT training. Research has also demonstrated that CIT officers have improved suicide assessment and de-escalation strategies by focusing on active listening skills and exhibiting patience during mental health crisis encounters (Canada et al., 2012). In the absence of In Vivo data, research also suggests that officers self-report less use of force and more successful implementation of de-escalation techniques to calm those in a mental health crisis compared to non-CIT officers (Browning et al., 2011; Cross et al., 2014; Hanafi et al., 2008; Morabito & Socia, 2015; Rogers et al., 2019). Compton et al. (2011) examined the responses of LEOs' use of physical force across three scenarios. Results indicated that CIT-trained officers consistently reported lower perceived effectiveness of physical force than non-CIT officers. When presented with scenarios involving a potentially violent individual who was actively psychotic, compared to the control group of officers, CIT officers were less likely to respond with force. Another study found that CIT positively affected the use of force and demonstrated that CIT officers' highest level of force used was verbal negotiation (Rogers et al., 2019). More recently, Hassell (2020) found that CIT significantly altered how officers interact with persons in crisis due to mental illness. Officers reported that the knowledge gained in training improved their communication by increasing patience and listening skills, ultimately de-escalating potentially volatile encounters (Hassell, 2020).

Despite these promising results, findings are divided regarding the impact CIT has on de-escalation (Bratina et al., 2020; Marcus & Stergiopoulos, 2022; Morabito & Socia, 2015; Taheri, 2016). For example, Morabito and Socia (2015), found that physical force and injury instances decreased. However, they were unable to determine whether CIT directly caused this reduction. A meta-analysis examining the use of force did not find a significant difference between CIT and non-CIT-trained officers (Taheri, 2016). Compton et al. (2014) examined CIT's effect on the use of force among LEOs and compared the highest level of force utilized by CIT and non-CIT officers. They reported that CIT officers used verbal negotiation as the highest level of force 20% of the time. Non-CIT officers used verbal negotiation as the highest level of force in only 11% of their encounters, which ultimately did not reflect a significant difference between groups.

Another meta-analysis revealed similar inconclusive results in overall public safety, including no evidence of reductions in the use of force by or against LEOs, or injuries to consumers or responding officers (Bratina et al., 2020). Surveys within the police department demonstrated that approximately 50% of officers did not believe that CIT officers were more effective at de-escalation than those not CIT trained (Yang et al., 2018). Further, Compton et al. (2017) evaluated whether CIT training outcomes differed among volunteers and officers assigned to the training. They did not find significant differences in the overall dispositions of encounters; however, officers who had volunteered were more likely to refer to a mental health facility rather than executing an arrest despite physical force being necessary for transport. Although research seems inconclusive, the issue may not be whether CIT's de-escalation techniques are effective, but whether this construct is being measured effectively. Therefore, more research should examine de-escalation tactics and improved methods to make this determination.

Overall Encounter Experience

As stated earlier, many LEOs have negative attitudes and perceptions of persons with mental illness, which also adds to the stigma of mental illness in general. Therefore, support for training and the feasibility of implementing CIT needs to be examined. Overall, it appears that officers rate CIT training positively. Bonfine et al. (2014) found that attitudes related to officer and community safety, access to services, preparedness to respond to mental health crisis calls, and learned skills and techniques were positively associated with LEOs' confidence in abilities and their perceptions of departmental effectiveness. Studies have also demonstrated that after CIT, many officers believed that they were: better prepared to respond to mental health incidents, aware of services available to those in crisis, and overall enhanced safety for themselves as well as the community (Bahora et al., 2008; Bonfine et al., 2014; Compton et al., 2006; 2008; Cross et al., 2014; Hanafi et al., 2008; Kubiak et al., 2017; Mulay et al., 2016). Increasing officer knowledge of common mental illnesses also seems to increase confidence in the identification of symptoms and reduces stereotypes, ultimately improving interactions with individuals in psychological distress (Compton et al., 2008).

Wells and Schafer (2006) assessed LEOs' perceptions of CIT before and after training. Results indicated significant increases in the perceived ability to manage incidents and communicate with psychologically distressed individuals (Wells & Schafer, 2006). Ritter et al. (2010) evaluated the feelings of preparedness of officers when confronted with those who have mental illness pre- and post-CIT training, as well as factors that predict improved self-efficacy. Overall, the results indicated increased feelings of preparedness from 26% pre-intervention to 97% post-intervention. The analysis also examined beliefs that officers held regarding their department's preparedness. Results showed that those who viewed mental illness as a significant issue for their department felt more prepared to handle mental crisis incidents after training (Ritter et al., 2010). This effect was also evidenced when examining confidence among various disorders. Bahora et al. (2008) found that LEOs with CIT training exhibited improved self-efficacy while interacting with individuals with depression, cocaine dependence, alcohol dependence, and schizophrenia. Officers also believed that they learned how to respond appropriately to a mental health crises and reduced arrest rates of those with mental illness by connecting individuals to the appropriate treatment services (Hanafi et al., 2008). Furthermore, LEOs who interact with individuals with mental illness appear to influence how CIT training is perceived in terms of improving safety and enhancing departmental effectiveness. As stated previously, Nick et al. (2022) were unable to find differences between their CIT and non-CIT trained officers; however, they attributed this to the exposure of persons with mental illness in the community. This result supports the notion that exposure and experience with this population can increase confidence when confronting mental illness. Hassell (2020) found that 87% of officers felt CIT training was useful because they learned a considerable amount of previously unknown information. Officers also felt better prepared to respond to mental health calls.

Changes in the self-efficacy and confidence of officers are integral when understanding the effects of CIT training. Low confidence in learned CIT skills may lead to snap decisions, increasing the use of force and arrests (Compton et al., 2011). Tully and Smith (2015) found that CIT-trained officers felt more prepared to deal with mental illness, but wanted more information regarding diversion programs in their community. Watson et al. (2021) observed that CIT responses increase the connection of those in psychological distress to care; however, most officers transported these individuals to an ED and requested more information for long-term solutions. This finding was one of the concerns reported in a survey to police chiefs and sheriffs over three months (Compton et al., 2015). Those in command believed that barriers to implementing CIT included not having a large enough force, the cost of training, officers taking five days to attend the training rather than being on patrol, and inadequate access to mental health services.

Continued Education and Online Training

CIT training in various forms (i.e., 40-hour, 8-hour training) is designed to be a one-time course, with many agencies not requiring officers to retake it. Although, limited refresher or continuing education courses are available, it is dependent on the agency and its requirements to reinforce such re-trainings. Department refresher courses typically range from 1 to 1.5 days and are offered to officers with at least one year of experience as an active CIT officer. During these courses, officers review de-escalation and active listening skills, updates on legal matters, self-care, and community resources. Officers also participate in scenario-based training to refresh their skills.

In response to the limited continuing education opportunities, CIT-Extension for Community Healthcare Outcomes (ECHO) was developed in 2015 (Crisanti et al., 2019). CIT ECHO was created for the needs from the Albuquerque Police Department (APD). In New Mexico, mental health-related calls received by APD increased by around 40% between 2010 and 2014. And in 2014, 43% of officer-involved shootings involved people with a serious mental illness. CIT ECHO is a videoconferencing network that uses case debriefings and supplemental training to promote best practices. This platform provides supplemental knowledge and skills development beyond the initial 40-hour CIT course. CIT ECHO holds weekly sessions for 90-minutes that includes a brief didactic presentation related to CIT policing or behavioral health (e.g., resource knowledge, psychiatric diagnoses, de-escalation and communication techniques, officer self-care, substance use, and special training), followed by case debriefings presented by officers who responded to mental health-related calls (Crisanti et al., 2019). This platform is not limited to LEOs as it is designed for other first responders who encounter mental health crises (e.g., firefighters, emergency medical services, correction officers, emergency communication officers and dispatchers, and mental health providers who work with first responders). According to Crisanti et al. (2019), ECHO is an evidence-based platform initially used to connect primary care physicians to a network of health care specialists. The adaptation of ECHO allows convenient access for officers to receive the necessary support regarding mental health-related encounters. The diverse team that provides support consists of psychiatrists, CIT detectives, crisis specialists, and project coordinators. Since its launch, CIT ECHO has expanded to various public safety services across the U.S., providing free and accessible networking and learning opportunities to first responders encountering, and responding to, mental health-related calls and crises.

To our knowledge, this is the only platform for continuing education that has been expanded nationwide. Other refresher courses are offered by departments, thus highlighting the variability in opportunities, availability, course topics, and overall training.

Application to Other First Responders

Emergency Communication Officers (ECOs)

ECOs are the first line of communication in emergency calls and, consequently, are frequently encountering people with mental illness. Therefore, they should be adequately trained in recognizing, responding to, and routing these calls (Compton et al., 2010). However, training varies based on agency requirements and opportunities. Other limitations to CIT training for ECOs are that law enforcement attendance is typically prioritized, and agencies may not have the staffing to allow ECOs to attend a 40-hour training. Compton et al. (2010) highlighted that agencies who have started to design and implement ECO-focused CIT training have developed shortened versions to accommodate staffing concern. According to the National Alliance on Mental Illness (NAMI) of Lee County, Florida (2023), CIT for ECOs provides mental health information and de-escalation techniques (e.g., active listening, patient questioning skills) which equips them with the appropriate skills needed to handle a crisis call. Topics covered in this training include the CIT model, the role of 911in the crisis response system, signs of mental health disorders, suicide assessment and intervention, crisis intervention strategies, call management, and scenario-based trainings via telephone (NAMI, 2023). Further evaluation and research are needed to address the difficulties regarding CIT training for ECOs and the effectiveness of such training.

Firefighters, Paramedics, and Emergency Medical Services (EMS)

Little research has examined fire rescue personnels' encounters with people suffering from mental illness; and even fewer CIT trainings are designed or offered for this first responder population. Given the nature of crisis-related calls, fire rescue and EMS frequently respond to calls for service involving a person experiencing a mental health crisis, assaults perpetrated by someone experiencing such a crisis, and restraint use on a person with a mental illness in crisis administered by personnel. Consequently, it has been suggested that CIT training should be extended to fire rescue and EMS (Ivancevich, 2015). According to Ivancevich (2015), 53.8% of EMS personnel reported an interest and willingness to complete CIT training, and 85.7% of EMS personnel noted that CIT training would be beneficial when responding to calls for service involving persons experiencing a psychological episode. It is unclear what CIT training for fire rescue and EMS personnel would include. However, the premise of this training is to provide de-escalation and active listening skills to personnel dealing with someone in a mental health crisis. More CIT research and program development are needed for these public safety groups to provide them with a level of preparedness, confidence, and a sense of safety when encountering an individual in a mental health crisis.

Corrections Officers (COs)

Given that the rates of mental health disorders among incarcerated individuals are significantly higher than that of the general population, CIT training is needed for COs. CIT training for COs is intended to improve on their understanding of mental illness, provide tools to support communication skills, and educate officers on interventions for use with those experiencing a crisis (McNeeley & Donley, 2020).

Regarding the efficacy of CIT training, research has yielded mixed results. According to the Public Health Research Institute (2005), COs appreciated the skills and information acquired from CIT training, and indicated they felt more prepared to handle mental health crises. Results also suggested that CIT-trained COs were more likely to use verbal de-escalation techniques and less likely to use physical force. CIT training was also found to improve COs' scores on tests on mental illness, self-efficacy in responding to crises, and self-perception of their verbal de-escalation techniques (Davidson, 2016). However, Davidson (2016) found a regression in self-efficacy and perception at follow-up. Other results revealed that CIT-trained officers were more successful in de-escalating situations, so that incarcerated individuals who were previously non-compliant eventually complied. Further, CIT training was not related to lower use of force (McNeeley & Donley, 2020). These findings suggest that CIT training equips COs with the knowledge needed to connect incarcerated people with necessary mental health care (McNeeley & Donley, 2020). CIT training has shown beneficial outcomes for both incarcerated individuals in crisis and with chronic mental illness as well as COs themselves.

Conclusion

CIT training for all first responders is a vital and practical progression since they frequently encounter individuals with mental illness. Research has shown CIT training to have many benefits, including improving law enforcement attitudes and perceptions towards persons with mental illness, and improving verbal or behavioral de-escalation techniques, (i.e., being empathetic, non-judgmental, and actively listening), and diversions. Further, CIT has demonstrated value in increasing safety for both the first responder, the individual in crisis or with a mental illness, and the community. However, there is still limited research concerning the utility and efficacy of CIT. Further, only some agencies and first responder groups receive such training due to various barriers, such as lack of sufficient staffing, limited financial support, and other agency-specific adversities. Therefore, it is suggested that CIT be offered, implemented, and adapted so that most, if not all, agencies have the opportunity for their personnel to receive this training. Despite the variability in mental health calls, agencies may also benefit if they receive a standardized training to ensure the CIT material is consistent across departments. It should also be noted that although CIT is primarily designed for law enforcement, other first responder groups (e.g., emergency communications officers, firefighters, corrections officers) benefit from this training. As CIT continues to be applied, more research regarding its efficacy is critical for continued advancement of this training.

References

Abramson, A. (2021). Building mental health into emergency response: More cities are pairing mental health professionals with police to better help people in crisis. *Monitor on Psychology, 52*(5), 30. https://www.apa.org/monitor/2021/07/emergency-responses

American Psychological Association. (2014). *Incarceration nation.* https://www.apa.org/monitor/2014/10/incarceration#:~:text=Mental%20illness%20among%20today's%20inmates,rampant%20and%20often%20co%2Doccurring

Bahora, M., Hanafi, S., Chien, V. H., & Compton, M. T. (2008). Preliminary evidence of effects of crisis intervention team training on self-efficacy and social distance. *Administration and Policy in Mental Health, 35*(3), 159–167. https://doi.org/10.1007/s10488-007-0153-8

Benbow, A. (2007). Mental illness, stigma, and the media. *Journal of Clinical Psychiatry, 68*(Suppl 2), 31–35.

Bonfine, N., Ritter, C., & Munetz, M. R. (2014). Police officer perceptions of the impact of crisis intervention team (CIT) programs. International Journal of Law and Psychiatry, 37(4), 341–350. https://doi.org/10.1016/j.ijlp.2014.02.004

Booth, A., Scantlebury, A., Hughes-Morley, A., Mitchell, N., Wright, K., Scott, W., & McDaid, C. (2017). Mental health training programmes for non-mental health trained professionals coming into contact with people with mental ill health: A systematic review of effectiveness. *BMC Psychiatry, 17*, 1–24.

Booty, M. D., Williams, R. G., & Crifasi, C. K. (2020). Evaluation of a crisis intervention team pilot program: Results from Baltimore, MD. *Community Mental Health Journal, 56*(2), 251–257. https://doi.org/10.1007/s10597-019-00474-w.

Bratina, M. P., Carrero, K. M., Kim, B., & Merlo, A. V. (2020). Crisis intervention team training: When police encounter persons with mental illness. *Police Practice & Research, 21*(3), 279–296. https://doi.org/10.1080/15614263.2018.1484290

Browning, S. L., Van Hasselt, V. B., Tucker, A. S., & Vecchi, G. M. (2011). Dealing with individuals who have mental illness: The crisis intervention team (CIT) in law enforcement. *The British Journal of Forensic Practice, 13*(4), 235–243. https://doi.org/10.1108/14636641111189990

Canada, K. E., Angell, B., & Watson, A. C. (2012). Intervening at the entry point: Differences in how CIT trained and non-CIT-trained officers describe responding to mental health related calls. *Community Mental Health Journal, 48*(6), 746–755. https://doi.org/10.1007/s10597-011-9430-9

Comartin, E. B., Swanson, L., & Kubiak, S. (2019). Mental health crisis location and police transportation decisions: The impact of crisis intervention team training on crisis center utilization. *Journal of Contemporary Criminal Justice, 35*(2), 241–260. https://doi.org/10.1177/1043986219836595

Compton, M. T., Bahora, M., Watson, A. C., & Oliva, J. R. (2008). A comprehensive review of extant research on crisis intervention team (CIT) programs. *Journal of the American Academy of Psychiatry and the Law Online, 36*(1), 47–55.

Compton, M. T., Bakeman, R., Broussard, B., D'Orio, B., & Watson, A. C. (2017). Police officers' volunteering for (rather than being assigned to) crisis intervention team (CIT) training: Evidence for a beneficial self-selection effect. *Behavioral Sciences & the Law, 35*(5-6), 470–479. https://doi.org/10.1002/bsl.2301

Compton, M. T., Bakeman, R., Broussard, B., Hankerson-Dyson, D., Husbands, L., Krishan, S., Stewart-Hutto, T., D'Orio, B. M., Oliva, J. R., Thompson, N. J., & Watson, A. C. (2014). The police-based crisis intervention team (CIT) model: II. Effects on level of force and resolution, referral, and arrest. *Psychiatric Services, 65*(4), 523–529. https://doi.org/10.1176/appi.ps.201300108

Compton, M. T., Broussard, B., Hankerson-Dyson, D., Krishan, S., Stewart, T., Oliva, J. R., & Watson, A. C. (2010). System- and policy-level challenges to full implementation of the crisis intervention team (CIT) model. *Journal of Police Crisis Negotiations, 10*(1-2), 72–85. https://doi.org/10.1080/15332581003757347

Compton, M. T., Broussard, B., Reed, T. A., Crisafio, A., & Watson, A. C. (2015). Surveys of police chiefs and sheriffs and of police officers about CIT programs. *Psychiatric Services, 66*(7), 760–763. https://doi.org/10.1176/appi.ps.201300451

Compton, M. T., Demir Neubert, B. N., Broussard, B., McGriff, J. A., Morgan, R., & Oliva, J. R. (2011). Use of force preferences and perceived effectiveness of actions among crisis intervention team (CIT) police officers and non-CIT officers in an escalating psychiatric crisis involving a subject with schizophrenia. *Schizophrenia Bulletin, 37*(4), 737–745. https://doi.org/10.1093/schbul/sbp146

Compton, M. T., Esterberg, M. L., McGee, R., Kotwicki, R. J., & Oliva, J. R. (2006). Brief reports: Crisis intervention team training: Changes in knowledge, attitudes, and stigma related to schizophrenia. *Psychiatric Services, 57*(8), 1199–1202. https://doi.org/10.1176/ps.2006.57.8.1199

Constantine, R. J., Petrila, J., Andel, R., Givens, E. M., Becker, M., Robst, J., Van Dorn, R., Boaz, T., Teague, G., Haynes, D., & Howe, A. (2010). Arrest trajectories of adult offenders with a serious mental illness. *Psychology, Public Policy, and Law, 16*(4), 319. https://doi.org/10.1037/a0020852

Cooper, V. G., Mclearen, A. M., & Zapf, P. A. (2004). Dispositional decisions with the mentally ill: Police perceptions and characteristics. *Police Quarterly, 7*(3), 295–310. https://doi.org/10.1177/1098611104267733

Council of State Governments Justice Center. (2021). *A matter of public health and safety: How states can support local crisis systems*. https://csgjusticecenter.org

Cowell, A. J., Broner, N., & Dupont, R. (2004). The cost-effectiveness of criminal justice diversion programs for people with serious mental illness co-occurring with substance abuse: Four case studies. *Journal of Contemporary Criminal Justice, 20*(3), 292–315. https://doi.org/10.1177/1043986204266892

Crisanti, A. S., Earheart, J. A., Rosenbaum, N. A., Tinney, M., & Duhigg, D. J. (2019). Beyond crisis intervention team (CIT) classroom training: Videoconference continuing education for law enforcement. *International Journal of Law and Psychiatry, 62*, 104–110.

Cross, A. B., Mulvey, E. P., Schubert, C. A., Griffin, P. A., Filone, S., Winckworth-Prejsnar, K., DeMatteo, D., & Heilbrun, K. (2014). An agenda for advancing research on crisis intervention teams for mental health emergencies. *Psychiatric Services, 65*(4), 530–536. https://doi.org/10.1176/appi.ps.201200566

Davidson, M. L. (2016). A criminal justice system-wide response to mental illness: Evaluating the effectiveness of the Memphis crisis intervention team training curriculum among law enforcement and correctional officers. *Criminal Justice Policy Review, 27*(1), 46–75. https://doi.org/10.1177/0887403414554997

Demir, B., Broussard, B., Goulding, S. M., & Compton, M. T. (2009). Beliefs about causes of schizophrenia among police officers before and after crisis intervention team training. *Community Mental Health Journal, 45*(5), 385–392. https://doi.org/10.1007/s10597-009-9194-7

Doulas, A. V., & Lurigio, A. J. (2010). Youth crisis intervention teams (CITs): A response to the fragmentation of the educational, mental health, and juvenile justice systems. *Journal of Police Crisis Negotiations, 10*(1-2), 241–263.

Ellis, H. A. (2014). Effects of a crisis intervention team (CIT) training program upon police officers before and after crisis intervention team training. *Archives of Psychiatric Nursing, 28*(1), 10–16. https://doi.org/10.1016/j.apnu.2013.10.003

Franz, S., & Borum, R. (2010). Crisis intervention teams may prevent arrests of people with mental illnesses. *Police Practice & Research: An International Journal, 12*(3), 265–272. https://doi.org/10.1080/15614263.2010.497664

Gard, B. A., & Ruzek, J. I. (2006). Community mental health response to crisis. *Journal of Clinical Psychology, 62*(8), 1029–1041.

Ghelani, A., Douglin, M., & Diebold, A. (2023). Effectiveness of Canadian police and mental health co-response crisis teams: A scoping review. *Social Work in Mental Health, 21*(1), 86–100.

Haigh, C., Kringen, A., & Kringen, J. (2018). Mental illness stigma: Limitations of crisis intervention team training. *Criminal Justice Policy Review, 31*(1), 42–57. https://doi.org/10.1177/0887403418804871

Hanafi, S., Bahora, M., Demir, B. N., & Compton, M. T. (2008). Incorporating crisis intervention team (CIT) knowledge and skills into the daily work of police officers: A focus group study. *Community Mental Health Journal, 44*(6), 427–432. https://doi.org/10.1007/s10597-008-9145-8

Hassell, K. D. (2020). The impact of crisis intervention team training for police. *International Journal of Police Science & Management, 22*(2), 159–170. https://doi.org/10.1177/1461355720909404

Hiday, V. A., & Burns, P. J. (2010). Mental illness and the criminal justice system. In T. L. Scheid & T. N. Brown (Eds.), *A handbook for the study of mental health: Social contexts, theories, and systems* (pp. 478–498). Cambridge University Press.

Ivancevich, D. M. (2015). Crisis intervention team (CIT) training for emergency medical services (EMS) personnel (publication no. 1598837) [Master's thesis, Florida Gulf Coast university]. Proquest Dissertations and Theses Global.

Klimley, K., Broj, B., Plombon, B., Haskamp, C., Christopher, R., Masias, E., Van Hasselt, V. B., & Black, R. A. (2021). Involuntary psychiatric admissions initiated by two us police departments: A descriptive analysis. *The Journal of Forensic Practice, 23*(4), 350–359. https://doi.org/10.1108/jfp-03-2021-0011

Kubiak, S., Comartin, E., Milanovic, E., Bybee, D., Tillander, E., Rabaut, C., Bisson, H., Dunn, L. M., Bouchard, M. J., Hill, T., & Schneider, S. (2017). Countywide implementation of crisis intervention teams: Multiple methods, measures and sustained outcomes. *Behavioral Sciences & the Law, 35*(5-6), 456–469. https://doi.org/10.1002/bsl.2305

Kubiak, S., Shamrova, D., & Comartin, E. (2019). Enhancing knowledge of adolescent mental health among law enforcement: Implementing youth-focused crisis intervention team training. *Evaluation and Program Planning, 73*, 44–52.

Kutylowski, M. (2020). Recommendations for improving encounters between law enforcement and mentally ill civilians.

Lattimore, P. K., Broner, N., Sherman, R., Frisman, L., & Shafer, M. S. (2003). A comparison of prebooking and postbooking diversion programs for mentally ill substance-using individuals with justice involvement. *Journal of Contemporary Criminal Justice, 19*(1), 30–64. https://doi.org/10.1177/1043986202239741

Lowder, E. M., Ray, B. R., & Gruenewald, J. A. (2019). Criminal justice professionals' attitudes toward mental illness and substance use. *Community Mental Health Journal, 55*, 428–439.

Marcus, N., & Stergiopoulos, V. (2022). Re-examining mental health crisis intervention: A rapid review comparing outcomes across police, co-responder and non-police models. *Health & Social Care in the Community, 30*(5), 1665–1679. https://doi.org/10.1111/hsc.13731

McNeeley, S., & Donley, C. (2020). Crisis intervention team training in a correctional setting: Examining compliance, mental health referrals, and use of force. *Criminal Justice and Behavior*. https://doi.org/10.1177/0093854820959394

Morabito, M. S., Kerr, A. N., Watson, A., Draine, J., Ottati, V., & Angell, B. (2012). Crisis intervention teams and people with mental illness: Exploring the factors that influence the use of force. *Crime & Delinquency, 58*(1), 57–77. https://doi.org/10.1177/0011128710372456

Morabito, M. S., & Socia, K. M. (2015). Is dangerousness a myth? Injuries and police encounters with people with mental illnesses. *Criminology & Public Policy, 14*(2), 253–276. https://doi.org/10.1111/1745-9133.12127

Mulay, A. L., Vayshenker, B., West, M. L., & Kelly, E. (2016). Crisis intervention training and implicit stigma toward mental illness: Reducing bias among criminal justice personnel. *International Journal of Forensic Mental Health, 15*(4), 369–381. https://doi.org/10.1080/14999013.2016.1208308

National Alliance on Mental Illness. (2023). Crisis intervention team (CIT) training. https://namilee.org/support-and-education/crisis-intervention-team-cit-training/

Nick, G. A., Williams, S., Lekas, H. M., Pahl, K., Blau, C., Kamin, D., & Fuller-Lewis, C. (2022). Crisis intervention team (CIT) training and impact on mental illness and substance use-related stigma among law enforcement. *Drug and Alcohol Dependence Reports, 5*, 100099. https://doi.org/10.1016/j.dadr.2022.100099

Park, K. (2019, August 30). *Poulsbo 'navigator' program partnering law enforcement with behavioral health specialists.* Bainbridge Island Review. https://www.bainbridgereview.com/news/poulsbo-navigator-program-partnering-law-enforcement-with-behavioral-health-specialists/

Peterson, J., Densley, J., & Erickson, G. (2020). Evaluation of 'the R-model' crisis intervention de-escalation training for law enforcement. *The Police Journal, 93*(4), 271–289.

Public Health Research Institute. (2005). Evaluation report of NAMI CIT implementation at the Androscoggin County jail

Puntis, S., Perfect, D., Kirubarajan, A., Bolton, S., Davies, F., Hayes, A., Harriss, E., & Molodynski, A. (2018). A systematic review of co-responder models of police mental health 'street' triage. *BMC Psychiatry, 18*(1), 1–11.

Ritter, C., Teller, J. L.S., Munetz, M. R., & Bonfine, N. (2010). Crisis intervention team (CIT) training: Selection effects and long-term changes in perceptions of mental illness and community preparedness. *Journal of Police Crisis Negotiations, 10*(1-2), 133-152. https://doi.org/10.1080/15332581003756992.

Rogers, M. S., McNiel, D. E., & Binder, R. L. (2019). Effectiveness of police crisis intervention training programs. *The Journal of the American Academy of Psychiatry and the Law, 47*(4), 414–421.

Shapiro, G. K., Cusi, A., Kirst, M., O'Campo, P., Nakhost, A., & Stergiopoulos, V. (2015). Co-responding police-mental health programs: A review. *Administration and Policy in Mental Health and Mental Health Services Research, 42*, 606–620.

Strauss, G., Glenn, M., Reddi, P., Afaq, I., Podolskaya, A., Rybakova, T., Saeed, O., Shah, V., Singh, B., Skinner, A., & El-Mallakh, R. S. (2005). Psychiatric disposition of patients brought in by crisis intervention team police officers. *Community Mental Health Journal, 41*(2), 223–228. https://doi.org/10.1007/s10597-005-2658-5

Taheri, S. A. (2016). Do crisis intervention teams reduce arrests and improve officer safety? A systematic review and meta-analysis. *Criminal Justice Policy Review, 27*(1), 76–96. https://doi.org/10.1177/0887403414556289

Teller, J. S., Munetz, M. R., Gil, K. M., & Ritter, C. (2006). Crisis intervention team training for police officers responding to mental disturbance calls. *Psychiatric Services, 57*(2), 232–237. https://doi.org/10.1176/appi.ps.57.2.232

Tully, T., & Smith, M. (2015). Officer perceptions of crisis intervention team training effectiveness. *The Police Journal, 88*(1), 51–64. https://doi.org/10.1177/0032258X15570558

US Department of Justice, Office of Public Affairs. (2015, April 16). *Justice department applauds adoption of police department-wide tactical de-escalation training program in Seattle* [Press release], 15–462.

Watson, A. C., Compton, M. T., & Draine, J. N. (2017). The crisis intervention team (CIT) model: An evidence-based policing practice? *Behavioral Sciences & the Law, 35*(5-6), 431–441.

Watson, A. C., Morabito, M. S., Draine, J., & Ottati, V. (2008). Improving police response to persons with mental illness: A multi-level conceptualization of CIT. *International Journal of Law and Psychiatry, 31*(4), 359–368.

Watson, A. C., Ottati, V. C., Draine, J., & Morabito, M. (2011). CIT in context: The impact of mental health resource availability and district saturation on call dispositions. *International Journal of Law and Psychiatry, 34*(4), 287–294. https://doi.org/10.1016/j.ijlp.2011.07.008

Watson, A. C., Owens, L. K., Wood, J., & Compton, M. T. (2021). The impact of crisis intervention team response, dispatch coding, and location on the outcomes of police encounters with individuals with mental illnesses in Chicago. *Policing (Oxford, England), 15*(3), 1948–1962. https://doi.org/10.1093/police/paab010

Wells, W., & Schafer, J. (2006). Officer perceptions of police responses to persons with a mental illness. *Policing: An International Journal of Police Strategies & Management, 29*, 578–601. https://doi.org/10.1108/13639510610711556

Wood, J., Swanson, J. W., Burris, S., & Robertson, A. G. (2011). *Police interventions with persons affected by mental illnesses*. Center for Public Health Law Research.

World Health Organization. (2022). Mental disorders. *World Health Organization.*. https://www.who.int/news-room/fact-sheets/detail/mental-disorders

Yang, S.-M., Gill, C., Kanewske, L. C., & Thompson, P. S. (2018). Exploring police response to mental health calls in a nonurban area: A case study of Roanoke County, Virginia. *Victims & Offenders, 13*(8), 1132–1152. https://doi.org/10.1080/15564886.2018.1512540

Chapter 8
Responding to Alzheimer's Disease Emergencies: Crisis Intervention Training for Law Enforcement

Jillian Crocker, Hannah Friedland, and Ashley Stripling

As the population ages and diversifies, police officers in the United States are facing increasing calls to respond to late-life crisis situations, including those brought on by Alzheimer's disease (Brown et al., 2017; Lachs et al., 2004; Tyuse et al., 2016). This chapter aims to provide context to better understand why these types of emergencies are happening more frequently, as well as, how to effectively recognize and react to crises involving individuals with Alzheimer's disease and related dementias to improve life for everyone involved.

> It is 4:30 on a Thursday afternoon and an officer is dispatched to the parking lot of the local Veterans Affairs Medical Center. Upon arrival, they discover a 72-year-old White man seated in his vehicle with a firearm. The nursing staff shares that he had recently received a diagnosis of Alzheimer's disease after his family insisted on testing due to concerns about his driving. It is revealed that he has difficulty hearing those around him and has had several minor car accidents. He has never seen a mental health professional and "doesn't see why he should start now." He has no history of homicidal thoughts or anger but appears to be experiencing severe suicidal ideation. It is also discovered that he has a family history of Alzheimer's disease and cared for both of his parents until they passed away. The staff reports that he "does not want to burden his family" and will "take care of it himself."

Americans are living longer than ever before, creating unique opportunities along with new challenges (Rajan et al., 2021; Congressional Budget Office, 2024; Vespa et al., 2020). These challenges, like the one above, translate into increased crisis calls to law enforcement (Brown et al., 2014, 2017; Lachenmayr et al., 2000; Liljegren et al., 2018; Sun et al., 2019; Tyuse et al., 2016). This chapter aims to provide context to better understand why crises involving individuals with Alzheimer's disease and related dementias are happening more frequently, as well as how to effectively recognize and react to these types of emergencies.

Present Address:
J. Crocker · H. Friedland · A. Stripling (✉)
College of Psychology, Nova Southeastern University, Fort Lauderdale, FL, USA
e-mail: astripling@nova.edu

V. B. Van Hasselt and M. L. Bourke (eds.), *Advances in First Responder Mental Health*,
Advances in First Responder Mental Health 1,
https://doi.org/10.1007/978-3-032-27978-1_8

Shifting Demographics

The first recorded case of Alzheimer's disease, over 100 years ago, involved a 50-year-old woman who displayed symptoms of paranoia, confusion, sleeping difficulty, memory impairment, and aggression (Hippius & Neundörfer, 2003). Upon her death, her brain was examined, and distinct abnormalities now recognized as plaques and neurofibrillary tangles associated with Alzheimer's disease were discovered (Hippius & Neundörfer, 2003). Today, our understanding of Alzheimer's disease, as well as the frequency of dementia-related emergencies handled by law enforcement, has increased significantly due to shifts in demographics and infrastructures (GBD 2021 Demographics Collaborators, 2024; Rajan et al., 2021; Sun et al., 2019).

Aging in America

Globally, life expectancy is projected to increase from 78.7 years to 82.2 years over the next 30 years (GBD 2021 Demographics Collaborators, 2024). In the United States, advancements in healthcare, shifts in birth rates and immigration patterns, and a reduction in mortality rates have collectively contributed to longer lifespans (GBD 2021 Demographics Collaborators, 2024; *The Demographic Outlook*, 2024). Estimates suggest that individuals in the United States will experience unprecedented longevity, living fulfilling lives well into their eighties (GBD 2021 Demographics Collaborators, 2024; Vespa et al., 2020). Consequently, older adults are anticipated to account for 23% of the United States population (United States Census Bureau, 2023), making the U.S. older than ever before. As the population demographic shifts, older adults, who are more likely to live with chronic illnesses such as Alzheimer's disease, find themselves in need of infrastructures that will provide appropriate support (2023 Alzheimer's Disease Facts and Figures [ADFF], 2023; Hacker, 2024). Unfortunately, the changing landscape of mental healthcare within the United States over the past 75 years has complicated the availability of care.

Deinstitutionalization and the Rise of Community Policing

In the 1950s, the United States began a process of deinstitutionalization, which involved the closure of public psychiatric hospitals and mental health facilities (Grob, 1991; Lamb & Bachrach, 2001; Tyuse et al., 2016). Deinstitutionalization altered the infrastructure available to support those with mental healthcare needs, including those with dementias, and placed increased responsibility on family, friends, and communities (Grob, 1991; Lamb & Bachrach, 2001; Tyuse et al., 2016). Since these informal systems often lacked prior training, law enforcement's role in addressing mental health crises or suicide threats, like the one at the start of this chapter, has grown to fulfill demand (Brown et al., 2014; Liederbach & Stelle, 2010; Tyuse et al., 2016). Specifically, due in part to deinstitutionalization and other geopolitical events of the 60s and the 70s, the expectation of law enforcement to address mental health needs through community policing practices has become the norm (Greene, 2000; Oliver, 1992). Today, police officers in the United States play a vital role in maintaining public order, enforcing laws, defending constitutional rights, preserving democratic values, and guarding communal well-being (American Bar Association, 2020; Schuck, 2024). This shift toward trust, mutual respect, and understanding between officers and citizens has built the foundation for public safety and community cooperation; however, it has also increased expectations and responsibilities (Hawdon et al., 2003; Peyton et al., 2019).

This increase in expectations and responsibilities for law enforcement officers can take a personal toll. The nature of police work inherently involves exposure to traumatic incidents, such as violence, life-threatening situations, and human tragedy (Haugen et al., 2012; Lee & Wu, 2024). The cumulative impact of police work can manifest psychologically as post-traumatic stress disorder, depression, anxiety, burnout, and other mental health concerns (Alves et al., 2023; Craddock & Telesco, 2022; Klimley et al., 2018; Syed et al., 2020). However, police officers are often resistant to acknowledge psychological distress, as they have been conditioned to maintain an image of toughness and emotional stoicism (Kirschman, 2007). Officers may feel compelled to internalize their stress, fearing that seeking help could be misconstrued as a sign of weakness or lead to doubts about their ability to fulfill their duties (Blum, 2000). The reluctance to discuss mental health openly within the force can lead to isolation, worsened symptoms, and contemplation of suicide (Wheeler et al., 2021).

In examining protective factors against these adverse effects, preparation, prior training, social support, and appropriate coping mechanisms have been identified as fostering resilience (Alves et al., 2023; Anders et al., 2022; Klimley et al., 2018; Syed et al., 2020). Given that training protocols can differ widely by state, the crisis management of late-life emergencies due to conditions like Alzheimer's disease is not uniformly addressed in the United States (Blumberg et al., 2019). This is unfortunate considering the positive impacts that late-life crisis training, including training on Alzheimer's disease, can have on police officer competence in providing assistance during these emergencies (American Psychiatric Association, 2022). The expected rise of these types of emergencies warrants educational programs, such as crisis intervention team programs, that focus on late-life issues (Hawley et al., 2005; Tyuse et al., 2016).

Alzheimer's Disease Training

Of the older adults encountered by crisis intervention team law enforcement officers, one in five have a diagnosis of dementia and one in three are suicidal (Tyuse et al., 2016). Although most older adults do not develop dementia like Alzheimer's disease or face other late-life mental health emergencies, such as depression and suicide, increased awareness of the signs and symptoms can prevent crises before they occur and ensure appropriate intervention (Ma et al., 2023). Thus, in line with best training practices (Hutter et al., 2023), the following section will provide education about Alzheimer's disease dementias and related mental health emergencies, as well as provide recommendations to optimize police training for crisis intervention involving Alzheimer's disease.

Alzheimer's Disease

Out of the 58 million older adults living in the United States, there are currently 6.7 million Americans living with Alzheimer's disease (2023 Alzheimer's Disease Facts and Figures [ADFF], 2023; United States Census Bureau, 2023), By the year 2060, the number of people living with Alzheimer's disease is expected to double to 13.8 million (2023 ADFF, 2023). Women currently account for almost two-thirds of Americans with Alzheimer's disease, which may be due to Alzheimer's disease's association with increased age and women's longer life expectancies (2023 ADFF, 2023). However, it is important to note that the chances of receiving a diagnosis may not accurately reflect the actual prevalence of Alzheimer's disease, as almost 40% of people with probable signs and symptoms are not diagnosed (Amjad et al., 2018). Although White Americans are diagnosed with Alzheimer's disease more frequently, other races and ethnicities are more likely to live with the disorder (Amjad et al., 2018; APA, 2022). Non-Hispanic Black and Hispanic individuals are at higher risk of developing Alzheimer's disease than White Americans but have lower chances of being diagnosed (APA, 2022). The variability between Alzheimer's disease symptoms and diagnosis rates complicates the determination of which older adults might be impacted, but understanding the causes and symptoms of Alzheimer's disease can help identify those at risk.

Alzheimer's disease is a type of neurocognitive disorder or dementia (American Psychiatric Association [APA], 2022). Dementias, or neurocognitive disorders, refer to a decline in cognitive functioning that causes a significant change in daily life and can be caused by Alzheimer's disease, cerebrovascular disease, traumatic brain injuries, and other medical conditions (APA, 2022). Since normal functioning can vary from person to person, an official diagnosis of Alzheimer's disease requires specialized assessment. The current diagnostic process for a neurocognitive disorder caused by Alzheimer's disease often involves clinical interviewing, genetic testing, and/or neuropsychological testing with the patient, family members, and healthcare professionals. The clinical interview may ask questions about changes in activities of daily living (e.g. managing medications, finances, taking care of oneself) to determine the extent to which cognitive impairment impacts independent functioning (APA, 2022). A diagnosis of major neurocognitive disorder is made when the impairment is severe enough that other people are needed to manage medications and healthcare (APA, 2022). Conversely, mild neurocognitive disorder, also known as mild cognitive impairment, is characterized by a less severe impact on independence (APA, 2022). At the mild stages, patients may have developed strategies to help compensate for difficulties (APA, 2022). Early diagnosis is crucial to help people and their families develop solutions and plan.

Currently, the prevention and development of Alzheimer's disease are unknown. However, researchers have identified that Alzheimer's disease involves the accumulation of a brain protein called beta-amyloid and the formation of neurofibrillary tangles (Rao et al., 2022). Brain damage is usually found in areas that are responsible for memory and starts 20 years before noticeable symptoms (Bateman et al., 2012; Rao et al., 2022). Initial symptoms often include cognitive changes, such as difficulty remembering novel information, reported by the individual or family members. Please see Table 8.1 for a full list. Symptoms typically start to appear between 70 and 89 years of age, presenting as memory difficulties that frequently co-occur with difficulty planning and organizing (APA, 2022). The disease can start earlier than 70 years old, but its prevalence increases with age (APA, 2022). As Alzheimer's disease progresses, cognitive impairments worsen and impact other areas of the brain, causing disorientation, impaired judgment and impulse control, and personality changes (APA, 2022).

Many individuals diagnosed with Alzheimer's disease have witnessed it in their siblings, parents, or grandparents. Alzheimer's disease is genetic, and one method of confirming the diagnosis is for the clinician to detect a family history of the disorder (APA, 2022). Like the Veteran's situation at the start of the chapter, many people diagnosed with Alzheimer's disease are already familiar with the disorder and can recognize the implications of being diagnosed. Although familiarity with the disease is not always present, the ability to learn and retain new information becomes challenging, resulting in a tendency to rely on memories from previous years (APA, 2022). Long-term memory usually remains intact at the initial stages of Alzheimer's disease, whereas short-term memory is impaired (APA, 2022). Therefore, the Veteran's memories of caring for his parents remain vivid.

It is also likely that the Veteran has been a caregiver for many years and is aware of what his family will experience. Individuals with Alzheimer's disease can live with the disease for as long as 20 years (APA, 2022). The level of care needed increases as the disease progresses, making the later stages especially difficult for caregivers to manage. The survival duration could potentially become longer than 20 years as treatments continue to advance, leading to a higher chance of living with the diagnosis. However, early diagnosis not only improves outcomes for those with Alzheimer's disease and their family, but could also prove important when effective treatments become available (Amjad et al., 2018). Importantly for crisis intervention and prevention, early diagnosis holds implications for mitigating safety risks and managing problematic behaviors (Amjad et al., 2018; Scogin & Mieskowski, 2015). Specifically, programs like the Safe Return registry through the national Alzheimer's Association and U.S. Department of Justice help to identify, locate, and return those who wander or become lost due to memory impairment (Bateman et al., 2012).

Table 8.1 Alzheimer's disease state and subsequent signs

Alzheimer's Disease State	Impairment	Signs
Mild Cognitive Impairment	Independent in everyday activities	• Behavioral symptoms (see Table 8.2) • Concerns of cognitive changes, such as difficulty remembering new things, reported by the individual or family members
Mild Neurocognitive Disorder	Capable of carrying out daily tasks independently, with potential development of strategies to help with cognitive changes	• Difficulty recalling recent events • Reliance on calendar/list • Becoming easily lost • Needs occasional reminders • Repeating to the same person over a few weeks • Loses track of bill payments • Difficulty multitasking or resuming tasks after being interrupted • Increased fatigue, especially from large social gatherings and multi-stage projects
Major Neurocognitive Disorder	Difficulty being independent in everyday activities due to cognitive impairment and concerns for safety	*Beginning Stages* • Repeats within the same conversation • Cannot keep track of lists or items • Requires frequent reminders to take medications
		Later Stages • Requires assistance to plan daily activities • Struggling with activities that were once familiar, such as using tools or driving • Gets lost in familiar places • Feels confused at dusk when shadows and reduced light levels change perception

At this time there is no cure for Alzheimer's disease, and since treatments can only manage symptoms, awareness and prevention programs are of the utmost importance. With regard to symptom management of Alzheimer's disease, cholinesterase inhibitors and N-methyl-D-aspartate receptor antagonists are commonly prescribed to ease the clinical symptoms (Bateman et al., 2012; Haddad et al., 2022). The search for additional medications is ongoing, and the National Institutes of Health (NIH, 2023) has allocated an additional $100 million to research Alzheimer's disease and

Table 8.2 Alzheimer's symptoms, descriptions, and related emergencies

Clinical symptom	Defined	Emergencies
Apathy	Lack of motivation and general indifference to one's surroundings	Delays accessing medical care, dangerous environment, hoarding, falls, abuse, and neglect
Depression	Depressed mood that can cause loss of interest or pleasure, changes in sleep and appetite, fatigue, feelings of worthlessness or excessive guilt, and thoughts of death	Financial exploitation, suicidal ideation, self-neglect, suicide attempts
Agitation	Disruptive, non-aggressive motor activity	Sleep disturbances, wandering
	Disruptive, non-aggressive vocal activity	Uncooperating
Aggression	Physically aggressive behaviors	Hitting, pushing, kicking, scratching, grabbing objects
	Verbally aggressive behaviors	Cursing, temper outbursts, unusual noises, screaming
Psychosis	Hallucinations, delusions, misidentifications	Paranoia and other delusions, accusing others of theft
Learning and memory	Ability to learn, remember, and recognize things from recently or long ago	Recognizing familiar people's names and faces, recalling events, stealing, becoming lost or disoriented, driving difficulties, managing finances, medication compliance

dementia in the 2024 fiscal year. Given the lack of effective treatment and the timeline of the disease, older adults who develop a neurocognitive disorder can be more vulnerable to crisis situations. Therefore, understanding the warning signs and nature of neurocognitive disorders, like Alzheimer's disease, can enhance awareness and facilitate communication, particularly during situations threatening safety.

Alzheimer's Disease Emergencies

The progressive decline of memory function in individuals with Alzheimer's disease is typically accompanied by a range of behavioral and psychological symptoms (BPSD) (Finkel et al., 1997). These symptoms are present in over 90% of dementia cases and can vary in severity and inappropriateness, ranging from physical and verbal aggressiveness to depression, anxiety, social isolation, and disrupted sleep (Cohen-Mansfield et al., 1995; Steinberg et al., 2003, 2008). These symptoms can be challenging to treat and recognize, as they may occur without any apparent trigger before a diagnosis of dementia is made (Table 8.1). As dementia progresses, impairments may impact the person's ability to communicate new symptoms.

Behavioral and psychological symptoms are often the primary reasons for Alzheimer's disease emergencies involving law enforcement, as dementia increases vulnerability to other stressors (e.g. medical problems, caregiver concerns, unsafe environments) (Kales et al., 2015; Tyuse et al., 2016). In examining crisis intervention calls for older adults, the most frequent reason for calls was for suicide, followed by "disturbance" and "welfare checks" (Tyuse et al., 2016). The manifestation and timing of symptoms vary from person to person, but have been linked to the stage of dementia (Table 8.2). For example, apathy typically emerges early in individuals with Alzheimer's disease, and as the disease progresses, agitation, aggression, delusions, and auditory hallucinations may ensue, creating a greater burden on caregivers (Ballard et al., 2009). When caregivers lack access to resources, their strain is increased, often resulting in suicide attempts, wandering, and physical altercations. In some of these cases, law enforcement becomes involved, especially if caregivers are not trained to handle the symptoms without imposing a threat. To wit, the highest proportion of emergency calls involving older adults are initiated by family caregivers, highlighting the complexity of managing the symptoms associated with dementia (Tyuse et al., 2016). Understanding the symptoms of Alzheimer's disease and the types of emergencies associated with them is vital for Alzheimer's disease law enforcement training programs, such as Alzheimer's Aware, to assess the needs and ensure the appropriate medical and social service referrals (Brown et al., 2017; Shanley et al., 2004).

Apathy

Apathy is a lack of motivation and general indifference to one's surroundings (APA, 2022). Alzheimer's disease and frontotemporal dementias are often associated with apathy, particularly for men (APA, 2022). Apathy persists throughout Alzheimer's disease progression, which complicates the management of other symptoms outlined below and often necessitates law enforcement involvement (Ballard et al., 2009). Given the extensive time spent with individuals with dementia and potential communication difficulties, caregivers are the front line in detecting and managing apathy-related crises (Burling et al., 2024). However, even with care, persistent apathy can result in the neglect of fundamental needs, leading to health crises and environmental hazards. Specifically, apathy associated with Alzheimer's disease and related dementias can compromise an individual's ability to effectively eat and drink, maintain personal hygiene (e.g. showering, shaving), and take medications as prescribed, potentially resulting in self-neglect (Pavlou & Lachs, 2008; Toot et al., 2013). Even in situations where a caregiver is involved, apathy may decrease an individual's ability to care for themselves despite multiple reminders, which increases the likelihood of hospitalization or even death (Toot et al., 2013; van der Linde et al., 2017).

Additionally, individuals with apathy caused by dementia may not be able to recognize environmental hazards that might increase their risk of falling, such as hoarding (Henstra et al., 2019). Take for example, Ms. A:

> First responders are dispatched to investigate a foul odor coming from an apartment, after being called by a next door neighbor. Upon arrival, Ms. A, a 91-year-old, White woman greets law enforcement at the front door. She appears well-groomed, and happy to see the officers but disoriented. In her home, there is an alarming amount of clutter to the point of posing a hazard to her health (i.e. large piles of unread newspapers by the door, no surface left uncluttered) and has a very foul odor. When she is questioned, she has problems speaking ("I have it on the back of my tongue"), with her memory ("Who are you again?"), and judgment ("I wasn't sure what to keep"). During the visit the phone began to ring, Ms. A immediately began rummaging through a large pile near the couch even though the ringing appeared to be coming from the other side of the room. As the ringing continues, she becomes quite agitated insisting "Don't just stand there find the "hook snicky before it gets away!"

What should the officer do?

Hoarding can lead to unsafe environments by increasing the risk of fires, infestations, gastrointestinal problems due to eating spoiled food, respiratory ailments due to dust/mold, and exacerbation of medical conditions (Hwang et al., 1998). Unfortunately, it can be a common dementia behavior that often results in a welfare check by first responders (Hwang et al., 1998). Welfare checks may become increasingly common as the neurocognitive disorder progresses, and caregivers may struggle to motivate or engage individuals with apathy even as they retain the ability to complete activities (Stanton & Carson, 2016). Luckily, in the case of Ms. A police officers on the scene were able to build trust and help facilitate her transitions to a safer living situation through the appropriate community referrals, thus preventing further crisis situations and welfare checks.

Agitation and Aggression

Individuals diagnosed with Alzheimer's disease may experience pain, fear, anger, disorientation, and confusion which are often expressed as agitation and aggression (Knight, 2004).

Physically Non-aggressive Behaviors. Psychomotor agitation is a persistent symptom in dementia characterized by aimless walking, pacing, restlessness, wandering, and repetitive actions, as well as difficulties with dressing, undressing, and sleeping (Ballard et al., 2009; Cohen-Mansfield et al., 1995). It is difficult to determine the exact cause of agitation, but restlessness is often observed after periods of inactivity or daytime naps (Zarit & Zarit, 2011). Agitation may also occur when the individual is uncomfortable (e.g. experiencing pain, hunger, boredom) and unable to communicate their needs, so the discomfort is expressed through increased behavioral problems (Zarit & Zarit, 2011). In certain situations, caregiving crises may require immediate help and emergency line contact. For example, consider:

> Its 10 on a Monday morning and an officer is dispatched to a busy street in a residential neighbor. Upon arrival, they discover an 81-year-old shirtless man pacing back and forth

> across an intersection disrupting traffic. Onlookers report they had tried to help him cross, but he continues to stop halfway and return to the curb almost causing multiple car accidents. Despite their attempts, no one has been able to communicate with him and he has just continued to mutter to himself "Got to get to the store" repeatedly.

What should the officer do?

Individuals with Alzheimer's disease can become unable to navigate familiar unfamiliar environments as the disease progresses; this paired with physical non-aggressive pacing can lead to wandering (Uc et al., 2004). In fact, it is estimated that approximately one in three of those living with Alzheimer's disease or related dementias living in the community will wander, which can lead to an increased risk of injury or death (Byard & Langlois, 2019; Jeong et al., 2016). In the case above, prior late-life crisis intervention training had made the officers aware of *The Safe Return program.* The program enabled them to use effective communication techniques to escort the gentleman to a safe location while they accessed the national database and contacted his daughter (Lachenmayr et al., 2000).

In addition to *The Safe Return program, Project Lifesaver* and *Silver Alert* were created due to the increasing concerns about missing persons (Petonito et al., 2013). Silver alerts broadcast information about missing older adults with Alzheimer's disease, dementia, or cognitive impairments to ensure their safe return (Petonito et al., 2013). *The Silver Alert* system distributes details and descriptions to the public primarily through television stations and radio, hoping that someone may recognize the individual and report their location (Petonito et al., 2013). Using a *Silver Alert* system, caregivers and families can add "eyes and ears" for the safe return of the older adult to their home (Petonito et al., 2013). Consider the above example with a different scenario with the *Silver Alert*:

> It is 9 on a Tuesday morning, and a caregiver notices their husband has gone missing. She calls 911, and first responders use the *Silver Alert* system to notify the public. Within an hour, an officer is dispatched to a local gas station where someone thinks they have located the missing man and his vehicle. Upon arrival, they identify the women's 77-year-old husband pacing across the parking lot. Onlookers report they had tried to help him, but he refused to go inside the gas station to get cool or return to his car. His wife comes to the scene, and the husband immediately goes to her, and he is safely returned home.

Verbally Non-aggressive Agitation. Individuals with Alzheimer's disease and related dementias may also exhibit disruptive but non-aggressive vocal behaviors, including constant demands for attention, verbal assertiveness, expressions of dissatisfaction, negativism, uncooperativeness, outbursts of anger, cursing, and screaming (Cohen-Mansfield et al., 1995). Such behaviors can generate crisis scenarios when individuals resist cooperation in caregiving situations or impede first responders' efforts to assist. Moreover, persistent behavioral resistance, even in the advanced stages of dementia, may result from people communicating with them in a condescending tone (Shaw & Gordon, 2021).

Aggression

As Alzheimer's disease progresses, individuals lose coping skills and conditions such as delirium become more prevalent, consequently increasing the likelihood of aggression (Knight, 2004). At this stage, agitation and aggression can be expressed verbally (i.e. cursing, temper outbursts, unusual noises, screaming) or physically (i.e. hitting, pushing, scratching, grabbing, kicking), necessitating the involvement of law enforcement for a "disturbance" (Cohen-Mansfield et al., 1995; Tyuse et al., 2016). Take for example, Mrs. D:

> It is 3 pm on a Saturday, when officers are dispatched to the residence of Mrs. D, who lives with her daughter. Mrs. D called 911 to report that she had been robbed and the intruder was still in the house. When the officers arrive at the home, Mrs. D almost falls letting them in. There is no sign of forced entry and the only other person inside the home is her caregiver. Mrs. D is not able to focus her attention and begins to act impulsively. She becomes physically aggressive during questioning and attempts to hit and push the officers out of her home. They notice that Mrs. D is not sweating despite the heat and lack of air-conditioning in the home. She begins to accuse them of trying to rob her daughter's home and starts shouting "How dare you! I don't need your help!"

What should the officer do?

A delirium induced by heat stroke can create a situation where Mrs. D initiated the call above. With proper training, the law enforcement at the scene were able to identify that Mrs. D required medical care and provided the appropriate referral and hand-off. Prior training allowed the police at the scene to understand the medical and social complexity of Mrs. D's care and to engage in a collaborative community approach (Brown et al., 2014; Liederbach & Stelle, 2010). Specifically, they were able to perceive that the aggression was not personal and used low, clear, calming tones to communicate with Mrs. D. Once her agitation and aggression reduced, they collaborated with her caregiver and integrated simple orientating statements, such as "It sure seems warm for April." This allowed her to drink water and remain safe until medical personnel arrived, despite her psychotic feature of paranoia.

Psychosis

Psychotic features are often observed in various neurocognitive disorders, including Alzheimer's disease, especially in the early to middle stages of the disease (APA, 2022). Although disorganized speech and behavior are uncommon, individuals may experience hallucinations and persecutory delusions (i.e. paranoia) (APA, 2022). For instance, people with memory loss might forget that they have given away an item or no longer have it (Knight, 2004). They may be more inclined to believe the item was stolen, especially if they have limited insight into their difficulties (Knight, 2004). They might act upon or believe these delusions to protect themselves, as exemplified by Mrs. D's aggressive behavior (APA, 2022; Knight, 2004). Caregivers and other people around the individual with a neurocognitive disorder can worsen these circumstances by arguing about the mistaken belief without considering the person's condition (Knight, 2004). In Mrs. D's example above, the initial call was made after her caregiver had removed her dishes from their cabinet for cleaning and Mrs. D believed them stole. By not directly confronting her belief that she had been robbed and maintaining calm tones, the officers were able to build a trusting relationship until medical personnel arrived.

Memory

Alzheimer's disease and related neurocognitive disorders can cause memory and learning difficulties, leading to potential crises. In the early stages of the disease, individuals may have trouble remembering recent events and recognizing familiar people (APA, 2022). As the disease progresses, recalling familiar routes can become more difficult, making driving dangerous (Uc et al., 2004). Difficulty in recognizing familiar surroundings can impact their ability to identify threatening situations, inadvertently putting them at risk (APA, 2022). For example, they may unknowingly let strangers or burglars into their homes by opening the door at night without knowing who is there (Toot et al., 2013) or unintentionally steal goods at the store if they forget to pay. Pathological stealing is associated with frontotemporal dementia in individuals as young as 48 years old, further complicating memory deficits (Mendez, 2011):

> It's 8:00 on a Thursday morning, when officers are dispatched to the local grocery store due to reports of theft. The manager called 911 to report that Ms. V had taken ice cream multiple times over the past month. Ms. V makes personal comments to strangers, takes items from other people's carts, and insists we need to prepare for the storm coming. When questioned by officers, Ms. V drops the ice cream and begins to walk away, mumbling under her breath. The officer asks where she lives, and Ms. V tells her she lives "right around the corner" and gives the officer her license. Upon closer look, it appears she lives over 30 minutes away. After reviewing her license, the officer became aware that Ms. V has had numerous reports of theft, including stealing mail and mangos from the neighbors.

What should the officer do?

Ms. V appears not orientated to the time or location and compulsively takes items from people's carts (Mendez, 2011). Memory and frontal lobe impairment caused Ms. V difficulty recalling answers when questioned by the manager and first responders, like in the cases presented in the chapter. The first responders may become aware that her problems impact her ability to remember familiar places, such as her local grocery store. She is becoming more reliant on her long-term memory to fill in the details of the incident (2023 ADFF, 2023). The officer could assess the situation to help her return the stolen goods and contact a family member or close friend. Memory difficulties may also lead individuals to forget to take their medications as prescribed, which can lead to further crises, such as delirium. In addition to adhering to medications, managing finances and keeping track of dates and tasks can become difficult (APA, 2022).

Depression

Self-neglect is common across various mental health conditions and is associated with late-life depression and dementia as the disease progresses (Abrams et al., 2002; Alexopoulos, 2003). Symptoms of depression, isolation, and anxiety may also serve as indicators of dementia even in individuals with no family history of the disease (Ballard et al., 2009). Depression is strongly associated with Alzheimer's disease, with prevalence rates ranging from 25 to 75% compared to 4.4% in the general population (APA, 2022; Chi et al., 2015; Ferrari et al., 2013; Li et al., 2014). Individuals with Alzheimer's disease experience depression at a rate approximately ten times higher, with women being at the highest risk (APA, 2022; Chi et al., 2015; Ferrari et al., 2013). However, depression often goes untreated in older adults due to a lack of recognition of its symptoms. Depression presents challenges in diagnosis as its symptoms may overlap with those of various neurocognitive disorders, leading to uncertainty regarding the underlying cause of cognitive impairment (APA, 2022).

Among older adults, depression has emerged as a significant predictor of financial exploitation (Lichtenberg, 2016; Lichtenberg et al., 2013). Financial exploitation involves the unauthorized use of an older adult's money and property, including theft, scams, abuse of trust, coercion, and financial mismanagement (Conrad et al., 2010; Lichtenberg, 2016). When an individual's social needs are unfulfilled, fraud is the highest among those with depression (Lichtenberg et al., 2013). The vulnerability to financial exploitation is especially pronounced in older adults with Alzheimer's disease in the mild stages, where susceptibility to scams is heightened due to subtle cognitive decline, particularly in episodic memory and perceptual speed (Boyle et al., 2012; Han et al., 2015). Vulnerability due to episodic memory deficits is a key cognitive feature of depression (Boyle et al., 2012; Han et al., 2015; James et al., 2021).

Furthermore, depression's association with suicidal ideation presents a significant concern, with almost a third of Crisis Intervention Team (CIT) calls related to suicide (Tyuse et al., 2016). The risk of suicide is particularly pronounced among older adults, especially men over 65, whose risk factors often intersect with those of neurocognitive disorders (APA, 2022). Older adults disproportionately account for more suicides, likely because their attempts are more lethal than younger adults (Conwell, 2014). Factors, such as physical illness, disability, and loss of independence, contribute to increased risks of suicide for older adults with Alzheimer's disease and related dementias.

Take for example, the veteran at the start of the chapter. In this case prior training in late-life depression and dementia-related emergencies allowed officers to maintain their safety while keeping the veteran safe. Specifically, officers on the scene had previously completed a lecture on crisis intervention for suicide, followed by role-plays where they practiced active listening and collaborative problem-solving to establish rapport and create a safe environment. Once the veteran was unarmed, they were able to use VA resources to provide the mental healthcare he needed.

Conclusion

The symptoms of Alzheimer's and related dementias increase healthcare costs, nursing home placement, and morbidity and diminish the quality of life for individuals with Alzheimer's and their families (Beeri et al., 2002; Banerjee et al., 2006; Kales et al., 2015; Ornstein & Gaugler, 2012; Wancata et al., 2003; Yaffe et al., 2002; Van Den Wijngaart et al., 2007). Given the increasing lifespan in the United States, people are living longer, and the impact of Alzheimer's disease has expanded to include entire communities, leading to increased Alzheimer's disease-related emergencies (Brown et al., 2017; Lachs et al., 2004; Tyuse et al., 2016). In response, several comprehensive trainings have been developed to prepare law enforcement agents to interact with individuals living with dementia (Bateman et al., 2012; Bennell et al., 2022; Brown et al., 2017; Petonito et al., 2013).

Much like this chapter, the initial step in many of these programs involve education about Alzheimer's disease and its associated symptoms (Center for Public Safety & Justice, 2015; Wisconsin Department of Health Services, 2016). Such knowledge enables officers to recognize the conditions and situations they may encounter. Following the lecture, training often applies the knowledge obtained through role-playing, discussion, and provision of health education resources (Brown et al., 2017; Lachenmayr et al., 2000). Role-plays or scenario-based training allows officers to familiarize themselves with stressful situations and safely practice skills with actors (Beinicke & Muff, 2019; Hutter, 2023; Oleszkiewicz et al., 2022). Realism and adaptability are utilized to foster techniques for questioning and interviewing people with Alzheimer's disease and effectively communicating in common crisis situations, such as wandering (Alzheimer's Association, 2019; Center for Public Safety & Justice, 2015). This multifaceted approach prepares officers to effectively protect and engage with individuals with Alzheimer's disease. More recently, online training and virtual reality have provided the ability to expand knowledge and replicate real-life situations (Kleygrewe et al., 2024). For example, the Alzheimer's Association offers a free online *Approaching Alzheimer's: First Responder Training* (alz.org/firstresponders). With input from first responders, the Alzheimer's Association developed a six-module course aimed at effectively identifying the disease and responding to dementia-related emergencies. This training emphasizes person-centered dementia care, preparing officers to engage with the unique social, behavioral, and safety needs of individuals with Alzheimer's disease, thus filling in gaps for those without departmental training (Alzheimer's Association, 2019).

It is the hope of the authors that this chapter will bring greater awareness to Alzheimer's and related dementia emergencies, as well as provide guidance and resources for their management, thus improving the lives and promoting thriving communities.

References

2023 Alzheimer's Disease Facts and Figures. (2023). *Alzheimer's & Dementia: The Journal of the Alzheimer's Association, 19*(4), 1598–1695.

Abrams, R. C., Lachs, M., McAvay, G., Keohane, D. J., & Bruce, M. L. (2002). Predictors of self-neglect in community-dwelling elders. *The American Journal of Psychiatry, 159*(10), 1724–1730.

Alexopoulos, G. S. (2003). Role of executive function in late-life depression. *The Journal of Clinical Psychiatry, 64*(Suppl 14), 18–23.

Alves, L., Abreo, L., Petkari, E., & Pinto da Costa, M. (2023). Psychosocial risk and protective factors associated with burnout in police officers: A systematic review. *Journal of Affective Disorders, 332*, 283–298. https://doi.org/10.1016/j.jad.2023.03.081

Alzheimer's Association. (2019, June). *Dementia training for first responders.* Alzimpact.org. https://act.alz.org/site/DocServer/4__Training_Standards_for_First_Responders.pdf?docID=49071

American Bar Association. (2020). *ABA CJS Police function standards.* https://www.americanbar.org/groups/criminal_justice/publications/criminal_justice_section_archive/crimjust_standards_urbanpolice/#:~:text=serious%20criminal%20offenses.-,Such%20other%20police%20tasks%20include%20protection%20of%20certain%20rights%20such,and%20vehicular%20traffic%2C%20resolution%20of

American Psychiatric Association. (2022). *Diagnostic and statistical manual of mental disorders* (5th ed., text rev.). https://doi.org/10.1176/appi.books.9780890425787

Amjad, H., Roth, D. L., Sheehan, O. C., Lyketsos, C. G., Wolff, J. L., & Samus, Q. M. (2018). Underdiagnosis of dementia: An observational study of patterns in diagnosis and awareness in US older adults. *Journal of General Internal Medicine, 33*(7), 1131–1138. https://doi.org/10.1007/s11606-018-4377-y

Anders, R., Willemin-Petignat, L., Rolli Salathé, C., Samson, A. C., & Putois, B. (2022). Profiling police forces against stress: Risk and protective factors for post-traumatic stress disorder and burnout in police officers. *International Journal of Environmental Research and Public Health, 19*(15), 9218. https://doi.org/10.3390/ijerph19159218

Ballard, C. G., Gauthier, S., Cummings, J. L., Brodaty, H., Grossberg, G. T., Robert, P., & Lyketsos, C. G. (2009). Management of agitation and aggression associated with Alzheimer disease. *Nature Reviews Neurology, 5*(5), 245–255. https://doi.org/10.1038/nrneurol.2009.39

Banerjee, S., Smith, S. C., Lamping, D. L., Harwood, R. H., Foley, B., Smith, P., Murray, J., Prince, M., Levin, E., Mann, A., & Knapp, M. (2006). Quality of life in dementia: More than just cognition. An analysis of associations with quality of life in dementia. *Journal of Neurology, Neurosurgery, and Psychiatry, 77*(2), 146–148. https://doi.org/10.1136/jnnp.2005.072983

Bateman, R. J., Xiong, C., Benzinger, T. L. S., Fagan, A. M., Goate, A., Fox, N. C., Marcus, D. S., Cairns, N. J., Xie, X., Blazey, T. M., Holtzman, D. M., Santacruz, A., Buckles, V., Oliver, A., Moulder, K., Aisen, P. S., Ghetti, B., Klunk, W. E., McDade, E., & Morris, J. C. (2012). Clinical and biomarker changes in dominantly inherited Alzheimer's disease. *New England Journal of Medicine, 367*(9), 795–804. https://doi.org/10.1056/NEJMoa1202753

Beeri, M. S., Werner, P., Davidson, M., & Noy, S. (2002). The cost of behavioral and psychological symptoms of dementia (BPSD) in community-dwelling Alzheimer's disease patients. *International Journal of Geriatric Psychiatry, 17*(5), 403–408. https://doi.org/10.1002/gps.490

Beinicke, A., & Muff, A. (2019). Effectiveness of simulation-based learning in basic police training innovations in law enforcement—Implications for practice, education and civil society: Learning innovation(s). *European Law Enforcement Research Bulletin, Special Issue, 4*, 207–212.

Bonnell, C., Jenkins, B., Blaskovits, B., Semple, T., Khanizadeh, A.-J., Brown, A. S., & Jones, N. J. (2022). Knowledge, skills, and abilities for managing potentially volatile police–public interactions: A narrative review. *Frontiers in Psychology, 13*, Article 818009. https://doi.org/10.3389/fpsyg.2022.818009

Blum, L. N. (2000). *Force under pressure.* Lantern Books.

Blumberg, D. M., Schlosser, M. D., Papazoglou, K., Creighton, S., & Kaye, C. C. (2019). New directions in police academy training: A call to action. *International Journal of Environmental Research and Public Health, 16*(24), Article 24. https://doi.org/10.3390/ijerph16244941

Boyle, P. A., Yu, L., Wilson, R. S., Gamble, K., Buchman, A. S., & Bennett, D. A. (2012). Poor decision making is a consequence of cognitive decline among older persons without Alzheimer's disease or mild cognitive impairment. *PLoS ONE, 7*(8), Article e43647. https://doi.org/10.1371/journal.pone.0043647

Brown, R. T., Ahalt, C., Rivera, J., Stijacic Cenzer, I., Wilhelm, A., & Williams, B. A. (2017). Good cop, better cop: Evaluation of a geriatrics training program for police. *Journal of the American Geriatrics Society, 65*(8), 1842–1847. https://doi.org/10.1111/jgs.14899

Brown, R. T., Ahalt, C., Steinman, M. A., Kruger, K., & Williams, B. A. (2014). Police on the front line of community geriatric health care: Challenges and opportunities. *Journal of the American Geriatrics Society, 62*(11), 2191–2198. https://doi.org/10.1111/jgs.13093

Burling, J. E., Katz, Z., Yuan, Z., Munro, C., Mimmack, K., Ma, G., Hanseeuw, B. J., Papp, K. V., Amariglio, R. E., Vannini, P., Rentz, D. M., Quiroz, Y. T., Johnson, K. A., Sperling, R. A., Blacker, D., Marshall, G. A., Yang, H.-S., & Gatchel, J. R. (2024). Study partner report of apathy in older adults is associated with AD biomarkers: Findings from the Harvard Aging Brain Study. *The American Journal of Geriatric Psychiatry, S1064748124000204*,. https://doi.org/10.1016/j.jagp.2024.01.020

Byard, R. W., & Langlois, N. E. I. (2019). Wandering dementia—A syndrome with forensic implications. *Journal of Forensic Sciences, 64*(2), 443–445. https://doi.org/10.1111/1556-4029.13885

Center for Public Safety and Justice. (2015). *Alzheimer's Aware: A guide for implementing a law enforcement program to address Alzheimer's in the community* [Brochure]. https://www.ojp.gov/ncjrs/virtual-library/abstracts/alzheimers-aware-guide-implementing-law-enforcement-program-address

Chi, S., Wang, C., Jiang, T., Zhu, X. C., Yu, J. T., & Tan, L. (2015). The prevalence of depression in Alzheimer's disease: A systematic review and meta-analysis. *Current Alzheimer Research, 12*(2), 189–198. https://doi.org/10.2174/1567205012666150204124310

Cohen-Mansfield, J., Werner, P., Watson, V., & Pasis, S. (1995). Agitation among elderly persons at adult day-care centers: The experiences of relatives and staff members. *International Psychogeriatrics, 7*(3), 447–458. https://doi.org/10.1017/S1041610295002195

Congressional Budget Office. (2024, January 18). *The demographic outlook: 2024 to 2054.* https://www.cbo.gov/publication/59899

Conrad, K. J., Iris, M., Ridings, J. W., Langley, K., & Wilber, K. H. (2010). Self-report measure of financial exploitation of older adults. *The Gerontologist, 50*(6), 758–773. https://doi.org/10.1093/geront/gnq054

Conwell, Y. (2014). Suicide later in life: Challenges and priorities for prevention. *American Journal of Preventive Medicine, 47*(3 Suppl 2), S244–S250. https://doi.org/10.1016/j.amepre.2014.05.040

Craddock, T. B., & Telesco, G. (2022). Police stress and deleterious outcomes: Efforts towards improving police mental health. *Journal of Police and Criminal Psychology, 37*(1), 173–182. https://doi.org/10.1007/s11896-021-09488-1

Ferrari, A. J., Charlson, F. J., Norman, R. E., Flaxman, A. D., Patten, S. B., Vos, T., & Whiteford, H. A. (2013). The epidemiological modelling of major depressive disorder: Application for the Global Burden of Disease Study 2010. *PLoS ONE, 8*(7), Article e69637. https://doi.org/10.1371/journal.pone.0069637

Finkel, S. I., Costa e Silva, J., Cohen, G., Miller, S., & Sartorius, N. (1997). Behavioral and psychological signs and symptoms of dementia: A consensus statement on current knowledge and implications for research and treatment. *International Psychogeriatrics, 8*(Suppl 3), 497–500. https://doi.org/10.1017/s1041610297003943

GBD 2021 Demographics Collaborators. (2024). Global age-sex-specific mortality, life expectancy, and population estimates in 204 countries and territories and 811 subnational locations, 1950–2021, and the impact of the COVID-19 pandemic: A comprehensive demographic analysis for the Global Burden of Disease Study 2021. *Lancet, 403*(10440), 1989–2056. https://doi.org/10.1016/S0140-6736(24)00476-8

Greene, J. R. (2000). Community policing in America: Changing the nature, structure, and function of the police. *Criminal Justice, 3*. https://www.ncjrs.gov/criminal_justice2000/vol_3/03g.pdf

Grob, G. N. (1991). From hospital to community: Mental health policy in modern America. *The Psychiatric Quarterly, 62*(3), 187–212. https://doi.org/10.1007/BF01955796

Hacker, K. (2024). The burden of chronic disease. *Mayo Clinic Proceedings. Innovations, Quality & Outcomes, 8*(1), 112–119. https://doi.org/10.1016/j.mayocpiqo.2023.08.005

Haddad, H. W., Malone, G. W., Comardelle, N. J., Degueure, A. E., Poliwoda, S., Kaye, R. J., Murnane, K. S., Kaye, A. M., & Kaye, A. D. (2022). Aduhelm, a novel anti-amyloid monoclonal antibody, for the treatment of Alzheimer's disease: A comprehensive review. *Health Psychology Research, 10*(3), 37023. https://doi.org/10.52965/001c.37023

Han, S. D., Boyle, P. A., James, B. D., Yu, L., & Bennett, D. A. (2015). Mild cognitive impairment and susceptibility to scams in old age. *Journal of Alzheimer's Disease, 49*(3), 845–851. https://doi.org/10.3233/JAD-150442

Haugen, P. T., Evces, M., & Weiss, D. S. (2012). Treating posttraumatic stress disorder in first responders: A systematic review. *Clinical Psychology Review, 32*(5), 370–380. https://doi.org/10.1016/j.cpr.2012.04.001

Hawdon, J. E., Ryan, J., & Griffin, S. P. (2003). Policing tactics and perceptions of police legitimacy. *Police Quarterly, 6*(4), 469–491.

Hawley, K. S., Garrity, A. W., & Cherry, K. E. (2005). Knowledge of normal versus pathological memory aging among police officers. *Educational Gerontology, 31*(1), 1–17. https://doi.org/10.1080/03601270590522161

Henstra, M. J., Rhebergen, D., Stek, M. L., Swart, K. M. A., van Dijk, S. C., Zillikens, M. C., Oliai Araghi, S., de Groot, L. C. M. G. M., van Schoor, N. M., & van der Velde, N. (2019). The association between apathy, decline in physical performance, and falls in older persons. *Aging Clinical and Experimental Research, 31*(10), 1491–1499. https://doi.org/10.1007/s40520-018-1096-5

Hippius, H., & Neundörfer, G. (2003). The discovery of Alzheimer's disease. *Dialogues in Clinical Neuroscience, 5*(1), 101–108. https://doi.org/10.31887/DCNS.2003.5.1/hhippius

Hutter, R. I., Renden, P. G., Kok, M., Oudejans, R., Koedijk, M., & Kleygrewe, L. (2023). Criteria for the high quality training of police officers. In M. S. Staller, S. Koerner, & B. Zaiser (Eds.), *Police Conflict Management, Volume II: Training and Education* (Vol. 2, pp. 7–32). Springer International Publishing. https://doi.org/10.1007/978-3-031-41100-7_2

Hwang, J. P., Tsai, S. J., Yang, C. H., Liu, K. M., & Lirng, J. F. (1998). Hoarding behavior in dementia. A preliminary report. *The American Journal of Geriatric Psychiatry: Official Journal of the American Association for Geriatric Psychiatry, 6*(4), 285–289.

James, T. A., Weiss-Cowie, S., Hopton, Z., Verhaeghen, P., Dotson, V. M., & Duarte, A. (2021). Depression and episodic memory across the adult lifespan: A meta-analytic review. *Psychological Bulletin, 147*(11), 1184–1214. https://doi.org/10.1037/bul0000344

Jeong, J. G., Song, J. A., & Park, K. W. (2016). A relationship between depression and wandering in community-dwelling elders with dementia. *Dementia and Neurocognitive Disorders, 15*(1), 1–6. https://doi.org/10.12779/dnd.2016.15.1.1

Kales, H. C., Gitlin, L. N., & Lyketsos, C. G. (2015). Assessment and management of behavioral and psychological symptoms of dementia. *BMJ (Clinical Research Ed.), 350*, Article h369. https://doi.org/10.1136/bmj.h369

Kirschman, F. (2007). *I love a cop: What police families need to know* (Rev. ed.). Guilford Press.

Kleygrewe, L., Hutter, R. I. V., Koedijk, M., & Oudejans, R. R. D. (2024). Virtual reality training for police officers: A comparison of training responses in VR and real-life training. *Police Practice and Research, 25*(1), 18–37. https://doi.org/10.1080/15614263.2023.2176307

Klimley, K. E., Van Hasselt, V. B., & Stripling, A. M. (2018). Posttraumatic stress disorder in police, firefighters, and emergency dispatchers. *Aggression and Violent Behavior, 43*, 33–44. https://doi.org/10.1016/j.avb.2018.08.005

Knight, B. (2004). *Psychotherapy with older adults.* SAGE Publications. https://doi.org/10.4135/9781452204574

Lachenmayr, S., Goldman, K. D., & Brand, F. S. (2000). Safe return: A community-based initiative between police officers and the Alzheimer's Association to increase the safety of people with Alzheimer's disease. *Health Promotion Practice, 1*(3), 268–278. https://doi.org/10.1177/152483990000100313

Lachs, M., Bachman, R., Williams, C., Kossack, A., Bove, C., & O'Leary, J. (2004). Older adults as crime victims, perpetrators, witnesses, and complainants: A population-based study of police interactions. *Journal of Elder Abuse & Neglect, 16*(4), 25–40. https://doi.org/10.1300/J084v16n04_02

Lamb, H. R., & Bachrach, L. L. (2001). Some perspectives on deinstitutionalization. *Psychiatric Services, 52*(8), 1039–1045. https://doi.org/10.1176/appi.ps.52.8.1039

Lee, N., & Wu, Y.-K. (2024). Work-related stress and psychological distress among law enforcement officers: The Carolina Blue Project. *Healthcare, 12*(6), 688. https://doi.org/10.3390/healthcare12060688

Li, X. L., Hu, N., Tan, M. S., Yu, J. T., & Tan, L. (2014, July 15). Behavioral and psychological symptoms in Alzheimer's disease. *BioMed Research International, 2014*, 927804. https://doi.org/10.1155/2014/927804

Lichtenberg, P. A. (2016). Financial exploitation, financial capacity, and Alzheimer's disease. *The American Psychologist, 71*(4), 312–320. https://doi.org/10.1037/a0040192

Lichtenberg, P. A., Stickney, L., & Paulson, D. (2013). Is psychological vulnerability related to the experience of fraud in older adults? *Clinical Gerontologist, 36*(2), 132–146. https://doi.org/10.1080/07317115.2012.749323

Liederbach, J., & Stelle, C. D. (2010). Policing a graying population: A study of police contacts with older adults. *Journal of Crime and Justice, 33*(1), 37–68. https://doi.org/10.1080/0735648X.2010.9721279

Liljegren, M., Landqvist Waldö, M., Rydbeck, R., & Englund, E. (2018). Police interactions among neuropathologically confirmed dementia patients: Prevalence and cause. *Alzheimer Disease & Associated Disorders, 32*(4), 346–350. https://doi.org/10.1097/WAD.0000000000000267

Ma, F., Heintz, H. L., Schmidt, N. E., Carpenter, B. D., Allen, R. S., Dzierzewski, J. M., Mlinac, M. E., Montepare, J. M., & Moye, J. (2023). Building the geropsychology workforce: A national survey and virtual conference define critical obstacles and steps forward. *Professional Psychology, Research and Practice, 54*(5), 361–371. https://doi.org/10.1037/pro0000524

Mendez, M. F. (2011). Pathological stealing in dementia: Poor response to SSRI medications. *The Journal of Clinical Psychiatry, 72*(3), 418–419. https://doi.org/10.4088/JCP.10l06440gry

National Institutes of Health (NIH). (2023). Estimates of funding for various research, condition, and disease categories (RCDC)—Table Published: Retrieved from March 31, 2023. https://report.nih.gov/funding/categorical-spending/

Oleszkiewicz, S., Weiher, L., & Mac Giolla, E. (2022). The adaptable law enforcement officer: Exploring adaptability in a covert police context. *Legal and Criminological Psychology, 27*(2), 265–282. https://doi.org/10.1111/lcrp.12209

Oliver, C. (1992). The antecedents of deinstitutionalization. *Organization Studies, 13*(4), 563–588. https://doi.org/10.1177/017084069201300403

Ornstein, K., & Gaugler, J. E. (2012). The problem with "problem behaviors": A systematic review of the association between individual patient behavioral and psychological symptoms and caregiver depression and burden within the dementia patient–caregiver dyad. *International Psychogeriatrics, 31*(10), 1536–1552.

Pavlou, M. P., & Lachs, M. S. (2008). Self-neglect in older adults: A primer for clinicians. *Journal of General Internal Medicine, 23*(11), 1841–1846. https://doi.org/10.1007/s11606-008-0717-7

Petonito, G., Muschert, G. W., Carr, D. C., Kinney, J. M., Robbins, E. J., & Brown, J. S. (2013). Programs to locate missing and critically wandering elders: A critical review and a call for multiphasic evaluation. *The Gerontologist, 53*(1), 17–25. https://doi.org/10.1093/geront/gns060

Peyton, K., Sierra-Arévalo, M., & Rand, D. G. (2019). A field experiment on community policing and police legitimacy. *Proceedings of the National Academy of Sciences, 116*(40), 19894–19898. https://doi.org/10.1073/pnas.1910157116

Rajan, K. B., Weuve, J., Barnes, L. L., McAninch, E. A., Wilson, R. S., & Evans, D. A. (2021). Population estimate of people with clinical Alzheimer's disease and mild cognitive impairment in the United States (2020–2060). *Alzheimer's & Dementia, 17*(12), 1966–1975. https://doi.org/10.1002/alz.12362

Rao, Y. L., Ganaraja, B., Murlimanju, B. V., Joy, T., Krishnamurthy, A., & Agrawal, A. (2022). Hippocampus and its involvement in Alzheimer's disease: A review. *3 Biotech, 12*(2), 55. https://doi.org/10.1007/s13205-022-03123-4

Schuck, A. M. (2024). Exploring the guardian mindset as a strategy for improving police-community relations. *Journal of Police and Criminal Psychology, 39*(1), 82–92. https://doi.org/10.1007/s11896-023-09617-y

Scogin, F., & Mieskowski, L. (2015). Evidence-based treatments and their status in geropsychology. In P. A. Lichtenberg, B. T. Mast, B. D. Carpenter, & J. Loebach Wetherell (Eds.), *APA handbook of clinical geropsychology, Vol. 1. History and status of the field and perspectives on aging* (pp. 101–133). American Psychological Association. https://doi.org/10.1037/14458-006

Shanley, C., Quirke, S., Shaw, L., & Sammut, A. (2004). Working with an organization to implement dementia awareness training for public contact staff. *American Journal of Alzheimer's Disease & Other Dementias, 19*(3), 166–171. https://doi.org/10.1177/153331750401900312

Shaw, C. A., & Gordon, J. K. (2021). Understanding elderspeak: An evolutionary concept analysis. *Innovation in Aging, 5*(3), igab023. https://doi.org/10.1093/geroni/igab023

Stanton, B. R., & Carson, A. (2016). Apathy: A practical guide for neurologists. *Practical Neurology, 16*(1), 42–47. https://doi.org/10.1136/practneurol-2015-001232

Steinberg, M., Shao, H., Zandi, P., Lyketsos, C. G., Welsh-Bohmer, K. A., Norton, M. C., & Tschanz, J. T. (2008). Point and 5-year period prevalence of neuropsychiatric symptoms in dementia: The Cache County Study. *International Journal of Geriatric Psychiatry, 23*(2), 170–177. https://doi.org/10.1002/gps.1858

Steinberg, M., Sheppard, J. M., Tschanz, J. T., Norton, M. C., Steffens, D. C., Breitner, J. C., & Lyketsos, C. G. (2003). The incidence of mental and behavioral disturbances in dementia: The Cache County Study. *The Journal of Neuropsychiatry and Clinical Neurosciences, 15*(3), 340–345. https://doi.org/10.1176/jnp.15.3.340

Sun, F., Gao, X., Brown, H., & Winfree, L. T., Jr. (2019). Police officer competence in handling Alzheimer's cases: The roles of AD knowledge, beliefs, and exposure. *Dementia, 18*(2), 674–684. https://doi.org/10.1177/1471301216688605

Syed, S., Ashwick, R., Schlosser, M., Jones, R., Rowe, S., & Billings, J. (2020). Global prevalence and risk factors for mental health problems in police personnel: A systematic review and meta-analysis. *Occupational and Environmental Medicine, 77*(11), 737–747. https://doi.org/10.1136/oemed-2020-106498

Toot, S., Hoe, J., Ledgerd, R., Burnell, K., Devine, M., & Orrell, M. (2013). Causes of crises and appropriate interventions: The views of people with dementia, carers and healthcare professionals. *Aging & Mental Health, 17*(3), 328–335. https://doi.org/10.1080/13607863.2012.732037

Tyuse, S. W., Cooper-Sadlo, S., & Underwood, S. E. (2016). Descriptive study of older adults encountered by crisis intervention team (CIT) law enforcement officers. *Journal of Women & Aging, 29*(4), 281–293. https://doi.org/10.1080/08952841.2016.1174513

Uc, E. Y., Rizzo, M., Anderson, S. W., Shi, Q., & Dawson, J. D. (2004). Driver route-following and safety errors in early Alzheimer disease. *Neurology, 63*(5), 832–837. https://doi.org/10.1212/01.WNL.0000139301.01177.35

United States Census Bureau. (2023). *2023 summary tables* [Data file]. https://www.census.gov/data/tables/2023/demo/popproj/2023-summary-tables.html

Van Den Wijngaart, M. A. G., Vernooij-Dassen, M. J. F. J., & Felling, A. J. A. (2007). The influence of stressors, appraisal and personal conditions on the burden of spousal caregivers of persons with dementia. *Aging & Mental Health, 11*(6), 626–636.

van der Linde, R. M., Matthews, F. E., Dening, T., & Brayne, C. (2017). Patterns and persistence of behavioural and psychological symptoms in those with cognitive impairment: The importance of apathy. *International Journal of Geriatric Psychiatry, 32*(3), 306–315. https://doi.org/10.1002/gps.4464

Vespa, J., Medina, L., & Armstrong, D. M. (2020). *Demographic turning points for the United States: Population projections for 2020 to 2060* (Population Estimates and Projections Current Population Reports No. P25-1144). Issued March 2018, Revised February 2020. U.S. Census Bureau.

Wancata, J., Windhaber, J., Krautgartner, M., & Alexandrowicz, R. (2003). The consequences of non-cognitive symptoms of dementia in medical hospital departments. *The International Journal of Psychiatry in Medicine, 33*(3), 257–271.

Wheeler, C., Fisher, A., Jamiel, A., Lynn, T. J., & Hill, W. T. (2021). Stigmatizing attitudes toward police officers seeking psychological services. *Journal of Police and Criminal Psychology, 36*(1), 1–7. https://doi.org/10.1007/s11896-018-9293-x

Wisconsin Department of Health Services. (2016). *Dementia-friendly law enforcement and first responders*. https://www.dhs.wisconsin.gov/publications/p01269e.pdf.

Yaffe, K., Fox, P., Newcomer, R., Sands, L., Lindquist, K., Dane, K., & Covinsky, K. E. (2002). Patient and caregiver characteristics and nursing home placement in patients with dementia. *JAMA, 287*(16), 2090–2097.

Zarit, S., & Zarit, J. M. (2011). *Mental disorders in older adults: Fundamentals of assessment and treatment*. Guildford Press.

Chapter 9
Police Training for Crisis Intervention with the Deaf and Hard-of-Hearing Community

David M. Feldman, Marissa Miller-Anguay, and Tali M. Shir

Introduction to the Deaf Community and American Sign Language Models of Deafness

Approximately 5% of the general population has some sort of hearing loss (Woodcock et al., 2007). However, this number includes any degree of hearing loss and does not account for the wide range of variability among deaf people. The word *deaf* can refer both to the physical condition as well as a cultural preference and linguistic identification typically indicated by the use of the upper or lower case "D" (Napier et al., 2006). Historically, there has been just these two categories in which deaf individuals were placed, Deaf, with a capital "D," referring to individuals who consider themselves a linguistic and cultural minority, and deaf, with a lowercase "d" referring to a pathological condition requiring correction (Kožuh et al., 2016). The term, or in this case condition, as denoted by a lowercase "d," refers to hearing loss alone and does not necessarily imply a connection to the Deaf Community (Padden & Humphries, 1988). There are a number of conventions with regard to whether or when to refer to deaf people as uppercase "Deaf" or lowercase "deaf" (Napier et al., 2006). In this chapter, "Deaf" is used only in reference to the collective entities of the Deaf community or Deaf culture.

D. M. Feldman (✉) · M. Miller-Anguay · T. M. Shir
College of Psychology, Nova Southeastern University, Fort Lauderdale, FL, USA
e-mail: dfeldman@nova.edu

M. Miller-Anguay
Harris County Sheriff's Office, Houston, TX, USA

V. B. Van Hasselt and M. L. Bourke (eds.), *Advances in First Responder Mental Health*, Advances in First Responder Mental Health 1,
https://doi.org/10.1007/978-3-032-27978-1_9

The Deaf Community, Deaf Culture, and Identity

The Deaf community is generally accepted as a minority culture that is composed of individuals with a variety of hearing loss, communication and language preferences, and cultural identities. This diversity makes the statistics of deaf people in the United States somewhat difficult to determine, as the actual number of anyone with a hearing loss may be very different (and much higher) than those that are culturally Deaf and/or utilize sign language as their means of communication. Membership in the Deaf community is typically more dependent on preference, cultural connection, sign language usage, and attitude than any specific degree or type of hearing loss (Bat-Chava, 2000).

The formation of a Deaf identity is a fluid and ambiguous process (De Clerck, 2017). The extent to which a person identifies as deaf, or Deaf, may range from those whose hearing is only slightly impaired, to individuals who are profoundly deaf. Within the Deaf community, there are also multicultural and diverse Deaf communities such as Black, Latino, LGBTQ+, and many others. Each of these with both a Deaf identity and "other" cultural identity have particular nuances of sign language. The Deaf community is also a group that varies across socioeconomic status, ethnicity, religion, and many other demographics (Foss, 2014; Pray & Jordan, 2010). The age of onset of hearing loss likely will be a factor in language development with those who are prelingually deaf being a different group than those "late-deafened." Prelingual deafness refers to deafness occurring before age three, where hearing cannot be used to learn language (Vernon & Raifman, 1997). These individuals who are Deaf are likely to have constricted vocabularies and poor English and literacy skills (Vernon & Raifman, 1997). While sign language proficiency may be acquired in either of these cases, the prelingual Deaf individual may find learning English to be more challenging.

From a practical standpoint, the cause of deafness is important and may have a significant effect on developmental etiology. Some causes of deafness may also include factors associated with intellectual disability and cognitive functioning. These may affect language development, which in turn could affect legal issues, such as understanding rights, the ability to provide informed consent, or the demonstration of competency to proceed.

American Sign Language (ASL)

While there are many forms of signed communication, American Sign Language (ASL) is the only one that is considered to be an actual language[1] as opposed to a form of signed communication. ASL is, in fact, the third most used language in the

[1] There are other *signed languages* utilized in other countries, such as British Sign Language (BSL), Australian Sign Language (AUSLAN), Langue des signes Québécoise (Quebec Sign Language or LSQ), and Spanish Sign Language (Lengua de Signos Española or LSE).

United States. It is typically passed on from Deaf parents to Deaf children and used as a means of instruction in Deaf schools or mainstream Deaf education programs. ASL is a major component of the social environment of the Deaf community and is considered to be an inseparable part of Deaf culture. However, traditionally outside of the Deaf community, ASL was rarely used or seen, and few hearing individuals ever achieved a mastery of ASL skills and abilities for effective communication.

ASL utilizes shapes and movements of the hands to provide communication that is visual rather than auditory. Some signs may be iconic, the shape of the hands representing and mimicking the shape or some characteristics of the object (e.g., milk, phone, cat), or be more abstract but express a specific concept or idea (e.g., want, thank you, happy). ASL is not just a collection of randomly assigned gestures, and there are strict rules of grammar, production, movement, and signing space. ASL not only uses signs based on handshapes to convey thoughts and ideas but is also largely reliant on the movements of the shoulders, body, and facial expressions to provide context and affect, which in spoken language is manifested in tone, pitch, and volume. In addition to the rules of handshapes, there are specific rules and meanings relating to hand placement, directionality, and movement.

ASL and English are not mutually translatable, and there are major differences between the two languages in terms of grammar, syntax, and presentation (Lane, 1999). English sentence order is *subject-verb-object* ("*I* am *going* to the *store*"), while in ASL, it is *object-subject-verb* ("*store I go*"). Many English words, including legal terms, do not have an ASL equivalent (e.g., "charges"). Some words, like "right," may be signed in multiple ways and with a different meaning (e.g., "right" as in *directional right turn, a correct response/choice, a legal right, or "it's all right*"). Accurate translation often depends on one's knowledge and understanding of ASL and the context of communication (Feldman et al., 2023).

Other Signed Communication Systems and Oral/Speech Reading

It should be noted that not every deaf person is proficient in or even uses ASL. There are several different methods of signed communication that may be used by deaf individuals, such as Signed Exact English (SEE), Cued Speech, and the Rochester Method. However, these are not universally compatible with each other and are independent of ASL. Some deaf individuals, depending on exposure, may prefer other signing systems to communicate in lieu of ASL. Some deaf individuals may prefer an oral or speech or lip-reading method without any use of signing (Stewart et al., 1998). Still, other deaf individuals may prefer to use real-time captioning (e.g., Communication Access Real-time Translation (CART)), which is a service that a trained captioner listens to, and instantaneously translates all speech to text similar to closed captioning on a television or computer screen read by the deaf individual (Humphries & Alcorn, 1994). However, real-time captioning requires proficiency in English reading to effectively access communication, and due to English and ASL differences, many deaf individuals read at approximately the fifth-grade level (Easterbrooks & Beal-Alvarez, 2012). Approximately 95% of deaf children have hearing parents who likely have either no, or very limited knowledge of ASL or other communication systems. This suggests that deaf children in these families will likely rely on speech/lip-reading, and this will be the deaf child's first exposure to communication which may cause language delays. In addition, most hearing parents have no personal experience, or even awareness of, Deaf culture, and little opportunity is provided for the child for social interaction or further sign language development.

The Deaf Community and Law Enforcement

Law Enforcement and the Lack of Knowledge About the Deaf Community and Culture

Research on interactions between law enforcement and the Deaf community or Deaf suspects is scarce, although some attempts have been made to better analyze and understand the nature and consequences of such interactions (Garner, 2019), as well as with other first responders (Engelman et al., 2013). The gaps in awareness, knowledge, and preparedness of the law enforcement profession when encountering someone from the Deaf community are only noticed through reported negative encounters and lawsuits.

In most cases, the first interaction between a Deaf individual and law enforcement will occur when an officer has either observed some infraction (e.g., traffic violation) or is called to investigate a reported or alleged crime. Deafness is not a visible condition, and law enforcement officers (LEOs) may not be aware that a suspect is Deaf until attempts at communication are made. Visual cues of hearing loss, such as hearing aids or cochlear implants, may not be seen or identified, and communication challenges or preferences will not be immediately known. Even when signed communication is observed, it may readily be identified as such by the officer and instead be seen as a non-compliant or threatening act (e.g., aggressive gestures, gang signs). While the decision to file charges is at the discretion of the office of the district or state's attorney, however, what transpires initially with law enforcement can mitigate or increase accusations and charges. Depending on the specifics of the allegations and the subsequent interactions between the officer and the Deaf suspect, this will be the first step in a process that may include questioning, criminal prosecution, court appearances, incarceration, or other legally determined punitive actions.

Few LEOs, or first responders, receive training on recognizing disabilities and understanding the needs of people with disabilities (Nelson, 2012). Typically, when these types of trainings are available, they are not focused specifically on the challenges faced by the Deaf community, but rather a general introduction to the subject. However, some law enforcement agencies have offered, and continue to offer, specific trainings on interacting with the Deaf suspects and the Deaf community to both their recruit classes and current officers. Training has also been provided at law schools and attorneys' offices on the Deaf community and legal rights. While sporadic, these trainings have been met with enthusiasm and appear to demonstrate at least some interest in addressing the potential challenges related to the interactions with Deaf suspects, witnesses, defendants, and victims. There is even a study from the United Kingdom which indicated that LEOs recognize their lack of knowledge of the Deaf community and have identified this as a need for training (Wakeland et al., 2019).

Unfortunately, for many agencies the reality is that such training and education is typically a reaction to such incidents or violations of Americans with Disabilities Act (ADA, 1990) rights rather than a proactive approach to well-rounded training. The reactive approach is due to greater systemic factors like lack of funding, resources, and staffing yet leaves agencies vulnerable to potential lawsuits and negative news headlines, further contributing to society's condemnation of the law enforcement profession. This underscores the need for comprehensive training on interacting with individuals who are Deaf or hard-of-hearing, as the consequences of not doing so can be severe.

The Deaf Community and the Lack of Knowledge About Law Enforcement and Procedure

Both Deaf suspects and victims, "face significant barriers in their interactions with the police" and that "these barriers can have a detrimental effect not only on Deaf individuals but also in how law enforcement conceptualizes cases" (McAnnany & Shah, 2011, p. 878).

Interactions with law enforcement can be anxiety-provoking for many individuals under any circumstance but are often heightened for individuals who are Deaf or hard-of-hearing. For many who are Deaf, the initial contact with LEOs is likely to be confusing, challenging, and even frightening due to language barriers and lack of access to information. For the Deaf suspect, the outcome of such interactions will likely be highly dependent on effective communication and cultural awareness that is not known to or recognized by most LEOs. Important and consequential information will need to be communicated to the Deaf suspect, and the Deaf suspect will need to communicate information back to the officer. Miscommunications and misunderstandings can occur at any of the various points of officer contact, beginning with the arrival on scene and continuing through arrest and questioning. At each of these stages, effective communication is essential to provide the Deaf suspect with instructions, information, and their rights. In addition, the Deaf suspect should be provided with the opportunity to ask questions and provide details related to the situation. Depending on the skills and ability of the officer and the Deaf suspect to communicate effectively, misunderstandings may occur, and the consequences for such misunderstandings could easily escalate the situation and result in arrest, additional charges, or physical altercations.

Many instances that involve the interaction of someone who is Deaf or hard-of-hearing with law enforcement usually start to go awry as individuals are not able to hear and thus obey the verbal commands being given by an officer. Consequently, these individuals are then viewed as non-compliant, engaging the officer's fight or flight response, leading to the determination of the need for the use of force. In such cases, officers may not realize that the person is Deaf or hard-of-hearing until further action is taken; however, the damage has been done. Such anxiety, fear, and frustration are due to a poor understanding, lack of preparedness, and communication gap between both the Deaf community and the law enforcement profession. Unfortunately, as emotions of anxiety and fear heighten among both parties during an interaction, the outcomes can vary from violation of rights to physical harm or death, ending in lawsuits, negative headlines, and condemnation of an already scrutinized profession.

Negative Outcomes

Absent or incomplete communication can lead to serious consequences for deaf individuals involved in criminal justice and legal systems. It can deprive them of fully understanding their due process and other rights under the law and constitution. It can also severely limit their ability to communicate with mental health professionals, law enforcement officials, attorneys, correctional officers, or the court (as a witness or defendant).

The inability to hear and therefore respond to commands made by officers has been noted in many instances where Deaf suspects and law enforcement have crossed paths resulting in negative outcomes for the Deaf suspect (Andone, 2017; Herman, 1997). Sadly, many examples of cultural and linguistic misunderstandings resulting in the abuse of Deaf suspects can be found through searches of the United States Department of Justice (2022), the American Civil Liberties Union (ACLU, 2022), and various media and disability advocacy groups (Hsu, 2017; Lewis, 2014; Smith, 2010).

Available data regarding the use of force from public records and media reports suggest that 33–50% of all use of force incidents involve an individual with a disability, including mental illness (Perry & Carter-Long, 2016). Headlines and stories involving such poor interactions suggest a "multitude of lawsuits have been filed against cities and police departments by Deaf or hard-of-hearing individuals for violations of their rights" (Bennett v. Aiken, City of et al., 2024; Blevins v. Town of Brighton, 2024; Mattchett et al. v. Brighton Police Department et al., 2024; Mistic v. Hanning et al., 2021; US v. Massachusetts State Police, 2022).

Perry and Carter-Long (2016) highlight that media coverage of Deaf victims of police brutality tends to be more sympathetic than that of other disabilities, explaining that society has an easier time understanding how being Deaf can lead to unwarranted escalation and violence. For instance, a Deaf man in Colorado was pulled over for running a stop sign, which quickly escalated to him being slammed to the ground, tased, and charged with second-degree assault on a police officer and resisting arrest, which were eventually dropped as a result, of the lawsuit (Tucker, 2021). The lawsuit sought compensation for physical and emotional harm, pain and suffering, economic damages, and punitive action against the officers involved for abusing authority and violating rights (Tucker, 2021). Another example of the quick escalation of such interactions is when North Carolina State Troopers attempt to pull a man over for speeding, ultimately leading to a pursuit before stopping. Once he pulled over, the driver exited his vehicle and continued to advance toward the trooper against commands, leading the trooper to shoot and kill the man (Rahman, 2016). Later information notes that he exited the vehicle to try and communicate through sign language with the trooper. His family and community expressed that the driver was afraid and lacked understanding of the situation, calling for further training of law enforcement on interacting with deaf people as many felt the trooper had other options but instead "shot first and asked questions later" (Rahman, 2016). Some specific "headline" media descriptions include the following:

- "A Colorado Man Who Couldn't Hear Police Commands Says He Was Tased, Spent Four Months in Jail" (Tucker, 2021)
- "State Trooper Shoots Dead an Unarmed Deaf Father Who Was Trying to Communicate via Sign Language After Being Pulled Over for a Speeding Violation" (Rahman, 2016)
- "Austin Jailer Breaks Elderly Deaf Woman's Arm After Misunderstanding at Airport" (Bingamon, 2023)
- "Deaf Advocates Call Oklahoma Police Shooting 'Tragic but Not Surprising'" (Chuck & Connor, 2017)

These are only a few of many stories that have been shared worldwide, sparking outrage in communities since law enforcement engaged in methods of force before identifying or acquiring knowledge that the person was Deaf or hard-of-hearing.

These cases have highlighted the clear and apparent need for systematic changes, training, and education for interacting with this vulnerable population. Lives of Deaf people have been lost over misunderstandings and unclear communication (Dollhopf, n.d.; Doubek, 2017). In the majority of cases, settlements were reached, imposing significant financial burdens. Moreover, these lawsuits have tarnished the reputations of the cities and departments, resulting in costly adjustments to their current accommodations for this population. It is important to understand that these lawsuits could have been prevented if the proper training and accommodations had been in place beforehand. This underscores the importance of taking proactive measures to ensure the rights and safety of Deaf and hard-of-hearing individuals.

Communication Between Deaf Individuals and Law Enforcement

Absent or incomplete communication can lead to consequences for Deaf individuals as there is limitation in their ability to communicate with various personnel within the criminal justice and legal systems. For instance, these gaps in communication may also create a highly stressful situation for both police officers and Deaf citizens (Silvasi, 2020). When a LEO gives a command, and it is not received or understood by the Deaf individual, it is confusing and can easily escalate the situation. Cultural awareness and sensitivity toward the Deaf community and the ability to recognize and adapt in situations with Deaf suspects appears to be a key factor until an interpreter can be obtained, and Deaf suspects who felt more at ease during their interaction with law enforcement also acknowledged that the officer accommodated their communication needs (Silvasi, 2020). This is similar to findings which found that communication accommodations from the police resulted in more citizen trust in the police and positive attitudes about complying with police requests (Hajek et al., 2008).

The majority of LEOs are well-trained in department policy and procedural regulations. They are adept at following a specific set of rules that govern their actions in the community and for safety of themselves, citizens, and suspects. While this may be efficient the more the average hearing individual encounters during a routine day, it will likely be much more challenging for situations involving the Deaf community. Police training will dictate that in certain situations an officer stands in a specific place, how they approach a situation, and when they can lawfully apply restraints, or what may justify physical contact. All of these procedures make sense from a policing perspective and are intended to ensure the safety of all involved. None of those procedures impedes communication between a police officer and a hearing suspect. However, they can be extremely challenging for a Deaf suspect when they cut off or impair communication and limit effective interactions between the Deaf suspect and the officer.

In a legal context, effective communication between the suspect and police officers is a prerequisite for the successful functioning of the law enforcement process. In summary:

- It is how an individual becomes aware of interactions with law enforcement.
- It is how an individual knows they are being arrested.
- It is how a suspect is made aware of their charges, their rights, and their entitlement to due process.
- It is how an arrestee, or inmate, learn the milieu and rules of jail and are made able to participate in activities and treatment.

As noted above, few police officers possess any knowledge of the Deaf community, and fewer still have any proficiency in sign language communication. This means that there will be little to no efficient direct communication between the Deaf suspect and the officer. Even officers who may have a rudimental knowledge of sign language will not likely be able to utilize this skill in an efficient enough manner to allow for meaningful communication of such complex and consequential information. Typically, in the initial interactions between the officer and the deaf individual, attempts are made using inefficient communication methods such as lip-reading, note-passing, gesture, or fingerspelling. LEOs should be cautioned about overestimating their ability to *effectively* communicate using any of these methods.

When Deaf suspects attempt to use sign language in order to communicate, this may be interpreted as a threat, resistance, or behavior that indicates mental disturbance. Perceiving these attempts at sign language in this way, LEOs may attempt to physically restrain or handcuff, the Deaf suspect, which in turn may lead to more frantic signing or gesturing viewed as "resistance," resulting in additional use of force and possibly additional charges (Scharper, 2009). Deaf suspects who attempt to adjust their position to better see the officer may be viewed as noncompliant, resistant, or aggressive, especially if the Deaf suspect did not hear a command to stay in place. In at least one case, a Deaf suspect's sign language attempts were mistakenly viewed by police as "flashing gang signs" (Herman, 1997). Deaf suspects will not be aware of officer's presence if approaching from behind and will have essentially cut-off communication if standing behind the Deaf suspect (Sandlin, 1995). Not following instructions may initially be viewed as noncompliance as opposed to the Deaf suspect's inability to hear the commands (Lewis v. Truitt, 1997). When hands are restrained, in front of or behind the back, the Deaf suspect has lost the ability to communicate through sign language and may struggle in ways that appear to be threatening and resisting arrest.

Typically, LEOs interacting with the Deaf community attempt to resolve these challenges in communication in the following ways:

1. They may try to utilize speech/lip-reading
2. They may try to use written forms of communication, such as notes
3. They may request the services of a sign language interpreter.

Speech/lip-reading, although preferred by some deaf individuals, has been shown to be an inefficient means of communication and not a satisfactory solution in almost all cases. Studies on this subject have concluded that "of the 42 phonemes that make up the sound of the English language, half look like some other sound as formed on the lips or else are invisible" (Davis & Hardick, 1981, pp. 59–60). In addition, Eckhardt and Anastas (2007) noted that "on average the Deaf adult will not understand more than 26–40% of one-on-one conversation through lip-reading" (p. 241), and the United States Department of Justice (2020) noted that "only about one-third of spoken words can be understood by speech reading" (p. 4). However, it is again important to recognize that some deaf individuals do not sign and may, in fact, choose lip-reading as their preferred mode of communication. Therefore, despite the controversy noted above, signed communication should not be imposed on someone who is Deaf if they express a preference for oral communication.

Similarly, writing notes in English to Deaf individuals does not equal full access to communication (Miller & Vernon, 2002; Vernon & Raifman, 1997). The ability to read and comprehend written English varies greatly among people who are Deaf and is dependent on such variables as level of education, early language development, and social networks. While reading English proficiently is certainly obtainable, many Deaf individuals read at approximately the fifth-grade level (Easterbrooks & Beal-Alvarez, 2012). Therefore, simply having a Deaf suspect read notes will not provide for equal access or comprehension of such important information.

A third option, requesting an ASL interpreter, is, in many cases, the best solution as long as the Deaf suspect has some degree of fluency in ASL. However, for most law enforcement agencies, this can be a lengthy and time-consuming process and is not required for all encounters. Many law enforcement agencies have a contract with a private community interpreting agency, and requesting an interpreter may involve a myriad of levels, departments, and supervisors. Even when an interpreter is provided, there may still be some language and communication concerns. As noted above, not all people who are deaf utilize sign language, and those that do may have various levels of proficiency or use systems other than ASL. Caution should be exercised as to ensuring the right interpreter is present or even required. This should always include asking the Deaf suspect about their signed communication preferences and as needed, seeking assistance from relevant others (e.g., family members, interpreters, case workers) to determine communication needs and appropriate accommodations. The Deaf individual should always be permitted to have input regarding the type of interpreter or accommodation that they prefer.

Law and Policy

The United States Department of Justice

Deaf suspects and defendants must be "afforded the same fundamental fairness as English-speaking defendants," and "the failure to do so deprives deaf Americans of their life or liberty without the due process guaranteed by the Fifth and Fourteenth Amendments" (Hoopes, 2006, p. 28). Otherwise, the Deaf suspect, defendant, or inmate is essentially being denied their right to due process (Vernon & Miller, 2001).

The U.S. Department of Justice (USDOJ), Office of Justice Programs has a video that aims to "inform police officers about the approaches that should and should not be used in the presentation of the Miranda warnings prior to the questioning of Deaf persons who are in police custody" (USDOJ, 2019). This video dramatizes several methods of administering the Miranda warnings and note "inadequacies" of administration through lip-reading ability, written copy, and even through the use of a sign language interpreter. The video goes on to advise that the police should "not even attempt" to administer the warnings until the suspects attorney is present and that all meetings between police, attorneys, and the Deaf suspect should be videotaped (USDOJ, 2019). Vernon et al. (1996b) has also developed a template of the Miranda warnings administration that they have suggested for use with Deaf suspects. Several states (Arizona, 2003; Oklahoma, 2007; Tennessee Code, 2010) have enacted requirements that a sign language interpreter be provided and recognizing the need for an interpreter that best fits the needs of the suspect.

The USDOJ also regulates the provision of interpreters for police departments receiving federal funding. Among other things, these regulations specifically state: "law enforcement agencies should provide for qualified interpreters to assist agencies when dealing with hearing-impaired persons"; and that "it is the responsibility of the law enforcement agency to determine uses ASL or signed English to communicate"; and "the law enforcement agency has an obligation under federal law to offer an interpreter to the arrestee with no cost" (USDOJ, 2019, p. 503). Furthermore, "complainants and victims are also entitled to have interpreters" (McEntee, 1995, p. 186).

The Americans with Disabilities Act

The Americans with Disabilities Act (ADA, 1990), which built upon the Civil Rights and the Rehabilitation Acts, identifies deafness as a disability and recognizes impairment in linguistic skills "if (they) do not speak or adequately understand English (or a comparable language) because of deafness" (Dubow & Geer, 1992). The ADA addresses the issue of access for people who are considered disabled, outlines the rubric by which accommodations must be made, and attempts to enable people with disabilities to participate fully in society (Clegg, 1999; Shapiro, 1994). The ADA established the protocol for both private and public entities regarding when reasonable accommodations must be provided to people with disabilities.

Under the ADA (1990), people with disabilities are entitled to the same services law enforcement provides to others. This includes effective communication with people who are Deaf or hard-of-hearing, as mandated by the National Association of the Deaf (NAD, 2024). To help agencies fulfill these obligations, the Department of Justice has developed information for officers to use as guides for communicating with people who are Deaf or hard-of-hearing in addition to the basic training in academies (NAD, 2024).

Attending a law enforcement training academy is standard for state and local agencies. The academies use varying training methods and prioritize certain subjects over others. The allotment of time dedicated to subjects taught in the academy is based on several factors, including the probability and frequency of usage. For instance, in 2018, the average length of a basic training program was 833 h and nearly all recruits were instructed on report writing (24 h on average), defensive tactics (61 h on average), firearm skills (73 h on average), and ethics and integrity (12 h on average) (Buehler, 2021). The average amount of time spent on community diversity was 14 h. Within this subject is where officers learn to interact with their community, including serving people with physical impairments (Buehler, 2021). Therefore, about an hour of their training is allotted to teach recruits briefly about physical impairments (i.e., mobility impairment, vision impairment, hearing impairment, speech impairment) and how to interact with individuals with such impairments.

As such, "reasonable accommodations" are required to be provided during various parts of the legal and criminal justice process. Generally, these take the form of sign language interpreters, although other modifications (e.g., CART) may also be provided. The ADA (1990, Sect. 36.303(c)(1)(ii)) specifies that the "type of auxiliary aid or service necessary to ensure effective communication will vary in accordance with the method of communication used by the individual; the nature, length, and complexity of the communication involved; and the context in which the communication is taking place." Furthermore, the standard that has been set for effective communication is that a person with a disability should be afforded a level of communication that is substantially equal to that afforded to a non-disabled person (Silva v. Baptist Health S. Fla., Inc., 2017).

Currently in some states, or jurisdictions, they place cards or indicators on a driver's license, which helps to identify the individual as Deaf, and are available from motor vehicle departments or other government agencies. Place cards can be left in the driver's side back window or kept in the glove or arm-rest compartment, or a window shade to be used as needed. While this may seem like a viable solution for both the Deaf community and law enforcement, it is not without challenges. Some Deaf individuals have expressed concern that the place cards, if left in the window, identify them as Deaf and make them more likely to become a victim of a crime. Others have expressed concern that leaving the card in the window or indicating "deaf" on a driver's license makes their private and personal information public and possibly subject to discrimination. The keeping of place cards in the glove or arm-rest compartment also raises concerns, as when stopped, a Deaf driver will be seen by the officer as reaching for "something" and not remaining still when ordered to do so. The impression they are reaching for a weapon and not following commands to stop will, in all likelihood, escalate the situation and possibly result in a deadly reaction from the officer who mistakenly feels their safety to be in jeopardy (Herman, 1997; Twersky-Glasner, 2006).

The Qualified Interpreter

The American Sign Language Interpreter

While many law enforcement agencies will contract with an interpreting agency, which will then provide interpreters as needed, it is still critical for the LEO to have some understanding of The Deaf community, ASL, and the role of the interpreter. Full and equal access to communication is essential, and LEOs may play an important role in assuring that this is considered and provided in legal settings.

At this time, there are no established state or federal licensure requirements or standards for professional interpreters. However, criteria for certification as an ASL interpreter have been established by the Registry of Interpreters for the Deaf (RID) and the Conference of Interpreter Trainers (CIT). Most Interpreter Training Programs

(ITP) in the United States are 2-year associate degree programs, with some being 4-year bachelor's degree programs. This certification includes not only training in ASL but also in the RID Code of Professional Conduct (RID, 2005). This ethical code for professional interpreters includes rules related to interpreter confidentiality, professional conduct, and competency guidelines.

Ultimately, the role of the interpreter is to facilitate communication, not to clarify misunderstandings, contribute to the conversation, or provide training to hearing professionals (Olsen & Kermit, 2014). The utilization of an interpreter alone is not a guarantee to equal access for the person who is Deaf (LaVigne & Vernon, 2003; Olsen & Kermit, 2014) and other factors must be considered relating to educational and developmental demographics.

A qualified interpreter for a legal assignment is able to "interpret effectively, accurately, and impartially, both receptively and expressively, using specialized vocabulary required in a legal setting" (ADA, 1990). The Registry of Interpreters for the Deaf has produced a standard practice paper for legal interpreting (RID, 2022) but imposed a moratorium on legally certified interpreters since 2016 (RID, 2016). However, a LEO should ask the interpreter or interpreting agency about specific legal experience and knowledge of legal terminology. Not every interpreter is qualified to interpret for legal situations, and if an appropriate interpreter is not available, then questioning, hearing, trial, or other legal activities may need to be rescheduled.

Not every person who can sign is a qualified interpreter, and even those who have Deaf families or have taken ASL classes may not have the proficiency to serve in this role. It is important to recognize that "interpreting English into ASL and vice-versa requires a great deal of skill" and that "relying on amateurs who know some sign language is a frequent error" (Dubow et al., 1986, p. 2). As a general rule, family members, friends, attorneys, LEOs, inmates, and other "invested" individuals, except in dire emergency situations, should never be utilized as interpreters. These could clearly create problems in such situations where there may be a victim of interpersonal violence, and the "interpreter" is the alleged abuser. In addition, information may need to be kept private, such as sensitive personal, financial, or medical information for which a non-professional interpreter may benefit.

In addition to in-person interpreters, video interpretation (e.g., telehealth, videophones) may be used by ASL interpreters. Video remote interpretations are usually acceptable in situations in which the connection is adequate, and the image does not lag (ADA, 1990). In addition, video remote interpreting is best when it is a one-to-one conversation but loses its effectiveness with multiple speakers or signers, when there is movement or background distractions, when people involved are off camera, or when the situation is extremely sensitive and emotional.

Certified Deaf Interpreters (CDI)

Some individuals who are Deaf may have educational, social, or additional disability deficits that affect their ability to understand any signed, spoken, or written language.

For these Deaf defendants who may not be proficient in any sign language, a more specialized form of intermediary interpreter must be utilized, known as a Certified Deaf Interpreter (CDI). The CDI facilitates communication between the deaf individual and the ASL interpreter, who then voices to the hearing person. CDIs are Deaf individuals who have been certified by the Registry of Interpreters of the Deaf as CDIs as a result of specific and specialized training. These interpreters have special linguistic skills in signed idioms and gestures used by deaf people who may have limited language skills (Vernon & Andrews, 2011). The need for a CDI can be determined by the practitioner and ASL interpreter through a preliminary interview with the Deaf individual.

The Consequences of Using Unqualified "Signers" as Interpreters

Considerations for accommodations are often not considered until after the situation has been initiated. Because of this, the needs of the Deaf suspect may be overlooked or not appropriately accommodated. Agencies may even attempt to take a cheaper and easier "good enough" approach instead of ensuring equal access to communication and due process. These solutions can often lead to unqualified individuals acting as an interpreter without sufficient documented skills, breeches in confidentiality, insufficient access to communication, or bias in communication. These have included:

- Utilizing officers as interpreters
- Utilizing other suspects or inmates as interpreters
- Utilizing family members as interpreters
- Utilizing note passing, texting, or other written communication exchanges
- Utilizing speech or lip-reading[2]

Without a qualified interpreter, the Deaf individual's ability to fully comprehend their legal situation, understand complex and important legal information, and their ability to make informed decisions may be impaired or compromised. When needed, ASL interpreters should be provided during all aspects of legal interaction.

Unfortunately, many Deaf suspects have been processed through the legal system without regard for language or cultural differences. They have been denied interpreters or provided with inappropriate interpreters or access to communication. Failure to provide for effective communication has led to wrongful arrests, unfair trials, systemic abuse, and documented instances of misdiagnosis and miscarriages of justice as a result (Maryland v. Barker, 1977; Oregon v. Mason, 1980; Tennessee v. Jenkins, 2002; Wisconsin v. Hindsley, 2000) (see Appendix A).

[2] It is important to note that deaf individuals who have been raised "orally" and do not utilize sign language may have a preference for an oral communication method.

The Challenges of Administering the Miranda Warnings Police Interrogations: An Example of the Difficulties in Conceptual Communication with Deaf Suspects

Under the justice system of the United States, all suspects are entitled to a Miranda warning at the time of arrest which outlines the rights and considerations afforded to the arrestee such as the right to an attorney and the right not to incriminate oneself (Miranda v. Arizona, 1966). This critical piece of due process provides protection to the suspect and allows them to be informed of the potential consequences of their choices or actions. This section is meant to illustrate the difficulties in communication and legal procedure between Deaf suspects and law enforcement, lack of awareness and its effects, and the complications of assuring due process to Deaf suspects.

Clearly, Deaf suspects and defendants must be "afforded the same fundamental fairness as English-speaking defendants" and "the failure to do so deprives Deaf Americans of their life or liberty without the due process guaranteed by the Fifth and Fourteenth Amendments" (Hoopes, 2006, p. 28). Historically, the Miranda warnings when administered to a Deaf suspect has rarely been presented in a manner that meets with the ideal of "fundamental fairness" (Andrews et al., 2007). In such cases, it is more likely to be done in a way that the Deaf suspect may not fully comprehend, or comprehend at all, and therefore they are not made truly aware of their rights. Studies of the comprehension of the Miranda warnings and Deaf suspects have found that approximately 30% "are not properly informed of their privilege against self-incrimination and their right to an attorney" (Anon, 1992a, 1992b). Therefore, much caution and consideration should be observed with Deaf suspects in the administration of the Miranda warnings and any subsequent questioning, interviews, or interrogations. There are many examples of the negative consequences resulting from inappropriately administered Miranda warnings by the police (see Appendix A; Maryland v. Barker, 1977; Oregon v. Mason, 1980; Tennessee v. Jenkins, 2002; Wisconsin v. Hindsley, 2000).

There are "three possibilities" for the presentation of the Miranda warnings to the Deaf suspect available to law enforcement (Vernon et al., 1996c, p. 122), although each present with specific challenges, and no one method is necessarily the best for all Deaf suspects, considering the variety of cultural and linguistic differences within the Deaf community as a whole.

Oral/Speech Reading Administration

The first option is for the officer to present the warnings to the Deaf suspect through verbally, as they would to any other suspect. However, this presumes that the Deaf suspect is able to read their speech/lips well enough to be considered effective communication and that they will be able to comprehend the meanings behind the warnings and be enabled to make an informed choice. As noted above, with the difficulties in his mouth-shape duplicity and rates of comprehension, this is not considered a satisfactory solution, and the likelihood of any deaf suspect fully understanding the meaning and intent of the warnings is remote. Clearly, the administration of the Miranda warnings in this format is grossly insufficient for Deaf suspects, especially those who prefer sign language.

However, it is important to note that some deaf people have been raised "orally" and do not utilize any form of signed communication. These deaf individuals may have a preference for an oral administration, and methods that involve signing may actually be less efficient in this circumstance. As always, care, caution, and consideration should be applied in determining communication preferences, and there should be input from the Deaf suspect as to their needs.

A Written/Read Administration

A second option is to administer a written format of the Miranda warnings for the Deaf suspect to read, typically on a note card. The ability to read and comprehend written English varies greatly among people who are Deaf and is dependent on such things as level of education, language development, education, and social exposure. Vernon et al. (1996a) noted that a reading level of eighth grade or higher is required for the "acceptable" comprehension of the Miranda warnings in printed form (p. 123), and data suggests that approximately 60% of Deaf individuals do not read well enough to comprehend the information provided in the Miranda warnings (Anon, 1992a, 1992b). Therefore, simply having the Deaf suspect read the warnings off a card will likely not be possible with the majority of Deaf suspects and certainly not be enough for the Deaf suspect to comprehend what they are reading for the warnings to have any real value.

As it is not possible for an arresting officer, an attorney, or an interpreter to know with certainty the reading level of the Deaf suspect from general interactions or conversation, caution in assuming reading ability is recommended.

Administration in ASL or Other Signed Communication

The third option would be to sign the Miranda warnings, and of the three this may be the best method in circumstances with a signing Deaf suspect. However, there are a still myriad of problems associated using sign language for such a complex task, and it is by no means a perfect solution for all Deaf suspects. In fact, there are many legal terms for which there are no signs, or the signs can be interpreted in multiple ways (Vernon et al., 1996b).

Administration in this format assumes that the Deaf suspect utilizes ASL and has proficiency in this language to make the warnings meaningful. This would need to be determined prior to the administration of the warnings as an interpreter signing to a Deaf suspect who does use ASL or another form of sign language would be of little or no value, for example, an interpreter signing to a Deaf suspect in ASL when that suspect uses Cued Speech would not likely provide full access to the meanings and contact of the warnings. To further complicate matters, ASL and English are not mutually translatable, and there are many terms for which there are no signs, or the signs are only known to better-educated deaf people possessing legal or academic backgrounds (Vernon et al., 1996a, 1996b, 1996c). Fingerspelling (e.g., manual alphabet) the Miranda warnings is also not an accurate or time-efficient administration if they are spelled to an illiterate or poorly educated Deaf suspect (Dubow & Geer, 1992) and would likely be exhausting both expressively and receptively. Some deaf suspects may have minimal or no measurable communication, and a specialist interpreter, such as the CDI, may be required.

Law Enforcement Training

Training for Law Enforcement

It is not practical to expect all, or even some, LEOs to become proficient enough in ASL for any meaningful or effective communication. In fact, it may not be recommended that officers use anything but the most basic signs or gestures only in emergency or life-threatening situations. Unless the LEO has some documented proficiency in ASL, attempting to communicate complex and legal information in this way is not advised.

In fact, it is not recommended that LEOs use anything but the most basic signs or gestures. Even the officers' assumption that because the suspect is Deaf and therefore uses sign language can be a huge, and costly, mistake. Unless the officer has some documented proficiency in a signed language, attempting to communicate in this way is not advised. As soon as the officer establishes that the suspect or victim is Deaf, attempts should be made to accommodate their communication preferences immediately. If a Deaf suspect has expressed a preference for sign language and requests a sign language interpreter, any questioning should be put on hold until the language and communication issues are resolved, and the requested interpreter arrives (Vernon et al., 2001). Several states (Arizona, 2003; Oklahoma, 2007; Tennessee Code, 2010) have all enacted requirements that a certified sign language interpreter be provided prior to a statement being taken and recognizing the need for an interpreter that best fits the needs of the suspect.

Few opportunities for training on successful interactions with the Deaf community are provided, leaving officers often unaware of how to get an interpreter or of any department policy or process for doing so. Department policies on the acquiring of interpreters or other accommodations are recommended, and it may be helpful for a single officer to be designated as a form of liaison to ensure the appropriate accommodations are requested and placed as quickly as possible.

As noted previously, few opportunities for training on successful interactions with the Deaf community are provided, leaving officers often unaware of the need for, and how to acquire, an interpreter or of any department policy or process for doing so. It is important that law enforcement agencies and individual LEOs are familiar with the reasons for an interpreter when to provide one, and the process by which they can acquire an interpreter prior to potential interactions with Deaf suspects. For this reason, law enforcement training in community relations with the Deaf community and department policies on the utilization of and provision of interpreters, or other accommodations, is recommended. When possible, it may be helpful for a single officer to be designated as a form of liaison between the department, the Deaf community, and the interpreting agency to ensure the appropriate accommodations are requested and in place as quickly as possible. It is also suggested that law enforcement agencies build relationships with interpreting agencies, Deaf Service Centers, and the Deaf Community, who can provide training and consultation.

Agencies and officers should note that it could be several hours before an interpreter is available to assist with the apprehension or initial questioning of a suspect or victim. During that time, the officer will likely be on their own and use a combination of department policy and professional judgment to help them navigate through communication with a Deaf suspect or victim. Training for law enforcement agencies in cultural awareness and relations with the Deaf community is very useful, and police-sponsored trainings for the Deaf community on the rationale for police actions and policies will also likely decrease misunderstandings that lead to the escalation of the situation.

Training for the Deaf Community

Community-based trainings specific to the Deaf community related to interactions and procedures with law enforcement would likely be beneficial. Often, the Deaf community is left out of educational and informational programs due to lack of awareness, language issues, and failure to include the Deaf community on the part of program organizers. These programs would serve to:

1. Facilitate awareness regarding the rationale for police procedures
2. Inform members of Deaf community their due process rights
3. Educate the Deaf community on how and when to ask for and make clear their communication and other accommodation preferences.

Furthermore, collaboration with the Deaf community has proven to be effective when training police on how to interact with this community in the field (Seek the World, 2020) (Refer to Appendix B). The Oregon Police Academy and the Department of Public Safety Standards and Training utilize a training facility to play out scenarios using Deaf actors. It trains law enforcement on how to interact and partner with the Deaf community. Starting more programs like the one in Oregon can be an effective method to begin bridging the gap in communication, training, and relations with law enforcement and the Deaf community.

Similarly, the Rochester Police Department has a Deaf and Police Integrative Committee that meets every month. They discuss issues or concerns related to procedures (Dollhopf, n.d.). This committee ensures that the policies and procedures used for the Deaf community are up to date and viable. Committees like this give the Deaf community a voice and allow them to collaborate effectively with the police to not only advocate for themselves but to hear multiple perspectives to come to an adequate solution.

Conclusion

As noted in this chapter, there are a myriad of ways in which interactions between law enforcement officers and Deaf suspects can be challenging. Statements obtained from Deaf suspects who were improperly administered the Miranda warnings would likely be inadmissible in court; miscommunications and misunderstandings could result in escalations and possibly physical confrontations; and improper or unprovided accommodations could result in serious negative consequences for the Deaf suspect and lead to a lack of trust and cooperation with law enforcement by the Deaf community. To avoid these difficulties, agencies and officers should strive to increase their cultural awareness when it comes to the Deaf community and to effectively accommodate communication needs. It has been suggested that this would increase the effectiveness of police interactions with Deaf suspects and the trust of the Deaf community in their local law enforcement agency. In his study, Silvasi (2020) found that misunderstandings and miscommunications contribute to a highly stressful situation for both police officers and Deaf citizens. In his application of the deference exchange theory (Bonner, 2015) to his findings, Silvasi (2020) concluded that when an officer gives a command and it is not received by the Deaf individual, it is perplexing and confusing for the officer and can escalate the situation if they do not have the appropriate cultural sensitivity to recognize and adapt to these events. Additionally, it was found that Deaf participants who indicated that they felt more at ease during their interaction with law enforcement also acknowledged that the officer accommodated their communication needs. This is similar to findings made by Hajek and colleagues (2008), who found that communication accommodations from the police resulted in more citizen trust in the police and predicted positive attitudes about complying with police requests.

Appendix A

Maryland v. Barker, 1977

Judge E. Mackall Childs found that the written and the signed presentation of the Miranda warnings were an insufficient communication of these rights to a prelingually deaf person of Mr. Barker's educational and linguistic limitations. In essence, this means the confessions were obtained involuntarily and are not admissible as evidence.

Oregon v. Mason, 1980

The trial court concluded from the evidence that while all four interpreters used by the police could, in one way or another, communicate with the defendant at a rudimentary level and receive from him simple responses and a sequential narrative of sorts, none of them possessed the training and expertise to interpret accurately in defendant's own language the concepts contained in the Miranda warnings:

> This defendant by reason of his lack of hearing has never been exposed to the commonplace materials of history, past or present, which give the Miranda warnings meaning for the simplest citizen who possesses sufficient attention span to watch television. His previous criminal case which involved a plea of guilty was not sufficient to provide for such background. The evidence here indicated that his lawyer who acted as his interpreter on that occasion knew no American Sign Language and conversed with him largely using Fingerspelling and Signed English. He also employed incorrect signs for important words such as 'rights.' Indeed, there was no evidence that Miranda warnings were given him on that occasion. To give Miranda warnings to this defendant so as to make an intelligent waiver possible would require an interpreter familiar with and competent in his primary language. This he did not have. Even more technically difficult would have been explanation of a polygraph examination and the interpretation of questions in a comprehensible manner for that examination.

Wisconsin v. Hindsley, 2000

At the close of the testimony, the trial court ruled that Hindsley's statement was voluntary, but Hindsley had not knowingly and intelligently waived his Miranda rights. A statement during a video-taped police interview led to his being charged and convicted of first-degree intentional homicide of his two-year-old son. However, the interpreter hired by the police transliterated the Miranda Rights and police questions into Signed English, rather than translating them into ASL. Hindsley used a contact language formed from ASL and Native American Indian Sign Language (NAISL). He could not read, write, or understand English and Signed English interpretation cannot be understood by people who are not already proficient English speakers (Eades, 2008). Several errors, principally arising from the use of Signed English and lack of ASL concerned the use and translation of pronouns, non-manual nods, various lexical items, and omissions.

Tennessee v. Jenkins, 2002

The defendant, who is deaf, was charged with first-degree murder and aggravated arson. On the morning after the residential fire that claimed the victim's life, a deputy sheriff entered the defendant's home, tapped him on the shoulder to awaken him, and asked, via gestures and a written note, that the defendant accompany him to the sheriff's department for questioning. Investigators at the department interviewed the defendant and took his statement through an interpreter of American Sign Language. The defendant argued that the statement should be suppressed on the grounds that it was taken without adequate *Miranda* warnings, in violation of his Fifth Amendment right to counsel, and that the State failed to prove that he had been given an adequate *Miranda* warning. Finding that the defendant voluntarily accompanied the deputy to the sheriff's department, but that he was in custody at the department during questioning, they granted the motion to suppress on Fifth Amendment grounds.

Appendix B

Marlee Matlin on Deaf and Police Interaction

https://www.youtube.com/watch?v=pAvewviVwjY

10 Signs for Law Enforcement to Learn in Engaging with Deaf/HH & Autistic Communities

https://www.youtube.com/watch?v=rKTZF2_eYOU&t=2s

Oregon Police Training: How to Communicate with Deaf in American Sign Language Better

haattps://waaww.youtube.com/watch?v=8hO80gZhULQ&t=4s

Position Statement on Accessible Emergency Management for Deaf and Hard-of-Hearing People

https://www.nad.org/about-us/position-statements/position-statement-on-accessible-emergency-management-for-deaf-and-hard-of-hearing-people/

References

American Civil Liberties Union. (2022). *ACLU asks DOJ to investigate accommodations for Deaf inmates*. https://www.accessibility.com/blog/aclu-asks-doj-to-investigate-accommodations-for-deaf-inmates

Americans with Disabilities Act of 1990, 42 U.S.C. § 12101 *et seq*. Section 36.303(c)(1)(ii) (1990).

Andone, D. (2017, September 21). 'He can't hear you': Officers shoot, kill deaf man after giving verbal orders. *CNN*. https://www.cnn.com/2017/09/21/us/police-shoot-deaf-man-oklahoma-citytrnd/index.htm

Andrews, J. F., Vernon, M., & LaVigne, M. (2007). The Bill of Rights, due process and the deaf suspect. *Journal of Interpreting, 2007*, 9–38.

Anon, L. (1992a). *Annual survey of deaf and hard-of-hearing children and youth.* Gallaudet University Press.

Anon, L. (1992b). *Deaf suspects and the Miranda warnings (Video).* Police Executive Research Forum.

Ariz. Rev. Stat. Ann. § 12–242(C) (2003).

Bat-Chava, Y. (2000). Diversity of deaf identities. *American Annals of the Deaf, 145*(5), 420–428.

Bennett v. Aiken, City of et al. 1:24-cv-03006. 446 Civil Rights. 42:12117 Americans with Disabilities Act (2024).

Bingamon, B. (2023, March 24). Austin jailer breaks elderly deaf woman's arm after misunderstanding at airport. *The Austin Chronicle.* https://www.austinchronicle.com/news/2023-03-24/austin-jailer-breaks-elderly-deaf-womans-arm-after-misunderstanding-at-airport/

Blevins v. Town of Brighton. 6:2024cv06080. 42 U.S.C. § 12101 Americans with Disabilities Act (2024).

Bonner, H. S. (2015). Police officer decision-making in dispute encounters: Digging deeper into the 'black box.' *American Journal of Criminal Justice, 40*(3), 493–522.

Buehler, E. D. (2021). State and Local Law Enforcement Training Academies, 2018 – Statistical Tables. *U.S. Department of Justice.* chrome-extension://efaidnbmnnnibpcajpcglclefindmkaj/https://bjs.ojp.gov/sites/g/files/xyckuh236/files/media/document/slleta18st.pdf

Chuck, E., & Connor, T. (2017, September 21). Deaf advocates call Oklahoma police shooting 'Tragic but Not Surprising'. *NBC News.* https://www.nbcnews.com/news/us-news/deaf-advocates-call-oklahoma-police-shooting-tragic-not-surprising-n803226

Clegg, R. (1999, Summer). The costly compassion of the ADA. *Public Interest*, pp. 100, 112.

Davis, J. M., & Hardick, E. J. (1981). *Rehabilitation audiology for children and youth.* John Wiley.

De Clerck, G. A. (2017). Introduction: Sign language, sustainable development, and equal opportunities. *American Annals of the Deaf, 162*(1), 34–38. https://doi.org/10.1353/aad.2017.0013

Dollhopf, J. (n.d.). *Police interaction with the deaf.* Center for Disability Rights. https://www.cdrnys.org/blog/advocacy/police-interaction-with-the-deaf/

Doubek, J. (2017, June 18). Oklahoma City police fatally shoot deaf man despite yells of "He can't hear". *KGOU*. https://www.kgou.org/oklahoma-news/2017-09-21/oklahoma-city-police-fatally-shoot-deaf-man-despite-yells-of-he-cant-hear

Dubow, S., & Geer, S. (1992). *Legal rights: The guide for deaf and hard of hearing people.* Gallaudet University Press.

Dubow, S., Goldberg, L., Geer, S., Gardner, F., Penn, A., Conlon, S., & Charmatz, M. (1986). *Legal rights of hearing-impaired persons* (3rd ed.). Gallaudet University Press.

Easterbrooks, S. R., & Beal-Alvarez, J. S. (2012). States' reading outcomes of students who are d/deaf and hard of hearing. *American Annals of the Deaf*, *157*(1), 27–40. http://www.jstor.org/stable/26235186

Eckhardt, E., & Anastas, J. (2007). Research methods with disabled populations. *Journal of Social Work, Disability, and Rehabilitation,* 241.

Eades, D. (2008). Language and disadvantage before the law. In G. John, & M. T. Teresa (Eds.), *Dimensions of forensic linguistics* (pp. 179–195). John Benjamins.

Engelman, A., Ilvey, S., Tseng, W., Dahrogue, D., Brune, J., & Neurhauser, L. (2013). Responding to the deaf in disasters: Establishing a need for systematic training for state-level emergency management agencies and community organizations. *BMC Health Services Research, 13*, 84. https://doi.org/10.1186/1472-6963-13-84

Feldman, D. M., Caggiano, C., & Beldon-Feldman, J. (2023). Why language matters: What forensic psychologists need to know about the deaf community, American Sign Language, and interpreters. *Practice Innovations, 8*(3), 249–264. https://doi.org/10.1037/pri0000219

Foss, K. (2014). Constructing hearing loss or "deaf gain?" voice, agency, and identity in television's representations of d/deafness. *Critical Studies in Media Communication, 31*(5), 426–447. https://doi.org/10.1080/15295036.2014.968603

Garner, J. (2019). *The deaf & law enforcement listening through deaf eyes: A grounded theory approach.* [Doctoral dissertation, Nova Southeastern University]. Nova Southeastern University ProQuest Dissertations & Theses.

Hajek, C., Giles, H., Barker, V., Lin, M. C., Zhang, Y. B., & Lee Hummert, M. (2008). Expressed trust and compliance in police-civilian encounters: The role of communication accommodation in Chinese and American settings. *Chinese Journal of Communication, 1*(2), 168–180.

Herman, B. (1997, December 14). Hearing impaired present special problems, opportunities for police. *Miami Herald.*

Hoopes, R. (2006). Trampling Miranda: Interrogating deaf suspects. In C. Lucas (Ed.), *Language and the law in deaf communities* (p. 28). Gallaudet University Press.

Hsu, S. (2017, October 1). D.C. jail held man for 77 days after his case was dropped until another inmate flagged an attorney. The *Washington Post.* https://www.washingtonpost.com/local/public-safety/dc-jail-held-man-for-77-days-after-his-case-was-dropped-until-another-inmate-flagged-an-attorney/2017/10/01/61235af2-9f0a-11e7-8ea1-ed975285475e_story.html

Humphries, J. H., & Alcorn, B. J. (1994). *So you want to be an interpreter: An introduction to sign language interpreting.* H & H Publishing.

Kožuh, I., Hintermair, M., & Debevc, M. (2016). Community building among deaf and hard of hearing people by using written language on social networking sites. *Computers in Human Behavior, 65*, 295–307.

Lane, H. (1999). *The mask of benevolence: Disabling the deaf community* (Rev. ed.). Dawn Sign Press.

LaVigne, M., & Vernon, M. (2003). An interpreter isn't enough: Deafness, language, and due process. *Wisconsin Law Review, 5*, 844–936.

Lewis, T. (2014). *Police brutality and deaf people.* American Civil Liberties Union (ACLU). https://www.aclu.org/blog/national-security/police-brutality-and-deaf-people

Lewis v. Truitt, 960 F. Supp. 175,176 (S.D. Ind. 1997).

Maryland v. Barker, Crim. Nos. 17,995 & 19,518 (Md. Cir. Ct. Dec. 8, 1977).

Mattchett et al. v. Brighton Police Department et al. 6:2024cv06001. 42 U.S.C. § 12101 Americans with Disabilities Act (2024).

McAnnany, K., & Shah, A. K. (2011). With their own hands: A community lawyering approach to improving law enforcement practices in the deaf community. *Valparaiso University Law Review, 45*(3), 875–926.

McEntee, M. (1995). Deaf and hard-of-hearing clients: Some legal complications. *Social Work, 40*(2), 183–187.

Miller, K., & Vernon, M. (2002). Linguistic diversity in deaf defendants and due process rights. *Journal of Deaf Studies and Education, 6*(3), 99.

Miranda v. Arizona, 384 U.S. 436 (1966).

Mistic v. Hanning et al. (2021).

Napier, J., McKee, R. L., & Goswell, D. (2006). *Sign language interpreting: Theory and practice in Australia and New Zealand.* Federation Press.

National Association of the Deaf. (2024). *Police and law enforcement.* https://www.nad.org/resources/justice/police-and-law-enforcement/

Nelson, P. (2012). Awareness is key for cops, awareness. *Times-Union.* http://www.timesunion.com/local/article/Awareness-key-for-cops-disabled3415737.ph

Olsen, T., & Kermit, P. (2014). Sign language, translation, and rule of law – deaf peoples experiences from encounters with the Norwegian criminal justice system. *Scandinavian Journal of Disability Research, 17*(1), 23–41.

Okla. Stat. tit. 63, § 2410(A) (Supp. 2 2007).

Padden, C., & Humphries, T. (1988). *Deaf in America: Voices from a culture.* Harvard University Press.

Perry, D. M., & Carter-Long, L. (2016). *The Ruderman white paper on media coverage of law enforcement use of force and disability.* Ruderman Family Foundation.

Pray, J. L., & Jordan, I. K. (2010). The deaf community and culture at a crossroads: Issues and challenges. *Journal of Social Work in Disability & Rehabilitation, 9*(2), 168–193. https://doi.org/10.1080/1536710X.2010.493486

Rahman, K. (2016, August 22). State trooper shoots dead an unarmed deaf father who was trying to communicate via sign language after being pulled over for a speeding violation. *Daily Mail.* https://www.dailymail.co.uk/news/article-3753378/North-Carolina-state-trooper-shoots-dead-deaf-mute-man.html

Registry of Interpreters for the Deaf. (2005). *Code of ethics.* Silver Spring, MD.

Registry of Interpreters for the Deaf. (2016). *Certifications under moratorium.* https://rid.org/about/certifications-under-moratorium/

Registry of Interpreters of the Deaf. (2022). *Standard practice papers.* https://rid.org/about/resources/

Sandlin, S, (1995). APD, Jail Change Handling of Deaf, ALBUQUERQUE J. (N.M.), Sept. 2.

Scharper, J. (2009, March 9). Eroding a wall between police, the deaf. *The Baltimore Sun.* https://www.baltimoresun.com/2009/03/09/eroding-a-wall-between-police-the-deaf/

Seek the World. (2020, February 11). Oregon police training: How to communicate with deaf in American Sign Language better [Video]. *YouTube.* https://www.youtube.com/watch?v=8hO80gZhULQ

Shapiro, J. (1994). *No pity: People with disabilities forging a new civil rights movement.* Times Books.

Silva v. Baptist Health S. Fla., Inc., 856 F.3d 824 (11th Cir. 2017).

Silvasi, P. M. (2020). *Warnings that fell on deaf ears: A three-pronged analysis of encounters between deaf Individuals and law enforcement.* Gallaudet University.

Smith, J. (2010, December 3). Tone deaf: Deaf Austinites say police can't seem to listen to reason. *The Austin Chronicles.* https://www.austinchronicle.com/news/2010-12-03/tone-deaf/#:~:text=Advocates%20in%20Austin%20and%20elsewhere,in%20the%20populations%20they%20serve

State of Oregon v. Mason, No. C 80–03–30821 (Or. Cir. Ct. May 27, 1980).

State of Tennessee v. Chester Lee Jenkins, No. E2001–01173-CCA-R9-CD (2002).

Stewart, A. D., Schein, J. D., & Cartwright, B. E. (1998). *Sign language interpreting: Exploring its art and science.* Allyn and Bacon.

Tennessee Code. (2010). *Title 71—welfare chapter 4—programs and services for handicapped persons, part 21—deaf and hard of hearing persons.*

Tucker, E. (2021, September 30). Deaf Colorado man who couldn't hear police commands says he was tased, spent 4 months in jail. *CNN.* https://www.cnn.com/2021/09/30/us/deaf-colorado-man-arrested-jailed-four-months/index.html

Twersky-Glasner, A. (2006). Miranda warnings and deaf suspects: It is not just a matter of translation. *Criminal Law Bulletin, 42*, 593.

United States Department of Justice (USDOJ). (2019). *Miranda and the deaf suspect.* Police Executive Research Forum, Washington Bureau. https://www.worldcat.org/title/miranda-and-the-deaf-suspect

United States Department of Justice (USDOJ). (2020). *Communication with people who are deaf or hard of hearing: ADA guide for law enforcement officers.* https://search.justice.gov/search/docs?affiliate=justice&dc=3851&query=Deaf

United States v. Massachusetts State Police. 28 C.F.R. § 3 5. 1 72(b). 42 U.S.C. §§ 12131–12134 (2022).

Vernon, M., & Andrews, J. (2011). *Basic legal issues in handling cases of defendants who are deaf.* The Champion. National Association of Criminal Defense lawyers.

Vernon, M., & Miller, K. (2001) Linguistic incompetence to stand trial: A unique condition in some deaf defendants. *Journal of Interpreting, Millennial Edition*, 99–120.

Vernon, M., & Raifman, L. (1997). Recognizing and handling problems of incompetent deaf defendants charged with serious crimes. *International Journal of Law and Psychiatry, 20*(3), 373–387.

Vernon, M., Raifman, L., & Greenberg, S. (1996a). The Miranda warnings and the deaf suspect. *Behavioral Sciences and the Law, 14*, 128.

Vernon, M., Raifman, L., & Greenberg, S. (1996b). The Miranda warnings and the deaf suspect. *Behavioral Sciences and the Law, 14*, 123.

Vernon, M., Raifman, L., & Greenberg, S. (1996c). The Miranda warnings and the deaf suspect. *Behavioral Sciences and the Law, 14*, 122.

Vernon, M., Raifman, L., Greenberg, S., & Monteiro, B. (2001). Forensic pretrial police interviews of deaf suspects avoiding legal pitfalls. *Journal of Law and Psychiatry, 24*(1), 43–59.

Wakeland, E., Rose, J., & Austin, S. (2019). Professionals experience of deaf offenders with mental health difficulties. *American Annals of the Deaf, 164*(1), 137–157.

Wisconsin v. Hindsley, 237 Wis. 2d 358 (2000). https://www.wicourts.gov/html/ca/99/99-1374.htm

Woodcock, K., Rohan, M. J., & Campbell, L. (2007). Equitable representation of deaf people in mainstream academia: Why not? *Higher Education, 53*(3), 359–379. https://doi.org/10.1007/s10

Chapter 10
The Interdiction for the Protection of Children Program in Indian Country

Michael L. Bourke, Jake Boyd, and Mac Di Rocco

The Interdiction for the Protection of Children Program in Indian Country

Child sexual exploitation (CSE) includes contact sexual offenses, technology-facilitated crimes, certain missing children cases, and commercial sexual exploitation. Youth may be victimized by a stranger or, more often, by a relative, family friend, or an adult in a position of authority (Cawson et al., 2000; Center for Sex Offender Management, n.d.; Cole & Sprang, 2015; Finkelhor et al., 2008; Richards, 2011).

Efforts to investigate CSE can be very challenging, not only because the acts typically occur in secrecy but, unlike most crimes against persons, the offenses are only infrequently reported and the victim may be unwilling or unable to participate. Children who are manipulated, groomed, or threatened could be confused about what occurred and may question their complicity in their own victimization. Their capacity to disclose may be affected by significant emotional turmoil, including embarrassment and shame, fears of retaliation and punishment, stigma, and concerns about impacts on their or their family's reputation (Belknap, 2010; Campbell, 2012; Chon, 2014; Rennison, 2002; Roesler & Wind, 1994). Since most sexual offenses go undetected, hundreds of thousands of victims of CSE remain in the shadows (Chon, 2014; Taylor & Gassner, 2010).

Given the context in which abuse and exploitation are likely to occur, it is unfair to place the burden of reporting on the child victim and unreasonable to wait for children to ask for help. The IPC program was created to provide public safety professionals

M. L. Bourke (✉) · M. Di Rocco
Raven, Dallas, United States
e-mail: MichaelBourkePhD@gmail.com

J. Boyd
Texas Department of Public Safety, Austin, Texas, USA

V. B. Van Hasselt and M. L. Bourke (eds.), *Advances in First Responder Mental Health*, Advances in First Responder Mental Health 1,
https://doi.org/10.1007/978-3-032-27978-1_10

with a new “lens” through which they are more likely to recognize signs something is amiss so they can take action to rescue children and prevent future harm.

At-Risk Youth

As defined by Bourke et al. (2016), an “at-risk youth” is “any individual younger than 18 years of age who is in a situation in which he or she is vulnerable for becoming a victim of sexual, physical, or emotional abuse; child neglect; or any form of sexual exploitation” (p. 69). Exploitative and abusive acts include rape, molestation, and fondling; being forced to perform a sexual act; and being photographed, videorecorded, or broadcast online for a sexual purpose. Some of the more common categories of victims include: (a) non-familial abductees; (b) endangered runaways; (c) critically endangered runaways; (d) lost, injured, or otherwise missing children; and (e) neglected children (Association of Public Safety Communications Officials, 2015; National Human Trafficking Resource Center, 2015; NCMEC, 2015a, 2015b; O’Leary & Howard, 2001).

High-Risk Threats to Children

High-risk threats to children are adults who have neglected, exploited, or abused any child. The abuse may be physical, psychological/emotional, sexual, or a combination of these types. An adult also may be considered a high-risk threat if his or her presence with a certain child, or perhaps any children, is specifically prohibited by law. Finally, the category includes cases where the individual does not match any of these descriptions but extant factors suggest he or she is likely to abuse, neglect, endanger, or exploit a juvenile. Examples include abductors, undetected sex offenders, known sex offenders, and sex traffickers.

Interdiction for the Protection of Children Program

The Interdiction for the Protection of Children (IPC) program is an innovative, proactive policing approach designed to prevent criminal offenses through active intervention as well as intelligence gathering. A description of the program was previously published by Bourke et al. (2016). Since the date of that publication, the program has expanded, and the number of children rescued from abuse and exploitation continues to grow.

On an operational level the program has three specific goals. First, it is designed to identify and rescue juvenile victims of child sexual abuse and sexual exploitation, as well as minors considered at risk for becoming victimized (e.g., runaways, youth in the custody of non-custodial adults). Second, the program is committed to the investigation of criminal activity and the identification of offenders and other individuals who pose a high risk to children (e.g., acquaintances, pimps, non-custodial relatives, sex offenders who are noncompliant with registries). The third priority is the gathering of intelligence for analysis by fusion centers, where the information is integrated with other data provided by local and national sources to prevent and respond to any crime-related suspicious activity.

Program Origins

Understanding the scope of CSE crimes has been hampered, in part, by poor record-keeping procedures in many states, but more especially by the low detection rates for these offenses. State troopers, border agents, park rangers, and county and municipal police officers are trained to look for signs of specific criminal behavior (e.g., driving while intoxicated, narcotics trafficking); unfortunately, for the most part, they are not taught how to recognize many indicators of child exploitation. As a result, crimes involving CSE occur in plain sight yet remain unidentified. The IPC program was designed to remedy this training deficit by providing specialized training in how to recognize signs of CSE, rescue at-risk and exploited minors, and facilitate the gathering of relevant intelligence on those who pose a high-risk threat to children.

The IPC Training Course

The focus of the two-day IPC program, as well as the five-day "train-the trainer" IPC course, has evolved over the past 15 years. Initially, one of the foremost areas of concern for the developers of IPC was child sex trafficking. Since most trafficked youth in the United States are transported on public roadways, the intervention training originally was focused on enhancing state troopers' ability to identify minors who were being exploited for commercial gain. The program has since broadened in scope to include a wider range of criminal activity.

The Texas Department of Public Safety has continued to maintain responsibility for the IPC training component, as well as for the ongoing development and improvement of the model. Some data collection efforts are performed in close collaboration with the Behavioral Analysis Unit (BAU) of the United States Marshals Service. The courses are led by experienced Texas DPS troopers who work with qualified instructors from other jurisdictions and other disciplines (e.g., clinical psychology, victim advocacy, law, social work). Participants learn how to more accurately recognize indicators of child sexual exploitation during the course of their duties, as well as more effective methods for identifying children who may be at particular risk of victimization from a sexually motivated crime.

Criminal Indicators

IPC is based on an obvious premise: it is better for police to prevent offenses from occurring rather than simply find more effective ways to investigate the crimes after the fact. While this is easier said than done, the IPC program attempts to prevent acts of harm by identifying *precursive behaviors* (i.e., those that are associated with and precede a target behavior) and *indicative signs* (i.e., things that correlate with, and may temporally co-exist with, factors of interest; in other words, indicators that "point toward" the presence of the target factor) (Bourke et al., 2016).

Sex Offender Characteristics

Sex offenders are found across all socioeconomic strata, within every profession, and in all racial and cultural groups (Center for Sex Offender Management [CSOM], 2015). Since they do not "burn out" and are capable of offending across the lifespan, they do not necessarily fall into any particular age group (CSOM, 2015). Put simply, they are the man or woman next door. Since most sex offenders are adept at compartmentalizing their deviance and appear quite normal, investigators must find ways to draw back this curtain.

Sex offenders are masters at creating a façade of normalcy, and typically there is a paucity of overt evidence to indicate these men and women are sexually attracted to children. The task of distinguishing potential offenders from non-offenders is, therefore, very challenging for law enforcement personnel, particularly when they are asked to make this distinction during the course of other policing activities. One might reasonably wonder if it is even possible during a brief traffic stop, or while assisting a motorist with a disabled vehicle, to reliably identify individuals who pose a high risk to children. Are there clues that can prompt an officer to suspect a minor in the back seat of a vehicle is the victim of a non-custodial abduction? Do adults traveling to meet a child for a sexual encounter exhibit specific behaviors? Are there signs that suggest a subject intends to exploit (or is already exploiting) runaway or homeless youth?

IPC Indicators

IPC indicators are signs observable to law enforcement officers during their interactions with one or more persons that might suggest something is amiss. While some signs are obvious, others are subtler; without training these indicators can easily be overlooked by even experienced officers. For example, individuals who sexually exploit others for commercial gain (e.g., pimps) may use certain symbols and tattoos to reflect their involvement in their particular criminal subculture. With training, law enforcement personnel learn to quickly recognize these symbols, just as gang investigators learn to recognize and interpret the cryptic graffiti and tattoos of street gang members. Other indicators might not mean anything by themselves; when viewing them in light of other factors, however, a more comprehensive picture can be formed.

The process of recognizing signs of CSE is a dynamic endeavor. IPC continues to identify potential indicators of CSE as well as indicators of *risk* for CSE. Anecdotal reports from the field, as well as results from data analysis, allow those involved with ongoing program development to improve detection methodology. The goal is to push this knowledge to the field to help officers more effectively identify crimes that have occurred or are occurring, in order to better engage in effective and proactive law enforcement. IPC concentrates on eight categories of indicators: (1) behaviors exhibited by the potential high-risk threat to children; (2) behaviors exhibited by any children who are present; (3) physical characteristics of the potential high-risk threat to children; (4) physical characteristics of children who are present; (5) property of the potential high-risk threat to children; (6) property of children who are present; (7) vehicle characteristics; and (8) situational characteristics.

Child Exploitation in Indian Country[1]

While "Indian Country" implies all tribal entities are more or less alike, in fact the term describes an amalgam of many different cultures, languages, beliefs, and ways of life. The U.S. government recognizes 566 tribes and 325 Native American reservations (U.S. Department of Health & Human Services, n.d.), and many face unique challenges. While some reservations struggle with poverty, for example, others do not. And whereas some Indian nations have lost, or are in danger of losing, their language and stories, others have experienced a resurgence in native language speakers and have taken measures to ensure the preservation of their cultural heritage. Some are policed by tribal agencies, others by local law enforcement, and still others by federal agencies (e.g., Bureau of Indian Affairs). Further, the degree to which tribal members adhere to traditional ways varies not only from one reservation to another, but from one home to the next.

A second observation, which is nearly always made in relevant studies, is that the statistics for abuse, exploitation, and human trafficking are under-reported on Indian lands. There are numerous challenges that interfere with accurate data collection, including a lack of resources, fear of consequences for reporting to authorities, issues related to the criminal justice system in Indian Country (Brown, 2024), as well as victim reluctance to participate, drug addiction (United States Government

[1] Federal law defines the term "Indian country" as all land within the limits of any Indian reservation under the jurisdiction of the U.S. government, all dependent Indian communities within U.S. borders, and all existing Indian allotments, including any rights of way running through an allotment. See 18 U.S.C. § 1151.

Accountability Office, 2017a), and the scattered nature of the communities (Nikkel & Parker, 2022).

A third point is that even when under-reporting is taken into consideration, Native American, Native Alaskan, and First Nations girls and women disproportionally are victims of sexual exploitation, violence, and human trafficking. Farley et al. (2011) studied Indian women involved with sex trafficking at four sites in the continental United States and Canada. They found up to 40% of survivors were Native American or First Nations women, although less than 10% of the overall population at each of those sites were Indigenous (Nikkel & Parker, 2022).

Risk Factors for Sexual Violence in Indian Country

Sex offenders seek out persons they view as vulnerable. While vulnerability comes in many forms, many of the identified risk factors for becoming a victim of sexual violence are more common in Indian country.

Poverty

According to U.S. Census Bureau numbers from 2022, 25% of Native Americans live in poverty, compared to 11.5% of the general population (Shrider & Creamer, 2023). The reservation poverty rate for Indian families is 36%, compared with the national family poverty rate of 9.2% (Administration for Native Americans, n.d.).

Maltreatment

Native American children from low-income families face much higher rates of maltreatment. In fact, Indian youth experience all forms of abuse and neglect more than five times as often as non-Native children. They are more than three times as likely to be abused and nearly seven times more likely to be neglected (Cooper, 2013).

Homelessness

According to a report by the Urban Institute, approximately 1 in 200 American Indian and Alaska Native people are homeless, compared with 1 in 1,000 people in the overall U.S. population (Biess, 2017). As of 2019, Native Americans account for approximately 1.5% of North America's population yet make up about 3.6% of the homeless population in the United States (Henry et al., 2020, p. 21). These statistics likely are underestimated; an additional 4 to 7% of Indian people would be homeless if a friend or family member had not taken them in (this practice, called "doubling up," makes homelessness in Indian Country less conspicuous) (Biess, 2017).

Substance Abuse

Overall, Native Americans have higher rates of alcohol and other drug abuse than any other racial and ethnic group (Substance Abuse and Mental Health Services Administration, 2019). Studies examining the lifetime prevalence of alcohol dependence on reservations have consistently shown high rates in nearly every tribe, with rates ranging from 21 to 56% of men, and 17 to 30% of women (Koss et al., 2003).

Adverse Childhood Experiences (ACEs)

ACEs are "traumatic or stressful events that include, but are not limited to, experiencing or witnessing physical or sexual abuse, physical and emotional neglect, and exposure to substance abuse in the household" (Felitti et al., 1998, in Luther, 2019). In a recent study, the average ACEs score among American Indians and Alaska Natives was 2.32 times higher than individuals identifying as White, Black, and Hispanic (Giano et al., 2021).

Native American people reported the greatest average number and variety of ACEs than people from any other racial/ethnic group and reported the highest rates of physical abuse, sexual abuse, parental substance abuse, and witnessing violence than members of any other racial/ethnic category (Richards et al., 2021). More than 84% of Indian and Alaskan Native women have experienced violence in their lives (Rosay, 2016).

Prior Sexual Victimization

Significantly higher rates of sexual violence were reported by Native American females compared to other groups; approximately 1 in 4 Native American females reported experiencing sexual violence (Basile et al., 2010; Richards et al., 2021), compared to 18% of American women, overall. Many of these victims do not come forward, and various explanations have been offered. In a report prepared by the U.S. Government Accountability Office (GAO), the reason most frequently cited by service providers who had encountered Native American human trafficking victims was shame (United States Government Accountability Office, 2017a). While this barrier to seeking services is also common among non-Indian victims, one tribal respondent noted that their tribe "has a very private culture" where "[k]eeping things quiet is very common and children are often taught to not tell about situations such as sexual assault and trafficking" (United States Government Accountability Office, 2017a, p. 22).

GAO survey respondents and tribal officials also noted that some Native American victims see their circumstances as an acceptable or inevitable lifestyle. Other barriers outlined in a companion report by GAO include situations where the victim: (a) fears retaliation from the trafficker; (b) is traumatized; (c) does not see herself or himself as a victim; (d) distrusts law enforcement; (e) is sentimentally attached to the trafficker; (f) is underage and does not want to return home; and (g) is addicted to drugs (one law enforcement official told researchers that Native American perpetrators use drugs as a tool to control their victims) (United States Government Accountability Office, 2017a, 2017b).

Involvement in Foster Care Programs

The socioeconomic challenges faced by many Native American communities, particularly high rates of poverty, have a significant bearing on child welfare outcomes. Research consistently demonstrates a strong correlation between poverty and increased involvement with the foster care system. In fact, professionals in child welfare suggest "the public child welfare system in America is populated almost exclusively by poor children" (Cooper, 2013).

Indian children enter foster care at twice the rate of all American children (United States Government Accountability Office, 2015). The disproportionate representation of Native American children in foster care systems has been a persistent issue, as indicated by statistics from the past decade. In 2013, for example, while Native American children constituted only 0.9% of the total U.S. child population, they accounted for 2% of children in foster care—more than double their representation in the general population. This disparity is even more alarming in states with larger Native American populations. South Dakota provides a striking example: Despite Native Americans comprising less than 15% of the state's overall population, they represent more than half the children in the state's foster care system (Cooper, 2013).

Another factor that appears to play a significant role in foster placement is parental use of drugs and alcohol. While Indigenous youth were less likely than non-Native children to be removed from their homes for sexual or physical abuse, child behavior concerns, or parents' inability to cope (Davis et al., 2023), nearly 20% of Indigenous children were in foster care because of a parent's misuse of alcohol. Davis and colleagues indicate the percentage of non-Indigenous youth who are removed for the same reason is about 5%, a disparity they describe as "staggering" (p. 297).

Lack of Resources or Support Systems

According to a 2017 GAO survey, nearly half (60 of 132) the tribal police agencies who responded indicated that undetected trafficking was occurring on Indian lands[2] (United States Government Accountability Office, 2017a). Some tribal officers attributed the increase to casinos on their land, or linked the sexual exploitation of minors and adults to drug trafficking. In addition, almost one-third (8 of 27) described a lack of resources needed to effectively combat human trafficking and support victims in Indian country. Some also mentioned a lack of effective interagency cooperation. Over half the tribal agencies surveyed (72 out of 132) identified specific types of assistance they needed to better address human trafficking in their jurisdictions, including additional training, technical assistance, and/or funding (United States Government Accountability Office, 2017a). Funding shortages directly impact staffing levels, with several tribal police departments reporting a desire for additional federal funding to hire more officers and support staff for investigations. The lack of adequate personnel and resources not only hinders the ability to investigate and prosecute trafficking cases, but also limits the capacity to provide necessary support services to victims.

IPC in Indian Country

In 2017, the U.S. GAO surveyed victim service providers about ways the federal government could support their efforts to serve Native American human trafficking victims. One of the top two responses was a request for additional training for service providers and law enforcement agencies. Respondents cited a need to train tribal police officers to identify victims as well as how to effectively work with Native American populations. Researchers noted that according to officials from one county agency located near a tribal community, "[O]fficers may not recognize that human trafficking is taking place, particularly when it occurs alongside another crime like drug trafficking" (United States Government Accountability Office, 2017a, p. 14).

IPC Training—Choctaw Nation

The IPC program was first introduced in Indian Country in 2022, when a program was given on tribal lands of the Choctaw Nation. Immediately following that training, a request for a second course was received, in which tribal officials indicated they would like to not only provide the class to officers who could not attend the first course, but also to invite law enforcement personnel from surrounding police agencies. Training for the larger group was held in late 2023.

Based on reports made to the National Center for Missing and Exploited Children (NCMEC), between 2018 and 2023 there were 123 incidents in which the victim was an enrolled member or was otherwise affiliated with the Choctaw Nation (NCMEC,

[2] An additional 29 agencies indicated they did not know if trafficking was occurring beyond what was being brought to their attention.

2023). The statistical trends are concerning in that it appears the problem is worsening; the number of missing child incidents more than doubled from 2021 ($n = 12$) to 2023 ($n = 30$). Perhaps even more alarming are the statistics that reveal how many of these Choctaw children were involved in probable sexual exploitation. While only one child was enticed online, and fortunately none were located deceased, almost half ($n = 22$) of the sample of 49 children where this information was provided were identified as victims of likely sex trafficking (NCMEC, 2023).

In their report about the plight of Native American women and girls in the area of human trafficking, Nikkel and Parker (2022) offer the reader a description of what Native women need. Among the pragmatic needs (e.g., shelters, job programs), the authors make a heartbreaking observation that this population is often simply overlooked. An important step to combat their invisibility and ally with them "is simply to see them—in all the complexity of their oppression and resilience. Understanding their stories, their heritage and values, and the injustices that have made them vulnerable can better equip us to prevent and respond to trafficking." Nikkel and Parker (2022) republished a statement by a survivor originally quoted by Farley et al. (2011):

> Women like myself need someone they feel they can trust without being judged by how they lived their life… We need someone to understand where we came from and how we lived and that half of us were raped, beat, and made to sell our bodies. We need people with hearts.

Case Example: Choctaw Nation Rescue

In June 2023, very soon after the completion of her IPC training, a graduate of the course was on patrol just outside tribal lands. At approximately 2:00 AM she was advised that a suspicious vehicle was flashing its headlights at passing drivers. When the officer arrived on scene and approached the vehicle, a pickup truck, she observed that the bed was loaded with what appeared to be bags and totes. She also noticed what appeared to be a handwritten paper tag (license plate).

A female exited the driver's side of the vehicle and walked toward the officer. She explained that she had run out of fuel and was trying to flag down someone for help. While speaking with her, the officer used her flashlight to illuminate the cab, where she observed an adult male laying down in the back seat, holding a male toddler. The man immediately placed his hands over the toddler's face and asked the officer to turn off her flashlight, explaining that the child was "autistic" and that "lights cause him to have seizures." The officer asked the male if he meant "epileptic," and he responded, "He's both." She thought this was an odd statement, and the male's nonverbal behavior suggested something was amiss.

The officer asked the adults if they were the legal guardians of the child, and they indicated they were. When additional clarification was sought and they were asked if they were the *biological* parents, the male initially affirmed that they were, but then corrected himself and said the female was not, but was the only woman the child knew as a maternal figure because the biological mother had abandoned the child. The female provided an out-of-state identification card, as well as a name and date of birth for the adult male. The officer asked the female if she had ever been in trouble, and the woman said she was previously charged with Racketeering and Solicitation.

The officer and her partner, who by then had responded to the scene, agreed the situation was suspicious. They were concerned for the well-being of the child as he was wrapped in a towel instead of a diaper, and the adults did not have anything to drink and were asking for water. The officer also noticed cockroaches crawling out of the bed of the truck. Recalling her IPC training, the officer decided the extant factors could be consistent with a high-risk situation, and she decided to contact the on-call caseworker for Child Protective Services.

During the next two hours both adults engaged in deception with the officers as well as the CPS investigator. When it was discovered that the male had multiple outstanding felony warrants from another state, he began to physically resist arrest until the officers were able to successfully take him into custody.

Later that morning, around 10:00 AM, the officer was still uncertain about whether the story the subjects provided about the biological mother (i.e., that she did not want anything to do with the child) was true. She began searching online for the biological mother and soon located the woman's Facebook page. She discovered that in May 2023, the biological mother posted a message in which she indicated the male subject and the female subject had left with her child without her permission.

The officer contacted the mother, who advised that she and the male had been in a relationship which ended due to his methamphetamine use and other criminal activity. She indicated that two months prior the male asked if he could spend some time with the child while she ran errands. She had agreed, and when she returned they were gone. She said she contacted her local police department and tried to report her child as missing or kidnapped, but was told it was a "civil matter."

The mother had a Bluetooth tracking device in the child's diaper bag, and she had followed the device across several states before the subjects dumped the bag and she was no longer able to locate them. The mother said she then filed a report with the National Center for Missing and Exploited Children (NCMEC). This was verified by NCMEC when the officer called to confirm.

At the request of CPS, the officer re-interviewed the female, who again claimed the biological mother wanted nothing to do with the child. The woman was placed under arrest, and upon further investigation it was learned that she had been indicted in a federal court for Sex Trafficking of Children by Force, Fraud, or Coercion; after she pled down to one count of Racketeering and Solicitation, she was sentenced to 60 months. It was also learned the woman was associated with a street gang.

As a result of the instincts and observational skills of the officers, as well as by the application of techniques they learned in the Choctaw Nation's IPC training, the child was safely reunited with his biological mother and his abductors were imprisoned for multiple charges, including Child Endangerment.

Discussion and Future Directions

As indicated, the IPC program is designed to provide police officers with a new lens through which to view situations they may come across. Since we tend to find what we look for, the class is focused more on altering officers' approach to their encounters with citizens and less on learning specific indicators that could change or might be context-dependent. As one graduate of the recent course on Choctaw lands noted, "As a law enforcement professional involved in [crimes against children] investigations for over 20 years, [IPC] was a new perspective."

There are aspects of the course that may require modification as we continue to expand IPC in Indian Country. These include increasing the time set aside to address complex legal issues pertaining to child exploitation on and around tribal lands. For example, it can be difficult, particularly roadside, to determine which law enforcement agency has investigative jurisdiction, or which social services agency can best serve the children involved. In addition, while the U.S. Supreme Court decision in *McGirt v. Oklahoma* restored tribes' ability to tailor their justice systems to their own customs and culture, it also has presented new challenges and adaptations (e.g., cross-deputation) that require additional education (Elkins, 2022).

It is important to note that the techniques and principles taught in the IPC course are not necessarily unique to traffic stops—they have been effectively applied in other settings. For example, several months after the IPC course was offered at the Choctaw Nation, an Oklahoma Probation and Parole Officer wrote to the instructors. He reported that the Probation and Parole Officers who attended to course immediately began applying what they had learned in the field, and within a few months they discovered that 22 sex offenders on probation or parole were violating the terms of their supervised release. The application of IPC principles during home visits prompted further investigation and new criminal charges for three of the 22 offenders, including possession of child sexual abuse images, and three additional parolees were under investigation. The officer concluded, "I cannot stress how much your class has helped our team."

As IPC training is provided to jurisdictions on or nearby tribal lands, an emphasis will be made on the need to provide culturally relevant and trauma-informed practices. In a "Trafficking in Indian Country" brief released by the National Congress of American Indians Policy Research Center (2016), many Native American human trafficking victims said they "felt they owed their survival to Native cultural practices and they wished for Native healing approaches to be integrated with mainstream services" (United States Government Accountability Office, 2017a, p. 21). We intend to continue to work closely with our Victim Services colleagues to ensure we address this issue appropriately in our training.

As Bourke et al. (2016) noted, "The beneficiaries of our collaborative efforts [as IPC-trained professionals] are children who otherwise would go unidentified and unrescued." One of the two attendees who made the rescue of the child in the case described above wrote:

> The training my partner and I received when we attended Interdiction for the Protection of Children (IPC) allowed us to take my investigation further, instead of just responding to a simple call for service in regards to a suspicious vehicle. The training I received at IPC allowed me to identify signs of deception, prepared me to ask the appropriate questions in regards to child safety, and allowed me to successfully recover an endangered child and return him to the biological mother.

The present program is committed to reaching out to each law enforcement officer to first help them understand the unique issues relating to exploitation in Indian Country, and then to equip them with the right tools to make a difference, one traffic stop at a time.

References

Administration for Native Americans. (n.d.). *American Indians and Alaska Natives – by the numbers*. U.S Department of Health & Human Services, Administration for Children & Families. https://www.acf.hhs.gov/ana/fact-sheet/american-indians-and-alaska-natives-numbers

Association of Public Safety Communications Officials. (2015). *Standard for public safety telecommunicators when responding to calls of missing, abducted, and sexually exploited children (APCO ANS 1.101.3-2015)*. http://www.missingkids.org/en_US/documents/911standards.pdf

Basile, K. C., Smith, S. G., Kresnow, M., Khatiwada S., & Leemis, R. W. (2010). *2010 national intimate partner and sexual violence survey*. National Center for Injury Prevention and Control, Centers for Disease Control and Prevention. https://www.cdc.gov/nisvs/documentation/nisvsReportonSexualViolence.pdf

Belknap, J. (2010). Rape: Too hard to report and too easy to discredit victims. *Violence Against Women, 16*, 1335–1344. https://doi.org/10.1177/1077801210387749

Biess, J. (2017). *Homelessness in Indian Country is a hidden, but critical, problem*. Urban Institute. https://www.urban.org/urban-wire/homelessness-indian-country-hidden-critical-problem

Bourke, M. L., Prestridge, D., & Malterer, M. B. (2016). Interdiction for the protection of children: Preventing sexual exploitation one traffic stop at a time. *Aggression and Violent Behavior, 30*, 68–75. https://doi.org/10.1016/j.avb.2016.07.009

Brown, B. J. (2024). *IHS Recognizes the importance of human trafficking prevention in Indian Country*. Indian Health Services Blog. https://www.ihs.gov/newsroom/ihs-blog/january-2024-blogs/ihs-recognizes-the-importance-of-human-trafficking-prevention-in-indian-country/

Campbell, R. (2012, December). *The neurobiology of sexual assault* [Seminar]. National Institute of Justice. https://nij.ojp.gov/media/video/24056

Cawson, P., Wattam, C., Brooker, S., & Kelly, G. (2000, November). Child maltreatment in the United Kingdom: A study of the prevalence of abuse and neglect. *NSPCC Inform*. https://www.nspcc.org.uk/globalassets/documents/research-reports/child-maltreatment-uk-executive-summary.pdf

Center for Sex Offender Management. (2015). *Understanding sex offenders: An introductory curriculum*. Office of Justice Programs, U.S. Department of Justice. http://csom.org/train/etiology/3/3_1.htm

Chon, D. S. (2014). Police reporting by sexual assault victims in Western and Non-Western countries. *Journal of Family Violence, 29*, 859–868. https://doi.org/10.1007/s10896-014-9644-z

Cole, J., & Sprang, G. (2015). Sex trafficking of minors in metropolitan, micropolitan, and rural communities. *Child Abuse & Neglect, 40*, 113–123. https://doi.org/10.1016/j.chiabu.2014.07.015

Cooper, T. A. (2013). Racial bias in American foster care: The national debate. *Marquette Law Review, 97*(2), 215–278. https://scholarship.law.marquette.edu/mulr/vol97/iss2/3

Davis, C. G., Dunnigan, A., & Stevens, B. B. (2023). Indigenous-centered racial disproportionality in American foster care: A national population study. *Journal of Public Child Welfare, 17*(2), 280–304. https://doi.org/10.1080/15548732.2021.2022565

Elkins, F. C. (2022, January). What does a recent Supreme Court decision mean for tribal, state, and federal law enforcement? *Dispatch, 15*(1). https://cops.usdoj.gov/html/dispatch/01-2022/McGirt_decision.html

Farley, M., Matthews, N., Deer, S., Lopez, G., Stark, C., & Hudon, E. (2011). *Garden of truth: The prostitution and trafficking of Native women in Minnesota.* Minnesota Indian Women's Sexual Assault Coalition. https://www.niwrc.org/sites/default/files/images/resource/Garden-of-Truth.pdf

Felitti, V. J., Anda, R. F., Nordenberg, D., Williamson, D. F., Spitz, A. M., Edwards, V., Koss, M. P., & Marks, J. S. (1998). Relationship of childhood abuse and household dysfunction to many of the leading causes of death in adults: The Adverse Childhood Experiences (ACE) Study. *American Journal of Preventive Medicine, 14*(4), 245–258. https://doi.org/10.1016/s0749-3797(98)00017-8

Finkelhor, D., Hammer, H., & Sedlak, A. J. (2008, August). *Sexually assaulted children: National estimates and characteristics.* U.S. Department of Justice, Office of Justice Programs, Office of Juvenile Justice and Delinquency Prevention. https://www.ncjrs.gov/pdffiles1/ojjdp/214383.pdf

Giano, Z., Camplain, R. L., Camplain, C., Pro, G., Haberstroh, S., Baldwin, J. A.,Wheeler, D. L., & Hubach, R. D. (2021). Adverse childhood events in American Indian/Alaska Native populations. *American Journal of Preventative Medicine, 60*(2), 213–221. https://doi.org/10.1016/j.amepre.2020.08.020

Henry, M., Watt, R., Mahathey, A., Ouelette, J., & Sitler, A. (2020, January). *The 2019 Annual Homeless Assessment Report (AHAR) to Congress.* U.S. Department of Housing and Urban Development. www.huduser.gov/portal/sites/default/files/pdf/2019-AHAR-Part-1.pdf

Koss, M. P., Yuan, N. P., & Dightman, D. (2003). Adverse childhood exposures and alcohol dependence among seven Native American tribes. *American Journal of Preventive Medicine, 25*(3), 238–244.

National Center for Missing and Exploited Children. (2015a). *Child sex trafficking in America: A guide for child welfare.* http://www.missingkids.com/en_US/documents/Fact_Sheet_Child_Welfare.pdf

National Center for Missing and Exploited Children. (2015b). *Key facts.* http://www.missingkids.org/KeyFacts

National Center for Missing and Exploited Children. (2023). *Choctaw report: 2018–2023.* Unpublished manuscript.

National Congress of American Indians Policy Research Center. (2016, Spring). *Human trafficking: Trends and responses across Indian Country.* Tribal Insights Brief. https://archive.ncai.org/policy-research-center/research-data/prc-publications/TraffickingBrief.pdf

National Human Trafficking Resource Center. (2015). *Human trafficking.* http://traffickingresourcecenter.org/type-trafficking/human-trafficking

Nikkel, M., & Parker, L. (2022). *Human trafficking in Native American communities.* The Exodus Road. https://theexodusroad.com/human-trafficking-in-native-american-communities/

O'Leary, C., & Howard, O. (2001). *The prostitution of women and girls in metropolitan Chicago: A preliminary prevalence report.* Center for Impact Research. http://www.thenightministry.org

Rennison, C. M. (2002). *Rape and sexual assault: Reporting to police and medical attention, 1992–2000 [NCJ 194530].* U.S. Department of Justice, Office of Justice Programs, Bureau of Justice Statistics. http://bjs.ojp.usdoj.gov/content/pub/pdf/rsarp00.pdf

Richards, K. (2011, September). *Misperceptions about sex offenders.* Australian Government, Australian Institute of Criminology, 429. http://aic.gov.au/media_library/publications/tandi_pdf/tandi429.pdf

Richards, T. N., Schwartz, J. A., & Wright, E. (2021). Examining adverse childhood experiences among Native American persons in a nationally representative sample: Differences among racial/ethnic groups and race/ethnicity-sex dyads. *Child Abuse & Neglect, 111*, Article 104812.

Roesler, T. A., & Wind, T. W. (1994). Telling the secret: Adult women describe their disclosures of incest. *Journal of Interpersonal Violence, 9*(3), 327–338.

Rosay, A. B. (2016, June 1). Violence against American Indian and Alaska Native women and men. *National Institute of Justice Journal.* https://nij.ojp.gov/topics/articles/violence-against-american-indian-and-alaska-native-women-and-men

Shrider, E. A., & Creamer, J. (2023). *Poverty in the United States: 2022.* U.S Census Bureau. https://www.census.gov/content/dam/Census/library/publications/2023/demo/p60-280.pdf

Substance Abuse and Mental Health Services Administration. (2019). *2018 national survey on drug use and health detailed tables.* https://www.samhsa.gov/data/report/2018-nsduh-detailed-tables

Taylor, S. C., & Gassner, L. (2010). Stemming the flow: Challenges for policing adult sexual assault with regard to attrition rates and under-reporting of sexual offences. *Police Practice and Research: An International Journal, 11*(3), 240–255.

U.S. Department of Health & Human Services. (n.d.). *American Indians and Alaska Natives – By the numbers.* https://www.acf.hhs.gov/ana/fact-sheet/american-indians-and-alaska-natives-numbers

United States Government Accountability Office. (2015, February 25). *Foster care: HHS needs to improve the consistency and timeliness of assistance to tribes,* GAO-15-273. https://www.gao.gov/assets/gao-15-273.pdf

United States Government Accountability Office. (2017a). *Human Trafficking. Information on cases in Indian Country or that involved Native Americans,* GAO-17-624. https://www.gao.gov/products/gao-17-624

United States Government Accountability Office. (2017b). *Supplemental material for GAO-17-624: Survey results for selected tribal and major city law enforcement agencies and victim service providers on human trafficking,* GAO-17-626SP. https://www.gao.gov/products/gao-17-626sp

Chapter 11
Peers as Law Enforcement Support for Correctional Officers: A Model Demonstration Program

Naysha Rivera-Hartley, Gabrielle L. LaRock, Gregory S. Tony, Quina Munson, Vincent B. Van Hasselt, and Ryan A. Black

Peer Support Training for COs: A Model Demonstration Program

Correctional Officers (COs) face significant occupational stress due to exposure to high-risk situations, mental and emotional challenges, and the inherent dangers of working in a correctional environment (Montoya-Barthelemy et al., 2021). The Peer Assistance and Law Enforcement Support (PALS-C) program was designed for COs to provide a structured support system to navigate personal and professional crises. By fostering a culture of peer support, resilience, and mental health awareness, PALS-C serves to enhance officer well-being, improve job performance, and reduce the stigma surrounding mental health challenges.

Modeled after the original Peers as Law Enforcement Support (PALS) program (Van Hasselt et al., 2019), PALS-C program is a voluntary initiative that enables law enforcement officers to receive confidential support from trained peers who understand the unique stressors of their chosen profession. This program acts as both a proactive and supportive resource, equipping COs with the tools needed to

The opinions expressed in this work are solely those of the authors and do not reflect or represent the views or official positions of Nova Southeastern University, Broward Sheriff's Office, or Miami-Dade Corrections and Rehabilitation.

N. Rivera-Hartley (✉) · G. L. LaRock · V. B. Van Hasselt · R. A. Black
College of Psychology, Nova Southeastern University, Fort Lauderdale, FL, USA
e-mail: nr1084@mynsu.nova.edu

G. S. Tony · V. B. Van Hasselt
Broward Sheriff's Office, Broward County, FL, USA

Q. Munson
Miami-Dade Corrections and Rehabilitation, Doral, FL, USA

V. B. Van Hasselt and M. L. Bourke (eds.), *Advances in First Responder Mental Health*, Advances in First Responder Mental Health 1,
https://doi.org/10.1007/978-3-032-27978-1_11

manage workplace stress and personal challenges. Further, PALS-C provides an internal network where officers can seek peer support during times of crisis, fostering resilience, reducing stigma concerning mental health, and promoting overall well-being within the workplace.

A training manual serves as a resource and guidebook for peer supporters. Its importance cannot be overstated as it serves as a compass to guide and remind participants of the program purpose and the importance of the work that they are doing. When providing a manual, it is ideal to personalize and address this communication by including a letter addressing the members of the team as follows:

To Members of the PALS-C Team,

Correctional Officers (COs) face numerous stressors, making peer support programs like PALS-C (Peers as Law Enforcement Support) essential. PALS-C provides confidential, peer-led support to help COs navigate personal and professional challenges, safeguarding their mental well-being and preventing the loss of valuable personnel.

*PALS-C operates on the principles of confidentiality, mutual respect, and emotional support. Selection is based on an officer's ability to understand behavioral health concerns and relate empathically to another individual, rather than on rank. Members receive specialized training to assist peers and refer them to professional resources when necessary. As of 2025, 38 states offer legal protections to peer support programs to maintain confidentiality and trust under their state statutes (*O'Dare et al., 2024*). For example, Florida Statute 111.09 provides confidentiality protections for first responders who are involved in peer support communications, guarding their communications from use in legal, administrative, or disciplinary procedures. Exceptions to this confidentiality include threats of harm, criminal activity, or if the responder consents to disclosure. The statute also defines and protects trained, non-clinical first responder peers and extends these protections to include dispatchers, and correctional officers* (Chapter 111-Public Officers General Provision Section 09-2024 Florida Statutes, 2024).

Beyond intervention, PALS-C emphasizes prevention by reducing the stigma surrounding mental health in law enforcement. Peer support members play a vital role in fostering a culture where seeking help is normalized. The camaraderie within the profession is strengthened through programs like PALS-C, ensuring officers have the support they need to continue serving with resilience and fortitude.

Your dedication to your fellow officers is deeply valued. Programs like PALS-C can make a lasting impact on law enforcement culture, reinforcing the importance of support, trust, and well-being for generations to come.

(Your signature here)

Mission Statement

Correctional institutions are recognizing the critical need for officer wellness and are increasingly establishing peer support programs to complement existing Employee Assistance Programs. These programs are designed to promote confidential, peer-led support for officers experiencing occupational stress, trauma, or other professional challenges.

The mission of PALS-C is to provide structured peer support that strengthens officers' mental health, professional resilience, and crisis management skills. By engaging in specialized training and peer mentorship, they are equipped with the tools to support one another, fostering a healthier work environment.

Providing a mission statement further illustrates the agency's dedication and commitment to the program. A mission statement used in PALS-C is as follows:

Mission Statement

[Name of Your Law Enforcement Agency] recognizes the critical need to support personnel as they navigate personal and professional challenges. To enhance the support services already offered through our Employee Assistance Program (EAP), (the agency's name) has launched the Peer Assistance and Leadership Support (PALS-C) program. This initiative is staffed by fellow officers who volunteer to undergo specialized training to assist any department member in need.

PALS-C offers a confidential, peer-led resource where officers can receive support from colleagues who deeply understand the unique stressors of law enforcement as lived experiences. The program aims to reinforce overall well-being and ensure that officers continue to thrive in their roles as productive members of [Name of Your Law Enforcement Agency].

PALS-C Overview

PALS-C equips peer support members with the skills necessary to address both routine stress and critical incidents, providing officers with essential emotional support, organized interventions, and referrals to suitable mental health resources when needed. A core component of the PALS-C is "just-in-time" crisis support, ensuring that officers in distress receive immediate peer assistance. Additionally, the program emphasizes resilience-building by promoting holistic wellness and effective stress management, and healthy or adaptive coping strategies. Confidentiality and trust are fundamental to the program, ensuring that all interactions remain private and that officers feel safe when seeking support. Crucial to the efficacy and "buy-in" of PALS-C is that the peer team members are sensitive to issues of trust, confidentiality, and anonymity for peers seeking assistance. It is emphasized that contacts and interactions involving a PALS team member and fellow police officer are confidential, with the exception of matters that violate the law (Van Hasselt et al., 2019, p. 2).

Peer supporters also receive specialized training in active listening and communication, preparing them to provide meaningful support to colleagues facing challenges. Additionally, the PALS-C program serves as a central link, connecting officers with mental health professionals when intervention is needed, reinforcing overall workforce well-being. Peer support programs like PALS-C are integral to behavioral health services within law enforcement agencies, serving as an additional layer of support that complements traditional resources such as Employee Assistance Programs. They maintain the highest standards of confidentiality and trust, ensuring that officers feel safe when seeking assistance.

Research indicates that peer support programs are effective in improving mental health outcomes and job satisfaction for law enforcement officers by providing a relatable and trustworthy support system (Carleton et al., 2017; McCanlies et al., 2018). The integration of peer-led initiatives with existing support services has proven beneficial in reducing the stigma associated with seeking help and enhancing the overall resilience of officers (Papazoglou & Andersen, 2014).

Occupational Risks in Corrections

COs encounter numerous occupational hazards that contribute to mental and physical strain. Research indicates that high levels of stress, frequent exposure to violence, and the need for physical intervention significantly impact officer wellness and job performance (Lee & Wu, 2024). Additionally, there are psychological impacts when COs face situations requiring the use-of-force, such as breaking up fights, restraining inmates, and responding to emergencies (Goulette et al., 2020). The psychological consequences of these incidents include increased risk of anxiety, and symptoms of traumatic stress (e.g., hypervigilance, emotional numbing, sleep disturbances), not to mention being subjected to agency-mandated use-of-force investigations.

Studies have found that officers who frequently engage in use-of-force may develop "moral injury" in which the individual struggles with actions taken in the line of duty that conflict with personal or professional ethics. This specific type of injury can be defined as a "… particular trauma syndrome including psychological, existential, behavioral, and interpersonal issues that emerge following perceived violations of deep moral beliefs by oneself or trusted individuals" (Jinkerson, 2016, p. 126). Providing peer support intervention allows officers to discuss and process these experiences in a safe and confidential environment. Further, COs experience a high risk of physical assaults, with incidents ranging from verbal threats to direct physical attacks. Prolonged exposure to such events increases the risk of burnout and compassion fatigue. Moreover, it may lead to heightened levels of aggression or detachment and increased reliance on negative coping mechanisms (e.g., alcohol use).

Implementing a peer support program within an agency enables officers to seek support before stress leads to severe psychological consequences, including suicidality. For example, Zimmerman et al. (2023) found factors contributing to this risk include long hours, unpredictable schedules, lack of access to mental health resources, and cumulative trauma from violent or high-stress situations. By normalizing mental health discussions, and help-seeking initiatives, peer support programs have the potential to mitigate isolation and self-destructive behaviors.

Benefits of a Peer Support Program

Implementing peer support in correctional facilities provides significant benefits for both individual officers and the agency as a whole. For officers, access to peer support improves mental health by early recognition of anxiety, depression, and PTSD symptoms. Research indicates that peer support programs contribute to better health outcomes by increasing mental health awareness, helping individuals recognize problems as a common experience, and reducing the stigma associated with seeking assistance (Fallon et al., 2023). It also fosters a sense of camaraderie and teamwork, leading to increased job satisfaction and a supportive work environment.

For the agency, a well-established peer support program may contribute to increased job satisfaction, resulting in higher personnel retention, thus reducing the costs associated with high turnover. According to Byrd et al. (2000), greater job satisfaction is associated with diminished turnover, emphasizing the value of a supportive work environment to enhance retention and workplace morale. A culture of peer support strengthens workplace morale by improving communication, trust, and collaboration among staff. Although direct evidence linking peer support programs to reduced absenteeism in law enforcement is scarce, related studies suggest that providing emotional support through such programs can enhance job engagement and potentially decrease absenteeism. Further research is needed to establish a direct causal relationship in the context of law enforcement (Milliard, 2020).

Peer Supporter

A peer supporter is an individual, often with lived experience and specialized training, who offers support, guidance, and encouragement to people experiencing similar challenges or situations. Their role involves offering emotional and social support by sharing experiences, instilling hope, and helping others navigate recovery or personal growth knowing that they are not alone in their struggles. By fostering connections based on empathy, active listening, and mutual respect, peer supporters empower individuals to advocate for themselves and take an active role in their welfare.

Unlike professional counselors or therapists, peer supporters may not have formal clinical training. However, their life experience allows them to offer a unique and relatable form of support, bridging gaps in traditional mental health and social services. Their assistance is grounded in the principle of "meeting people where they are," emphasizing mutual respect, non-judgment, and a partnership approach (Johns Hopkins Medicine, 2018).

Program Objective

The primary goal of peer support programs is to enhance the overall well-being, emotional safety, and performance of officers by providing a source of trusted support, resources, and services. The programs are designed to assist officers in managing personal or professional challenges that may affect their social and occupational functioning. This initiative seeks to create a supportive environment where officers feel encouraged to discuss issues, ultimately fostering a more positive workplace culture (Careless, 2023).

PALS-C was designed to prevent and alleviate the negative impact of stress and trauma among officers by offering trained peer support, and information on coping strategies and resources. The program's volunteers are trained in stress management, critical incident response, communication, and behavioral health. PALS-C, like the original PALS program, provides immediate and ongoing support through one-on-one interactions, on-scene responses, and post-incident care, helping officers manage the emotional aftermath of their experiences.

Benefits of Peer Support

Enhanced job satisfaction, safety, and health: Peer support can help reduce the impact of traumatic experiences, decrease burnout, and contribute to overall job satisfaction and safety. Implementing peer support programs by virtue of improving personnel job satisfaction can support agency efforts to decrease costs associated with recruitment and training by improving officer retention rates (Milliard, 2020).

Increased resources for officers and their families: The program offers officers and their families' access to a variety of resources and support systems, providing alternative options for managing personal and professional challenges. These objectives and benefits highlight the critical role of peer support in promoting the mental and emotional well-being of law enforcement personnel.

Program Goals

These following goals were established to create a comprehensive support system that addresses the diverse needs of COs and facility personnel, promoting resilience, well-being, and a positive work environment.

I. Provide Crisis Support: Serve as a familiar and accessible resource for employees experiencing crises in either their personal lives or professional roles, ensuring timely intervention and assistance during critical moments.

II. Promote Holistic Health and Wellness: Encourage and support the social, physical, emotional, and mental well-being of officers through various resources and peer-led activities designed to promote a healthy work-life balance and reduce stress.
III. Conflict Resolution and Emotional Support: Help identify and assess conflicts or challenging situations that officers may face, actively listen, and offer non-judgmental support, guidance, and referrals when necessary.
IV. Model Effective Communication and Relational Trust: Promote an environment of open dialogue, encouragement, and trust by modeling effective communication skills and maintaining confidentiality to strengthen the peer support network among officers.
V. Offer Assistance During and After Traumatic or Stressful Event: Provide ongoing support during and following incidents that cause personal or professional distress, ensuring that those in need receive assistance and resources to recover.
VI. Act as a Liaison to EAP Resources: Serve as a conduit between officers and external resources, facilitating access to services and support that address various personal and professional difficulties.
VII. Promote Mental Health Awareness and Education: Increase awareness and normalize mental health challenges; provide education on recognizing signs of stress, trauma, and burnout. This goal aims to create a culture where help seeking is normalized and stigma is reduced.
VIII. Enhance Team Cohesion and Increase Morale: Strengthen team dynamics by fostering a sense of community and mutual support, encouraging positive interactions, and contributing to a cohesive and resilient workforce. This promotes relational safety, enhances overall morale, and helps officers feel supported and valued within the organization.

Program Policies

1. *Voluntary Participation*: Joining PALS-C is completely voluntary. Participants are required to complete the curriculum.
2. *Role and Limitations:* PALS-C members are not professional therapists or counselors. They provide support, and possible resources when needed, but are not a replacement for professional mental health services.

Responsibilities

1. *Ongoing Support:* PALS-C members offer continuous help to officers dealing with emotional or behavioral issues and provide support during and after critical incidents like injuries, fatalities, or any event causing serious emotional impact.

2. *Connecting to Resources:* When additional help is needed, PALS-C members guide officers to appropriate resources such as counseling services or community support programs.

Confidentiality

1. *Confidentiality Commitment*: PALS-C members maintain confidentiality to build trust and ensure officers feel safe using the service. This confidentiality is respected by both command staff and colleagues.
2. *Exceptions to Confidentiality:* There are specific cases where confidentiality cannot be maintained, including situations involving danger to oneself or others, suspected child or elder abuse, and suspected abuse of individuals with intellectual disabilities.

PALS-C includes trained volunteers from within the department who offer peer support. They have specialized training to help identify and address issues such as stress, substance use, and psychological reactions to incidents like inmate attacks, fights, or suicides.

PALS-C Member Responsibilities

PALS-C members are known and selected for their good rapport with peers, effective listening skills, and empathy. They are committed to maintaining confidentiality and providing support for officers dealing with crises, mental health challenges, or everyday stress. Participation is voluntary, and members can step down at any time, but must notify their PALS-C team leader immediately. They also receive regular training to keep their skills current. Communication within the program remains confidential between officers and PALS-C members, and referrals are made when necessary. Officers can contact PALS-C personnel directly or be recommended for services by others. However, no further action is taken to ensure privacy if an officer declines support.

Additional Responsibilities and Involvement

PALS-C members may assist in shaping program policies, creating materials like brochures, and educating others about the program. They hold regular meetings to discuss changes and provide support to each other. Members also promote the program through station visits and presentations.

PALS-C Program Modules

PALS-C is provided over two, eight-hour days. Taking frequent breaks during peer support training for COs is essential to maintaining engagement and maximizing learning. Unlike individuals accustomed to prolonged seated instruction, COs are used to high-energy, fast-paced environments where constant movement is the norm. Long training sessions without breaks can lead to restlessness, reduced attention, and decreased information retention. By incorporating regular breaks, trainees have the opportunity to reset mentally, process the material more effectively, and return to the session with renewed focus. These breaks also serve as a chance for informal peer interaction, reinforcing camaraderie and the importance of self-care which are key principles of peer support itself.

The training incorporates various learning methods, including PowerPoint modules, mental health videos, and scenario-based exercises, covering the "Big 6" mental health topics: Anxiety, Depression, Substance Use, Sleep Problems, PTSD, and Suicide Awareness. Active Listening and Resilience/Post-Traumatic Growth are also covered (Fig. 11.1).

Module 1: Active Listening Skills

Active listening is a fundamental skill for peer support members. Given the unique stressors COs encounter, such as exposure to violence, high-pressure environments, and a culture that often discourages open discussion of mental health, effective peer support requires more than just casual conversation. Active listening fosters trust, encourages openness, and helps COs feel truly heard and understood. By utilizing techniques, such as open-ended questioning, minimal encouragers, and reflection/mirroring, peer supporters can create a safe and judgment-free space where officers feel comfortable sharing their struggles. This is particularly important in law enforcement settings, where seeking professional mental health services may be stigmatized.

Fig. 11.1 The Big 6: core peer support training modules

Fig. 11.2 Active listening skills

By demonstrating empathy and avoiding communication blockers, peer supporters can ensure that their colleagues receive the validation and support they need while also guiding them toward appropriate resources when necessary.

Further, teaching active listening skills helps peer supporters avoid common pitfalls, such as offering unsolicited advice, minimizing concerns, or equating personal experiences with those of their peers. COs experiencing distress may be hesitant to open up, and a poorly handled conversation can deter them from assistance in the future. Active listening techniques (see Fig. 11.2), such as emotional labeling, paraphrasing, and effective use of silence, help peer supporters acknowledge the emotions underlying their peers' words, promoting deeper understanding and connection.

Active Listening Skills Checklist for PALS-C

Establish a Positive Training Environment

- Ensure the setting is private and free from distractions.
- Display open body language (e.g., uncrossed arms, steady eye contact).
- Create a welcoming space that encourages the speaker to feel comfortable.

Show Genuine Interest

- Use verbal and non-verbal cues, such as nodding and maintaining eye contact.
- Minimize distractions—put away your phone and give your full attention.
- Avoid interrupting or finishing the other person's sentences.

Practice Reflective Listening

- Paraphrase what the speaker has said to show understanding (e.g., "It sounds like you're feeling frustrated because…").
- Use Summaries to review key points (e.g., "So, if I'm hearing you correctly, you're saying that…").

- Ask Clarifying Questions when something is unclear (e.g., "Can you explain more about what happened then?").

Use Open-Ended Questions

Encourage deeper conversation by asking Open-Ended Questions such as:

- "Can you tell me more about how that made you feel?"
- "What was that experience like for you?"

Avoid yes/no questions unless you are confirming facts.

Validate Feelings and Emotions

- Use empathetic statements like, "That sounds really tough," or "I can see why you'd feel that way."
- Avoid minimizing or dismissing their emotions. Show acceptance, even if you don't agree.

Avoid Judgment and Advice-Giving

- Refrain from making judgments or giving unsolicited advice.
- Focus on understanding rather than evaluating or diagnosing.
- Use supportive language such as, "I'm here to listen and support you."

Be Aware of Your Own Biases and Reactions

- Reflect on your own emotional reactions and avoid projecting them onto the speaker.
- Stay present and manage any personal biases or assumptions that may affect your listening.

Use Silence Effectively

- Allow for pauses in the conversation without rushing to fill the silence.
- Use silence as a tool to encourage the speaker to continue and share more.

Provide Encouragement and Affirmation

- Use affirming phrases like, "You're doing great sharing this," or "I appreciate your honesty."
- Show that you recognize and value their willingness to open up.

Follow up and Offer Continued Support

- Offer continued support by checking in on the speaker at a later time.
- Ask if there are any additional ways you can support them going forward.

Module 2: Depression

Teaching COs peer supporters about depression is essential, as it is one of the most common and misunderstood mental health conditions in this population. Depression goes beyond temporary sadness. It can present as persistent irritability, anger, impulsivity, and isolation, which are most prevalent among law enforcement officers. Many COs may not recognize their symptoms as depression, assuming instead that they are simply stressed or "burned out." By educating peer supporters on the signs, risk factors, and gender differences in depression, they can better identify when a fellow officer is struggling and offer meaningful support. Since law enforcement culture often discourages vulnerability, peers play a crucial role in normalizing depression as a medical condition rather than a personal weakness.

Understanding depression is also critical because it is a major risk factor for suicide, with a majority of individuals who die by suicide having a previously diagnosable mental health condition (Hawton et al., 2013). COs face elevated levels of job strain, social isolation, and trauma exposure, all of which increase their likelihood of experiencing depression and suicidal ideation. Teaching peer supporters to recognize behavioral changes, such as increased risk-taking, withdrawal, or sudden shifts in mood, can be lifesaving. By fostering open conversations, offering emotional support, and guiding their peers toward professional resources, peer support team members can help break the stigma surrounding mental health and encourage officers to seek help before their struggles escalate into a crisis. It is important to understand that while it is normal to "feel down" sometimes, if that feeling lasts for more than a few days, it might be a sign of depression. Major depression is more than just feeling sad; it involves symptoms like persistent sadness or a loss of interest in previously pleasurable activities for at least two weeks, and it can interfere with everyday life. It is not a sign of weakness or a bad attitude, but rather a common mental health condition that can be treated.

Depression can be triggered by different things, such as a stressful life event (e.g., losing a job, death of a loved one) or having a chronic illness. People with depression often experience sadness or a lack of interest in things they used to enjoy. They may also feel guilty, worthless, hopeless, or have thoughts of death or suicide. Physical symptoms, such as significant weight changes, low energy, trouble sleeping, or persistent aches and pains, can also be present.

Men and women can show disparate signs of depression. Men often feel tired, irritable, and lose interest in work or hobbies, while women might feel more sadness, guilt, and a sense of worthlessness. This difference can affect how they cope: while men might turn to alcohol or drugs more often, women are more likely to seek assistance. Regardless of gender, depression can become overwhelming and make it hard to think, behave, and function normally. Figure 11.3 provides a chart summarizing some common symptoms of depression. Symptoms under the blue shade represent physical symptoms; symptoms under the pink shade are emotional symptoms. Symptoms that fall in the white portion are those that overlap physical and emotional presentations of depression.

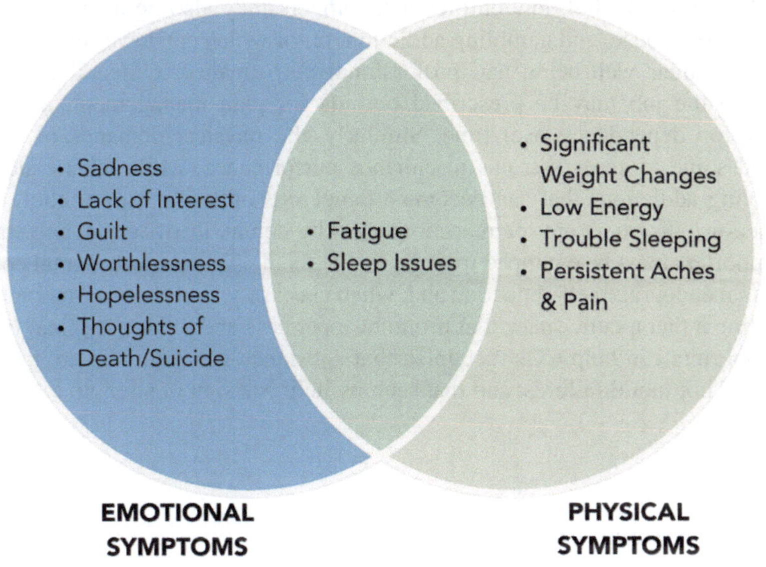

Fig. 11.3 Symptoms of depression

Module 3: Substance Use

Teaching peer support volunteers about the prevalence of substance use in the law enforcement community is crucial, as it has historically been viewed as a culturally acceptable coping mechanism. COs face high levels of occupational stress, trauma exposure, and shift work, all of which contribute to an increased risk of substance use, particularly alcohol abuse. Research indicates that while approximately 8% of the general population experience alcohol-related problems, this number rises to 16–18% among law enforcement officers (Ballenger et al., 2010). Drinking is frequently normalized as a way to bond with colleagues, decompress after a shift, or cope with the emotional burdens of the job. However, this normalization can prevent officers from recognizing when their use has escalated into a problem, leading to increased risk of dependence, impaired judgment, and long-term mental and physical health consequences. Additionally, these conditions can seriously affect a CO's job performance, decision-making, and personal relationships. It is crucial to recognize these symptoms early and provide support through mental health and addiction services (Correctional Officers: Behavioral Health Concerns, Emergency Response, and Trauma–Suicide Prevention Resource Center, 2018). Peer support team members must understand these dynamics to recognize when a fellow officer may be using substances as a way to self-medicate rather than utilizing healthier coping strategies.

In addition to alcohol, law enforcement officers may also be at risk of opioid misuse, steroid abuse, and gambling addiction, all of which can have serious consequences for their well-being and professional performance. Officers who suffer injuries on the job may be prescribed opioids for pain management, and some may develop dependency over time. Similarly, the physical demands of the job may lead some to abuse steroids to enhance performance, while others succumb to gambling addictions that can become a dangerous outlet for stress relief. Since substance-use disorders are often accompanied by denial, justification, and stigma, peer supporters must be equipped to engage officers in open, nonjudgmental conversations that encourage self-reflection and, when necessary, professional intervention. By creating a therapeutic space that promotes openness and reduces stigma, trained peer supporters can help COs recognize that substance-use disorders are treatable conditions, not moral failures, and that seeking help is a sign of strength rather than weakness.

Module 4: Anxiety and PTSD

Educating peer support volunteers about the heightened risk of PTSD and anxiety in the CO community is critical, as these conditions are common due to the nature of the job. COs are frequently exposed to high-stress environments, violent incidents, and traumatic experiences, which can contribute to the development of PTSD. Unlike acute stress reactions that naturally subside within 30 days, PTSD symptoms persist, often surfacing months or years after a traumatic event, perhaps even after retirement. Officers suffering from PTSD may experience hypervigilance, flashbacks, emotional numbness, or avoidance behaviors that interfere with daily life and job performance. Anxiety can present as excessive worry, irritability, difficulty concentrating, and physical symptoms such as restlessness or sleep disturbances. By recognizing the warning signs, peer supporters can provide early intervention, thus reducing the potential long-term impact of these disorders and encouraging officers to seek professional help.

Additionally, PTSD and anxiety can lead to secondary complications, such as substance use, social withdrawal, and burnout, which further diminish an officer's mental and emotional resilience. Compassion fatigue, a condition where individuals become emotionally drained from supporting others, is also common in law enforcement. If not properly addressed, these mental health struggles can negatively impact decision-making, increase aggression, and strain on personal relationships. This highlights the importance of peer supporters offering compassion and understanding when assisting officers who are facing difficulties. Teaching peer supporters effective ways to engage with colleagues, for example, by allowing open conversations without judgment, avoiding dismissive or devaluing statements, and offering practical coping strategies, can create a culture of support within the correctional system.

Module 5: Suicide Awareness

Educating peer support volunteers about the heightened risk of suicide within the CO community is essential. Violanti (2017) noted that "suicide rates among correction officers were found to be 39% higher than the national average" and that "more correctional officers die by suicide than are killed in the line of duty." The unique pressures of the job, such as chronic exposure to trauma, high-stakes decision-making, and a culture that discourages vulnerability, can create an environment in which officers may struggle in silence. According to BlueHelp.org, a non-profit organization that tracks first responder suicides, 123 COs have died by suicide since 2019 (Blue H.E.L.P., 2025). Many experience undiagnosed depression, PTSD, and substance-use issues, which are risk factors for suicidal ideation. The stigma surrounding mental health in law enforcement often prevents personnel from seeking help, thereby reinforcing feelings of isolation and hopelessness. By training peer supporters to recognize warning signs such as mood shifts, social withdrawal, increased alcohol use, or uncharacteristic expressions of despair, they can step in early and provide crucial support. Encouraging open conversations and normalizing mental health challenges can make officers feel less alone and more willing to reach out for assistance before they reach a crisis point.

Peer supporters must understand that suicidal thoughts are often concealed, especially in a profession where emotional and physical resilience is highly valued. Many officers may not explicitly state that they are struggling; however, indirect cues (i.e., giving away personal belongings, reckless behavior, or talking about being a burden) should be taken seriously. Volunteers trained in suicide risk assessment and prevention can play a key role in disrupting these thought patterns by providing a safe space for officers to express their distress without judgment.

Figure 11.4 highlights the critical issue of suicide in COs, underscoring the urgent need for mental health support and intervention. Johnson et al. (2022) identify ten primary reasons why COs take their own lives, including occupational stress, cumulative trauma exposure, PTSD, depression, substance use, relationship breakdowns, financial difficulties, fear of seeking help due to stigma, lack of coping resources, and easy access to firearms. The Ruderman White Paper, a 2018 publication focused on keeping first responders' mental health at the forefront of public attention, further underscores the contention that both COs and police officers experience significantly higher suicide rates than the general population, largely due to the intense psychological burden of their profession (Bar Nissim et al., 2022). These findings emphasize the importance of proactive peer support programs that address the risk factors, reduce stigma, and provide accessible mental health resources tailored to the unique challenges encountered by COs. Unlike other law enforcement personnel who leave the scene after an incident, COs remain immersed in the same high-tension atmosphere, increasing their risk for chronic stress, PTSD, and emotional exhaustion. A strong peer support system provides a safe outlet for the processing of their experiences, thus reducing isolation and encouraging early intervention before struggles escalate into a crisis.

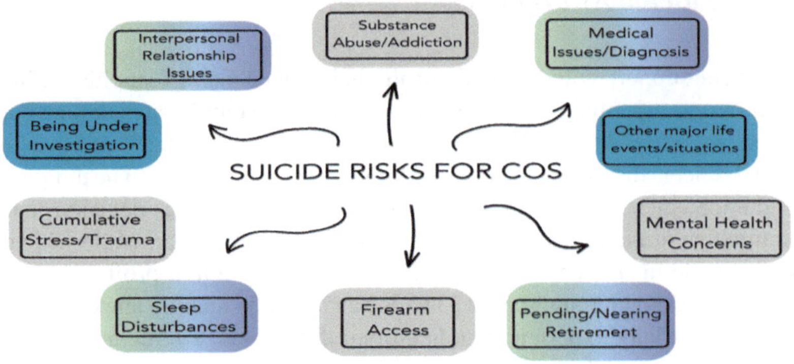

Fig. 11.4 Suicide risks for COs

Module 6: Resilience and Post-Traumatic Growth

Resilience is the ability to recover from adversity; it plays a critical role in determining how officers cope with traumatic experiences. While some may develop chronic stress or PTSD, others are able to process difficult events and integrate them into a meaningful framework. Understanding resilience allows peer supporters to help officers recognize their own stress responses, develop healthy coping strategies, and avoid maladaptive behaviors (e.g., social avoidance, substance use). By incorporating self-awareness techniques, stress-reduction strategies, and mindfulness practices (e.g., meditation, deep breathing), peer supporters can guide their colleagues toward healthier ways to manage job-related pressures.

While exposure to trauma can have serious negative effects, it can also lead to "post-traumatic growth"—positive psychological changes that occur as a result of overcoming adversity. For COs, post-traumatic growth may include a greater appreciation for life, improved relationships, and a renewed sense of purpose in life and in their work. By focusing on both resilience and post-traumatic growth, they can not only recover from aversive situations, so they can also grow and find new meaning through their experiences. With regular practice and support, COs can build and maintain resilience, enhancing their ability to cope with stress and trauma in both their personal and professional lives.

Post-traumatic growth goes *beyond* resilience by emphasizing how individuals can paradoxically emerge from adversity *stronger* and *more self-aware*. When COs are provided with the right support and coping tools, they can develop a deeper appreciation for life, strengthen personal relationships, and find meaningfulness in their work. Teaching peer supporters about this concept helps shift the narrative from trauma as solely damaging to an opportunity for personal growth.

Viktor E. Frankl's "Man's Search for Meaning" offers profound insights into transforming traumatic experiences into opportunities for personal growth. A profound quote that underscores the concept of post-traumatic growth is: "In some ways suffering ceases to be suffering at the moment it finds a meaning, such as the meaning of a sacrifice" (Frankl, 2013, *Man's Search for Meaning*, p. 113). This perspective can be particularly relevant for COs who, after enduring traumatic events, may find deeper purpose and resilience by attributing meaning to their experiences. Encouraging activities, such as goal setting, guided imagery, and mindfulness exercises, can empower officers to take control of their mental health and build long-term emotional endurance. By fostering a culture that promotes growth rather than merely survival, peer support volunteers can play a crucial role in helping COs maintain psychological well-being throughout their careers. The unique demands of the profession make it essential for them to develop resilience skills to maintain their well-being and continue performing their duties effectively.

Resilient Responders Are Better Equipped to:

- Access resources and support systems more efficiently.
- Experience fewer missed workdays and maintain better job attendance.
- Manage their emotions during and after critical events without relying on harmful coping behaviors, like excessive alcohol consumption, smoking, or isolation.
- Maintain positive relationships with family, friends, and colleagues.
- Achieve greater job satisfaction and extend their career longevity.

Building Resilience: Key Strategies

Several strategies can help individuals build resilience and manage stress. One of the most important factors is having a strong support system, which can include family, friends, co-workers, or a professional network. A good support system helps individuals feel connected and provides a safe space to share feelings and seek help. Other factors contributing to resilience include having a positive self-image, confidence in one's abilities, effective communication, problem-solving skills, and the ability to manage emotions.

COs can incorporate the following strategies into their daily routines to build resilience:

Establish Healthy Routines: Maintain regular sleep, exercise, and eating patterns to reduce the buildup of stress, anxiety, and depressive symptoms.
Practice Positive Coping Techniques: Engage in activities such as meditation, mindfulness, exercise, journaling, and hobbies to decrease stress.
Utilize Mental Health Resources: Seeking assistance through peer support, counseling, or Employee Assistance Programs (EAPs).
Avoid Negative Coping Mechanisms: Resist using drugs, alcohol, or other unhealthy behaviors as temporary solutions to manage stress.

The Role of Resiliency Training in First Responder Wellness

Resiliency training is a structured way to teach first responders how to effectively manage stress and trauma. It can include stress management techniques, role-playing exercises, and learning about the psychological impact of trauma. Such training makes first responders more self-aware, allowing them to identify when they need help and to seek support without concern about stigma. Incorporating resiliency training before and after deployment to high-stress situations can prepare responders to handle intense experiences and recover more quickly. Developing a personal action plan with steps and coping strategies is a practical way to reinforce resilience skills.

Program Utilization

To measure and provide continuous improvement to PALS-C is critical to implement a system of measuring program utilization. Peer support logs are designed to track interactions while maintaining confidentiality and respecting the privacy of those seeking support. Instead of collecting names or identifying information, peer supporters typically document the date of the interaction, the form of communication (e.g., in-person, phone, text), and the general category of concern, such as stress or burnout, family or relationship issues, sleep disturbances, substance use, depression or anxiety, exposure to a critical incident, grief and loss, or career-related concerns. A brief, non-identifying description of the support provided is included, noting actions such as active listening, offering psychoeducation, or connecting the individual to appropriate resources. The log also indicates whether a referral was made (e.g., to an Employee Assistance Program, chaplain, or licensed clinician), whether follow-up is needed, and any additional notes relevant to supporting continuity of care. This approach ensures accountability and consistency in peer support programs while preserving the trust and confidentiality essential to their effectiveness.

Continuing Education

As the program is launched and utilized, PALS-C members may find it helpful to continue to grow their skills as peer supporters. This can be achieved through regular team meetings where challenges are discussed as an exploration for areas in which to grow. "We suggest that peer support teams should receive ongoing mandatory trainings to retain and reinforce knowledge of the mental health problems and responses, and continue scenario-based trainings to maintain key support skills (e.g., active listening)" (Van Hasselt et al., 2019). These opportunities not only reinforce core competencies but also allow members to stay updated on best practices. Continuing education also promotes team cohesion, mitigates the risk of secondary traumatic stress among peer supporters, and models a culture of ongoing growth and accountability within the agency (Benedek et al., 2007).

Program Evaluation

A Course Evaluation is administered following the program to gather participant feedback on the training experience. This structured assessment approach allows for an objective evaluation by the participants of the training's effectiveness and highlights areas where additional learning opportunities may be beneficial (Fig. 11.5).

Summary

This chapter outlined a peer support training model specifically tailored for COs, addressing their unique occupational stressors and mental health needs. The Peers as Law Enforcement Support for Corrections (PALS-C) program serves as a framework for fostering resilience, emotional well-being, and a culture of support within correctional institutions. This model prioritizes peer-provided support, ensuring that officers receive guidance from colleagues who understand the difficulties of their profession. The structured training curriculum, focused on active listening, depression, substance use, PTSD, suicide awareness, and resilience, equips peer supporters with essential skills to recognize distress, offers support and intervention, and facilitates access to professional resources. This collaborative approach not only empowers officers; it also reduces the stigma surrounding mental health by normalizing conversations about emotional well-being.

A key strength of this model lies in its integration with existing correctional systems, ensuring sustainability and institutional buy-in. By engaging officers at multiple levels (peer supporters, leadership, and command staff), PALS-C fosters an environment of trust and confidentiality. However, challenges remain, particularly in maintaining consistent engagement, overcoming cultural barriers to seeking help, and ensuring long-term program sustainability. The correctional environment presents unique difficulties, such as restricted confinement and prolonged exposure to high-stress situations, making mental health interventions all the more critical. Future research should explore the long-term impact of PALS-C, assess officer retention and well-being outcomes, and identify best practices for program fidelity. Additionally, continued leadership support and policy advocacy will be essential in ensuring that peer support remains an integral part of correctional officer wellness strategies and not just as a tool that is used in response to facility crises.

Peers as Law Enforcement Support (PALS-C) Training Evaluation Survey

Thank you for participating in the PALS-C training. Your feedback is valuable and will help us improve future training sessions. Please indicate your level of agreement with the following statements by selecting the most appropriate response.

Scale:
1 - Strongly Disagree
2 - Disagree
3 - Neutral
4 - Agree
5 - Strongly Agree

Training Content
1. The training provided relevant and useful information.
2. The topics covered (Depression, Anxiety, PTSD, Suicide, Sleep, and Active Listening Skills) were valuable to my role.
3. The training materials were well-organized and easy to understand.
4. The training objectives were clearly defined and met.

Instructor Effectiveness
5. The instructors demonstrated expertise in the subject matter.
6. The instructors were engaging and encouraged participation.
7. The instructors effectively answered questions and clarified key points.
8. The pace of the training was appropriate.

Engagement & Interaction
9. The interactive components (discussions, case studies, role-playing) were helpful in understanding the material.
10. The training encouraged collaboration and peer support.
11. I felt comfortable asking questions and sharing my thoughts.

Practical Application
12. I feel more confident in applying what I learned to real-world situations.
13. The training provided practical strategies for supporting peers in law enforcement.
14. The scenarios and case studies were realistic and applicable.

Overall Experience
15. The training met my expectations.
16. I would recommend this training to my colleagues.
17. The length of the training was appropriate.
18. I would be interested in attending additional training sessions on similar topics.

Additional Comments
Please share any additional feedback or suggestions to improve future training sessions:

Thank you for your feedback!

Fig. 11.5 Course survey

References

Ballenger, J. F., Best, S. R., Metzler, T. J., Wasserman, D. A., Mohr, D. C., Liberman, A., Delucchi, K., Weiss, D. S., Fagan, J. A., Waldrop, A. E., & Marmar, C. R. (2010). Patterns and predictors of alcohol use in male and female urban police officers. *The American Journal on Addictions, 20*(1), 21–29. https://doi.org/10.1111/j.1521-0391.2010.00092.x

Bar Nissim, H. S., Dill, J., Douglas, R., Johnson, O., & Folino, C. (2022). *The ruderman white paper update on mental health and suicide of first responders*. Ruderman Family Foundation. https://rudermanfoundation.org/white_papers/the-ruderman-white-paper-update-on-mental-health-and-suicide-of-first-responders/

Benedek, D. M., Fullerton, C., & Ursano, R. J. (2007). First responders: Mental health consequences of natural and human-made disasters for public health and public safety workers. *Annual Review of Public Health, 28*, 55–68. https://doi.org/10.1146/annurev.publhealth.28.021406.144037

Blue H.E.L.P. (2025). *The numbers.* Retrieved April 21, 2025, from https://bluehelp.org/the-numbers/

Byrd, T. G., Cochran, J. K., Silverman, I. J., & Blount, W. R. (2000). Behind bars: An assessment of the effects of job satisfaction, job-related stress, and anxiety on jail employees' inclinations to quit. *Journal of Crime and Justice, 23*(2), 69–93. https://doi.org/10.1080/0735648x.2000.9721123

Careless, J. (2023, January 2). *Why building trust is critical to building an effective officer wellness program.* Police1. https://www.police1.com/smash-the-stigma/articles/why-building-trust-is-critical-to-building-an-effective-officer-wellness-program-tDjZSzXXveVCyjVo/

Carleton, R., Afifi, T. O., Turner, S., Taillieu, T., Duranceau, S., LeBouthillier, D. M., Sareen, J., Ricciardelli, R., MacPhee, R. S., Groll, D., Hozempa, K., Brunet, A., Weekes, J. R., Griffiths, C. T., Abrams, K. J., Jones, N. A., Beshai, S., Cramm, H. A., Dobson, K. S., ..., Asmundson, G. G. (2017). Mental disorder symptoms among public safety personnel in Canada. *The Canadian Journal of Psychiatry, 63*(1), 54–64. https://doi.org/10.1177/0706743717723825

COs: Behavioral Health Concerns, Emergency Response, and Trauma—Suicide prevention Resource Center. (2018). https://sprc.org/online-library/first-responders-behavioral-health-concerns-emergency-response-and-trauma/

Fallon, P., Jaegers, L. A., Zhang, Y., Dugan, A. G., Cherniack, M., & El Ghaziri, M. (2023). Peer support programs to reduce organizational stress and trauma for public safety workers: A scoping review. *Workplace Health & Safety, 71*(11), 523–535. https://doi.org/10.1177/21650799231194623

Florida Statutes § 111.09. (2024). https://m.flsenate.gov/statutes/111.09

Goulette, N., Denney, A. S., Crow, M. S., & Ferdik, F. V. (2020). Anything can happen at any time": Perceived causes of correctional officer injuries. *Criminal Justice Review, 47*(1), 17–33. https://doi.org/10.1177/0734016820952521

Hawton, K., Comabella, C. I., Haw, C., & Saunders, K. (2013). Risk factors for suicide in individuals with depression: A systematic review. *Journal of Affective Disorders, 147*, 1–3. https://doi.org/10.1016/j.jad.2013.01.004

Jinkerson, J. D. (2016). Defining and assessing moral injury: A syndrome perspective. *Traumatology, 22*(2), 122–130. https://doi.org/10.1037/trm0000069

Johns Hopkins Medicine. (2018). *Roadmap to peer support.* https://www.hopkinsmedicine.org/armstrong-institute/peer-support-roadmap/four-parts/implement/peer-supporters#role

Johnson, O., Papazoglou, K., Violanti, J., & Pascarella, J. (Eds.). (2022). *Practical considerations for preventing police suicide.* Springer International Publishing. https://doi.org/10.1007/978-3-030-83974-1

Lee, N., & Wu, Y.-K. (2024). Work-related stress and psychological distress among law enforcement officers: The Carolina Blue Project. *Healthcare, 12*(6), 688. https://doi.org/10.3390/healthcare12060688

McCanlies, E. C., Gu, J., Andrew, M. E., & Violanti, J. M. (2018). The effect of social support, gratitude, resilience and satisfaction with life on depressive symptoms among COs following Hurricane Katrina. *International Journal of Social Psychiatry, 64*(1), 63–72. https://doi.org/10.1177/0020764017746197

Milliard, B. (2020). Utilization and impact of peer-support programs on police officers' mental health. *Frontiers in Psychology, 11.* https://doi.org/10.3389/fpsyg.2020.01686

Montoya-Barthelemy, A., Gibson, B. R., Lee, C. D., Bade, A. M., Butler, J. W., Smith, E., Skipworth, D., Gutekunst, J., Segula, M., Wicken, C., Friedman, E., Darbari, I., Menegas, S., Thatai, S., & Wheeler, L. (2021). Occupational and environmental hazards of correctional settings. *Journal of Occupational & Environmental Medicine, 64*(3), e172–e182. https://doi.org/10.1097/jom.0000000000002440

O'Dare, K., Mathis, A., Tawk, R., Atwell, L., & Jackson, D. (2024). State level policies on first responder mental health in the U.S.: A scoping review. *Administration and Policy in Mental Health, 51*(4), 579–596. https://doi.org/10.1007/s10488-024-01352-8

Papazoglou, K., & Andersen, J. P. (2014). A guide to utilizing police training as a tool to promote resilience and improve health outcomes among police officers. *Traumatology: An International Journal, 20*(2), 103–111. https://doi.org/10.1037/h0099394

Van Hasselt, V. B., Klimley, K. E., Rodriguez, S., Themis-Fernandez, M., Henderson, S. N., & Schneider, B. A. (2019). Peers as law enforcement support (PALS-C): An early prevention program. *Aggression and Violent Behavior, 48*, 1–5. https://doi.org/10.1016/j.avb.2019.05.004

Violanti, J. M. (2017). Suicide behind the wall: A national analysis of corrections officer suicide. *Suicidology Online, 8*(1), 58–64.

Zimmerman, G. M., Fridel, E. E., & Frost, N. A. (2023). Examining differences in the individual and contextual risk factors for police officer, correctional officer, and non-protective service suicides. *Justice Quarterly, 41*(2), 190–217. https://doi.org/10.1080/07418825.2023.2188063

Chapter 12
Training Police Officers in Suicide Risk Assessment and Intervention

Taylor Tejera, Juliette Hubbard, and Scott Poland

Training Police Officers in Suicide Risk Assessment and Intervention

Suicide is a pressing public health concern worldwide. The World Health Organization (WHO) estimated that 703,000 individuals died by suicide internationally in 2019 and placed it as the fourth leading cause of death for ages 15 to 29 (WHO, 2021). The alarming suicide prevalence has directed attention to the need for more research on crisis situations, the pathways individuals experiencing suicidality undergo, and effective strategies to prevent suicide. One research area emphasizes improving the relationship between police officers (POs) and those who are suicidal or have a mental illness, as POs are frequently the first people to interact with those experiencing crisis. Rates of mental health calls vary by region. A systematic review showed that 1% of all calls pertained to those with mental illness, with approximately a quarter of people with mental health conditions arrested by police in their life, and 12% having police involved in their pathway to care (Livingston, 2016). Within the scope of mental health (MH) related calls, a significant portion is related to suicidal thoughts and behaviors (Wood et al., 2023). A survey of over 800 law enforcement officers (LEOs), the majority being patrol officers and sergeants, found that 95% of the sample had responded to suicide cases throughout their career (Cerel et al., 2019). Another study of 828 police officers in Ireland, Portugal, and Germany found that approximately 36% had responded to individuals at risk for suicide in the

T. Tejera · J. Hubbard · S. Poland (✉)
College of Psychology, Nova Southeastern University, Fort Lauderdale, FL, USA
e-mail: spoland@nova.edu

T. Tejera
e-mail: tt1119@mynsu.nova.edu

J. Hubbard
e-mail: jh2688@nova.edu

V. B. Van Hasselt and M. L. Bourke (eds.), *Advances in First Responder Mental Health*,
Advances in First Responder Mental Health 1,
https://doi.org/10.1007/978-3-032-27978-1_12

past year (Arensman et al., 2016). Because prior mental illness and legal issues are established risk factors for suicidal thoughts and behaviors (Steele et al., 2018), it is of critical importance that officers responding to calls where the subject is believed to be struggling with mental health issues are prepared to ask questions and respond effectively to a crisis.

Assessment and Training for Police

Given the pervasive nature of suicide as a global health concern and the front-facing role of law enforcement, it is crucial that suicide prevention training for officers be implemented. Calls where suicidality is at issue occur within the broader framework of training, policies, and procedures for responding rather than distinct assessment techniques. MH professionals have described the skills needed for effective suicide prevention (Cramer et al., 2023) and several stand out as being particularly relevant for law enforcement including managing attitudes and reactions toward suicide, and developing and maintaining a collaborative, empathetic stance. This is a key factor in effectively responding to an individual in crisis as recipients of service have indicated a desire for police to have greater understanding of mental illness and its effects as well as increased compassion for individuals with mental health concerns (Livingston et al., 2014). Other steps including determining level of risk, forming and enacting a collective evidence-based treatment plan, and notifying and involving other persons may be reframed in a criminal justice context as police personnel are increasingly tasked with determining the best method of resolving MH-related calls (e.g., arrest, hospitalization, connection to other community support) and connecting individuals to needed services.

In line with the recommendations articulated above, suicide prevention practices increasingly focus on helping POs understand and identify the signs of mental illness and suicidal distress, helping officers de-escalate situations where mental health is at issue, and diverting service users from arrest. Mental health and suicide related training for police personnel is likely vast and may differ across departments, focusing on the needs of their communities and mindful of available resources. Despite the difficulty in reviewing all training given the diversity that exists in this area, some training courses are widely known. The following programs, Crisis Intervention Team (CIT), Co-Responder Models, and Gatekeeper Trainings (GKT), are among those frequently disseminated. With this in mind, an overview of popular models for responding to individuals with mental health issues is provided with relevant outcome data as well as general best practices in risk assessment which can be incorporated into any of these models or utilized by individual officers. The information provided does not make implications for a favored application of a training but rather discusses its possible utility and effectiveness based on peer-reviewed research.

Crisis Intervention Team (CIT)

With over 3000 CIT programs worldwide, the CIT model, otherwise known as the Memphis Model, is one of the most widely used programs aimed at building a community response to mental health crisis (Usher et al., 2019). In their best practice guide, Usher and colleagues (2019) describe CIT as a program which aims to improve crisis response by developing strong community based mental health services, including law enforcement and dispatchers, mental health professionals, emergency departments, receiving facilities, and mental health advocates, such as individuals and families of people with mental illness. As part of this expansive network, officers who pass a selection process to become CIT certified are trained to respond compassionately and strategically to a mental health crisis where safety or criminal activity is a concern and to divert individuals away from arrest when possible. This model offers a complete, one-time, 40-h training to officers and covers several topics, including how to identify symptoms of mental health diagnoses, recognize possible co-occurring conditions, psychiatric medications, drug abuse, legal criteria for emergency apprehension, and de-escalation skills (Watson & Wood, 2017). While most CIT research has been done in the U.S., promising research from a CIT program in Liberia suggests that implementation of CIT programs may be viable in non-U.S. countries with limited resources (Boazak et al., 2020; Kohrt et al., 2015).

The CIT program is often considered the "gold standard" of crisis training for LEOs and dispatchers (Peterson & Densley, 2018). CIT training aims to enhance identification of risk factors and promote empathy through its core training goals of increasing knowledge about mental illness and sensitivity to the lived experiences of those with mental health issues (Usher et al., 2019). This is accomplished both through didactic training and interactions with individuals who have mental health conditions and their families (Watson & Wood, 2017). Evidence exists that CIT training is successful in accomplishing these goals as CIT trained officers showed improvements in knowledge about mental illness and better attitudes toward people with mental health issues (Compton et al., 2014; Ellis, 2014). Further, surveyed officers had beneficial impressions of CIT training as they believed it enhanced skills, knowledge about mental illness, prepared officers to handle MH-related calls, and promoted greater confidence among CIT officers (Bonfine et al., 2014). Police confidence is important as it is a characteristic that may result in effective decision making during emotionally charged situations and can contribute to preventing suicides.

Findings related to subjective outcomes of CIT (e.g., knowledge about mental illness, attitudes toward persons with mental illness, preparedness to handle incidents involving persons with mental illness) are generally positive (Seo et al., 2021). However, there is considerable heterogeneity in research that examines more objective outcomes, such as reduced arrests and referrals to services (Seo et al., 2021; Taheri, 2016). In one study, the majority of officers surveyed believed that CIT training improved effective de-escalation and increased the likelihood that officers would facilitate referrals to appropriate services (Yang et al., 2018). There is minimal consistent support that CIT results in diminished arrest rates, use of force, or results in a solution on scene with no further involvement (Marcus & Stergiopoulos,

2022). While some studies have found that CIT officers made significantly fewer arrests (Compton et al., 2014), others have indicated that CIT-trained officers had approximately double the arrest rates as non-CIT-trained officers (Boddy et al., 2024). Even with CIT training, many officers report fear for their safety and perceive individuals with mental health issues as fearful of police, a factor which may contribute to resistance and disproportionately high use of force on these types of calls (Yang et al., 2018).

In some cases, CIT training improves referral to services (Kane et al., 2018) and sometimes assists with transportation to care (Watson et al., 2021). Other studies have found that CIT and non-CIT trained officers were equally likely to facilitate outreach to a mental health professional, but that CIT trained officers were more likely to initiate involuntary hospitalization (Boddy et al., 2024). When looking specifically at calls related to suicidality, CIT trained officers chose to take the individual to an emergency department (ED) in 96% of cases and, in the rare case that an individual was apprehended, 86% were taken to the ED beforehand (Tyuse, 2020). While this does represent a connection to care, there is disagreement among researchers as to whether increased hospitalization by LEO's represents an accurate analysis of the suicidal individual's needs (Boddy et al., 2024) or whether hospitalization is something to be avoided, if possible, in favor of alternative means of treatment (Kerr et al., 2022).

There are several limitations to the CIT model noted in the literature. As such, in places where there is a dearth of community resources or partnerships, referral rates may be low or officers may choose to resolve calls on the scene through more informal measures (Marcus & Stergiopoulos, 2022; Watson & Wood, 2017). The model is also a "one-time" format with limited opportunity for continuing education and less importance placed on in-service training (Crisanti et al., 2022). Crisanti and colleagues (2022) aimed to combat this issue and investigated the efficacy of CIT ECHO (Extension for Community Healthcare Outcomes), a continuing education program for LEOs. Overall, continued CIT training was associated with an increase in knowledge about mental illness and community resources, greater confidence in working with those with mental illness, using techniques, such as de-escalation and knowing who to contact about how to appropriately respond to situations, and less stigmatizing attitudes toward these populations. Therefore, continuing education may be important when developing or improving training for POs. Though the evidence supporting CIT as "evidence-based" is inconsistent (Peterson & Densley, 2018), this model can still provide advantages and skills to use to begin limiting the increasing problem of suicide.

Co-responder Models

Co-responder models describe programs that involve at least one PO and one mental health practitioner responding to mental health calls together (Morabito et al., 2018). While CIT programs predominate in research in the U.S., co-response models (e.g.,

Street Triage in the UK, Mobile Crisis Team in Canada) may be more popular internationally (Seo et al., 2021). Co-responder teams are different across departments but regardless of the varying modalities, the overarching goal is to use the skills of each professional to effectively handle crisis situations by reducing escalation, protecting people in crisis, connecting people to services, and limiting undue responsibility placed on the criminal justice system in responding to the ever-growing public mental health concerns (Shapiro et al., 2015). Notably, Usher and colleagues (2019) cautioned against an embedded co-response model (i.e., mental health professionals ride along with officers) as they believe this may exacerbate the over-reliance on law enforcement as a service provider and entrench the belief that mental health services are inaccessible without law enforcement contact. They actually suggest a co-response model where CIT officers and a mobile crisis team may be dispatched independently or together based on the judgment of the emergency communication center.

Within a co-responder model, officers gain skills in understanding mental health issues through accompanying training and observing the co-responder in the field (Shapiro et al., 2015). The presence of a co-responder with advanced mental health knowledge and practice communicating with individuals who are in crisis was particularly valued by service users (Lamanna et al., 2018). A mental health clinician may also help mitigate the burden on the justice system by reducing the amount of time that officers spend handling MH calls (Shapiro et al., 2015; Yang et al., 2024). Furthermore, co-responder's skills in de-escalation strategies may improve use of force outcomes (Blais & Brisebois, 2021).

There are mixed or unclear conclusions regarding outcomes, arrest rates, and hospital transport for this model. Though varied, there is some reduction in apprehension rates in studies evaluating co-response in comparison to police-only situations, and possible positive implications for arrest rates for co-response teams (Marcus & Stergiopoulos, 2022; Puntis et al., 2018). Other studies have not found any significant differences between the two groups regarding arrest rates (Blais & Brisebois, 2021; Lowder et al., 2024). Co-responder models are generally viewed positively by officers who feel that it improves de-escalation and reduces the pressure to utilize an emergency custody order or temporary detention order (ECO/TDO; Yang et al., 2024). However, studies have been inconsistent as to whether a co-responder model actually reduces hospitalizations in favor of other mental health resources (Kerr et al., 2022). Nevertheless, while hospitalizations may be higher in co-responding teams, more of these escorts may be voluntary (Lamanna et al., 2018).

A parallel goal of co-response models is to improve connection to helpful services in the hopes of providing relief to individuals in crisis and reducing MH related follow-up contacts with law enforcement. Some research indicates that this program helps with connections to community services for people with mental illness (Shapiro et al., 2015). Co-response models also appear to enable more resolutions achieved by connecting individuals to support via their social networks (Blais & Brisebois, 2021), an intervention which is highly desirable according to individuals with mental health concerns (Boscarato et al., 2014). Nevertheless, while many service users find the immediate availability of mental health workers beneficial, others have felt that formal treatment following the intervention was lacking or ineffective (Kerr et al., 2022; Puntis et al., 2018). Individuals experiencing suicidal ideation can oscillate between low-risk states and high-risk states during the course of their lifetime (Bryan et al., 2020). As such, appropriate follow-up and treatment are a critical concern for risk management.

Service users routinely rate co-response, particularly embedded co-response models highly (Kerr et al., 2022; Lamanna et al., 2018). However, there are notable limitations to a co-response model. Most notably, lack of availability of community mental health services and clinicians is routinely noted as an issue for consistent implementation (Watson et al., 2019). Officers may also feel responsible for safeguarding the clinician's safety (Morabito et al., 2018). Furthermore, there are limitations as to the efficacy and follow-through with connections to alternative mental health service providers as some studies suggest that follow-up contact was similar whether or not individuals (including those endorsing suicidal ideation) had been connected to treatment by a co-responding mental health clinician (Yang et al., 2024). It should be noted that this may not be a weakness of the co-response model per se as treatment attrition was high even after individuals were connected to services. Nevertheless, this factor should be considered in any agency considering a co-response model.

Gatekeeper Trainings (GKTs)

GKTs are programs that teach community members, particularly those who are likely to be in frequent contact with people in crisis, known as "gatekeepers" (e.g., teachers, POs, etc.), the warning signs of suicide, how to determine if someone is in crisis, and how to direct these individuals to appropriate help or services (Plöderl et al., 2023). This is critical given the prevalence of people who have limited understanding about suicide and endorse misconceptions about the topic. For instance, findings from a sample of LEOs showed that while they felt they were knowledgeable about suicide prevention, many lacked accurate information (Osteen et al., 2020). Additionally, almost 53% expressed that suicide could not be prevented (Osteen et al., 2020).

GKTs demonstrate some efficacy, enhancing understanding about suicide (Adams et al., 2018; Patel et al., 2021; Plöderl et al., 2023), attitudes (Patel et al., 2021; Plöderl et al., 2023), perceptions that knowledge and GKT skills advanced (Patel et al., 2021), and self-efficacy (Plöderl et al., 2023; Sylvara & Mandracchia, 2019). However, while the GKT framework is sound and leads to these improvements, its long-term outcomes are limited and sometimes neglected in studies. For example, one study found that one online GKT produced better readiness and self-efficacy to employ GKT techniques, in addition to reducing stigma about suicide among college students (Hill et al., 2024). However, long-term outcomes were not measured (Hill et al., 2024). Holmes and colleagues (2019) suggested that GKT only produced some long-term knowledge and self-efficacy impacts. Yet, another study showed that increases in knowledge, self-assurance, and attitudes about interacting with suicidal individuals were represented in data six months after the GKT (Plöderl et al., 2023).

Research regarding a widely used GKT known as Question, Persuade, and Refer (QPR) shows promising results. QPR teaches individuals to question those who seem at risk for suicidal ideation regarding their thoughts to end their life, persuade them to seek help, and refer them to the necessary services available (Gryglewicz et al., 2024). QPR has been found to improve knowledge about suicide and leads to greater self-efficacy to help individuals who may be suicidal across multiple studies (Gryglewicz et al., 2024). It has also increased people's belief that they are capable of questioning whether a person is suicidal, persuading them to not die by suicide, and their inclination to engage with an individual in crisis (Aldrich et al., 2018). Tailored QPR training for law enforcement has significantly improved knowledge on how to identify and engage with a suicidal person and diminished negative attitudes about suicide and suicide prevention (Osteen et al., 2021). Notably, Osteen and colleagues (2021) reported that QPR for law enforcement was not associated with any changes in suicide intervention behaviors, such as asking if the individual is having suicidal thoughts. The effects of police participation in a GKT focusing on suicidality and depression displayed similar findings, indicating reduced stigmatizing beliefs and increases in knowledge of suicide intervention and depression and confidence (Arensman et al., 2016). Despite these outcomes, LEOs have endorsed a slight decline in positive views following QPR and overall implementation of QPR has been believed to be challenging to incorporate in the police profession (Gryglewicz et al., 2024).

General Best Practices

Suicide Assessment

In general, the key to suicide assessment is asking direct questions about suicide ideation, intent, and plan. Direct discussion limits the opportunity for people to be confused and give inaccurate information on their current state. This also reduces the stigma that surrounds the subject of suicide. Coming across as hesitant can potentially frustrate the individual as well (Accinni et al., 2021). POs are also encouraged to utilize standardized assessment tools, such as the Columbia-Suicide Severity Rating Scale (C-SSRS), which is free, translated into several languages (The Columbia Lighthouse Project, n.d.-a), shows moderate to strong reliability across studies (Nam et al., 2024), and is considered an evidence-based and validated measure (The Columbia Lighthouse Project, n.d.-b). The C-SSRS *Brief* screening includes six questions. Answers endorsing intent to act on suicidal thoughts (in the past month), having thought about carrying out a plan (in the past month), and preparing to end life (in the past three months) are indicative of high risk for a suicide attempt and should receive immediate help (The Columbia Lighthouse Project, n.d.-a).

Notably, suicide crisis can look different across people. The Suicide Prevention Resource Center (SPRC, n.d.) lists various warning signs that may be important to know in the case any relevant information is provided to dispatchers or identified on scene. Red flags include, expressing significant pain, interest in death, feelings of hopelessness or burdensomeness, and heightened negative emotions (e.g., anger, guilt). Even though police are only responding to crisis situations and may not be directly exposed to these signs, it is still essential to be aware that dramatic changes in behavior or mood, such as giving away possessions, demonstrating rage, changes in eating or sleeping, saying good-bye to others, and withdrawing are pivotal signs of risk (SPRC, n.d.). Other signs noted by SPRC (n.d.) are having attempted suicide, substance use, poor hygiene, or recklessness. Contextual factors will also play a role in assessment. POs should be mindful to use their skills to collect information and piece together situations to avoid mislabeling an individual as suicidal or having a mental health crisis, potentially leading to unjustified hospitalization, harm, or detainment.

De-escalation

De-escalation will be a core component in managing many crisis situations. In these cases, POs are encouraged to engage in usual cautious behaviors, such as introducing themselves and keeping an appropriate physical distance. When interacting with suicidal individuals, Accinni and colleagues (2021) suggest remaining calm and utilizing verbal skills, such as a consistent tone of voice. The authors also emphasize the importance of expressing genuine empathy, being mindful of establishing some eye contact, and possibly discussing other topics besides their suicidality. Being perceived as confident and reliable is pertinent as well (Accinni et al., 2021). Furthermore, it is best practice to stay with the individual and evidently remove any objects that can cause harm to a suicidal person or others.

Active listening is a common tool used to build trust with people and a core component of successful de-escalation. It elicits greater feelings of being understood in comparison to receiving suggestions or any acknowledgment (Weger et al., 2014). Connors (2021) outlines active listening skills, emphasizing the importance of giving people space to speak about their thoughts without interruption. Connors (2021) also suggested refraining from expressing any judgment, presenting appropriate listening nonverbal behaviors, (e.g., directed eye contact and body language), and paraphrasing what was stated. Moreover, instilling hope may be another useful de-escalation technique that POs could practice, as research indicates that greater hope reduces the impact of hopelessness on having suicidal thoughts (Huen et al., 2015).

Myths About Suicide

Though suicidality manifests in many ways and there are different conceptualizations of suicide, there are still common misconceptions surrounding the subject. Police training in assessment and intervention for interacting with suicidal persons should outline these myths to develop a better understanding of the matter which can directly prevent suicide. A misconception people often endorse is that suicide is not preventable (Fuller, 2020; Suicide Awareness Voices of Education [SAVE], n.d.) and that people will always express suicidality (Fuller, 2020). However, suicidality changes over time, meaning there are opportunities to intervene and support people who are at risk (Bryan et al., 2020). Another common myth is that suicide is selfish (Fuller, 2020; SAVE, n.d.). According to the interpersonal therapy of suicide, a key experience that forms the desire for suicide is feeling that you are a burden to others, demonstrating the actual selflessness of suicidal ideation (Joiner, 2005). The belief that talking about suicide increases the likelihood someone will complete their plan is also inaccurate (Fuller, 2020; SAVE, n.d.), as there is no adequate empirical support suggesting that speaking about suicide encourages it (Dazzi et al., 2014). In fact, a study showed the contrary, that discussing suicide reduces suicidal thoughts and promotes help-seeking (Dazzi et al., 2014).

Lethal Means Safety

Lethal means safety is an approach to suicide prevention geared toward diminishing an individual's access to resources that can be used to complete suicide (Substance Abuse and Mental Health Services Administration [SAMHSA], 2023). Dr. Michael Anestis, the executive director of the New Jersey Gun Violence Resource Center, stated, "separating an individual from the method that they are intending on using for suicide is the most powerful tool we have to keep suicidal people alive" (Poland & Hauser, 2019, p. 5). Lethal means safety is a crucial problem globally, as 20% of suicides around the world are attributed to pesticide poisoning and other frequent methods involve hanging or firearms (WHO, 2023). This topic is especially important in the U.S. given that in 2021, over 50% of suicides involved a firearm (Centers for Disease Control & Prevention, 2024). POs are encouraged to be made aware of the importance of lethal means safety, policies pertaining to this issue, and their influence in implementing this practice. In the U.S., Extreme Risk Protection Orders (ERPO) legally limit a person who is at risk for suicide or harming another from being able to access a firearm (SAMHSA, 2023). Police can also practice lethal means safety in good faith by encouraging individuals and families to safely store medications, firearms, or other means away from the person at risk or even take these means outside of the home.

Special Considerations

Populations at Risk

While suicide can affect anyone, there are populations that may be more susceptible to suicide which police training should emphasize. For instance, on top of suicide being the fourth leading cause of death among those aged 15 to 29 globally (WHO, 2021), youth and young adult suicide in countries, such as the U.S. and those in Central-Latin America and Australasia have particularly shown increasing suicide rates (Bertuccio et al., 2024). Research has also suggested some connection between police interaction and youth suicidality. Based on data from the UK, teens who were stopped by police by 14 years old, had a greater chance of harming themselves and attempting suicide by age 17 (Jackson et al., 2021). Therefore, conducting suicide assessments when interacting with youth during any police interaction may be pertinent in suicide prevention.

On the contrary, older adults have the highest suicide rates across regions of the world (Naghavi, 2019). The rate is especially high for individuals over the age of 85 (Naghavi, 2019). The National Council on Aging (2024) indicates many possible reasons as to why this population has such a high rate of suicide including, loneliness, losing a loved one, declining independence, illness or pain, cognitive decline, and financial struggles. Tyuse and colleagues (2017) examined encounters involving this population and CIT officers, concluding that around 32% of police calls pertained to suicide attempts or threatening suicide, with the most frequent choice for suicide attempt or plan to be the use of medication. When responding to calls involving mental health calls by older adults, POs should be aware of these red flags and connect older adults to available resources.

Autism spectrum disorder (ASD) is a neurodevelopmental condition characterized by deficits in social communication and interaction and restricted, repetitive behaviors (American Psychological Association, 2022). People with this diagnosis comprise close to 1% of the world's population (Salari et al., 2022). While it is difficult to determine a consistent prevalence of suicide risk among those with ASD, data indicates that this population is three times more likely to engage in self-injurious behavior and suicidality than those without ASD (Blanchard et al., 2021). Unfortunately, people with this diagnosis are also in frequent contact with police, with estimates suggesting that 19.5% of people diagnosed with ASD are stopped by the police by age 21 and nearly 4.7% are arrested by that age (Rava et al., 2017). Approximately 60% of LEOs noted they responded to at least one call including an individual diagnosed with ASD in the last year, but many had no formal education in the condition (Gardner & Campbell, 2020). POs should be aware of ASD related symptoms, such as difficulties with socially appropriate eye contact, engaging in reciprocal conversation, understanding others' speech or cues, and struggles with transitions, rigidity, and self-expression (Leydier, 2022). When interacting with those with ASD, Autism Speaks (n.d.) recommends officers to maintain distance, abstain from making sudden movements, noises, and engage in physical touch as much as possible, keeping speech simple, and more simply, practicing patience.

Studies across several countries also show that marginalized populations, such as Lesbian, Gay, Bisexual, Transgender, Intersex, and Queer (LGBTIQ) individuals are at greater risk of suicide ideation and non-suicidal self-injury in comparison to those who do not identify as LGBTIQ (Marchi et al., 2022). Moreover, while determining whether suicide disparities exist across ethnicities is challenging given the diversity among research, high-quality studies show that individuals of an ethnic minority community may present with a higher likelihood of dying by suicide than individuals from a majority identity (Troya et al., 2022). Indigenous populations appear to have the highest likelihood of dying by suicide (Troya et al., 2022). Furthermore, there is increasing attention on the relationship between race and ethnicity, mental health, and law enforcement. A U.S. study showed that non-white individuals, and particularly Black and those who identified as other races or multiracial, were more likely to be involuntarily hospitalized than White individuals (Shea et al., 2022). POs should be aware of the increased suicide risk marginalized communities may experience as well as have tailored training encouraging anti-discriminatory interactions with these populations.

Suicide by Cop

A separate subset of suicide cases that are complex and call for training is "suicide by cop," a term used to describe a scenario in which an individual intentionally acts in a threatening manner toward POs in an effort to provoke them into using lethal force (Jordan et al., 2020). These individuals may be not as likely to demonstrate suicidal ideation before the encounter (Patton & Fremouw, 2016). Research also suggests that perpetrators of suicide by cop are likely to be killed (Patton & Fremouw, 2016); however, data from one department concluded that 3% of people were injured and 1% died by police (Jordan et al., 2020). Among suicide by cop scenarios in which police used force, aggressive actions, a criminal history, not surrendering, inebriation, domestic issues, and interpersonal crisis influenced the choice to use force (Lord, 2014). More recent research about this phenomenon is needed but the gravity for training in this area due to its potentially harmful consequences is unequivocal.

Conclusion

Police officers are a vital connection between individuals in crisis and much needed services. While programs exist to aid LEO's in developing the needed competencies for positive interactions, appropriate assessment, and beneficial intervention, each has limitations that must be taken into consideration. Each model incorporates best practice recommendations of awareness of mental health symptoms and compassionate de-escalation. Furthermore, the available evidence underscores the importance of a strong community mental health network in order for diversions to be successful. Regardless of the preferred model, it is clear that law enforcement officers around the world appreciate training which improves their knowledge and awareness of mental health issues and bolsters their confidence in handling a crisis effectively. To this end, robust interdisciplinary collaboration with mental health practitioners and resources provides an excellent general use framework to promote competency in identifying risk factors, asking directly, and removing access to lethal means, all critical foundational skills which can be incorporated into any existing practice. While further research is needed, one thing is beyond doubt—the intervention of police officers can be lifesaving for an individual in crisis.

References

Accinni, T., Papadogiannis, G., & Orso, L. (2021). De-escalation Techniques in Various Settings. In Biondi, M., Pasquini, M., & Tarsitani, L. (Eds.), *Empathy, normalization and de-escalation.* Springer. https://doi.org/10.1007/978-3-030-65106-0_5

Adams, L. M., Nguyen, T., Morgan, K. B., & Gumbleton, C. (2018). RU OK: Evaluating the effectiveness of a gatekeeper training program. *Journal of College Student Development, 59*(5), 614–617. https://doi.org/10.1353/csd.2018.0056

Aldrich, R. S., Wilde, J., & Miller, E. (2018). The effectiveness of QPR suicide prevention training. *Health Education Journal, 77*(8), 964–977. https://doi.org/10.1177/0017896918786009

American Psychiatric Association. (2022). *Diagnostic and statistical manual of mental disorders* (5th ed., text rev.). https://doi.org/10.1176/appi.books.9780890425787

Arensman, E., Coffey, C., Griffin, E., Van Audenhove, C., Scheerder, G., Gusmao, R., Costa, S., Larkin, C., Koburger, N., Maxwell, M., Harris, F., Postuvan, V., & Hegerl, U. (2016). Effectiveness of depression–suicidal behaviour gatekeeper training among police officers in three European regions: Outcomes of the optimising suicide prevention programmes and their implementation in Europe (OSPI-Europe) study. *International Journal of Social Psychiatry, 62*(7), 651–660. https://doi.org/10.1177/0020764016668907

Autism Speaks. (n.d.). *Teaching first responders the signs of autism is an important first step toward preventing unfortunate situations.* https://www.autismspeaks.org/information-law-enforcement

Bertuccio, P., Amerio, A., Grande, E., La Vecchia, C., Costanza, A., Aguglia, A., Berardelli, I., Serafini, G., Amore, M., Pompili, M., & Odone, A. (2024). Global trends in youth suicide from 1990 to 2020: An analysis of data from the WHO mortality database. *EClinicalMedicine, 70*, 102506. https://doi.org/10.1016/j.eclinm.2024.102506

Blais, E., & Brisebois, D. (2021). Improving police responses to suicide-related emergencies: New evidence on the effectiveness of co-response police-mental health programs. *Suicide & Life-Threatening Behavior, 51*(6), 1095–1105. https://doi.org/10.1111/sltb.12792

Blanchard, A., Chihuri, S., DiGuiseppi, C. G., & Li, G. (2021). Risk of self-harm in children and adults with autism spectrum disorder: A systematic review and meta-analysis. *JAMA Network Open, 4*(10), Article e2130272. https://doi.org/10.1001/jamanetworkopen.2021.30272

Boazak, M., Yoss, S., Kohrt, B. A., Gwaikolo, W., Strode, P., Compton, M. T., & Cooper, J. (2020). Law enforcement and mental health clinician partnerships in global mental health: Outcomes for the Crisis Intervention Team (CIT) model adaptation in Liberia, West Africa. *Global Mental Health (Cambridge, England), 7*, Article e2. https://doi.org/10.1017/gmh.2019.31

Boddy, K., Athaide-Victor, E., Law, F. M., & Sharp, J. (2024). CIT training among law enforcement: Does it work? *Journal of Police and Criminal Psychology*. https://doi.org/10.1007/s11896-024-09660-3

Bonfine, N., Ritter, C., & Munetz, M. R. (2014). Police officer perceptions of the impact of Crisis Intervention Team (CIT) programs. *International Journal of Law and Psychiatry, 37*(4), 341–350. https://doi.org/10.1016/j.ijlp.2014.02.004

Boscarato, K., Lee, S., Kroschel, J., Hollander, Y., Brennan, A., & Warren, N. (2014). Consumer experience of formal crisis-response services and preferred methods of crisis intervention. *International Journal of Mental Health Nursing, 23*(4), 287–295. https://doi.org/10.1111/inm.12059

Bryan, C. J., Butner, J. E., May, A. M., Rugo, K. F., Harris, J., Oakey, D. N., Rozek, D. C., & Bryan, A. O. (2020). Nonlinear change processes and the emergence of suicidal behavior: A conceptual model based on the fluid vulnerability theory of suicide. *New Ideas in Psychology, 57*. https://doi.org/10.1016/j.newideapsych.2019.100758

Centers for Disease Control and Prevention. (2024, April 25). *Suicide data and statistics*. https://www.cdc.gov/suicide/facts/data.html

Cerel, J., Jones, B., Brown, M., Weisenhorn, D. A., & Patel, K. (2019). Suicide exposure in law enforcement officers. *Suicide and Life-Threatening Behavior, 49*(5), 1281–1289. https://doi.org/10.1111/sltb.12516

The Columbia Lighthouse Project. (n.d.-a). *About the protocol*. https://cssrs.columbia.edu/the-columbia-scale-c-ssrs/about-the-scale/

The Columbia Lighthouse Project. (n.d.-b). *Evidence*. https://cssrs.columbia.edu/the-columbia-scale-c-ssrs/evidence/

Compton, M. T., Bakeman, R., Broussard, B., Hankerson-Dyson, D., Husbands, L., Krishan, S., Stewart-Hutto, T., D'Orio, B. M., Oliva, J. R., Thompson, N. J., & Watson, A. C. (2014). The police-based Crisis Intervention Team (CIT) model: I. Effects on officers' knowledge, attitudes, and skills. *Psychiatric Services, 65*(4), 517–522. https://doi.org/10.1176/appi.ps.201300107

Connors, K. (2021, September 29). *How to talk (and listen) to someone experiencing suicidal thoughts*. https://www.nami.org/relationships/how-to-talk-and-listen-to-someone-experiencing-suicidal-thoughts/

Cramer, R. J., Hawgood, J., Kaniuka, A. R., Brooks, B., & Baker, J. C. (2023). Updated suicide prevention core competencies for mental health professionals: Implications for training, research, and practice. *Clinical Psychology: Science and Practice*. Advance online publication. https://doi.org/10.1037/cps0000172

Crisanti, A. S., Fairfax-Columbo, J., Duran, D., Rosenbaum, N. A., Melendrez, B., Trujillo, I., Earheart, J. A., & Tinney, M. (2022). Evaluation of ongoing Crisis Intervention Team (CIT) training for law enforcement using the ECHO Model. *Journal of Police and Criminal Psychology, 37*, 863–875. https://doi.org/10.1007/s11896-022-09529-3

Dazzi, T., Gribble, R., Wessely, S., & Fear, N. T. (2014). Does asking about suicide and related behaviours induce suicidal ideation? What is the evidence? *Psychological Medicine, 44*(16), 3361–3363. https://doi.org/10.1017/S0033291714001299

Ellis, H. A. (2014). Effects of a Crisis Intervention Team (CIT) training program upon police officers before and after Crisis Intervention Team training. *Archives of Psychiatric Nursing, 28*(1), 10–16. https://doi.org/10.1016/j.apnu.2013.10.003

Fuller, K. (2020). *5 common myths about suicide debunked*. National Alliance on Mental Illness. https://www.nami.org/stigma/5-common-myths-about-suicide-debunked/

Gardner, L., & Campbell, J. M. (2020). Law enforcement officers' preparation for calls involving autism: Prior experiences and response to training. *Journal of Autism and Developmental Disorders, 50*(12), 4221–4229. https://doi.org/10.1007/s10803-020-04485-5

Gryglewicz, K., Garrison, C. M. T., Childs, K. K. Labouliere, C. D., & Karver, M. S. (2024). Examining individual and service delivery context variables and their association with the effectiveness of QPR suicide prevention gatekeeper training. *Administration and Policy in Mental Health Services Research, 51*, 47–59. https://doi.org/10.1007/s10488-023-01308-4

Hill, R. M., Picou, P., Hussain, Z., Vieyra, B. A., & Perkins, K. M. (2024). Randomized controlled trial of an online suicide prevention gatekeeper training program. *Crisis, 45*(1), 57–64. https://doi.org/10.1027/0227-5910/a000917

Holmes, G., Clacy, A., Hermens, D. F., & Lagopoulos, J. (2019). The long-term efficacy of suicide prevention gatekeeper training: A systematic review. *Archives of Suicide Research, 25*(2), 177–207. https://doi.org/10.1080/13811118.2019.1690608

Huen, J. M., Ip, B. Y., Ho, S. M., & Yip, P. S. (2015). Hope and hopelessness: The role of hope in buffering the impact of hopelessness on suicidal ideation. *PLoS ONE, 10*(6), Article e0130073. https://doi.org/10.1371/journal.pone.0130073

Jackson, D. B., Testa, A., Fix, R. L., & Mendelson, T. (2021). Adolescent Police Stops, Self-Harm, and Attempted Suicide: Findings From the UK Millennium Cohort Study, 2012–2019. *American Journal of Public Health, 111*(10), 1885–1893. https://doi.org/10.2105/AJPH.2021.306434

Joiner, T. (2005). *Why people die by suicide*. Harvard University Press.
Jordan, A., Panza, N. R., & Dempsey, C. (2020). Suicide by cop: A new perspective on an old phenomenon. *Police Quarterly, 23*(1), 82–105. https://doi.org/10.1177/1098611119873332
Kane, E., Evans, E., Mitsch, J., Jilani, T., Quinlan, P., Cattell, J., & Khalifa, N. (2018). Police interactions and interventions with suspects flagged as experiencing mental health problems. *Criminal Behaviour and Mental Health, 28*(5), 424–432. https://doi.org/10.1002/cbm.2078
Kerr, K., Heffernan, E., Hawgood, J., Edwards, B., & Meurk, C. (2022). Optimal care pathways for people in suicidal crisis who interact with first responders: A scoping review. *International Journal of Environmental Research and Public Health, 19*(18), 11510. https://doi.org/10.3390/ijerph191811510
Kohrt, B. A., Blasingame, E., Compton, M. T., Dakana, S. F., Dossen, B., Lang, F., Strode, P., & Cooper, J. (2015). Adapting the Crisis Intervention Team (CIT) model of police-mental health collaboration in a low-income, post-conflict country: Curriculum development in Liberia, West Africa. *American Journal of Public Health, 105*(3), e73–e80. https://doi.org/10.2105/AJPH.2014.302394
Lamanna, D., Shapiro, G. K., Kirst, M., Matheson, F. I., Nakhost, A., & Stergiopoulos, V. (2018). Co-responding police-mental health programmes: Service user experiences and outcomes in a large urban centre. *International Journal of Mental Health Nursing, 27*(2), 891–900. https://doi.org/10.1111/inm.12384
Leydier, T. B. (2022). Policing along the spectrum: Reducing risk and improving service delivery. *International Journal of Police Science & Management, 24*(4), 427–436. https://doi.org/10.1177/14613557221119117
Livingston, J. D. (2016). Contact between police and people with mental disorders: A review of rates. *Psychiatric Services (Washington, D.C.), 67*(8), 850–857. https://doi.org/10.1176/appi.ps.201500312
Livingston, J. D., Desmarais, S. L., Verdun-Jones, S., Parent, R., Michalak, E., & Brink, J. (2014). Perceptions and experiences of people with mental illness regarding their interactions with police. *International Journal of Law and Psychiatry, 37*(4), 334–340. https://doi.org/10.1016/j.ijlp.2014.02.003
Lord, V. B. (2014). Police responses in officer-involved violent deaths: Comparison of suicide by cop and non-suicide by cop incidents. *Police Quarterly, 17*(1), 79–100. https://doi.org/10.1177/1098611114522040
Lowder, E. M., Grommon, E., Bailey, K., & Ray, B. (2024). Police-mental health co-response versus police-as-usual response to behavioral health emergencies: A pragmatic randomized effectiveness trial. *Social Science & Medicine, 345*, Article 116723. https://doi.org/10.1016/j.socscimed.2024.116723
Marchi, M., Arcolin, E., Fiore, G., Travascio, A., Uberti, D., Amaddeo, F., Converti, M., Fiorillo, A., Mirandola, M., Pinna, F., Ventriglio, A., Galeazzi, G. M., & Italian Working Group on LGBTIQ Mental Health. (2022). Self-harm and suicidality among LGBTIQ people: A systematic review and meta-analysis. *International Review of Psychiatry, 34*(3–4), 240–256. https://doi.org/10.1080/09540261.2022.2053070
Marcus, N., & Stergiopoulos, V. (2022). Re-examining mental health crisis intervention: A rapid review comparing outcomes across police, co-responder and non-police models. *Health & Social Care in the Community, 30*(5), 1665–1679. https://doi.org/10.1111/hsc.13731
Morabito, M. S., Savage, J., Sneider, L., & Wallace, K. (2018). Police response to people with mental illnesses in a major U.S. city: The Boston experience with the co-responder model. *Victims & Offenders, 13*(8), 1093–1105.
Naghavi, M. (2019). Global, regional, and national burden of suicide mortality 1990 to 2016: Systematic analysis for the Global Burden of Disease Study 2016. *BMJ, 364*(l94). https://doi.org/10.1136/bmj.l94
Nam, S., Um, B., Jeong, J., Rodriguez, M., & Lardier, D. (2024). Score reliability generalization of the Columbia-Suicide Severity Rating Scale (C-SSRS): A meta-analysis. *Measurement and*

Evaluation in Counseling and Development, 57(2), 173-185. https://doi.org/10.1080/07481756.2023.2301285

National Council on Aging. (2024, January 9). *Suicide and older adults: What you should know.* https://www.ncoa.org/article/suicide-and-older-adults-what-you-should-know

Osteen, P. J., Oehme, K., Morris, R. C., Arciniegas, J., Frey, J. J., Woods, M., & Forsman, L. R. (2021). Suicide intervention training with law enforcement officers. *Suicide and Life-Threatening Behavior, 51*(4), 785–794. https://doi.org/10.1111/sltb.12763

Osteen, P. J., Oehme, K., Woods, M., Forsman, R. L., Morris, R. C., & Frey, J. (2020). Law enforcement officers' knowledge, attitudes, self-efficacy, and use of suicide intervention behaviors. *Journal of the Society for Social Work and Research, 11*(4), 509–527. https://doi.org/10.1086/712495

Patel, R., Mehta, R., Dave, K., & Chaudhary, P. (2021). Effectiveness of gatekeepers' training for suicide prevention program among medical professionals and medical undergraduate students of a medical college from Western India. *Industrial Psychiatry Journal, 30*(2), 217–223. https://doi.org/10.4103/ipj.ipj_31_21

Patton, C. L., & Fremouw, W. J. (2016). Examining "suicide by cop": A critical review of the literature. *Aggression and Violent Behavior, 27*, 107–120. https://doi.org/10.1016/j.avb.2016.03.003

Peterson, J., & Densley, J. (2018). Is Crisis Intervention Team (CIT) training evidence-based practice? A systematic review. *Journal of Crime and Justice, 41*(5), 521–534. https://doi.org/10.1080/0735648X.2018.1484303

Plöderl, M., Fartacek, C., Kapitany, T., Schrittwieser, U., & Niederkrotenthaler, T. (2023). Effects of gatekeeper trainings from the Austrian national suicide prevention program. *Frontiers in Psychiatry, 14*, 1118319. https://doi.org/10.3389/fpsyt.2023.1118319

Poland, S., & Hauser, K. (2019). Guns and suicide: Interview with Dr. Michael Anestis. *Office of Suicide & Violence Prevention Quarterly Newsletter—Fall 2019*, 3–9. https://nsuworks.nova.edu/cgi/viewcontent.cgi?article=1022&context=suicideprevention

Puntis, S., Perfect, D., Kirubarajan, A., Bolton, S., Davies, F., Hayes, A., Harriss, E., & Molodynski, A. (2018). A systematic review of co-responder models of police mental health 'street' triage. *BMC Psychiatry, 18*(1), 256. https://doi.org/10.1186/s12888-018-1836-2

Rava, J., Shattuck, P., Rast, J., & Roux, A. (2017). The prevalence and correlates of involvement in the criminal justice system among youth on the autism spectrum. *Journal of Autism and Developmental Disorders, 47*(2), 340–346. https://doi.org/10.1007/s10803-016-2958-3

Salari, N., Rasoulpoor, S., Rasoulpoor, S., Shohaimi, S., Jafarpour, S., Abdoli, N., Khaledi-Paveh, B., & Mohammadi, M. (2022). The global prevalence of autism spectrum disorder: A comprehensive systematic review and meta-analysis. *Italian Journal of Pediatrics, 48*(112). https://doi.org/10.1186/s13052-022-01310-w

Seo, C., Kim, B., & Kruis, N. E. (2021). Variation across police response models for handling encounters with people with mental illnesses: A systematic review and meta-analysis. *Journal of Criminal Justice, 72*, Article 101752. https://doi.org/10.1016/j.jcrimjus.2020.101752

Shapiro, G. K., Cusi, A., Kirst, M., O'Campo, P., Nakhost, A., & Stergiopoulos, V. (2015). Co-responding police-mental health programs: A review. *Administration and Policy in Mental Health, 42*(5), 606–620. https://doi.org/10.1007/s10488-014-0594-9

Shea, T., Dotson, S., Tyree, G., Ogbu-Nwobodo, L., Beck, S., & Shtasel, D. (2022). Racial and ethnic inequities in inpatient psychiatric civil commitment. *Psychiatric Services, 73*(12), 1322–1329. https://doi.org/10.1176/appi.ps.202100342

Steele, I. H., Thrower, N., Noroian, P., & Saleh, F. M. (2018). Understanding suicide across the lifespan: A United States perspective of suicide risk factors, assessment, & management. *Journal of Forensic Sciences, 63*(1), 162–171. https://doi.org/10.1111/1556-4029.13519

Substance Abuse and Mental Health Services Administration. (2023, September 29). *Lethal means safety for suicide prevention.* https://www.samhsa.gov/blog/lethal-means-safety-suicide-prevention

Suicide Awareness Voices of Education. (n.d.). *Common misconceptions*. https://www.save.org/learn/common-misconceptions/

Suicide Prevention Resource Center. (n.d.). *Warning signs of suicide*. https://sprc.org/warning-signs-for-suicide/

Sylvara, A. L., & Mandracchia, J. T. (2019). An investigation of gatekeeper training and self-efficacy for suicide intervention among college/university faculty. *Crisis: The Journal of Crisis Intervention and Suicide Prevention, 40*(6), 383–389. https://doi.org/10.1027/0227-5910/a000577

Taheri, S. A. (2016). Do Crisis Intervention Teams reduce arrests and improve officer safety? A systematic review and meta-analysis. *Criminal Justice Policy Review, 27*(1), 76–96. https://doi.org/10.1177/0887403414556289

Troya, M. I., Spittal, M. J., Pendrous, R., Crowley, G., Gorton, H. C., Russell, K., Byrne, S., Musgrove, R., Hannah-Swain, S., Kapur, N., & Knipe, D. (2022). Suicide rates amongst individuals from ethnic minority backgrounds: A systematic review and meta-analysis. *EClinicalMedicine, 47*, 101399. https://doi.org/10.1016/j.eclinm.2022.101399

Tyuse, S. W. (2020). Crisis Intervention Team (CIT) programs and suicide. *Journal of Psychosocial Rehabilitation and Mental Health, 7*, 221–229. https://doi.org/10.1007/s40737-020-00186-5

Tyuse, S. W., Cooper-Sadlo, S., & Underwood, S. E. (2017). Descriptive study of older adults encountered by Crisis Intervention Team (CIT) law enforcement officers. *Journal of Women & Aging, 29*(4), 281–293. https://doi.org/10.1080/08952841.2016.1174513

Usher, L., Watson A. C., Bruno, R., Andriukaitis, S., Kamin, D., Speed, C., & Taylor, S. (2019). *Crisis Intervention Team (CIT) programs: A best practice guide for transforming community responses to mental health crises*. CIT International. citinternational.org/bestpracticeguide.

Watson, A. C., Compton, M. T., & Pope, L. G. (2019). *Crisis response services for people with mental illnesses or intellectual and developmental disabilities: A review of the literature on police-based and other first responder models*. The Vera Institute. https://www.vera.org/downloads/publications/crisis-response-services-for-people-with-mental-illnesses-or-intellectual-and-developmental-disabilities.pdf

Watson, A. C., Owens, L. K., Wood, J., & Compton, M. T. (2021). The impact of Crisis Intervention Team response, dispatch coding, and location on the outcomes of police encounters with individuals with mental illnesses in Chicago. *Policing, 15*(3), 1948–1962. https://doi.org/10.1093/police/paab010

Watson, A. C., & Wood, J. D. (2017). Everyday police work during mental health encounters: A study of call resolutions in Chicago and their implications for diversion. *Behavioral Sciences & the Law, 35*(5–6), 442–455. https://doi.org/10.1002/bsl.2324

Weger, H., Castle Bell, G., Minei, E. M., & Robinson, M. C. (2014). The relative effectiveness of active listening in initial interactions. *International Journal of Listening, 28*(1), 13–31. https://doi.org/10.1080/10904018.2013.813234

Wood, L. L., Barrenger, S., & Bonfine, N. (2023). Contextual factors of mental health crisis calls to law enforcement: A brief report. *Community Mental Health Journal, 60*, 403–409. https://doi.org/10.1007/s10597-023-01185-z

World Health Organization. (2021). *Suicide worldwide in 2019: Global health estimates*. https://iris.who.int/bitstream/handle/10665/341728/9789240026643-eng.pdf?sequence=1#:~:text=In%202019%2C%20an%20estimated%20703,100%20000%20(Figure%201).

World Health Organization. (2023). *Suicide*. https://www.who.int/news-room/fact-sheets/detail/suicide

Yang, S., Gill, C. E., Kanewske, L. C., & Thompson, P. S. (2018). Exploring police response to mental health calls in a nonurban area: A case study of Roanoke County, Virginia. *Victims & Offenders, 13*(8), 1132–1152. https://doi.org/10.1080/15564886.2018.1512540

Yang, S., Gill, C. E., Lu, Y., Azam, M., & Kanewske, L. C. (2024). A police-clinician co-response team to people with mental illness in a suburban-rural community: A randomized controlled trial. *Journal of Experimental Criminology*. https://doi.org/10.1007/s11292-023-09603-8

Chapter 13
Mental Health Training for Police Officers

Christopher E. Powell

Mental Health Training for Police Officers

Officer Ramirez pulled up to what dispatch called a simple noise complaint, yet the heavy thuds and overlapping voices behind the metal door told a different story. He took cover by the door frame and radioed for a second unit—no one knew whether weapons were inside. Between crashes, he heard a woman plead, "He stopped taking his meds–please help us!" A second, strained voice shouts back, "They're watching me; keep them away!".

The mix of fear and confusion signaled a likely psychotic episode, so when backup arrived, Ramirez quickly detailed the safety risks, unknown layout, possible delusions, children present, and their priorities: secure the scene and connect the man to medical care. He knocked and announced, "Police–we're here to keep everyone safe and get you the help you need." The response—a startled silence, then quiet sobs—underscored both the danger for officers entering an unpredictable environment and the family's urgent need for mental-health intervention.

This scene plays out all over the world as society continually asks police officers to do the unimaginable: help people with their mental illness. Often, this request is just that, a simple ride to a hospital, and a kind word is all it takes. Unfortunately, some end up tragically, leaving all involved asking the hard question, "What could we have done better?"

The nexus between law enforcement and mental health represents a crucial, yet challenging, domain within the criminal justice system. While many encounters culminate in individuals receiving appropriate assistance, others tragically result in

C. E. Powell (✉)
School of Criminal Justice, Nova Southeastern University, Fort Lauderdale, FL, USA
e-mail: CPowelletal@gmail.com

V. B. Van Hasselt and M. L. Bourke (eds.), *Advances in First Responder Mental Health*, Advances in First Responder Mental Health 1,
https://doi.org/10.1007/978-3-032-27978-1_13

unfavorable outcomes. These negative incidents, widely disseminated through media cycles, raise critical questions regarding potential solutions. Can increased training, improved understanding, and more substantial support from communities and agencies contribute to more positive outcomes for everyone involved? This includes not only the individuals experiencing mental illness, but also their families and the first responders who intervene.

The Importance of Experience and Recognition

Mental illness encompasses a broad spectrum of health conditions affecting an individual's emotions, thinking, or behavior (or a combination thereof). These disorders can greatly affect a person's well-being and ability to function in daily life, causing distress and hindering social, work, or family activities (American Psychiatric Association, 2022). First responders, due to the nature of their work, are frequently on the front line of encountering individuals experiencing mental health crises. This chapter aims to equip first responders with a foundational understanding of the most commonly encountered mental illnesses, their associated signs and symptoms, and the importance of recognizing these indicators for effective intervention. It also provides trainers with guidelines for training.

Police officers approach each interaction informed by their cumulative personal and professional experiences. Consider this analogy: A seasoned race car driver, unlike a newly licensed driver, possesses the experience and honed skills for safe operation in a complicated situation. Similarly, experienced mental health officers can better recognize and respond effectively to the immediate crises.

Misunderstandings and Missed Cues: Escalation and Equitable Solutions

Mental health-related police encounters can escalate due to misinterpretations of behavior. Officers might misjudge non-compliance as defiance, potentially missing important cues that could indicate a mental health issue.

Law enforcement provides up to one-third of all mental health referrals (Borum et al., 1998). Studies suggest that a significant portion of police interactions involves individuals experiencing mental illness. Individuals with a mental illness are almost twice as likely to be arrested as those without for similar behavior (Teplin, 1984). A 2005 study found the New York Police Department responded to a person with a mental illness every 6.5 min (Reuland & Cheney, 2005, as cited in Roesch &

Goossens, 2021). This highlights the need for first responders, particularly law enforcement officers, to be equipped with the knowledge and skills to navigate these encounters effectively. A recent study found that of 126 police officers who were surveyed, 90% responded that the topic of mental illness was either fairly or very important (Vermette et al., 2005).

Prevalence of Mental Illness

The high rate of mental illness in the U.S. underscores the critical need for first responder awareness. According to the National Alliance on Mental Illness (NAMI), approximately 1 in 5 U.S. adults experience mental illness each year (*Mental Health by the Numbers*, n.d.). Notably, these numbers are even more concerning for young people, with 1 in 6 youths aged 6–17 experiencing a mental health disorder annually. Further, statistics reveal that half of all lifetime mental illnesses begin by age 14, with a staggering 75% manifesting by age 24. Tragically, suicide is the second leading cause of death among 10- to 14-year-olds because of untreated mental illness.

Mental Health Disorders: A Primer for First Responders

We will examine the specific mental disorders predominantly encountered by first responders. It is important to acknowledge that this is not an exhaustive list, as the focus will be on recognizing key signs and symptoms.

Equipping first responders with knowledge about mental health disorders is crucial for successful interventions and positive outcomes when encountering individuals in crisis. Recognizing signs and symptoms associated with various mental illnesses allows first responders to approach situations with greater awareness and empathy. This understanding, training, and de-escalation techniques can immensely contribute to the safety and well-being of the individual experiencing the crisis and the first responders themselves.

Spectrum of Mental Health Disorders

First responders often encounter individuals experiencing a variety of mental health disorders, including:

- *Anxiety Disorders*. Characterized by excessive worry, fear, and physical symptoms such as rapid heart rate and difficulty breathing.

- *Depressive Disorders.* Manifesting as persistent feelings of sadness, hopelessness, and a loss of interest in activities once enjoyed.
- *Bipolar Disorders.* Characterized by extreme mood swings, ranging from manic episodes with high energy and racing thoughts to depressive episodes with low mood and lethargy.
- *Attention Deficit Hyperactivity Disorder (ADHD).* Presenting with symptoms of inattention, hyperactivity, and impulsivity.
- *Obsessive–Compulsive Disorder (OCD).* Characterized by intrusive thoughts and repetitive behaviors aimed at reducing anxiety.
- *Schizophrenia.* A severe mental illness involving a disconnect from reality, with symptoms such as hallucinations and delusions.
- *Post-traumatic Stress Disorder (PTSD).* Develops after exposure to a traumatic event, with symptoms such as flashbacks, nightmares, and hypervigilance.

Anxiety Disorders

Anxiety disorders encompass a broad spectrum of mental health conditions characterized by excessive and persistent worry, fear, and physical symptoms. These disorders greatly impact an individual's quality of life and daily activities.

Anxiety – Trainers Toolbox
• **Excessive, hard-to-control worry** that persists most days. • **Restlessness or a constant "keyed-up" feeling.** • **Muscle tension and other somatic complaints** (e.g., headaches, gastrointestinal upset). • **Difficulty concentrating** or episodes of the mind "going blank." • **Sleep disturbance,** such as trouble falling or staying asleep.

Common Anxiety Disorders

Generalized Anxiety Disorder (GAD). Marked by persistent and excessive worry about a variety of everyday situations and activities.

Panic Disorder. Characterized by recurrent and unexpected panic attacks, which are sudden episodes of intense fear or discomfort accompanied by physical symptoms such as heart palpitations, shortness of breath, and dizziness.

Phobias. Intense and persistent fears of specific objects or situations.

Shared Features of Anxiety Disorders

Despite their differences, these anxiety disorders share common features of excessive fear and anxiety. The American Psychiatric Association (2022) defines fear as an "emotional response to a real or perceived imminent threat" and anxiety as "an anticipation of future threats" (p.216). This distinction is important, as individuals with anxiety disorders may experience heightened worry and apprehension even in the absence of a present danger.

Panic Attacks

Panic attacks are a hallmark symptom of some anxiety disorders, but they can also occur in other mental illnesses. During a panic attack, individuals may experience a range of physical and psychological symptoms that can be frightening and overwhelming. First responders encountering individuals experiencing anxiety attacks may observe behaviors such as increased vigilance and a sense of being watched or followed, fears of being harmed or killed, difficulty concentrating and focusing, and restlessness and agitation.

Understanding the core features of anxiety disorders, particularly the distinction between fear and anxiety, is crucial for first responders. Recognizing the signs and symptoms associated with these disorders allows for a more informed and empathetic approach during encounters with individuals in crisis.

Potential Triggers

- Generalized Anxiety Disorder (GAD):
  - Stressful life events (job loss, relationship problems, financial strain)
  - Health concerns (personal or family)
  - Uncertainty about the future
  - Social situations
  - Caffeine or other stimulants

  Panic Disorder:
  - Crowded or confined spaces
  - Loud noises or bright lights
  - The sensation of being trapped
  - Thoughts or memories of past panic attacks
  - Physical sensations (e.g., increased heart rate)
- Phobias:
  - Specific objects or situations (e.g., animals, heights, flying)
  - Exposure to the feared stimulus

– Even the thought or anticipation of the feared stimulus

Depressive Disorders

Depressive disorders, particularly Major Depressive Disorder (MDD), represent a prevalent mental health concern encountered by first responders. We will explore the core features of depression, emphasizing its impact on individuals and recognition by first responders.

Symptoms and Impact of Depression

The definition of depression is:

> a negative affective state, ranging from unhappiness and discontent to an extreme feeling of sadness, pessimism, and despondency, that interferes with daily life. Various physical, cognitive, and social changes also tend to co-occur, including altered eating or sleeping habits, lack of energy or motivation, difficulty concentrating or making decisions, and withdrawal from social activities. It is symptomatic of a number of mental health disorders. (*APA Dictionary of Psychology*, n.d.)

It is crucial to recognize depression in the general population, as individuals in crisis may require intervention. Common symptoms of depression include persistent low mood or sadness, anhedonia (loss of pleasure in activities previously enjoyed), changes in appetite or sleep patterns, difficulty concentrating or making decisions, feelings of hopelessness or worthlessness, fatigue or lack of energy, and suicidal ideation or thoughts of death.

Challenges in Identifying Depression

Individuals experiencing depression may not always exhibit a stereotypical "flat affect" or constant sadness. Some may display periods of excitement or euphoria, particularly in the presence of others. This can be a deceptive symptom, potentially masking underlying depression. A sudden shift from a flat affect to excessive cheerfulness can be a red flag for suicidal ideation, particularly in individuals previously expressing hopelessness.

Information Gathering

First responders may be unable to observe a person's emotional range during an encounter. Therefore, gathering information from family and friends about an individual's recent behavior and emotional state is crucial. This collaborative approach can help identify potential indicators of depression and facilitate the connection to appropriate mental health resources.

Depression – Trainers Toolbox

- **Persistent low mood or pervasive feelings of sadness.**
- **Marked loss of interest or pleasure in previously rewarding activities.**
- **Significant changes in appetite or weight (increase or decrease).**
- **Sleep disturbances—insomnia or hypersomnia nearly every day.**
- **Feelings of worthlessness, inappropriate guilt, or recurrent thoughts of death**

Understanding the characteristics of depression and its potential masking symptoms is essential for first responders. This knowledge allows for more informed interactions with individuals in crisis and the identification of potential suicide risks. By recognizing the signs of depression and collaborating with others, first responders can play a significant role in promoting help-seeking behaviors and positive outcomes.

Potential Triggers

- Loss or grief (death of a loved one, loss of a job, end of a relationship)
- Social isolation or loneliness
- Chronic pain or illness
- Hormonal changes
- Negative self-talk and rumination
- Stressful life events

Bipolar Disorder

Bipolar disorder, formerly known as manic-depressive illness, is a chronic mental health condition characterized by distinct mood episodes. First responders are continually on the front line of encountering individuals experiencing bipolar episodes, and recognizing the key features is crucial for effective intervention.

Bipolar – Trainers Toolbox
• **Extreme mood swings cycles of manic and depressive lows** • **Inflated self-esteem or grandiosity during manic phases** • **Decreased need for sleep yet feeling unusually energetic** • **Racing thoughts and rapid speech that jump between topics** • **Impulsive or high-risk behaviors** like spending sprees and reckless driving

Cyclical Mood Shifts: Mania and Depression

Bipolar disorder is characterized by the cyclical nature of its mood episodes. These episodes can be broadly categorized as: (a) manic episodes characterized by elevated or irritable mood, (b) racing thoughts, increased energy levels, (c) psychomotor agitation (increased physical activity), (d) decreased need for sleep, (e) grandiose thinking, (f) depressive episodes—marked by persistent sadness or loss of interest (anhedonia), (g) feelings of hopelessness or worthlessness, (h) changes in sleep or appetite, fatigue, difficulty concentrating, and (i) suicidal ideation (American Psychiatric Association, 2022).

Challenges in Recognizing Bipolar Disorder

It is important to acknowledge that individuals with Bipolar Disorder may not always be experiencing a full-blown manic or depressive episode. First responders may encounter individuals in an euthymic state, characterized by relatively normal mood and functioning. However, recognizing the potential for Bipolar Disorder is crucial, as individuals may experience hypomanic symptoms (less severe than mania) or subsyndromal depression (symptoms that do not meet the full criteria for a major depressive episode) (American Psychiatric Association, 2022).

Understanding the cyclical nature of Bipolar Disorder and its distinct mood episodes is essential for first responders. This knowledge allows for a more informed approach during encounters when these people are in crisis.

Potential Triggers

- Manic Episode:
  - Lack of sleep
  - Stressful life events
  - Changes in medication
  - Substance use
- Depressive Episode:
  - Stressful life events
  - Seasonal changes
  - Hormonal changes
  - Withdrawal from social activities

Attention Deficit Hyperactivity Disorder (ADHD)

Attention Deficit Hyperactivity Disorder (ADHD) is a common neurodevelopmental disorder often associated with childhood. However, recent research suggests that ADHD can persist into adulthood, affecting a significant portion of the population (American Psychiatric Association, 2022). First responders may encounter adults experiencing symptoms of ADHD, and recognizing these symptoms is crucial for effective interaction and de-escalation.

Core Signs of Adult ADHD

Clinicians commonly classify ADHD as a neurodevelopmental disorder characterized by a persistent pattern of inattention and/or hyperactivity-impulsivity that interferes with functioning or development. These core symptoms manifest differently in adults compared to children.

ADHD – Trainers Toolbox
• **Chronic inattention,** such as frequent distractibility, difficulty sustaining focus, and careless errors. • **Poor executive organization,** evident in persistent disorganization, losing items, and trouble following sequential tasks. • **Excessive motor activity or restlessness,** including fidgeting, inability to remain seated, or feeling internally "driven" to move. • **Impulsive behaviors,** manifested by interrupting others, blurting out answers, or difficulty waiting one's turn. • **Time-management and forgetfulness issues,** leading to missed deadlines, late arrivals, or forgetfulness in daily routines.

Inattention. Adults with ADHD may struggle to sustain focus, easily become distracted, and have difficulty completing tasks that require sustained mental effort.

Hyperactivity-Impulsivity. While hyperactivity may be less pronounced in adults, restlessness, fidgeting, and a sense of inner turmoil can be present. Additionally, adults with ADHD may exhibit impulsiveness in decision-making or difficulty waiting their turn.

Prevalence and Impact

While statistics on the exact prevalence of adult ADHD vary, studies suggest that approximately 4–5% of adults in the U.S. meet criteria for the disorder (Kessler et al., 2006). Untreated ADHD can considerably impact an individual's life, leading to difficulties with work performance, relationships, and self-esteem.

Recognizing ADHD in First Responder Encounters

First responders encountering adults in crisis may observe behaviors associated with ADHD, including (a) difficulty following instructions or staying focused during the conversation, (b) restlessness or fidgeting, (c) difficulty waiting their turn or interrupting conversations, and (d) making impulsive decisions or acting without considering consequences.

Recognizing potential ADHD symptoms in adults allows first responders to adjust their communication style and de-escalation techniques. For example, providing clear and concise instructions, allowing conversation breaks, and offering choices to promote self-control can be beneficial strategies. ADHD is not solely a childhood disorder, and its presence in adults can affect behavior.

Potential Triggers

- Stress
- Lack of structure or routine
- Overstimulation (e.g., noisy environments)
- Tasks that require sustained attention
- Time pressure or deadlines
- Interpersonal conflict

Obsessive–Compulsive Disorder (OCD)

Obsessive–compulsive disorder (OCD) is a common mental health disorder often portrayed in media as a collection of quirky habits or "ticks." This stereotypical portrayal can be misleading, as the core features of OCD involve intrusive thoughts (obsessions) and repetitive behaviors (compulsions) that are distressing and interfere with daily life (American Psychiatric Association, 2022). Recognizing the true nature of OCD is crucial for first responders, as they may encounter individuals whose behaviors stem from this disorder.

OCD – Trainers Toolbox
• **Intrusive, unwanted obsessions**—recurrent thoughts or images (e.g., contamination, harm) that cause marked distress. • **Compulsive rituals or mental acts** performed repetitively to neutralize anxiety (e.g., excessive hand-washing, checking, counting). • **Time-consuming behaviors** that occupy ≥ 1 hour per day and interfere with normal functioning. • **Recognition that obsessions/compulsions are excessive,** yet experiencing strong pressure to perform them. • **Pronounced anxiety or distress** whenever rituals are delayed, disrupted, or resisted.

Individuals with OCD experience intrusive thoughts, images, or urges that are unwanted and cause significant anxiety. These obsessions may involve various themes, including contamination fears, symmetry, orderliness, or harm to oneself or others (American Psychiatric Association, 2022). To ease the anxiety associated with these obsessions, individuals engage in repetitive behaviors or mental acts known as compulsions.

While repetitive behaviors can be a feature of OCD, it is crucial to recognize that these behaviors are not simply quirky habits. They are driven by a strong need to reduce anxiety associated with the obsessions. For example, someone fearing contamination may not simply touch a doorknob multiple times. They may experience a distressing obsession about germs and feel compelled to engage in a handwashing compulsion to reduce their anxiety temporarily.

OCD Manifestations in First Responder Encounters

First responders encountering individuals in crisis may misinterpret behaviors as deliberate defiance or a lack of cooperation. These behaviors may stem from OCD. Below are some examples:

Maintaining excessive physical distance. An individual with a fear of germs might consistently step back during a conversation because of an underlying obsession with contamination.

Repeatedly checking belongings. Someone with an obsession about losing things might frequently check their pockets for their phone, even if they have already confirmed it is there.

Organizing objects meticulously. An individual with an obsession with order might rearrange objects in their environment to achieve a specific sense of symmetry, even during an interaction with a first responder.

Recognizing OCD

A more informed approach is possible by recognizing the potential for OCD-related behaviors in first responders' encounters. Techniques such as maintaining a respectful distance, offering clear and concise instructions, and avoiding confrontational language can improve communication and de-escalation efforts.

OCD is a complex mental health disorder that can manifest in diverse ways. Equipping first responders with knowledge about OCD beyond stereotypical portrayals is essential for effective interaction with individuals in crisis. This understanding can contribute to positive outcomes for the person and the first responder.

Potential Triggers

- Triggers are highly specific to the obsession:
  - **Contamination Obsessions**: Exposure to perceived contaminants (e.g., germs, dirt)
  - **Symmetry/Orderliness Obsessions**: Disorganized or asymmetrical environments
  - **Harm Obsessions**: Thoughts or images of violence or danger
  - **Intrusive Thoughts**: Thoughts that violate the person's values.
  - **Stress**

Schizophrenia

Schizophrenia is a severe and chronic mental illness characterized by a disruption in an individual's perception of reality. The core features involve hallucinations and delusions, significantly affecting an individual's thoughts, emotions, and behaviors (American Psychiatric Association, 2022). First responders are occasionally called upon to interact with individuals experiencing schizophrenia, and understanding the disorder is crucial for effective and safe intervention.

Schizophrenia – Trainers Toolbox
• **Auditory or other sensory hallucinations,** most commonly "hearing voices" perceived as real. • **Fixed delusions,** such as persecutory or grandiose beliefs held despite clear contrary evidence. • **Disorganized speech and thought,** reflected in incoherence, loose associations, or tangential answers. • **Markedly disorganized or catatonic behavior,** ranging from unpredictable agitation to rigid immobility. • **Negative symptoms**—blunted affect, reduced motivation (avolition), and social withdrawal.

Hallucinations and Delusions

Hallucinations are sensory experiences that occur in the absence of an external stimulus. In schizophrenia, auditory hallucinations (hearing voices) are most common, but visual, tactile, olfactory, and gustatory hallucinations can also occur. People with delusions hold fixed beliefs that are not based in reality, and these beliefs persist despite contradictory evidence. Delusions can be grandiose (e.g., believing one is a famous figure) or persecutory (e.g., believing one is being followed or targeted).

Recognizing Schizophrenia

Recognizing the symptoms of schizophrenia allows first responders to prioritize safety and de-escalation during interactions. This understanding can also help to: (a) differentiate Schizophrenia from other mental health conditions, and (b) facilitate access to appropriate mental health services.

Schizophrenia is a complex mental illness requiring a specialized approach. By equipping first responders with knowledge about the disorder's core features and effective communication techniques, interactions with individuals experiencing schizophrenia can be safer and more productive for all parties involved.

Maintaining Rapport and De-escalation

Interactions with individuals experiencing schizophrenia require a delicate balance. First responders should not directly contradict a person's delusions to avoid seeming confrontational and potentially escalating the situation. Instead, a more therapeutic approach involves:

Active listening. Demonstrating genuine interest and empathy through attentive listening can foster rapport and trust.

Open-ended questions. Asking questions that encourage elaboration on the person's experience ("Tell me more about being heir to the throne") can provide valuable insights into their current reality.

Validation. Acknowledging the person's emotional state without validating the content of their delusions ("It sounds like you believe you are royalty. Can you tell me more about that feeling?") can de-escalate tension.

Potential Triggers

- These are more about exacerbating symptoms or triggering episodes:
  - Stress
  - Substance use (especially stimulants)
  - Lack of sleep
  - Changes in medication
  - Highly stimulating environments

Post-Traumatic Stress Disorder (PTSD)

Post-traumatic Stress Disorder (PTSD) is a debilitating mental health condition that can develop following exposure to a single traumatic event or many small events. Considering its significance, this chapter explores the historical context of PTSD and its core features.

Historical Context and Recognition

The concept of PTSD has a long and evolving history. World War I originally termed the disorder "shell shock," and various names have recognized it throughout history. However, advancements in research have led to a more comprehensive understanding of its symptoms and impact. While soldiers returning from war are often associated with PTSD, it is crucial to recognize that the disorder can develop in anyone who experiences a traumatic event.

Core Features of PTSD

A cluster of symptoms that can impair an individual's daily life characterizes PTSD. These core features include (American Psychiatric Association, 2022):

Re-experiencing symptoms. Flashbacks, nightmares, and intrusive thoughts related to the traumatic event.

PTSD – Trainers Toolbox
• **Intrusive trauma memories and flashbacks** that replay the event with vivid sensory detail and trigger intense distress. • **Avoidance of trauma-related stimuli,** including people, places, conversations, or thoughts connected to the event. • **Negative shifts in cognition and mood,** such as persistent guilt, detachment from others, or loss of interest in activities. • **Hyperarousal and exaggerated startle response,** manifested in irritability, hypervigilance, and difficulty concentrating. • **Sleep disturbances and recurrent nightmares,** leading to chronic fatigue and further emotional dysregulation.

Avoidance symptoms. Deliberately avoiding situations or stimuli associated with the trauma.

Negative alterations in cognitions and mood. Difficulty remembering key aspects of the trauma, negative self-perception or worldview, emotional detachment, and persistent feelings of fear, sadness, or anger.

Hyperarousal and reactivity. Increased alertness, difficulty concentrating, sleep disturbances, and hypervigilance.

Potential Triggers

- Trauma-Related Stimuli:
  - Sounds (e.g., loud noises, sirens)
  - Sights (e.g., uniforms, specific locations)

  - Smells
  - Tastes

- Anniversaries of the traumatic event
- Discussions or media portrayals of trauma
- Feeling trapped or helpless
- Interactions that resemble the trauma

Responding to Mental Health Crises: Challenges and Opportunities for First Responders

Mental health crises represent a significant public health concern, and first responders are often at the forefront of intervention. We will discuss the complexities of responding to people in mental health crises and the challenges and opportunities for improved outcomes below. Law enforcement is routinely called upon to address mental health crises, often because of the lack of readily available mental health services in the community. While families and individuals in crisis may seek help, this absence of resources can lead to police involvement. The reliance on law enforcement raises concerns about the potential for criminalization of individuals with mental illness (Slate et al., 2021).

Prevalence of Mental Illness Encounters

Empirical analysis shows that interactions with individuals exhibiting signs of mental illness constitute a meaningful subset of routine police activity. A survey of 174 U.S. municipal law enforcement agencies, Deane et al. (1999) found that roughly 7% of all officer—citizen contacts were identified as involving persons believed to have a mental illness.

Challenges in Recognition and Stigma

A key challenge lies in the potential for officers to misinterpret or fail to recognize the signs and symptoms of mental illness. Stigma surrounding mental illness can further hinder effective intervention. Research suggests that the public may hold negative views of individuals with mental illness, potentially influencing police perceptions during interactions (Slate et al., 2021).

Training in Mental Health

Training programs focusing on mental health awareness and de-escalation techniques are crucial for first responders. Encounters are less likely to escalate to violence when officers possess strong communication skills, employ negotiation tactics, and maintain a positive demeanor while managing their own stress levels. Trained officers who spend appreciably more time on scene were 58% less likely to use force that causes injury to citizens (White et al., 2023). It is important to dispel the misconception that individuals with mental illness are inherently violent. Research shows they are more likely to be victims of violence than perpetrators (Slate et al., 2021). A compassionate and empathetic approach is essential for first responders interacting with individuals in crisis.

Collaboration and Specialized Services

Effective responses to mental health crises require collaboration between first responders and mental health professionals. The availability of specialized mental health crisis response teams and accessible treatment options can improve outcomes for both individuals in crisis and first responders (Marcus & Stergiopoulos, 2022).

By encouraging collaboration and prioritizing de-escalation strategies, first responders can play a vital role in positive outcomes for all parties involved. Effective communication and de-escalation techniques are paramount for law enforcement officers responding to individuals experiencing a mental health crisis. Practical verbal and nonverbal communication skills are crucial in rapport building, reducing tension, and promoting favorable resolutions during these encounters.

De-escalation and Communication Techniques

De-escalation is a crucial skill for all first responders, but it takes on particular importance when encountering individuals experiencing a mental health crisis. It emphasizes active listening, rapport building, demonstrating empathy, and identifying potential triggers to prevent escalation. Active listening is a cornerstone of successful de-escalation. Officers should focus on truly understanding the individual's perspective, focusing on both verbal and nonverbal cues. This involves maintaining eye contact, using open-ended questions to encourage elaboration, and avoiding interruption.

Verbal and Nonverbal Communication

Mastery of both verbal and nonverbal communication skills is essential for de-escalation. Officers must be attentive to verbal cues, such as the content and tone of speech, while also recognizing nonverbal cues like posture, facial expressions, and gestures. A lack of verbal communication can be a potential indicator of heightened emotional states and a precursor to violence. Silence during a heated confrontation may represent an emotional "tipping point," requiring officers to adjust their approach.

Rapport Building

Rapport building involves showing empathy and acknowledging the individual's emotions without judgment. Taking the time to establish rapport with individuals experiencing a mental health crisis is necessary for a favorable resolution. This involves active listening, demonstrating empathy, and avoiding confrontational language. Building trust allows officers to gather information, assess the situation, and employ de-escalation techniques tailored to the individual's specific needs. Several techniques can help build rapport, including:

Open-ended questions. This technique invites narrative control, signaling respect and curiosity rather than interrogation. *Example*—"Can you tell me what's happening to you right now?" instead of "Why did you do this?".

Reflective Listening. Demonstrates accurate receipt of content and emotion, encouraging deeper disclosure. *Example*—"You sound overwhelmed by what happened at work, and you don't know who to trust."

Emotion labeling. Naming feelings can help subjects organize chaotic emotions and show empathic attunement. *Example*: "You seem frustrated and scared." Pause to let the label settle; allow correction.

Validation Without Agreement. Acknowledges the subject's reality while maintaining professional neutrality. *Example*: "Given what you just described, I can see why you feel trapped."

Empowerment via Choice Architecture. Small choices restore a sense of control, reducing oppositional behavior. *Example*: Offer binary, low-stakes options: "Would you prefer to sit in the patrol car or on the curb while we talk?".

Self-Disclose in Micro-Doses. Brief, professional disclosures can humanize the responder and shift the hierarchical dynamic toward partnership. *Example*: "I've had times I felt out of options, too. Let's figure this out together."

Future-Oriented Hope Statements. Crisis constricts temporal perspective; pointing gently toward next steps widens it. *Example*: "We're here to make sure you're safe tonight. After that, we can look at support that might help tomorrow."

Timely Intervention and Hasty Decisions

Traditional police training may emphasize the swift resolution of incidents. However, encounters with individuals in crisis often necessitate a more patient approach. Officers arriving on the scene should resist the urge to make immediate decisions and instead prioritize establishing rapport and using isolation techniques as needed. This deliberate approach can improve the chances of a successful outcome.

Effective communication and de-escalation techniques are fundamental tools for law enforcement officers interacting with individuals experiencing mental illness. By prioritizing rapport building, active listening, and nonverbal awareness, officers can navigate these situations more effectively, promoting safety for all involved parties.

Law Enforcement Response Options in Mental Health Crises: A Critical Analysis

First responders, especially law enforcement officers, are commonly called upon to address mental health crises. These situations require careful assessment and a nuanced understanding of response options. This section analyzes the various options available to law enforcement.

The optimal response option depends on the specific circumstances of each case. Decision-making is influenced by factors such as the severity of the mental health crisis, the presence of immediate danger, and the availability of mental health resources.

Balancing Competing Demands

First responders face the challenge of balancing the safety and well-being of the individual in crisis, public safety concerns, and the needs of the law enforcement agency itself. A variety of response options exists, each with its own set of implications.

Informal Resolution. In certain situations, officers may resolve the crisis informally through de-escalation techniques, active listening, and collaboration with on-scene mental health professionals.

Arrest. Arrest may be necessary if they have committed a crime. However, arrest should not be the default response for mental health crises.

Involuntary Hospitalization. Emergency psychiatric evaluations may authorize involuntary hospitalization for people considered a danger to themselves or others. This approach causes collaboration with mental health professionals and typically occurs when a first responder "Baker Acts" an individual and transports them to a psychiatric receiving facility or hospital.

Do Nothing. In some cases, where the individual is not an immediate threat to themselves or others, minimal or no intervention might be the most appropriate response.

Exercise/Role Plays

Scenario-based training immerses first responder students in lifelike, time-pressured situations marked by ambiguous cues and evolving subject behavior. Instructors can coach self-regulation strategies like controlled breathing or tactical positioning—strategies that conventional classroom methods cannot evoke—because they can pause, repeat, and debrief these exercises. This situated practice accelerates knowledge transfer to field performance and inoculates officers against the performance-degrading effects of acute stress.

Experimental evidence corroborates these benefits. In a randomized trial, officers who completed high-fidelity role-plays combined with stress management coaching made 38% more correct shoot/no shoot decisions and exhibited tighter psychological control six weeks later than peers who received standard firearm refreshers (Andersen & Gustafsberg, 2016).

A well-designed, feedback-rich role-play is a validated mechanism for sharpening judgment, communication, and motor execution under operational stress, enabling officers to make swifter, more accurate, and proportional decisions when the stakes are highest.

Role-Playing Examples

Below are sample role-plays for each disorder:

Anxiety Disorder (Panic Disorder)

- **Disorder**: Panic Disorder
- **Scenario**: Officers respond to a call about a disturbance in a grocery store. They find a young man hyperventilating, clutching his chest, and shouting, "I can't breathe! I'm going to die!" Customers are staring, and the man is becoming increasingly agitated.
- **Observed Symptoms**: Rapid breathing, chest pain, dizziness, trembling, sweating, fear of dying, agitation.
- **Potential Triggers**: Crowds, bright lights, loud noises, feeling trapped, medical concerns.
- **De-escalation Techniques**:
  - Speak in a calm, reassuring tone.
  - Clear the area to reduce stimulation.

- Offer simple, direct instructions (e.g., "Try to take slow, deep breaths with me").
- Acknowledge his distress ("I understand you're feeling scared, but I'm here to help").
- Avoid dismissing his feelings or telling him to "calm down."

- **Learning Points**:
  - Panic attacks can mimic medical emergencies.
  - Empathy and a calm demeanor are crucial.
  - Focus on the present moment and grounding techniques.

Depressive Disorder (Major Depressive Disorder)

- **Disorder**: Major Depressive Disorder
- **Scenario**: Officers are called to a residence for a welfare check. They find a middle-aged woman sitting in a darkened room, unresponsive to their questions. She has not been eating or sleeping and has expressed feelings of hopelessness to a family member.
- **Observed Symptoms**: Low mood, withdrawal, lack of eye contact, slowed speech, fatigue, neglect of personal hygiene.
- **Potential Triggers**: Loss (job, relationship), isolation, anniversary of a traumatic event.
- **De-escalation Techniques**:
  - Use a gentle, patient approach.
  - Allow for pauses in the conversation.
  - Ask simple, direct questions.
  - Express concern and offer help.
  - Avoid being overly cheerful or dismissive of her feelings.

- **Learning Points**:
  - Depression can impair communication and motivation.
  - Patience and empathy are essential.
  - Gather information from family/friends if possible.
  - Be aware of suicide risk.

Bipolar Disorder (Manic Episode)

- **Disorder**: Bipolar Disorder (Manic Episode)
- **Scenario**: Officers respond to a report of a man causing a disturbance in a public park. He is running around, shouting, and handing out money to strangers. He is grandiose, believing he is a famous celebrity, and becomes irritable when officers try to intervene.
- **Observed Symptoms**: Elevated mood, hyperactivity, rapid speech, impulsivity, inflated self-esteem, decreased need for sleep.
- **Potential Triggers**: Lack of sleep, stress, changes in medication.
- **De-escalation Techniques**:

- Use a calm but firm approach.
- Keep instructions simple and direct.
- Avoid arguing with his delusions.
- Try to redirect his energy into a less disruptive activity.
- Be aware that he may become easily agitated.
- **Learning Points**:
  - Mania can impair judgment and lead to risky behavior.

  Safety is a priority, both for the individual and the public.
- Monitor for potential exhaustion.

Attention Deficit Hyperactivity Disorder (ADHD)

- **Disorder**: Attention Deficit Hyperactivity Disorder
- **Scenario**: Officers respond to a call involving a traffic accident. One of the drivers is having difficulty staying focused, is interrupting the officers, and seems unable to follow instructions. He is fidgeting and appears restless.
- **Observed Symptoms**: Inattention, impulsivity, hyperactivity, difficulty with organization.
- **Potential Triggers**: Stress, sensory overload, complex instructions.
- **De-escalation Techniques**:
  - Give clear, concise instructions.
  - Repeat information as needed.
  - Minimize distractions.
  - Allow him to move around if it doesn't compromise safety.
  - Be patient and avoid taking his behavior personally.
- **Learning Points**:
  - ADHD can affect adults and impair their ability to follow directions.
  - Simple communication and a structured approach are helpful.

Obsessive–Compulsive Disorder (OCD)

- **Disorder**: Obsessive–Compulsive Disorder
- **Scenario**: Officers are called to a house where a woman is refusing to leave. She is repeatedly checking the locks on the door and washing her hands, even though they are visibly clean. She is distressed and anxious.
- **Observed Symptoms**: Repetitive behaviors (compulsions), anxiety, distress when rituals are interrupted.
- **Potential Triggers**: Stress, contamination concerns, feeling a lack of control.
- **De-escalation Techniques**:
  - Be patient and avoid interrupting her rituals unless there is an immediate safety concern.
  - Acknowledge her distress.
  - Use a calm and reassuring tone.
  - Avoid judgment or criticism of her behavior.

  - Keep a respectful distance.

- **Learning Points**:

  - OCD rituals are driven by anxiety, not a desire to be difficult.
  - Interfering with rituals can increase anxiety.
  - Focus on communication and de-escalation.

Schizophrenia

- **Disorder**: Schizophrenia
- **Scenario**: Officers respond to a call about a man talking to himself and acting erratically in a park. He is having auditory hallucinations, claiming that he hears voices telling him to be careful. He also expresses delusions that people are following him.
- **Observed Symptoms**: Hallucinations, delusions, disorganized speech, paranoia, agitation.
- **Potential Triggers**: Stress, lack of medication, substance use.
- **De-escalation Techniques**:

  - Speak calmly and simply.
  - Do not argue with his delusions or hallucinations.
  - Focus on his feelings rather than the content of his thoughts.
  - Maintain a safe distance.
  - Be patient and understanding.

- **Learning Points**:

  - Schizophrenia can severely distort a person's perception of reality.
  - Communication should be clear, simple, and non-confrontational.
  - Prioritize safety and de-escalation.

Post-Traumatic Stress Disorder (PTSD)

- **Disorder**: Post-Traumatic Stress Disorder
- **Scenario**: Officers respond to a domestic disturbance call. One of the individuals, a veteran, becomes agitated and aggressive when officers try to question him. He has flashbacks to his time in combat and misinterprets the officers' actions as a threat.
- **Observed Symptoms**: Agitation, irritability, hypervigilance, flashbacks, emotional numbness.
- **Potential Triggers**: Loud noises, physical contact, feeling trapped, aggressive questioning.
- **De-escalation Techniques**:

  - Use a calm and non-threatening approach.
  - Avoid sudden movements or loud noises.
  - Give him space and allow him to have some control.
  - Acknowledge his feelings and validate his experience.
  - Be patient and understanding.

- **Learning Points**:
  - PTSD can cause heightened reactivity and misinterpretations of threats.
  - Trauma-informed communication is essential.
  - Officer safety is paramount, but avoid unnecessary force.

Challenges and Considerations

Collaboration between law enforcement and mental health professionals is essential for effective responses to mental health crises. Investing in improved relationships and communication channels between these agencies can facilitate timely access to appropriate care for individuals in crisis. Advocating for increased resources and training for first responders to address mental health issues is crucial.

Law enforcement officers face problematic challenges when responding to mental health crises. A critical analysis of available response options and improved collaboration with mental health professionals are essential for promoting safety and facilitating access to appropriate care for individuals in crisis. Investing in resources and training can empower law enforcement agencies to navigate these situations more effectively.

Summary

This chapter surveys the intersection of policing and mental health training by (1) contextualizing the prevalence of mental health related encounters in law enforcement, (2) detailing observable signs and symptoms of common disorders, (3) outlining evidence-based de-escalation and communication techniques, (4) presenting role-play and scenario-based training as high-yield tools, and (5) analyzing response options ranging from information resolutions to civil commitment. Comprehensive skills-focused training in mental health can enhance officer safety, improve clinical outcomes for individuals in crisis, and strengthen community trust.

Taken together, the material shows that behavioral-health competence shapes contemporary police work as much as traditional law enforcement expertise. Scientific data confirms officers will routinely encounter individuals with psychiatric, developmental, or substance-use conditions that influence their behavior. Accurate recognition of symptom clusters, augmented by structured decision trees and checklists, enables officers to tailor their approach, avoid unnecessary escalation, and activate medical or social-service pathways. De-escalation and crisis-communication curricula grounded in cognitive-behavioral and stress inoculation principles further reduce the likelihood of injury to all parties, especially when reinforced through high-fidelity role-play that recreates the field's sensory, temporal, and emotional pressures.

Scenario-based training emerges as a pedagogical linchpin. By allowing instructors to pause, rewind, and debrief critical decision points, well-designed scenarios expose tacit reasoning, illuminate alternative tactical outcomes, and cultivate psychological self-regulation under stress. This chapter's modular toolbox of disorder-specific cues and tactical reminders provides students and practitioners with actionable resources that translate classroom learning into operational competence. Equally important, the discussion of response options underscores the legal and ethical frameworks that guide discretionary authority in mental health encounters.

Nevertheless, several challenges remain. The development of evidence on long-term training efficacy is ongoing, especially concerning skill decay and the sequencing of refresher training. Cultural-competence considerations, language access, and the needs of neurodiverse populations warrant a deeper integration into future curricula. Finally, sustained progress will require rigorous program evaluation, linking training inputs to measurable outcomes such as the reduced use of force, lower injury rates, improved referral uptake, and expanding collaborative models that embed mental health professionals alongside frontline officers.

In sum, policing and mental health are no longer peripheral to one another; they occupy a convergent domain when public safety, public health, and civil liberties intersect. By grounding training in empirical evidence, experiential learning, and cross-sectional collaboration, departments can better prepare officers to navigate this domain with professionalism, compassion, and accountability, ultimately safeguarding the community's well-being and officer resilience.

References

American Psychiatric Association. (2022). *Diagnostic and statistical manual of mental disorders* (5th ed., text rev.). American Psychiatric Pub Inc.

Andersen, J. P., & Gustafsberg, H. (2016). A training method to improve police use of force decision making. *SAGE Open, 6*(2). https://doi.org/10.1177/2158244016638708

APA Dictionary of Psychology. (n.d.). https://dictionary.apa.org/

Borum, R., Williams Deane, M., Steadman, H. J., & Morrissey, J. (1998). Police perspectives on responding to mentally ill people in crisis: Perceptions of program effectiveness. *Behavioral Sciences & the Law, 16*(4), 393–405. https://doi.org/10.1002/(sici)1099-0798(199823)16:4%3c393::aid-bsl317%3e3.0.co;2-4

Deane, M., Steadman, H. J., Borum, R., Veysey, B. M., & Morrissey, J. P. (1999). Emerging partnerships between mental health and law enforcement. *Psychiatric Services, 50*(1), 99–101. https://doi.org/10.1176/ps.50.1.99

Kessler, R. C., Adler, L. A., Barkley, R. A., Biederman, J., Conners, C., Demler, O., Faraone, S. V., Greenhill, L. L., Howes, M. J., Secnik, K., Spencer, T., Üstün, T., Walters, E. E., & Zaslavsky, A. M. (2006). The prevalence and correlates of adult adhd in the United States: Results from the national comorbidity survey replication. *American Journal of Psychiatry, 163*(4). https://doi.org/10.1176/ajp.2006.163.4.716

Marcus, N., & Stergiopoulos, V. (2022). Re-examining mental health crisis intervention: A rapid review comparing outcomes across police, co-responder and non-police models. *Health & Social Care in the Community, 30*(5), 1665–1679. https://doi.org/10.1111/hsc.13731

Mental Health by the Numbers. (n.d.). NAMI. https://www.nami.org/about-mental-illness/mental-health-by-the-numbers/

Roesch, R., & Goossens, I. (2021). Improving police procedures for dealing with mental illness. In *Police psychology* (pp. 173–188). Elsevier. https://doi.org/10.1016/b978-0-12-816544-7.00009-7

Slate, R., Frailing, K., Johnson, W., & Buffington, J. (2021). *The criminalization of mental illness: Crisis and opportunity for the justice system* (3rd ed.). Carolina Academic Press.

Teplin, L. A. (1984). Criminalizing mental disorder: The comparative arrest rate of the mentally ill. *American Psychologist, 39*(7), 794–803. https://doi.org/10.1037/0003-066X.39.7.794

Vermette, H. S., Pinals, D. A., & Appelbaum, P. S. (2005). Mental health training for law enforcement professionals. *Journal of the American Academy of Psychiatry and the Law Online, 33*(1), 42–46. Retrieved March 19, 2024, from https://web.archive.org/web/20190214170011id_/http://jaapl.org:80/content/jaapl/33/1/42.full.pdf

White, M. D., Orosco, C., & Watts, S. (2023). Can police de-escalation training reduce use of force and citizen injury without compromising officer safety? *Journal of Experimental Criminology, 21*(1), 45–70. https://doi.org/10.1007/s11292-023-09584-

Part III
Clinical Practice

Chapter 14
Understanding Clinical and Non-Clinical Trends and Observations Among Public Safety Candidates

Elizabeth Morris and Victoria Tumilty

An open folder sitting on a hiring manager's desk contains the personnel files of two individuals who have just finished interviewing for a job in a fast-paced, high-stress environment that focuses on collaboration and service to others. The first applicant came across as someone who is self-assured and confident in their abilities, has clear career goals, and can see themselves in a position of leadership in the future. They also presented with a powerful demeanor and appeared physically fit. On the other hand, the second applicant came across as friendly, possessing a deep desire to help those around them, and displaying flexibility with their future career goals. This second person also presented as more mild-mannered and appeared less physically fit. Which individual should the manager consider hiring?

What if the job in the abovementioned fast-paced, high-stress environment, that focuses on collaboration and service to others, was that of a law enforcement officer? Now, which applicant should be hired? Does one candidate appear more well-suited to be a police officer than the other?

Upon discovering that the position was for a law enforcement officer, most readers probably would select the first individual as the best police candidate. This is most likely because when asked to envision a public safety officer, a particular image comes to mind: a physically fit person with a commanding presence and an authoritative personality. Many in the general public have historically imagined this description, but it does not necessarily apply to public safety candidates today. Both individuals represent current examples of candidates under consideration for public safety employment.

This chapter aims to bring awareness to current trends observed among public safety candidates pre- and post-pandemic. Public safety candidates are individuals

E. Morris · V. Tumilty (✉)
The FMRT Group, Winston-Salem, NC, USA
e-mail: victoria@fmrt.org

V. B. Van Hasselt and M. L. Bourke (eds.), *Advances in First Responder Mental Health*, Advances in First Responder Mental Health 1,
https://doi.org/10.1007/978-3-032-27978-1_14

applying for positions in law enforcement, fire services, wildland fire services, corrections, and emergency medical services (EMS; NORA Public Safety Sector Council, 2019). We will discuss clinical and non-clinical trends in the areas of mental health and behavioral patterns that have been observed by licensed clinical psychologists and public safety support administrative staff from across the public safety industry. Observations provided by law enforcement recruiters will also be examined to determine if they coincide with these observations. Lastly, a discussion of the implications these trends pose to law enforcement agencies will follow as the authors offer best practices and recommendations for how to best develop and support law enforcement officers and candidates.

Our Research

The information reported throughout this chapter was obtained from a combination of preliminary survey and field research data conducted from April to June 2024 by a public safety support company headquartered in North Carolina. This company has facilitated more than 115,000 comprehensive pre-hire and post-hire psychological and medical evaluations for safety-sensitive employers over 20 years of business working with over 700 agencies. Participants included clinical psychologists and administrative staff from the public safety support company, other police and public safety psychologists throughout the United States, and police recruiters from several law enforcement agencies across the state of North Carolina.

The first part of our research consisted of a survey inquiring about clinical trends and observations. It was distributed electronically to 30 psychologists; 28 responses were returned. A non-clinical survey was distributed to 16 administrative staff from a public safety support company, and 6 responses were collected. The second component of our research consisted of field research, where the first author of this chapter conducted face-to-face interviews with approximately 10 police recruiters from three of the largest agencies in NC. Although this was a small convenience sample, we believe there is value in our preliminary findings. The results were analyzed via descriptive statistics. Examples of questions asked in the survey sent to clinical personnel include "What percentage of safety-sensitive applicants present with mental health concerns during interviews?" and "Which of the following mental health issues do you commonly encounter in safety-sensitive applicants?" Examples of questions asked in the non-clinical survey include "What percentage of safety-sensitive applicants arrive to their interview without the necessary forms and documentation?" and "Do safety-sensitive applicants typically demonstrate appropriate professional behavior and etiquette during interactions with staff?" While our research assessed several factors, descriptions of the full results are beyond the scope of this chapter, and only key findings will be discussed throughout the following pages.

Clinical Expertise

Before exploring the clinical observations, one may wonder what expertise these professionals have regarding behavioral concerns affecting current public safety candidates. It is well-documented that public safety employees work in some of the most dangerous and stressful environments (Hartley et al., 2011; NORA Public Safety Sector Council, 2019; North Carolina Association of Chiefs of Police, 2024; Stogner et al., 2020). Because of this work environment, pre-employment psychological evaluations (PPEs) have become a common tool utilized by public safety agencies across the United States (Ben-Porath et al., 2011; Holzman & Kirschner, 2003; Marshall et al., 2020; Mitchell, 2020). These evaluations serve to identify individuals who may not adjust well to law enforcement's fast-paced and highly stressful environment (Holzman & Kirschner, 2003; Marshall et al., 2020). A standard PPE covers areas including emotional functioning, behavior, personality, cognitive skills, and psychosocial support system (Holzman & Kirschner, 2003; International Association of Chiefs of Police, 2020). By delving into these areas, psychologists can get a more holistic snapshot of the candidate and their likelihood of successful occupational adjustment in a public safety role.

The utilization of PPEs is not a new practice. Mental health professionals across the United States have assisted public safety agencies in conducting these evaluations for nearly 100 years (Mitchell, 2020). A nationwide survey (Cochrane et al., 2003) of municipal police departments found that over 90% of these departments required their recruits to have a psychological evaluation (Mitchell, 2020). Almost a decade after this initial 2003 survey, nearly all law enforcement agencies in the United States required the utilization of PPEs, regardless of whether a state law with this requirement existed (Mitchell, 2020; Reaves, 2010). Since nearly all law enforcement agencies require psychological evaluations, it is no surprise that every year in the United States, thousands of mental health professionals, either working independently or contractually with businesses that specialize in offering public safety services, conduct PPEs on public safety candidates (Mitchell, 2020).

Clinical Trends and Observations

Candidates' Mental Health

The survey data found several common themes among the public safety candidates referred for their PPEs. The first clinical trend revolves around candidates' mental health. As a result of the inherently stressful work environment, public safety employees have an increased risk of experiencing a wide range of mental health problems (North Carolina Association of Chiefs of Police, 2024; Sadulski, 2024; Stogner et al., 2020). Research indicates these employees suffer from post-traumatic stress disorder (PTSD), depression, anxiety, and substance-related issues at a greater rate than the general population and employees of other occupations (Bennett et al., 2005; Berger et al., 2011; Marshall et al., 2020; North Carolina Association of Chiefs of Police, 2024; Petrie et al., 2018; Sadulski, 2024; Stogner et al., 2020). While this phenomenon of public safety employees experiencing mental health problems due to their line of work has been heavily researched, our survey data found a new and potentially alarming trend surrounding public safety candidates' mental health.

In our experience, candidates not only are exposed to factors that can affect their mental health while on the job, but they are also presenting with more mental health concerns than previous candidates. Current survey data suggests that 64% of evaluating clinicians reported that roughly 25% of applicants with no prior law enforcement experience referred for PPEs present with mental health concerns. Of this 25%, the most common mental health concerns encountered among applicants included depression (93%) and anxiety (89%). U.S. Department of Veteran Affairs (VA) PTSD ratings (54%) and substance use issues (39%) were also commonly encountered among these applicants. Moreover, clinicians observed an increase in attention-deficit/hyperactivity disorder (ADHD). This indicates that public safety departments are starting with a group of applicants who have yet to put on a uniform but already have mental health concerns.

One possible explanation for the stark increase in mental health presentations among current public safety candidates could be the lasting effects of the COVID-19 pandemic. The pandemic was marked with grave uncertainty and fear. As restrictions began lifting, a tremendous amount of research began to examine how the COVID-19 pandemic affected mental health. One study found that, globally, people began experiencing more symptoms of anxiety, depression, and substance use disorder during the pandemic than ever before (National Institute of Mental Health, 2024a; Stogner et al., 2020; World Health Organization, 2022). According to the World Health Organization (WHO, 2022), there was a 25% increase in the global prevalence of both depression and anxiety following the first year of the pandemic, reflecting the stresses and fears that were felt by millions. The main causes of this increase were the alteration of social norms due to social distancing requirements and the subsequent social isolation of many (Stogner et al., 2020; World Health Organization, 2022). Moreover, research suggests that younger people were most impacted by the pandemic in terms of experiencing lasting mental health implications (National Institute of Mental Health, 2024a; World Health Organization, 2022). Younger people, in particular, saw their ability to go about their normal routines, engage in their communities via sports and extracurricular activities, and interact with their peers abruptly halted.

The observations collected from the current survey data appear consistent with prior research that explored the pandemic's effect on overall mental health. Many candidates disclosed during their PPEs that they first began experiencing depression-like symptoms during the pandemic, which ultimately led to the use of psychotropic medication to manage their symptoms. The pandemic appeared to contribute to a lack of social interaction among young adults across the applicant pool, which had lasting effects. For example, younger people went out on fewer dates, and they were not in classrooms with their peers.

Voluntary and Involuntary Commitments

A second clinical trend ascertained by the current survey data suggests that public safety candidates have experienced an increase in both voluntary and involuntary commitments to mental health treatment programs or facilities. Clinicians reported that approximately 25% of applicants revealed a history of involuntary or voluntary commitments. This history of commitments, particularly involuntary commitments, also typically involves some element of suicidality, whether that be serious thoughts or active attempts. Knowing that an applicant already has an established baseline of contemplating suicide when faced with overwhelming life circumstances, how might the applicant handle the numerous hardships and stressors that await them in their future public safety career? In our experience, these disclosures also have led to an increase in medical release requests. These types of requests require more time to obtain and review records to assist in making a determination regarding a candidate's job suitability. One psychologist reported that more than 400 pages of records from the Veterans Administration (VA) needed to be reviewed before deciding on the candidate's suitability. The increased influx of medical and psychiatric records that need to be reviewed adds time to the overall evaluation process.

Further, this increase in both mental health commitments indicates that public safety candidates are seeking help from mental health professionals by receiving medication to help better manage their symptomatology. The most prevalent mental health concerns that public safety candidates are seeking help for include anxiety, depression, and PTSD. While much has been mentioned about the current pool of candidates having an increased history of mental health diagnoses and presentations, they do not necessarily equate to an automatic not suitable recommendation for a position within a public safety agency. Instead, it is the role of the evaluator to determine the likelihood of these issues impacting job performance.

The topic of job suitability will be explored later in this chapter. However, let's consider the example of a law enforcement candidate who revealed during their evaluation that they experience panic attacks. The *Diagnostic and Statistical Manual of Mental Disorders* (5th ed., text rev.; DSM-5-TR; American Psychiatric Association, 2022) defines panic attacks as "an abrupt surge of intense fear or discomfort that reaches a peak within minutes and during which time 4 or more of 13 physical and cognitive symptoms occur" (p. 242). One can see that panic attacks could pose problems for an individual working in a public safety occupation. The individual could freeze while pursuing a suspect or when facing a stressful and potentially life-threatening situation. This would be something the evaluator would want to discuss with the candidate.

Disclosure Patterns and Stigma

A third trend that emerged from our research centers on public safety candidates' mixed disclosure patterns of mental health concerns. Approximately half (52%) of the surveyed psychologists indicated that the majority of candidates typically hint at experiencing mental health struggles, but do not use explicit statements. Psychologists also noted that some candidates are not willing to admit having mental health problems at all, or they minimize their issues, while a few are willing to offer full disclosures.

Why are public safety candidates unwilling to fully disclose their mental health issues? Why do some candidates minimize their struggles, or outright avoid the topic during their PPEs? The answer, for many, has to do with stigma.

According to the National Institute of Mental Health (2024b), one in five adults in the United States suffers from a mental illness. With such a high incidence, one would think that there would be a greater openness in our society to speaking about one's mental health struggles. However, this is generally not the case. Broadly speaking, mental health stigma encompasses negative stereotypes, prejudices, and discriminatory behaviors toward individuals who suffer from mental health problems (Prizeman et al., 2024; Rüsch et al., 2005; Singhal, 2024). It serves as a major barrier to help-seeking, as more than half of people suffering from a mental illness do not seek help for fear of being judged, treated differently, or for fear of losing their job (Singhal, 2024). Research has identified several types of mental health stigma: public, self, and structural (Grupe, 2023; Prizeman et al., 2024; Singhal, 2024). *Public stigma* includes both the negative beliefs and discriminatory attitudes that members of the general public may hold about mental illness. *Self-stigma* is composed of negative attitudes that one who suffers from a mental illness may hold regarding their own condition, such as internalized shame. *Structural stigma* is more systemic in nature. It includes policies of organizations that either intentionally or unintentionally restrict opportunities for individuals suffering from mental illness (Grupe, 2023; Prizeman et al., 2024; Singhal, 2024). The stigmatization surrounding mental health can pose dangerous and even life-threatening consequences, such as reducing the likelihood of seeking treatment, which can consequently worsen an individual's symptoms and suffering (Singhal, 2024).

Mental health stigma in the workplace, particularly within certain occupations, remains a major problem. A national poll conducted by the American Psychiatric Association found that 52% of employees feel they cannot openly discuss mental health with their supervisors or coworkers due to fears of judgment or differential treatment (Singhal, 2024). One profession that particularly struggles with mental health stigma is public safety. A survey of law enforcement officers (Drew & Martin, 2021; National Council for Mental Wellbeing, 2023) found that 90% of the officers reported stigma as a barrier to seeking help. A plethora of both qualitative and quantitative research has found that both public and self-stigma are strong barriers to help-seeking behaviors among law enforcement (Drew & Martin, 2021; Grupe,

2023; Newell et al., 2021; Ricciardelli et al., 2018). Help-seeking among law enforcement is often viewed negatively due to police culture (Grupe, 2023; Tuckey et al., 2011). Police culture is built upon stoicism and maintaining control of one's emotions (Drew & Martin, 2021; Grupe, 2023; Tuckey et al., 2011), which causes many officers to avoid reaching out for help for fear of appearing weak or unfit to perform their duties (Drew & Martin, 2021; Grupe, 2023; Lilly, 2023; National Council for Mental Wellbeing, 2023; Tuckey et al., 2011).

Mental health stigma poses challenges to those employed in public safety agencies, but it also carries over and affects public safety candidates, as well. Similar to law enforcement officers not wanting to appear weak or unfit to work in this occupation, many candidates may minimize or avoid their mental health struggles altogether. This would explain why the current data indicates a mixed disclosure pattern among candidates. However, while the stigma of mental health still impacts candidates' willingness to make mental health disclosures, a positive outlook is on the horizon.

In our experience, the current public safety candidates appear to be discussing their mental health more openly than previous candidates. This observation aligns with the American Psychological Association's (2019) findings that people today are more willing than ever to discuss mental illness. This willingness comes as campaigns promoting the message "it is okay not to be okay" become more widespread due to the generational shifts toward recognizing mental health struggles and greater acceptance of help-seeking behaviors.

During our PPE process, candidates must complete several pre-employment assessment materials before their evaluations. They tend to provide more detail on these forms regarding their mental health histories and current struggles because it is easier for them to disclose on paper rather than one-on-one with the psychologist. The additional information is advantageous because it allows the evaluator to more thoroughly explore the issues during the interview portion of the evaluation. Psychologists report that when candidates are asked about their written disclosures, they are more willing to discuss these issues more directly.

While the openness to discuss mental health struggles is a positive clinical trend, one disclosure type presents a possible cause for concern. Our research revealed that the current candidate pool is more openly discussing suicidality with psychologists during their PPEs. Clinicians reported hearing about suicide attempts or ideations from candidates on a weekly basis. The disclosures are both negative and positive. Ultimately, while mixed disclosure patterns are occurring with public safety candidates due to stigma, they are more willing to discuss mental health struggles, including suicidality, compared to previous candidates.

Job Suitability

A fourth clinical trend that emerged from the survey data focuses on the impact of public safety candidates' mental health on job suitability. When asked how mental health information impacts a candidate's job suitability, 95% of the psychologists we surveyed indicated that it depends on several circumstances. Various pieces of information need to be considered. The example provided above describes a law enforcement candidate who is prone to experiencing panic attacks. What would the evaluating psychologist need to know about these panic attacks before determining job suitability?

Psychologists would want to know whether the individual is currently taking medication for the panic attacks, as well as whether he or she is receiving or actively seeking therapy to help manage his or her symptoms. If a candidate reveals a history of mental health troubles or indicates they are currently struggling with their mental health, an inquiry should be made to determine how the candidate is handling the concerns. Someone who was involuntarily committed to a psychiatric facility within the last six months would present a greater concern regarding suitability and successful job adjustment than an individual who is taking anxiety medication and seeking therapy.

Survey respondents indicated they are seeing an increase in candidates with high VA PTSD ratings due to prior military service. However, with this increase, psychologists report seeing minimal to no treatment history related to these prior diagnoses and ratings. Should there be a concern with these ratings alone? Should the date of these ratings and the credentials of the evaluators be considered? Should the concern lie more with how candidates currently present in their evaluations? Or should concern be more focused on whether the candidates are receiving help for their symptoms? Each of these questions is considered by evaluating psychologists when determining the impact a public safety candidate's mental health has on job suitability.

Alpha vs. Beta Personality Types

The fifth and final clinical trend presents the most drastic change observed among the current public safety candidate pool and is focused on the candidates' personalities. One of the PPE assessments utilized by the surveyed psychologists is the California Psychological Inventory-260-Police and Public Safety Selection Report (CPI-260-PPSR). This specialized report was designed to assist in the assessment of "normal" personality traits of applicants applying for public safety positions as compared to the general population and those already employed in this profession (Johnson, Roberts, & Associates, Inc., 2024; Roberts et al., 2018). While the CPI-260-PPSR is based on the CPI-260, this specialized report includes many features from the CPI-434, such as the CPI Type designations (Johnson, Roberts, & Associates, Inc., 2024). There are four CPI Type designations an applicant can be classified as based on the interaction of their scores, which describes the applicant's approach to the world: *alpha/implementor*, *beta/supporter*, *gamma/innovator*, and *delta/visualizer* (Roberts et al., 2018).

Using the personality constructs as stipulated within the CPI-260-PPSR, the surveyed clinicians reported encountering a higher prevalence of beta personality designations among public safety candidates. This comes in direct opposition to previous candidates who displayed more stereotypical alpha personalities, which are more traditionally drawn to law enforcement. In the opening scenario of this chapter, the first individual was described as having an alpha personality type, while the second had more of a beta personality. One personality type is not necessarily better than the other; however, beta personalities differ drastically from alpha personalities. Traditional alpha (implementor-type) candidates are action-oriented, ambitious, goal-directed, and charismatic leaders, whereas, beta (supporter-type) candidates are more patient, empathetic, conscientious, and motivated by a desire to help others (The Myers-Briggs Company, 2024). Because of their empathetic and supportive nature, our experience indicates that beta candidates can struggle with conflict, which may lead to a lack of physical resiliency needed for law enforcement.

The environment in which applicants were raised, both during and after the pandemic, may help explain the rise in beta personality types. This period saw a shift in societal views on law enforcement following the murder of George Floyd (Brantingham et al., 2022). This highly publicized event caused public perception of law enforcement to worsen, with political pressures pushing law enforcement agencies to change how they operate (Karch, 2024; Vitro et al., 2022). This push led many departments to enact more community-oriented approaches to policing. This change in approach appears to align more with beta personalities, so we posit that this is why more individuals with this personality type are applying to public safety positions than ever before. While beta candidates are willing to help and serve their community, we believe these individuals may need additional training for situations requiring physical altercations and engagement.

Another shift currently observed with this uptrend in candidates with beta personalities centers on career goals and expectations. Beta candidates have very different mindsets regarding their careers in public safety agencies than previous candidates with alpha personality types. When asked about their futures within the public safety agency they applied to, beta candidates often expressed a desire to help wherever needed rather than aiming for specific roles, like SWAT or K-9 units. Although this sentiment indicates a more amiable and flexible approach, superiors may perceive the individual as lacking drive. This differs drastically from what previous alpha personality candidates would express. When asked about their futures, the alpha candidates were very direct with clearly outlined career goals. Many of these candidates expressed a desire to ultimately work in a specific unit or see themselves eventually in a leadership position within the agency. Alpha candidates openly stated that they see working in a public safety occupation as a lifelong career. On the other hand, many of the current beta candidates view law enforcement as a temporary job, which presents a challenge in retention. This temporary career outlook creates more push-back, with candidates being unwilling to work rotating or night shifts. These beta candidates indicate their desire to feel appreciated and maintain a better-balanced quality of life.

Non-Clinical Observations

In addition to examining clinical observations, our research also focused on examining several non-clinical factors. While the above clinical trends were observed directly by licensed psychologists, the following non-clinical observations were gathered from the survey responses of administrative staff. The most salient observations fall into the categories of preparedness, problem-solving skills, and professionalism.

Preparedness, Problem-Solving Skills, and Professionalism

The most significant non-clinical trend affecting law enforcement candidates centers around a lack of preparedness. Roughly 67% of candidates arrive at their PPE appointments without the necessary forms. This is the case regardless of whether the appointment is for a PPE or a PPE combined with a physical examination. This lack of preparedness reflects an increase in what was seen among prior candidates.

Additionally, those in more recent applicant pools tend to lack basic problem-solving skills. It was reported that about half of all candidates needed reminders or clarifications regarding their scheduled appointments. Many frequently required additional guidance for completing the required pre-evaluation assessments, and they placed multiple calls requesting directions to the office locations where their respective appointments were scheduled. Again, this lack of basic problem-solving skills represents an increase compared to what administrative staff saw previously.

Lastly, a slight decrease in punctuality and overall level of professionalism was observed. Previously, candidates consistently arrived on time, or early, for their scheduled appointments. These candidates also came dressed in business or business casual attire. However, the administrative staff now report seeing a wider range of dress, including some candidates coming straight from the gym or arriving in shorts and "flip-flops," despite instructions to dress in business or business casual attire for their evaluations. Candidates are also arriving late for their appointments. However, this lack of professionalism was not observed among all of the current candidate pool; approximately 84% of current candidates arrived dressed in a professional manner.

Causes and Significance

One might question why there is an increase in these non-clinical issues among more recent candidate pools. A possible explanation is that applicants are not reading their appointment emails and reminders as carefully compared to previous applicants. When an appointment for a PPE is scheduled, the administrative staff sends very detailed emails to the applicants, which outline in depth all the information regarding their appointments. This includes all the necessary forms that need to be completed prior to arrival; the pre-evaluation assessment materials and how to access them; their appointment date, time, and office location; dress code; and advice for when they should plan to arrive. We posit that these emails are not read thoroughly because applicants fail to allocate sufficient time to the task, coupled with a lack of motivation to engage with the materials they are sent. This lack of diligence and attention to detail directly contributes to the observed increases.

It is important to note that the observed non-clinical issues can potentially negatively impact the clinical factors described above. The lack of preparedness may appear trivial, but it presents a potential cause for concern. Candidates who fail to complete all the necessary assessments prevent the psychologist from reviewing applicable information in advance of the interview. This inhibits proper preparation, which can make the psychologist's job more difficult and could lead to the candidate being inaccurately portrayed. This could potentially lead to problems for both the candidate and the candidate's hiring agency down the road.

What Recruiters Are Noticing

In addition to the preliminary survey data collected, our field research, consisting of in-person interviews, was also conducted with several law enforcement recruiters across the state of North Carolina to obtain an understanding of what changes these professionals have noticed among their recruits. Before diving into what these recruiters observed, it is important to acknowledge that police recruiting has faced many challenges in recent years. In 2020, the public increasingly viewed the law enforcement profession negatively, with many calling to defund the police. This led to public and political pressures urging law enforcement to change their tactical operations (Brantingham et al., 2022; Karch, 2024; Vitro et al., 2022). The criticisms facing law enforcement created an environment of negativity and a lack of support that resulted in many resignations and retirements (Karch, 2024). A report by the Police Executive Research Forum (2021) indicated there was an 18% increase in resignations and a 45% increase in law enforcement retirements between 2020 and 2021 (Karch, 2024). This large exit of employees led to a massive recruitment movement nationwide. The proposed solution to increase the candidate pool was to reduce hiring standards; however, the short-term benefits this solution provided did not outweigh the long-term costs. Instead, law enforcement departments had to "play the long game" by developing recruiting pipelines that focused on rebuilding positive community relations—the key to rebuilding a stronger and larger workforce within this profession (Karch, 2024). The law enforcement recruiters who participated in our field research indicated they have embarked on playing the long game.

The recruiters reported several common themes emerging from the candidates they are encountering. Younger candidates are performing better academically, particularly with testing through both the Academy and Basic Law Enforcement Training (BLET) than previous recruits. Recent recruits reportedly also exhibit more empathy. However, they are less physically fit, lack emotional maturity and basic life skills, have less resiliency and critical thinking skills, and are less adaptable than previous recruits. Recruiters also report a decline in candidates' ability to have face-to-face engagements. They are seeing candidates demonstrate an overreliance on their phones to communicate, along with a lack of comfort with face-to-face conversations. The overall takeaway is that many of the trends align with the increase in beta personalities the surveyed psychologists observed.

Implications

The increase in beta personality candidates has several positive implications as well as several areas of concern. On the positive side, these candidates may have better interactions with community members due to their greater empathy. It also appears that beta candidates are more open and honest about their mental health, an observation that suggests they may be better able to handle the stressors of the job as they enter their public safety role. On the other hand, a major cause for concern with these applicants is their impaired ability to engage in physical altercations and the lack of a strong command presence. Because of their empathic nature, they may not have the inherent skills or motivations needed to engage in physical altercations, which often causes candidates to fail the field training officer (FTO) process. Law enforcement agencies now, more than ever before, need to incorporate different training methods into their process that are more geared toward teaching beta candidates. Another concern centers around their failure to follow directives, particularly with face-to-face communication. These candidates increasingly rely on their cell phones and have greater comfort communicating electronically, which poses a concern for how effectively they will engage with community members in the field.

The increase in beta personalities also calls for public safety agencies to consider different leadership styles. In a podcast episode, featuring author Stephen Covey, Jan Griffiths discussed the difference between *inspire* leadership versus *command-and-control* leadership (Griffiths, 2022). The inspire model is ideal for beta personalities, who join public safety agencies for the culture, community orientation, and quality of life; alpha personalities, in contrast, are drawn to a more militant environment. Ideally, law enforcement departments should create an environment that accommodates both styles. We challenge public safety agencies to look at their recruitment departments and consider matching candidates with mentors they can relate to based on their personality types. Although a paramilitary environment like law enforcement requires command and control, inspire leadership is not about lacking control. It is about creating clarity around vision, direction, expectations, and accountability, while simultaneously trusting individuals to use their developed skills. A command presence and the ability to act on clear directives are imperative in high-risk situations. However, day-to-day inspire leadership can be more motivating and productive for beta personalities, as it allows them to leverage their skills within a structured framework. Inspire leadership is not about eliminating structure. It is about giving individuals the freedom to excel within it. This approach could increase investment and retention among younger beta candidates attracted to the agency's culture and community orientation.

Recommendations

We want to impart recommendations and best practices to support both public safety agencies and their candidates (see Fig. 14.1). Some agencies may already employ these practices within their agency; if not, it is recommended that mental and physical preparedness training be integrated into training academies. This preparation training will allow candidates to strengthen their skills before starting the job. A second recommendation is for agencies to establish peer mentor teams. Mentors can provide a "softer touch" to assess how candidates are doing, alongside their FTOs and trainers who prepare them for the challenges ahead. Younger officers and candidates, particularly those with beta personalities, appreciate being asked how they feel, and they want support from their leadership. Solutions outside the agency could include implementing required mental wellness appointments. It is crucial to assess candidates' well-being throughout their careers with regular check-ins. Lastly, it is recommended that public safety agencies create peer support teams. Agencies with these teams in place often see a decrease in fitness-for-duty referrals for behavioral problems and suicidal ideation or attempts. Being proactive rather than reactive can lead to positive outcomes, including creating a better workplace culture, increasing retention, and attracting the right candidates for public safety agencies.

Fig. 14.1 Recommendations and best practices to support public safety agencies and candidates

Conclusion

Thousands of individuals apply to public safety agencies every year. Our preliminary research found many clinical and non-clinical trends and observations among current public safety candidates. The two trends we believe should be studied further are: (a) the increase in mental health concerns among current candidates; and (b) the uptrend in beta personalities. These two trends have both positive and negative implications for law enforcement. The recommendations provided in this chapter could help law enforcement agencies better support their employees and candidates. If administered, these practices can help build a supportive environment, which will not only better the workplace culture in terms of officer retention but will also strengthen the recruitment of candidates to these agencies.

References

American Psychiatric Association. (2022). Anxiety disorders. In *Diagnostic and statistical manual of mental disorders* (5th ed., text rev.). https://doi.org/10.1176/appi.books.9780890425787.x05_Anxiety_Disorders

American Psychological Association. (2019). *Survey: Americans becoming more open about mental health* [Press release]. https://www.apa.org/news/press/releases/2019/05/mental-health-survey

Bennett, P., Williams, Y., Page, N., Hood, K., Woollard, M., & Vetter, N. (2005). Associations between organizational and incident factors and emotional distress in emergency ambulance personnel. *British Journal of Clinical Psychology, 44*(2), 215–226. https://doi.org/10.1348/014466505x29639

Ben-Porath, Y. S., Fico, J. M., Hibler, N. S., Inwald, R., Kruml, J., & Roberts, M. R. (2011). Assessing the psychological suitability of candidates for law enforcement positions. *The Police Chief,* 64–70.

Berger, W., Coutinho, E. S., Figueira, I., Marques-Portella, C., Luz, M. P., Neylan, T. C., Marmar, C. R., & Mendlowicz, M. V. (2011). Rescuers at risk: A systematic review and meta-regression analysis of the worldwide current prevalence and correlates of PTSD in rescue workers. *Social Psychiatry and Psychiatric Epidemiology, 47*(6), 1001–1011. https://doi.org/10.1007/s00127-011-0408-2

Brantingham, P. J., Mohler, G., & MacDonald, J. (2022). Changes in public–Police cooperation following the murder of George Floyd. *PNAS Nexus, 1*(5), 189–200. https://doi.org/10.1093/pnasnexus/pgac189

Cochrane, R. E., Tett, R. P., & Vandecreek, L. (2003). Psychological testing and the selection of police officers: A national survey. *Criminal Justice and Behavior, 30*(5), 511–537. https://doi.org/10.1177/0093854803257241

Drew, J. M., & Martin, S. (2021). A national study of police mental health in the USA: Stigma, mental health and help-seeking behaviors. *Journal of Police and Criminal Psychology, 36*, 295–306. https://doi.org/10.1007/s11896-020-09424-9

Griffiths, J. (Host). (2022). 'Trust and inspire' over 'command and control': A conversation on authentic leadership with Stephen Covey [Video podcast episode]. In *Finding gravitas*.

Grupe, D. W. (2023). Mental health stigma and help-seeking intentions in police employees. *Journal of Community Safety and Well-Being, 8*(Suppl 1), S32–S39. https://doi.org/10.35502/jcswb.290

Hartley, T. A., Burchfiel, C. M., Fekedulegn, D., Andrew, M. E., & Violanti, J. M. (2011). Health disparities in police officers: Comparisons to the U.S. general population. *International Journal of Emergency Mental Health, 13*(4), 211–220.

Holzman, A., & Kirschner, M. (2003). Pre-employment psychological evaluations. *Law and Order, 51*(9), 85–87.

International Association of Chiefs of Police. (2020). *Pre-employment psychological evaluation guidelines.* Police Psychological Services Section. https://www.theiacp.org/resources/resolution-on-preemployment-psychological-evaluations

Johnson, Roberts, & Associates, Inc. (2024). *California Psychological Inventory (CPI).* JRA, INC. https://www.jra-assessment.com/cpi.html

Karch, T. (2024). *Playing the long game: Law enforcement recruitment.* Federal Bureau of Investigations. https://leb.fbi.gov/articles/featured-articles/playing-the-long-game-law-enforcement-recruitment

Lilly, Z. (2023). *Reducing the stigma surrounding mental health.* Federal Bureau of Investigations. https://leb.fbi.gov/articles/featured-articles/reducing-the-stigma-surrounding-mental-health

Marshall, R. E., Milligan-Saville, J. S., Steel, Z., Bryant, R. A., Mitchell, P. B., & Harvey, S. B. (2020). A prospective study of pre-employment psychological testing amongst police recruits. *Occupational Medicine, 70*(3), 162–168. https://doi.org/10.1093/occmed/kqaa008

Mitchell, C. L. (2020). Pre-employment psychological screening of police officer applicants. *Research Anthology on Rehabilitation Practices and Therapy,* 579–601. https://doi.org/10.4018/978-1-7998-3432-8.ch029

National Council for Mental Wellbeing. (2023). *Dismantling mental health stigma in public safety.* Mental Health First Aid. https://www.mentalhealthfirstaid.org/2023/08/dismantling-mental-health-stigma-in-publicsafety/#:~:text=A%20staggering%2090%25%20of%20police,as%20part%20of%20their%20jobs.

National Institute of Mental Health. (2024a). *Covid-19 and mental health.* U.S. Department of Health and Human Services, National Institute of Health. https://www.nimh.nih.gov/health/topics/covid-19-and-mental-health

National Institute of Mental Health. (2024b). *Mental illness.* U.S. Department of Health and Human Services, National Institute of Health. https://www.nimh.nih.gov/health/statistics/mental-illness

Newell, C. J., Ricciardelli, R., Czarnuch, S. M., & Martin, K. (2021). Police staff and mental health: Barriers and recommendations for improving help-seeking. *Police Practice and Research, 23*(1), 111–124. https://doi.org/10.1080/15614263.2021.1979398

NORA Public Safety Sector Council. (2019). *National occupational research agenda for public safety.* Center for Disease Control and Prevention. https://www.cdc.gov/nora/councils/pubsaf/pdfs/National_Occupational_Research_Agenda_for_Public_Safety_Feb_2019-508.pdf

North Carolina Association of Chiefs of Police. (2024). *North Carolina law enforcement – Performance & wellness funding grant.* Grant Information: North Carolina Association of Chiefs of Police. https://ncacp.org/grant-information

Petrie, K., Milligan-Saville, J., Gayed, A., Deady, M., Phelps, A., Dell, L., Forbes, D., Bryant, R. A., Calvo, R. A., Glozier, N., & Harvey, S. B. (2018). Prevalence of PTSD and common mental disorders amongst ambulance personnel: A systematic review and meta-analysis. *Social Psychiatry and Psychiatric Epidemiology, 53*(9), 897–909. https://doi.org/10.1007/s00127-018-1539-5

Police Executive Research Forum. (2021). *PERF Special Report*: Survey on police workforce trends. https://www.policeforum.org/workforcesurveyjune2021

Prizeman, K., McCabe, C., & Weinstein, N. (2024). Stigma and its impact on disclosure and mental health secrecy in young people with clinical depression symptoms: A qualitative analysis. *PLoS ONE, 19*(1), 1–22. https://doi.org/10.1371/journal.pone.0296221

Reaves, B. A. (2010). *Local police departments: 2007.* The U.S. Department of Justice, Office of Justice Programs, Bureau of Justice Statistics. https://bjs.ojp.gov/library/publications/local-police-departments-2007

Ricciardelli, R., Carleton, R. N., Mooney, T., & Cramm, H. (2018). "Playing the system": Structural factors potentiating mental health stigma, challenging awareness, and creating barriers to care for Canadian public safety personnel. *Health: An Interdisciplinary Journal for the Social Study of Health, Illness and Medicine, 24*(3), 259–278. https://doi.org/10.1177/1363459318800167

Roberts, M. D., Roberts, R., & Johnson, M. (2018). *CPI-434® Police and public safety selection report (CPI-434-PPSR): Technical manual* (2nd ed.). JRA, Inc.

Rüsch, N., Angermeyer, M. C., & Corrigan, P. W. (2005). Mental illness stigma: Concepts, consequences, and initiatives to reduce stigma. *European Psychiatry, 20*(8), 529–539. https://doi.org/10.1016/j.eurpsy.2005.04.004

Sadulski, J. (2024). *Why stress management skills are so important for police officers.* American Public University. https://www.apu.apus.edu/area-of-study/public-safety/resources/why-stress-management-skills-important-for-police-officers/#:~:text=Post-traumatic%20stress%20disorder%20(PTSD,due%20to%20stress%20in%20policing

Singhal, N. (2024). *Stigma, prejudice and discrimination against people with mental illness.* American Psychiatric Association. https://www.psychiatry.org/patients-families/stigma-and-discrimination

Stogner, J., Miller, B. L., & McLean, K. (2020). Police stress, mental health, and resiliency during the COVID-19 pandemic. *American Journal of Criminal Justice, 45*(4), 718–730. https://doi.org/10.1007/s12103-020-09548-y

The Myers-Briggs Company. (2024). *The California psychological inventory™ (CPI™).* https://www.themyersbriggs.com/en-US/Products-and-Services/CPI#:~:text=They%20tend%20to%20be%20seen,Resources

Tuckey, M. R., Winwood, P. C., & Dollard, M. F. (2011). Psychosocial culture and pathways to psychological injury within policing. *Police Practice and Research, 13*(3), 224–240. https://doi.org/10.1080/15614263.2011.574072

Vitro, C., Clark, D. A., Sherman, C., Heitzeg, M. M., & Hicks, B. M. (2022). Attitudes about police and race in the United States 2020–2021: Mean-level trends and associations with political attitudes, psychiatric problems, and COVID-19 outcomes. *PLoS ONE, 17*(7), 1–27. https://doi.org/10.1371/journal.pone.0271954

World Health Organization. (2022). *Covid-19 pandemic triggers 25% increase in prevalence of anxiety and depression worldwide.* https://www.who.int/news/item/02-03-2022-covid-19-pandemic-triggers-25-increase-in-prevalence-of-anxiety-and-depression-worldwide

Chapter 15
Clinician's Awareness Program: Training in Firefighter Culture for Mental Health Practitioners

Olivia Wallman and Dustin Hawkins

Clinician's Awareness Program: Training in Firefighter Culture for Mental Health Practitioners

Firefighters are routinely exposed to occupational stressors that place them at a high risk of developing stress and trauma reactions, including anxiety, depression, substance abuse, and posttraumatic stress disorder (PTSD) (e.g., Gibbs et al., 2023; Johnson et al., 2020). Critical incidents, in particular, can produce considerable distress and overwhelm a firefighter's coping skills (Everly & Mitchell, 2008). Moreover, it is typical for firefighters to experience numerous critical incidents over the course of their career; and these repeated exposures can negatively impact their mental health and overall well-being. Further, since serious (and often undiagnosed) mental health problems increase the risk for suicidal ideation, attempts, and completion (Martin et al., 2017; Stanley et al., 2015), it is imperative to conduct periodic culturally appropriate evaluations of firefighters' psychological adjustment to determine the possible need for prevention and intervention.

Illustrative of the research in this area is a study examining the consequences of repeated exposure to trauma that asked 341 firefighters about symptoms of PTSD, depression, and alcohol use disorder (Harvey et al., 2016). Thirteen percent reported moderate symptoms of PTSD and 11% indicated they were experiencing moderate symptoms of depression. When asked about alcohol use, 24% acknowledged unsafe drinking habits (i.e., consuming more than 20 alcoholic drinks per week). Firefighters who responded to more than 20 fatalities over the course of their career tended

O. Wallman (✉)
College of Psychology, Nova Southeastern University, Fort Lauderdale, FL, USA
e-mail: ow122@mynsu.nova.edu

D. Hawkins
Indian River County Fire Rescue Department, Vero Beach, FL, USA

V. B. Van Hasselt and M. L. Bourke (eds.), *Advances in First Responder Mental Health*, Advances in First Responder Mental Health 1,
https://doi.org/10.1007/978-3-032-27978-1_15

to endorse symptoms of PTSD and depression. In addition, the more fatalities the firefighters witnessed, the higher likelihood they were suffering from a mental health and co-occurring alcohol use disorder.

Jitnarin et al. (2022) studied rates of PTSD and other mental health comorbidities to ascertain occupational stressors associated with the former disorder. Participants included 624 male firefighters ranging in age from 21 to 65 years. About one-quarter of the sample were administrators or Chiefs; time in the fire service ranged from one to 44 years. Using the PTSD Checklist (Blanchard et al., 1996), Jitnarin et al. (2022) found that nearly 7% of the sample met PTSD diagnostic criteria. Firefighters who met criteria for PTSD also met criteria for at least one other mental health disorder, namely anxiety, depression, panic disorder, and alcohol use or dependence.

More recently, Gibbs et al. (2023) reported findings of the National Wellness Survey for Public Safety Personnel administered to 1210 firefighters across the United States to determine: (1) prevalence and severity of occupational stressors, anxiety, depression, PTSD, alcohol use, and suicidal ideation, (2) access to mental health resources, and (3) actual and perceived barriers to treatment. Findings indicated high levels of both occupational and individual stressors in the respondents. Results also revealed that about 40% of the firefighters experienced clinically significant levels of anxiety and depression. More than 10% were experiencing similar levels of PTSD at rates well beyond the general population. In addition to being at an increased risk for the development of mental health difficulties, firefighters often have expressed difficulty in accessing mental health services when they do reach out for help.

Case Example

Dustin Hawkins, a Firefighter/Lieutenant with Indian River County Fire Rescue, and co-author of this chapter, has been a firefighter for 23 years in Vero Beach, Florida. His story is pivotal in the development of the Clinician's Awareness Program. In May, 2014, while on duty on the agency's fire boat, a flash fire ignited in the bilge and he sustained second and third degree burns to his arms, neck, and face while working in a compartment below deck. He was flown to a local trauma center in Fort Pierce where his condition deteriorated, and he was air transported to Orlando Regional Burn Center. He survived and redefined his understanding of what pain truly is during the debridement and reconstructive grafting process. The amazing group of angels at Orlando Regional painstakingly worked to guide him and his family through the long recovery process. However, Dustin's journey to recovery quickly challenged him with difficulties he had not experienced before.

As he attempted to integrate his physical self back into the fire service, he was ignoring the dynamic effect his injury had caused to his psychological self. As the shifts wore on, he experienced the trauma of his burns each and every time his station tones would go off. He heard the sounds of his own screams during debridement, and actually felt the pain of his burns or the ignition sound of the flash fire the day he was burned, instead of the call for service. The occasional uneasy night turned into an incessant score of sleepless nightmares, because of the fear inside caused by re-living my pain every time he fell asleep. After seven months of this newfound suffering and feeling that he had to keep this problem hidden, he convinced himself that, "I can't let anyone know, they will think I am crazy, or a coward, and I can't do this job anymore."

After a seemingly endless cycle of spiritual torture and physical exhaustion, the call that breached his cumulative mental scar tissue had arrived. He responded to a structure fire call in his station's response area. He arrived on scene of what he thought was going to be a routine event but was intersected with the painful unseen injury that he had been ignoring. As he walked up the driveway with the entire crew and supporting law enforcement agency to assess the situation a young man came stumbling down the driveway with severe burns. The burn victim grabbed onto his arms and yelled "You have to help me! You don't know what this feels like!" As they helped him to the ground and his grip released, the skin on his hand came off and stuck to Dustin's skin grafts.

According to Dustin, at this moment time stopped, every sound disappeared, the dispatcher on the radio echoed and then vanished, and he turned his head away from the sight of this raw meat that was now stuck on his own scarred arm. He was alone and he did not mean this as a euphemism. What he saw at that moment confused him. It was just him; he could not see a single person around, no crew, no trucks, nothing, they were gone. The officer that was right next to him vanished. He thought, "Did I just lose my mind? Where is everyone? Why can't I hear anything?" What felt like hours to Dustin was most likely just a few seconds and as quickly as everything had "vanished" before his eyes all now came back as abruptly as a sledgehammer to his chest. With the exception of his hearing, the trucks and radios were just a muffled noise and all he could hear was "Hey, Dustin you, ok?" As he stared at the burnt flesh on his arm, he heard the question over and over again but could not answer it.

He slowly lifted his head to look back at the patient; he could feel the tears already running down his face. He was not prepared for what he was going to see. He no longer saw the young man who just a moment ago was sitting in front of him. What he saw was himself, in the charred uniform he was wearing the day he was burned, with hair singed to his head and skin hanging off of him. He described it as clear and vivid, as if he were staring in a mirror. It was even his voice yelling back at him, screaming "You don't know what this feels like!" The only words he could manage were, "Yes, yes I do."

He told the Lieutenant standing next to him that he was going to head inside to check for fire extension. He did not want anyone to see him falling apart. As he entered the house and closed the door behind him, the sound of the strike on the door jarred him and dropped him to his knees. Instead of the sound of a door latching, he heard the whooshing ignition sound of the fire that burned him. The same sound he heard every night hundreds of times over and over for the past seven months. There he knelt on the floor in full gear and cried. He is grateful for his brother who first recognized that he was not "ok"; it was his captain, who took him straight out of the scene and directly to his home and to his family.

He explained that the next few attempts toward healing were not seamless. He was given the number for their Employee Assistance Program (EAP) which he called immediately. He recognized that he needed help, and he needed it now! He couldn't stop crying.... "not even if you gave me a million dollars to stop for one second," he just could not do it. After a brief phone conversation with the counselor, and sharing with her the mental and emotional pain he had been experiencing, he received silence on the phone. He then asked, "Hello...are you there?"

The silence was broken on the other end of the phone by listening to tears being shed. All he had done was share his nightmares with the counselor. This response made him feel even more lost than ever. He was reaching out for help to the people he thought were the experts and now they were crying too. After being transferred to several counselors over four days with no improvement to his spirit, he received the news that the counselors could not see him anymore due to the fact his department was no longer a customer with them as an EAP provider.

He remembered clear as day, sitting on the porch exhausted, tired, and for the first time in his life, simply broken. After a few phone calls to his administration, he discovered that he was provided with an old EAP number from a service provider the department had not used in years. He was back at square one. With his phone in hand, he dialed and prayed for it to be the right number, or at least a counselor who would not cry when he shared the nightmares in his head. He realized that after being asked repeatedly each time he called within the first 30 seconds, "Do you feel like harming yourself or others?" That was starting to sound like a good idea. Never in his life had he been in such an isolated and dark place. The answers offered from the clinicians available were a mix of medication and sedation during the waiting period until they could get him help.

He was given the direction and support through his workers compensation and administration to find his own clinician, due to the fact there were no professionals within network capable of treating posttraumatic stress disorder (PTSD). Through his exhaustingly painful healing process he learned culturally competent clinicians are an imperative link in the resiliency chain; and, when paired with a proactive behavioral health access program they can be an invaluable component of a first responders post-traumatic growth trajectory. He is forever thankful to his family for finding him the help he needed. Over a long period of discovery and growth, he had been given the gift through painful perspective to change from a victim to a survivor.

Development of Clinician's Awareness Program

After experiencing his own challenges with mental health, Dustin felt it was time to bring PTSD and the effects on his career out of the darkness. Dustin explains, "Humans are not hardwired to continually immerse themselves in grief and death and be unscathed. The most unique aspects I have witnessed of firefighters as well as law enforcement officers is they have an entire conversation within the first five seconds of meeting each other without ever saying word. Because they instantly recognize that the other has experienced the same painful perspective."

Following the suicide of a fellow firefighter and close friend, Battalion Chief Jeremy Hurd and Retired Captain Larry Doelling with Palm Beach County Fire Rescue together with Lieutenant Dustin Hawkins developed CAP. Given that the target audience for the program is doctoral and master's level mental health clinicians, the course was later enhanced by UCF Restores to integrate clinician focused material and information.

Dustin acknowledged the need for the community to make a shift to provide appropriate and skilled mental wellness services for our firefighters and police officers. He felt this might be possible through implementation of statewide peer-to-peer support programs, as well as curriculum augmentation to better equip clinicians in the unique culture and treatment of PTSD in first responders. He recognized that a collaborative and accessible effort statewide would be the most effective approach toward healing and prevention. As firefighters, they utilize a unified incident command system across the country to standardize the dissemination of information, mitigate disasters and ultimately save lives. It is designed to efficiently and safely utilize all assets and tactics with repeatable results. Dustin questioned why the same type of approach to create a system to educate, protect, and heal the people who protect our community was not being utilized. Dustin believed that it was time to bring clinicians alongside them through the same training process to help foster a unified language and understanding of the unique culture pre-crisis.

Experiences like Dustin's draw awareness to the need for mental wellness professionals to be well versed in firefighter culture to facilitate the bond between the provider and responder in need. An empowering tool for firefighters and police officers alike is having trained peers who can recognize signs of emotional trauma early and refer to vetted clinicians.

Clinician's Awareness Program: Objectives

Given the challenges that firefighters encounter while seeking and obtaining mental health resources, the Clinician's Awareness Program (CAP) was designed to address and mitigate these challenges. Additionally, firefighters are an under-represented group in academic literature (Fraess-Phillips et al., 2017). Further, they are clearly a group that would benefit from mental health counselors having a better understanding of their unique work culture and the complexity of the firefighting profession (Gulliver et al., 2019; Johnson et al., 2020). As a result of repeated exposure to trauma and occupational stressors (i.e., physical strain, shift work that results in disrupted sleep schedules), firefighters experience an increased prevalence rate of a variety of psychological disorders as well as suicidality (Henderson et al., 2016; Johnson et al., 2020).

Not only does CAP provide education on firefighter culture, it also gives clinicians opportunities to participate in simulated experiences to facilitate further understanding of what a day could look like as a firefighter. The program utilizes guest speakers including both active and retired first responders, and real-life events to prepare clinicians for what they may hear from a firefighter. CAP has taken the initiative to "troubleshoot" the difficulties of finding a competent mental health provider through their respective EAP's. While the main objective is to improve cultural competence among clinicians, there are several secondary objectives that are addressed over the course of CAP.

CAP has initiated the "Redline Rescue Mission" in an attempt to combat the difficulties firefighters face when seeking help through their EAP's. Redline Rescue ensures that all clinicians have attended the two-day program and have also devoted 10 documented hours to participating in ride times. CAP provides the materials/ opportunities to assist in development of competent clinicians. The goal of the Redline Rescue is to also deploy vetted clinicians if there are large scale incidents. (Redline Rescue mission is discussed below in the "Clinical Applications" Section). Redline Rescue was developed on the foundation of connecting firefighters and their families to trained Peer providers and culturally competent clinicians in their times of need. The site is operated by University of Central Florida (UCF) Restores and was developed through collaboration with Florida Firefighters Safety and Health Collaborative. UCF Restores is a nonprofit clinical research center and treatment clinic established to change the way posttraumatic stress disorder (PTSD) and other trauma-related concerns are understood, diagnosed, and treated. The site currently collaborates with several other partners such as the Firefighter Peer Support Network, Bureau of Fire Standards and Training, Florida Fire Chiefs Association, and The second Alarm Project. Firefighters in need will be able to search for peer support providers on personal characteristics, physical location, and experience with a variety of stressors. For clinicians, first responders will be able to search based on physical location, insurances accepted, availability of a sliding fee scale, and areas of clinical expertise.

There are requirements to become a provider with Redline Rescue. Again, one may become a provider as a peer or a clinician. To become a peer provider, you will need to complete a recognized peer support training course (e.g., UCF REACT, IAFF, NOVA, Illinois, and North Carolina) and then provide information on areas in which you feel you can provide expertise. As for a clinician, one must complete the cultural competency workshop known as the clinician's awareness program. In addition to completing the workshop, one must complete a 10-hour ride-along at a fire rescue department.

Course Outline

The course is conducted over two days. Day one is mainly conducted in a classroom setting or online and the second day consists of an in person hands-on experience. The course is led and informed by several fire rescue personnel who volunteer their time.

Training Day 1

Firefighter Culture and Hierarchy

One of the main reasons for developing CAP was to educate civilians on firefighter culture. This culture is paramilitaristic (e.g., hierarchical structure of Captains and Lieutenants and clear lines of authority). This structure includes a strong organizational ideology that discourages questioning of traditional arrangements (Blau & Meyer, 1971). However, the incorporation of Emergency Medical Services (EMS) and Paramedic training has shifted toward encouraging or questioning traditional arrangements and practices as the practices are derived from a medical model (Lucas & Kline, 2008). Organizational change that alters the existing values within a culture and differentially affects groups within the organization can lead to resistance (Trader-Leigh, 2002). Considering the research on organizational change and the unique cultural differences discussed bridging the gap between mental health and the fire service requires extensive knowledge and flexibility on the clinician's side. Overall, CAP's mission is to address the resistance toward mental health, but at the same time making mental health professionals aware of their role in the resistance.

Although the occupational cultures are distinct, there are some similarities observed as well. Both occupations exhibit characteristics of a "hero" culture. The groups consist of individuals who approach situations that most persons would try to escape. Another characteristic of the "hero" culture is a sense of urgency; the need to "fix something and fix it now" (Lucas & Kline, 2008). Firefighters are trained to help others which may make it more difficult to reach out for help for themselves. They may not be looking for signs in themselves that could indicate they need help, or they may assume they can fix their problems on their own. Understanding this about fire rescue personnel aids in understanding their mentality. In a career that is solution-oriented/problem-solving, one can assume that their outlook on mental health may be similar. Therefore, if they are not able to solve their own mental health difficulties, they may experience increased symptoms before asking for help. The concept of a "rescue personality" is primarily attributed to the work of Mitchell et al. (1990). Mitchell and Bray (1990) use the term rescue personality as a way of describing characteristics of individuals who serve in the emergency services and describe emergency service workers as inner-directed, action oriented, obsessed with high standards of performance, traditional, socially conservative, easily bored, and highly dedicated. Mitchell (1988) also indicates that practitioners working with emergency service populations must be aware of "the unique personalities of emergency personnel and the special jobs they perform." This information surrounding personality traits is then supplemented with a video in which firefighters speak about their culture and "firefighter personality."

Communication and Shift Work

Language and unique work schedules are discussed next. Firefighter's use several acronyms and terms that differ from civilian language. CAP provides clinicians with a "Rosetta Stone" to help bridge this language gap. The Rosetta Stone is sent to clinicians in a PDF so the document can be saved and studied at any time. During the two-day CAP training, the Rosetta Stone is applied to facilitate learning and encourage clinicians to become familiar with certain terms. Terms included in the document include accelerant, call firefighter vs. career firefighter, engineer, SAR, etc. Knowing and using such language when working with fire personnel can build and strengthen the therapeutic alliance. On the other hand, a lack of awareness of such terms may impede the relationship leading the client to feel as though the whole session was devoted to explaining terms to the clinician.

In addition to being familiar with the language used among firefighters, it is imperative that clinicians develop an understanding of the schedule that firefighters keep and the effect this can have on their physical and mental health. CAP devotes a portion of the course to explaining the shift work employed in most fire departments. Career firefighters working 24-hour shifts are susceptible to increased risk of developing physical conditions such as hypertension and high blood pressure (Choi et al., 2016), and mental health conditions including insomnia and chronic stress. Cognitive functioning can also be affected by these factors. Chronic sleep disruption can lead to fatigue, resulting in decreased overall job performance and decision-making (Banks & Dinges, 2007). Neuropsychological testing also showed reaction time, processing speed, short-term visual memory, psychomotor speed, and visual-motor coordination are all affected by disrupted sleep and could potentially put a firefighter at risk for suboptimal performance or work accidents. In addition to its physiological effects, stress is associated with the development of depression and PTSD (Marin et al., 2011) among other mental health problems such as anxiety, PTSD, substance use, and suicide (Van Hasselt et al., 2021).

Moreover, shift work can adversely affect familial relationships. Career firefighters often work 24-hour shifts following 48 hours off. Firefighters are expected to use the time-off to recover from any sleep deficit, while balancing social, family, and home responsibilities (Watkins, 2021). Due to the nature of emergency response, they do not have holidays or weekends off. Many firefighters may work several holidays one year and none the next, depending on when their shift falls. This can be an adjustment for the family unit as firefighters may not be present for their children's birthdays, anniversaries, holidays, etc. While this can be accommodated, it requires support, flexibility, and understanding from the firefighter's family. For example, Watkins et al. (2021) found that spouses can help improve sleep of firefighters by creating opportunities for recuperative sleep at home. However, spouses also conveyed underlying tones of "resentment" relating to their firefighter being unavailable for emotional and instrumental support.

Trauma and PTSD

The next topic covered during Day One emphasizes exposure to trauma and development of PTSD. Firefighter's careers are unique and challenging in many ways. Recent research has been conducted on the effects of repeated trauma exposure on fire service personnel. The research indicates that firefighters experience several traumatic events throughout their careers, let alone on one shift (Kessler et al., 2017). Indeed, the general population is likely to experience an average of 3.2 traumatic events in their lifetime. Fire personnel may experience three or more traumatic events on a given shift. Consequently, it should not be surprising to a clinician when a firefighter describes a memorable call that contains details that may be "disturbing" to the civilian population.

Moreover, CAP provides examples of traumatic events that may be more likely to result in the development of PTSD. It is often the traumatic events that have personal meaning to the firefighter. For example, events involving children may exacerbate stress reactions of a firefighter who is also a parent. There is also an emphasis on compounded risk in firefighters as their exposure to multiple traumatic events over time makes it difficult to identify stress reactions related to a single event (Lewis-Schroeder et al., 2018).

The concept of "moral injury" is especially prevalent in firefighters and is discussed within the CAP curriculum. When firefighters are faced with repeated traumas, they may experience moral injury. While the term moral injury is not a mental health diagnosis, it is implicated in PTSD outcomes (Litz et al., 2009), and is even more likely a component that drives those suffering from PTSD to suicide (Bryan et al., 2014; Kerr, 2001; Nazarov et al., 2015). Moral injury includes the expression of shame, anger, inappropriate guilt, spiritual/existential conflict, loss of trust, and secondary symptoms of depression, anxiety, self-harm, and social alienation that manifest after witnessing or engaging in traumatic events that defy a person's sense of humanity (Jinkerson, 2016).

A problem arises when the clinician is caught off guard by such stories and recollections, and they allow their feelings of the event to be evident and influence the client. Therapists should take special care to recognize their strong emotional reactions to patient, both positive and negative; this is an opportunity to ask themselves how much of what the patient is processing matches the therapist's prior experiences or pre-existing opinions (Prasko et al., 2010). For example, a therapist who is not accustomed to working with individuals who have experienced severe trauma may not be aware that these experiences may bring up certain positive or negative feelings within themselves. Controlling such feelings is crucial to maintain the therapeutic alliance between clinician and client. A clinician who allows their emotions to overwhelm them (e.g., crying) while the client is explaining a trauma, may make the client feel uncomfortable and less likely to open up further in order to protect the clinician's emotions. This is an experience shared and communicated by many firefighters.

Firefighters relay their encounters in which mental health professionals have asked "What is the worst thing you've seen?" or repeatedly used statements such as, "I understand." In a career where there is a heavy stigma toward mental health, it is important for clinicians to be mindful of common mistakes that have deterred firefighters from seeking help in the past. CAP incorporates mental health professionals who have experience working with firefighters. They are there to provide insight on how they have adapted their therapeutic style to better suit those individuals.

CAP incorporates actual footage and audio from traumatic calls to which firefighters have responded. For example, program attendees are played audio from a fire in which a firefighter lost his air supply, was not able to get out of the fire, and subsequently died. Additionally, audio was played from a pediatric drowning call. While clinicians may not be able to be on scene during such traumatic events, the audio recordings and videos are able to capture the raw, unfiltered emotions and long-lasting effects associated with them. CAP also introduces attendees to firefighters in the area who are willing to take them on ride times for an in-person experience.

Special Population

During lunch break, a video is shown that draws attention to a special population within the firefighter community: retired firefighters. The research done on retired firefighters demonstrates significantly higher prevalence rates of many major psychological disorders than those found in the general population (Pepper et al., 2024). The research also finds that participants who were forced into retirement, those who felt financially unstable, and those who felt they did not have access to adequate, affordable, and comprehensive health insurance, all suffered from significantly worse overall psychological functioning (Pepper et al., 2024).

Prevention and Mitigation of Trauma

Firefighters experiencing a mental health problem are likely to want a solution as soon as possible in order to resume their jobs and lives that may have been affected. This finding and observations of firefighter mentality have resulted in the use of techniques derived from Solution-Focused Brief Therapy (De Shazer & Berg, 1997). These techniques can be seen in Critical Incident Stress Management (CISM) training employed following a traumatic event. When using Solution-Focused Crisis Intervention (SFCI), the emphasis on peer support changes from focusing on the trauma to building solutions for recovery through active listening, building strengths, and developing coping skills (Hopson & Kim, 2004). The SFCI approach is based on Solution Focused Brief Therapy (SFBT), which assumes that the client knows what works best and individuals are the experts of their own recovery (Hopson & Kim, 2004).

Critical Incident Stress Management (CISM) is usually led by a fellow firefighter or law enforcement officer. The foundation of CISM is to reinforce the shared beliefs and culture of the group. While mental health professionals and chaplains are often called to assist with the intervention, the original structure is designed around the importance of peer support. While many of the tools and interventions utilized in CISM groups are founded in psychotherapy, the delivery is deemed more effective by a peer. It is a form of psychological "first aid" (PFA). PFA has emerged as a mainstay for early psychological intervention with survivors of disasters and extreme events (Forbes et al., 2011; Ruzek et al., 2007). In simple terms, PFA includes the provision of information, comfort, emotional care, and instrumental support to those exposed to an extreme event, with assistance provided in a step-wise fashion tailored to the person's needs (Forbes et al., 2011).

Peer support has been defined as a program which incorporates specifically trained sworn or civilian colleagues, who are not counselors or therapists. It is designed to provide one-on-one emotional, social, or practical support and referrals to additional professional services when needed (International Association of Chiefs of Police, 2020). Illustrative is the Firefighter Intervention and Response Support Team (FIRST), FIRST was collaboratively developed by the Broward Sheriff's Office Fire Rescue and Emergency Services' Division of Health and Safety and Nova Southeastern University's College of Psychology, both in Fort Lauderdale, Florida (Henderson et al., 2018). Participants in FIRST receive training to address issues related to behavioral health that may be common or problematic among firefighters and referral resources for more significant clinical problems. An important aspect of being a FIRST member is the responsibility of team members to maintain the anonymity, trust, and confidentiality of their peer's seeking assistance (Henderson et al., 2018). For all participants, communications between a FIRST member and a fellow firefighter are considered confidential and privileged, except for matters that violate the law. Research has demonstrated that firefighters have a strong sense of in vs out-group. In and out-group theory describes the human tendency to categorize people into groups: an "in-group" (those we identify with) and an "out-group" (those we do not). This categorization can lead to biases, where we favor our in-group and view out-groups negatively, even if the groups are based on arbitrary distinctions. Five main themes emerged in a literature review on the interaction between peer support and post-traumatic growth: (1) peer support assists with processing of traumatic events, (2) peers provide support with organizational stressors, (3) social support increases the use of coping strategies, (4) active engagement with peers encourages growth, and (5) relational safety encourages disclosure by the trust within groups between groups (Donovan, 2022).

Behavioral Health Training (BHT; Steinkopf et al., 2016) has been implemented as a preventative strategy for firefighters. BHT was created to address the challenges firefighters and paramedics experience. BHT serves as a resource for firefighters through presentations that target stress, depression, substance use, PTSD, and suicide. Different visuals are used (e.g., videos) to express the severity of behavioral health issues. The stress presentation encompasses education on the physiological effects of stress and statistics on cardiac deaths in firefighters. In addition, this presentation includes myths about stress, different expressions of stress, and interventions that can aid in the reduction of stress. The topic of substance abuse typically includes discussion of terminology (dependence, tolerance, withdrawal); use vs. abuse; statistics (general population vs. firefighters); history of alcohol and drug use in the fire service; indicators of substance abuse; steroids; and gambling. A module on anxiety and PTSD includes definitions/signs and symptoms (panic disorder, generalized anxiety disorder, PTSD); causes and levels; impact of trauma exposures; symptoms of PTSD in firefighters; compassion fatigue/burnout; strategies to reduce risk; resiliency factors; and resources. The depression module includes definitions and types (e.g., major depressive, bipolar, and dysthymic disorders); myths and facts; signs and symptoms; risk and protective factors; depression in firefighters; gender differences; depression and suicide; the grief process; hopelessness and depression. Finally, a module on suicide prevention discusses national statistics; theories of suicide; risk and protective factors; role of social support; facts regarding suicide in the fire service; reasons for not seeking help (e.g., denial, anger, pride, fear, stigma, culture); warning signs/checklist; assessment (mood, behavior, events); verbal and nonverbal cues; prevention/intervention (e.g., taking action, questions to ask); resources are also given to help those who have suicidal thoughts, intent, or plans (Steinkopf et al., 2016).

Implementing Psychological Treatment for Trauma-Related Disorders

An overview of interventions for trauma-related disorders is provided. Evidence-based exposure therapies are traditionally utilized to treat PTSD. Exposure therapy is a psychological treatment that was developed to help people confront their fears (American Psychological Association, 2019). When people are fearful of something, they tend to avoid the feared objects, activities or situations as seen in individuals with PTSD. Although this avoidance might help reduce feelings of fear in the short term, over the long term it can make the fear become even worse; in the case of PTSD, the event may not be fully processed. In such situations, a psychologist might recommend a program of exposure therapy in order to help break the pattern of avoidance and fear. In this form of therapy, psychologists create a safe environment in which to "expose" individuals to the things they fear and avoid. The exposure to the feared objects, activities, or situations in a safe environment helps reduce fear, decrease avoidance, and guide emotional processing (American Psychological Association, 2017). These psychotherapies include cognitive behavioral therapy with a trauma focus (CBT-TF) (generic), cognitive processing therapy (CPT), cognitive therapy (CT), eye movement desensitization and reprocessing (EMDR), and prolonged exposure (PE) (Bisson & Olff, 2021).

Sleep interventions are also discussed as they relate to shift work and unique disruptions of circadian rhythms making first responders more susceptible to insomnia. Sleep hygiene skills outlined in Cognitive Behavioral Therapy for Insomnia (CBT-I) are reviewed. Anger management therapy is also presented as a common treatment as the research shows common signs of depression, anxiety, and PTSD in first responders are an increase in irritability and anger. Lastly, behavioral activation for depression is covered.

Options for treatment settings are discussed. Treatment settings ranging from standard outpatient to crisis situations are explored. The standard outpatient setting for mental health services typically involves visiting a therapist or counselor in a doctor's office, a clinic, or a hospital outpatient department. These visits are scheduled, and treatment can range from once a week to more frequent sessions, depending on the individual's needs. An Intensive Outpatient Program (IOP) is a type of mental healthcare that is considered one step up from traditional outpatient therapy where you see a therapist once or maybe twice a week in their office. An IOP is a program where you will likely be in therapy (both group and individual) somewhere between two to three hours a day, three to five days a week. Crisis situations on the other hand would typically involve inpatient or residential settings where the individual can receive more frequent monitoring and intensive care. Unique to first responder and military mental health is the concept of "field deployment." The term refers to providing mental health services outside of a traditional clinic or hospital setting, often during a crisis or in a remote area. These include, peer support groups, critical incident teams, or providing psychological first aid following critical incidents or natural disasters. To end Day One, an information video outlines a roadmap for clinicians operating within the Fire Service.

Training Day 2

On Day 2, the clinicians participate in a training simulation. The clinicians are expected to dress in full gear while navigating the simulation. One simulation involves clinicians utilizing full face positive pressure masks and working as a team to navigate a smoky and enclosed space to find and rescue a person. This simulation is designed to "put clinicians in the shoes" of fire rescue personnel specifically in a situation that requires fast thinking under pressure, maintaining composure, and working as a team in conditions that are frightening disorienting and dangerous to civilians.

Prior to engaging in the simulation, the clinicians are given a demonstration of what a scene of a "live burn" may look like. The example scene included a multi-story building that was on fire and there were several people and children inside. A unique aspect of the scene that many clinicians may not have thought about otherwise is the emotions and reactions of family who are fearing for their loved one's life. These individuals can be seen crying, screaming, running onto the scene, etc. Not only are fire rescue personnel intended to put out the fire and save lives they are simultaneously put in a position of comforting family members and keeping the scene workable.

A tour of a fire station is provided. The tour highlights the living quarters and the unique aspects of living in a firehouse. For example, waking up in the middle of the night to an alarm signaling a call and the importance of the kitchen as a place where firefighters often cook meals together. In addition to the inside of the station, participants are also given a tour of the rescue truck and the ambulance.

Clinical Applications

Attending and completing CAP has proven to be beneficial for both clinician's and firefighters. The program provides clinicians with a new perspective on how to apply their clinical skills with a unique population: firefighters. Based on the objectives of the program, clinicians have the opportunity to be providers through the organization's Redline Rescue mission with the completion of a few additional requirements. Not only will clinicians have this opportunity; they will also learn and develop skills that will make their addition to teams more appealing.

Once a clinician completes the workshop and ride time, they will be eligible to provide services through Redline Rescue and become a valuable asset to any fire department if they choose. CISM teams typically include a mental health professional. Completing CAP in addition to the Critical Incident Stress Management Training will increase a clinician's value to the department. The clinician is trained on how to organize and conduct debriefings and is culturally competent when discussing details of a critical incident. A clinician's role on a CISM team is invaluable as they will be able to provide brief psychotherapy or PFA and make direct referrals to other providers if necessary. One of the main objectives of the CAP is to increase cultural competence among clinicians who work with fire rescue personnel. Therefore, after a clinician completes the CAP they may look into joining a department's Employee Assistance Program (EAP).

On the other hand, attending CAP may provide clarity for some clinicians that they, in fact, do not want to work with fire rescue. This could be for a multitude of reasons. Clinicians may not adhere to a solution-focused approach which is not the only option but nonetheless an effective orientation to utilize when working with first responder populations. A clinician may not be comfortable with the degree of flexibility required to navigate relationships within this population. As mentioned previously, firefighter culture is founded on trust and shared experience. Some clinicians may not be comfortable utilizing an appropriate amount of self-disclosure to build such trust. A provider working with fire rescue may not have the luxury of working within an office, a provider may need to spend time at the station, or on calls addressing certain events related and unrelated to the job. There are several factors that can deter clinicians from seeking a career in fire rescue, and CAP provides participants with necessary information to make that decision. Either way, the clinician will leave CAP with a better understanding of the fire rescue field and its alignment with their own clinical orientation.

Future Directions and Research

The Clinician's Awareness Program provides opportunities for growth and research. While it provides the initial introduction to the cultural and occupational stressors of fire rescue, it is important to see how clinicians continue their involvement with fire rescue. For example, research could be conducted with past participants to determine whether they have continued to work with fire rescue personnel in other capacities (e.g., CISM team members, EAP providers, ride time participation). Clinicians may also benefit from continued education in the field to maintain their cultural competence. Attending training on new fire legislation, schooling, or policies may ensure that clinicians continue to provide culturally competent treatment.

Clinicians who are included in an EAP for fire rescue personnel might be required to complete the workshop and the ride time requirement. However, if a clinician is providing services for a whole city and not solely firefighters, the training may not seem necessary especially if their clientele is not largely composed of firefighters. Clinicians should always be trying to improve cultural competency to serve all members of an area; adding CAP will ensure this competency for not only fire rescue, but to a certain extent, aid in understanding cultural themes within law enforcement and military personnel.

To further bridge the gap between mental health professionals and firefighters, it may be beneficial to implement Behavioral Health Trainings with an emphasis on stress management within fire departments. Not only does this provide firefighters with practical skills they can use to regulate their stress response; it also exposes firefighters to mental health professionals outside of a therapeutic setting. Such training can be delivered at the departments' stations to increase convenience and attendance. Moreover, further data should be collected on diverse populations within the fire rescue profession. Most career firefighters are Caucasian males. While the current data are informative and applicable to most, it is difficult to apply findings to women or ethnically diverse individuals. It may be beneficial to identify a department located in an area that would have higher rates of minorities and women to gather data on trainings and behavioral health.

References

Banks, S., & Dinges, D. F. (2007). Behavioral and physiological consequences of sleep restriction. *Journal of Clinical Sleep Medicine: JCSM: Official Publication of the American Academy of Sleep Medicine, 3*(5), 519. https://doi.org/10.5664/jcsm.26918

Bisson, J. I., & Olff, M. (2021). Prevention and treatment of PTSD: The current evidence base. *European Journal of Psychotraumatology, 12*(1), 1824381. https://doi.org/10.1080/20008198.2020.1824381

Blanchard, E. B., Jones-Alexander, J., Buckley, T. C., & Forneris, C. A. (1996). Psychometric properties of the PTSD checklist (PCL). *Behaviour Research and Therapy, 34*(8), 669–673. https://doi.org/10.1016/0005-7967(96)00033-2

Blau, P., & Meyer, M. W. (1971). *Bureaucracy in modern society*. Random House.

Bryan, A. O., Bryan, C. J., Morrow, C. E., Etienne, N., & Ray-Sannerud, B. (2014). Moral injury, suicidal ideation, and suicide attempts in a military sample. *Traumatology, 20*(3), 154. https://doi.org/10.1037/h0099852

Choi, B., Schnall, P., & Dobson, M. (2016). Twenty-four-hour work shifts, increased job demands, and elevated blood pressure in professional firefighters. *International Archives of Occupational and Environmental Health, 89*, 1111–1125. https://doi.org/10.1007/s00420-016-1151-5

De Shazer, S., & Berg, I. K. (1997). 'What works?' Remarks on research aspects of solution-focused brief therapy. *Journal of Family Therapy, 19*(2), 121–124. https://doi.org/10.1111/1467-6427.00043

Donovan, N. (2022). Peer support facilitates post-traumatic growth in first responders: A literature review. *Trauma, 24*(4), 277–285. https://doi.org/10.1177/14604086221079441

Everly, G. S., & Mitchell, J. T. (2008). *Integrative crisis intervention and disaster mental health*. Chevron Publishing.

Forbes, D., Lewis, V., Varker, T., Phelps, A., O'Donnell, M., Wade, D. J., & Creamer, M. (2011). Psychological first aid following trauma: Implementation and evaluation framework for high-risk organizations. *Psychiatry: Interpersonal & Biological Processes, 74*(3), 224–239. https://doi.org/10.1521/psyc.2011.74.3.224

Fraess-Phillips, A., Wagner, S., & Harris, R. L. (2017). Firefighters and traumatic stress: A review. *International Journal of Emergency Services, 6*(1), 67–80. https://doi.org/10.1108/IJES-10-2016-0020

Gibbs, T. S., Bourke, M. L., Van Hasselt, V. B., & Black, R. A. (2023). *Professional firefighters: Findings from the National Wellness Survey for public safety personnel*. Unpublished manuscript, Nova Southeastern University. https://doi.org/10.1037/ser0000900

Guideline Development Panel for the Treatment of PTSD in Adults, & American Psychological Association. (2019). Summary of the clinical practice guideline for the treatment of posttraumatic stress disorder (PTSD) in adults. *The American Psychologist, 74*(5), 596–607. https://doi.org/10.1037/amp0000473

Gulliver, S. B., Pennington, M. L., Torres, V. A., Steffen, L. E., Mardikar, A., Leto, F., Ostiguy, W., Zimering, R. T., & Kimbrel, N. A. (2019). Behavioral health programs in fire service: Surveying access and preferences. *Psychological Services, 16*(2), 340–345. https://doi.org/10.1037/ser0000222

Harvey, S. B., Milligan-Saville, J. S., Paterson, H. M., Harkness, E. L., Marsh, A. M., Dobson, M., Kemp, R., & Bryant, R. A. (2016). The mental health of firefighters: An examination of the impact of repeated trauma exposure. *Australian and New Zealand Journal of Psychiatry, 50*(7), 649–658. https://doi.org/10.1177/0004867415615217

Henderson, S. N., Burns, A., Van Hasselt, V. B., Leduc, T. J. (2018, September). FIRST Response: The Firefighter Intervention and Response Support Team. *Fire Engineering*. https://digital.fireengineering.com/fireengineering/201809/MobilePagedArticle.action?articleId=1423594#articleId1423594

Hopson, L. M., & Kim, J. S. (2004). A solution-focused approach to crisis intervention with adolescents. *Journal of Evidence-Based Social Work, 1*(2–3), 93–110. https://doi.org/10.1300/J394v01n02_07

IACP. (2020). *Employee mental health and wellness*. International Association of Chiefs of Police. https://www.theiacp.org/sites/default/files/2020-05/Employee%20Mental%20Health%2005-06-2020.pdf

Jinkerson, J. D. (2016). Defining and assessing moral injury: A syndrome perspective. *Traumatology, 22*(2), 122–130. https://doi.org/10.1037/trm0000069

Jitnarin, N., Jahnke, S. A., Poston, W. S. C., Haddock, C. K., & Kaipust, C. M. (2022). Posttraumatic stress disorder (PTSD) and mental health comorbidity in firefighters. *Journal of Workplace Behavioral Health, 37*(3), 147–168. https://doi.org/10.1080/15555240.2022.2081172

Johnson, C. C., Vega, L., Kohalmi, A. L., Roth, J. C., Howell, B. R., & Van Hasselt, V. B. (2020). Enhancing mental health treatment for the firefighter population: Understanding fire culture, treatment barriers, practice implications, and research directions. *Professional Psychology: Research and Practice, 51*(3), 304–311. https://doi.org/10.1037/pro0000266

Kerr, L. K. (2001). Foucault and the care of the self: Educating for moral action and mental illness. *Philosophy of Education Yearbook*. ISSN: 8756–6575.

Kessler, R. C., Aguilar-Gaxiola, S., Alonso, J., Benjet, C., Bromet, E. J., Cardoso, G., Degenhardt, L., de Girolamo, G., Dinolova, R. V., Ferry, F., Florescu, S., Gureje, O., Haro, J. M., Huang, Y., Karam, E. G., Kawakami, N., Lee, S., Lepine, J. P., Levinson, D., Navarro-Mateu, F., & Koenen, K. C. (2017). Trauma and PTSD in the WHO world mental health surveys. *European Journal of Psychotraumatology, 8*(sup5), 1353383. https://doi.org/10.1080/20008198.2017.1353383

Lewis-Schroeder, N. F., Kieran, K., Murphy, B. L., Wolff, J. D., Robinson, M. A., & Kaufman, M. L. (2018). Conceptualization, assessment, and treatment of traumatic stress in first responders: A review of critical issues. *Harvard Review of Psychiatry, 26*(4), 216–227. https://doi.org/10.1097/HRP.0000000000000176

Litz, B. T., Stein, N., Delaney, E., Lebowitz, L., Nash, W. P., Silva, C., & Maguen, S. (2009). Moral injury and moral repair in war veterans: A preliminary model and intervention strategy. *Clinical Psychology Review, 29*(8), 695–706. https://doi.org/10.1016/j.cpr.2009.07.003

Lucas, C., & Kline, T. (2008). Understanding the influence of organizational culture and group dynamics on organizational change and learning. *The Learning Organization, 15*(3), 277–287. https://doi.org/10.1108/09696470810868882

Marin, M. F., Lord, C., Andrews, J., Juster, R. P., Sindi, S., Arsenault-Lapierre, G., Fiocco, A. J., & Lupien, S. J. (2011). Chronic stress, cognitive functioning and mental health. *Neurobiology of Learning and Memory, 96*(4), 583–595. https://doi.org/10.1016/j.nlm.2011.02.016

Martin, C. E., Tran, J. K., & Buser, S. J. (2017). Correlates of suicidality in firefighters/EMS personnel. *Journal of Affective Disorders, 208*, 177–183. https://doi.org/10.1016/j.jad.2016.08.078

Mitchell, J. T. (1988). Development and functions of a critical incident stress debriefing team. *Journal of Emergency Medical Service, 13*, 43–46. PMID: 10291126.

Mitchell, J. T., & Bray, G. P. (1990). *Emergency services stress: Guidelines for preserving the health and careers of emergency services personnel*. Prentice Hall. ISBN: 0893036870.

Nazarov, A., Jetly, R., McNeely, H., Kiang, M., Lanius, R., & McKinnon, M. C. (2015). Role of morality in the experience of guilt and shame within the armed forces. *Acta Psychiatrica Scandinavica, 132*(1), 4–19. https://doi.org/10.1111/acps.12406

Pepper, J. S., Van Hasselt, V. B., Black, R. A., & Schneider, B. A. (2024). Assessment of psychological functioning in retired firefighters. *Psychological Services, 21*(1), 120. https://nsuworks.nova.edu/cps_stuetd/148

Prasko, J., Diveky, T., Grambal, A., Kamaradova, D., Mozny, P., Sigmundova, Z., & Vyskocilova, J. (2010). Transference and countertransference in cognitive behavioral therapy. *Biomedical Papers, 154*(3), 189–197.

Ruzek, R. I., Brymer, M. J., Jacobs, A. K., Layne, C. M., Vemberg, E. M., & Watson, P. J. (2007). Psychological first aid. *Journal of Mental Health Counseling, 29*(1), 17–49. https://doi.org/10.17744/mehc.29.1.5racqxjueafabgwp

Stanley, I. H., Horn, M. A., Hagan, C. R., & Joiner, T. E. (2015). Career prevalence and correlates of suicidal thoughts and behaviors among firefighters. *Journal of Affective Disorders, 187*, 163–171. https://doi.org/10.1016/j.jad.2015.08.007

Steinkopf, B. L., Klinoff, V. A., Van Hasselt, V. B., Leduc, T. J., & Couwels, J. (2016). Behavioral health training for fire rescue personnel. *Fire Engineering, 169*(12), 59–67.

Trader-Leigh, K. E. (2002). Case study: Identifying resistance in managing change. *Journal of Organizational Change Management, 15*(2), 138–155. https://doi.org/10.1108/09534810210423044

Van Hasselt, V. B., Bourke, M. L., & Schuhmann, B. B. (2021). Firefighter stress and mental health: Introduction to the special issue. *Behavior Modification, 46*(2), 259–266. https://doi.org/10.1177/01454455211064955

Wagner, S. L., Martin, C. A., & McFee, J. A. (2009). Investigating the "rescue personality". *Traumatology, 15*(3), 5–12. https://doi.org/10.1177/1534765609338499

Watkins, S. L., Shannon, M. A., Hurtado, D. A., Shea, S. A., & Bowles, N. P. (2021). Interactions between home, work, and sleep among firefighters. *American Journal of Industrial Medicine, 64*(2), 137–148. https://doi.org/10.1002/ajim.23194

Chapter 16
Using Simulations, Games, and Apps to Support the Mental Health of First Responders

David Englert, Daniel Sachau, and Andi Lassiter

This chapter summarizes how simulations, games, and mobile applications (apps) can be used to improve the performance, engagement, and mental health of employees who work in emergency settings. More specifically, we describe how technology can increase motivation and workplace fun. We discuss how simulations, games, and apps can enhance training, and finally, we summarize ways technology can be used to supplement wellness and mental health initiatives.

A Short History from Simulations to Apps

Industry started using basic computer simulations in the 1940s (Mourtzis et al., 2014), but the use of simulations expanded dramatically in the 1970s, particularly in educational settings. An early researcher in this area, Clark C. Abt, labeled this expansion the *serious games movement* (Abt, 1970). This term refers to games and simulations developed for educational rather than entertainment purposes. For instance, the early computer game Oregon Trail (1971) was created to teach eighth-grade students about the harsh realities pioneers faced while traveling between Missouri and Oregon. Other notable developments in serious games included those used to teach flying (SFS1 Flight Simulator, 1979), driving military vehicles (Bradley Trainer, 1981), English (Reader Rabbit, 1984), geography (Where in the World is Carmen Sandiego? 1985), history (Civilization, 1991), and diabetes management (Captain Novolin, 1992).

D. Englert
USAF Special Operations Command, Hurlburt Field, FL, USA

D. Sachau (✉) · A. Lassiter
Minnesota State University, Mankato, MN, USA
e-mail: daniel.sachau@mnsu.edu

V. B. Van Hasselt and M. L. Bourke (eds.), *Advances in First Responder Mental Health*, Advances in First Responder Mental Health 1,
https://doi.org/10.1007/978-3-032-27978-1_16

By the early 2000s, marketers, instructors, and employers were finding they did not need to create full simulations or develop entire games to shape behavior. Instead, they could use elements of games such as points, leaderboards, and performance levels to affect learning, buying, and productivity. Nick Pelling (2011), a British computer programmer, coined the term *gamification t*o describe this partial application of game elements to non-game activities. The term gamification is a bit vague because it is difficult to identify elements that are part of every game. That said, most games include competition, a challenging goal, an uncertain outcome, a strategy to reach the goal, feedback indicating progress toward the goal (e.g., points, levels), and player control of the action. This is all performed within the boundaries of rules and a game setting (e.g., board, court, virtual world). Frankly, defining a game is like defining obscenity: As Supreme Court Justice Stewart wrote, it's hard to define, "but I know it when I see it." (Jacobellis v. Ohio, 1964, p. 378). On a less theoretical level, gamification in the workplace involves applying leaderboards, points, puzzles, bingo, trivia, avatars, hidden objects, word games, role-playing, arcade-style games, board games, card games, and casino-style games to learning and work activities.

Mobile applications, or apps, are programs developed primarily for mobile devices. The first mobile app was introduced in 1997 for the Nokia 6110 phone and was a variation of the arcade game Snake (1976). Mobile technology was advanced by the introduction of BlackBerry in 2002; however, apps took off when the iPhone was released in 2007 and the Apple App Store opened in 2008. When it launched, the Apple App Store offered 500 apps. As of 2024, there are 1.96 million apps available for download in the Apple App Store and 2.87 million apps available in the Google Play Store. Fifty percent of people open an app more than 11 times per day (Buildfire, 2024). It's tempting to say that apps are only the medium for simulations and gamification, however, gamification is integral to so many kinds of apps (and vice versa) that it is difficult to separate the game from the medium.

Do Simulations, Gamification, and Apps Facilitate Learning?

Literature reviews and meta-analyses show that simulations are useful for training across a variety of settings including medical (Cook, 2014; Mitchell & Ivimey-Cook, 2023), military (National Research Council, 1998), higher education (Chernikova et al., 2020), psychiatry (Piot et al., 2020), heavy equipment operation (Vahdatikhaki et al., 2019), flying (Hays et al., 1992), and driving (Martín-delosReyes et al., 2019) (see Table 16.1 for additional examples). The most effective simulations involve realism (i.e., fidelity), freedom to make choices, choices tied to outcomes, and outcomes rich in performance feedback. Further, good simulations are challenging with increasing levels of difficulty as the player's mastery progresses. Simulations provide players with multiple learning trials accompanied by low to zero costs for making mistakes.

There has been considerable research on the benefits of gamification. Meta-analyses of 78 education studies (Sailer & Homner, 2020; Yildirim & Sen, 2021)

Table 16.1 Simulation and gamification examples in various settings

Education	Health	Marketing	Workplace
A number of companies sell software that allows students to respond in the classroom to teacher-generated polls.	Apple's Fitbit (2007) tracks steps and provides owners with health stats.	McDonald's Monopoly (1987) game gave customers tokens that correspond with properties on a Monopoly board.	Employees earn badges for completing training programs and display them on the company's internal social media profile.
Jeopardy-style competitions are used to help students review for a test.	DietBet (2017) allows dieters to enter a competition and win money for losing weight.	eBay popularized the idea of "winning" an auction.	Augmented reality, like Pokémon Go (2016) is used to teach employees how to use machines.
Stornaway (2020) software allows teachers to create interactive adventure films that change depending on students' choices.	NordicTrack (2024) takes riders on virtual rides in scenic locations.	Delta airlines awards bronze, silver, and gold medallion status to frequent fliers.	Virtual reality headsets are used to teach fabricators how to weld.
	Mango health app (2020) reminds patients to take their meds and rewards them with coupons for doing so.		

and 16 exercise studies (Mazeas et al., 2022) show positive, modest benefits to using gamification to facilitate learning and adherence to exercise programs. Similarly, in a literature review of 25 studies of the gamification of employee training, Hamari et al. (2014) found that gamification, again, had positive, modest benefits, particularly when games were first introduced.

Because apps are relatively new, and many gamified training activities are on apps, it is difficult to disentangle the benefits of apps versus the benefits of games; however, the research is promising and generally supports the benefits of gamified apps for learning (Sailer & Homner, 2020). Such apps allow learners to proceed at their own pace and away from the workplace.

How Do Simulations, Games, and Apps Affect Employee Engagement?

We suggest there are three primary ways that simulations, apps, and games contribute to learning and behavioral change on the job: they contribute to a fun environment, they increase engagement/motivation, and they facilitate social connections. The following sections outline several examples and evidence from practice and research to describe the ways games contribute to employee engagement.

Contribute to a Fun Environment

Thanksgiving is a busy day for 911 dispatchers. There are frequent calls for traffic accidents (the days before and after the holiday are busy travel days), fires, cooking burns, cuts, heart attacks, and family violence. Job strain is compounded on Thanksgiving because most dispatchers would rather be at home with their families than at work. To make matters worse, dispatchers receive many nuisance calls on Thanksgiving; for example, the most common nuisance call is from a citizen who has waited too long to remove the turkey from the freezer and needs advice about how to defrost it.

One manager of a call center in a large Southeastern U.S. city dealt with the nuisance call problem by making light of it. He bought a large, frozen turkey and traditional side dishes and announced that whoever received the most calls about turkey preparation would win the prize dinner. Tracking turkey calls became a very popular game; instead of being upset, employees were more easily able to laugh off the interruption as they "ticked" calls on the turkey tally sheet.

After discussing the turkey game with employees, the manager realized that nuisance calls are not limited to holidays, but are daily distractions and sources of frustration. To help employees better tolerate calls throughout the year, the manager created Bingo cards for nuisance calls. The cards included squares for multiple calls about the same accident, false burglar alarms, unintentional calls, random dialing, questions about the exact time of day, directions to an event, or day for garbage pick-up, etc. There were three levels of Bingo. Once an employee filled in a card, he/she received the first level prize and a second card. The second card came with a slightly better prize, and the third card with the best prize. Employees did not compete but completed cards at their own leisure, allowing them to win all three prizes.

Games like Turkey Bingo can be used to create a fun environment at work. Researchers define workplace fun as playful social, interpersonal, or task activities at work that provide individuals with amusement, pleasure, or enjoyment (Ford et al., 2004; Lamm & Meeks, 2009). Workplace fun can involve a wide variety of activities including, among many others, foosball tables in the office, happy hour events, daily jokes, cooking classes, participation in charitable events, birthday parties, costume days, bring your pet to work day, and office Olympics. Developing job-specific games, such as Turkey Bingo, can promote workplace fun and improve employee engagement.

The benefits of workplace fun have been examined in hospitality (Chan, 2010; Choi et al., 2013; Tews et al., 2013, 2014; Tetteh et al., 2022), retail (Chan & Mak, 2016; Karl & Peluchette, 2006b), banking (Mousa, 2021), healthcare (Karl & Peluchette, 2006a), human resources (Ford et al., 2004) and customer service (Hammedi et al., 2021) settings. Across these studies, researchers find that efforts to create a fun workplace lead to modest improvements in employee engagement and job satisfaction (Becker & Tews, 2016; Chan & Mak, 2016; Choi et al., 2013; Ford et al., 2004; Karl & Peluchette, 2006a; Ruangkanjanases & Chen, 2019), attachment to the organization (Becker & Tews, 2016), hope, efficacy, resilience, optimism (Tetteh et al., 2022), wellbeing (Georganta & Montgomery, 2016), trust in management (Chan & Mak, 2016; Karl et al., 2005), service quality (Karl & Peluchette, 2006a, 2006b), lowered turnover intentions (Karl et al., 2008; Tetteh et al., 2022; Tews et al., 2014), applicant attraction (Tews et al., 2012), teamwork, creativity (Ford et al., 2004), and productivity (Choi et al., 2013; Ruangkanjanases & Chen, 2019; Tews et al., 2013).

Increase Motivation

Games are motivating for a variety of reasons. First, simulations and games cause players to attend to activities they might otherwise ignore. Second, games involve goal setting, include feedback toward those goals, and reward players for obtaining those goals (Armstrong & Landers, 2017). A long history of research on goal setting shows that goals can be an effective tool for managing employees (Latham & Locke, 2007). Third, games involve competition. The simple act of competing can increase both intrinsic and extrinsic motivation in the activity (Harackiewicz & Sansone, 1991; Sansone & Harackiewicz, 2000). Finally, successful performance on a game or simulation can increase perceived competence on the job which, in turn, will increase interest in the job (Deci & Ryan, 1985). For example, Lindquist et al. (2021) created a phone-based trivia game to train 212 emergency medical technicians on prehospital procedures. The game was composed of 12 weekly challenges, with each challenge containing 10 questions. The authors report most participants enjoyed the game and said it made them feel better prepared for their jobs.

Provide Social Connections

Competition, team games, and games played over social media platforms have an important social function—they connect the players. Whether it is a game like Turkey Bingo to make something fun out of nuisance calls for emergency responders, or leaderboards to create a *race-to-the-top* for salespeople, these activities help build a social network which is important in an era when more and more employees are working remotely. Games played with partners can also create accountability. For example, Chen et al. (2014) found that when pairs of exercisers used the *Healthy Together app* (2024), public goals and mutual encouragement helped people stick to walking regimes. In these ways, games can foster a sense of team cohesion and enhance organizational identity when employees compete against each other or work with teams from another organization (Rees et al., 2015; Sherif, 1956).

Simulations, Games, and Apps to Support Mental Health

In this section, we discuss how simulations, games, and apps have been used to promote wellness for employees who work specifically in frontline and first responder jobs.

Provide Distraction and Flow

Playing a game can provide a distraction from obsessive thoughts and intrusive memories. Butler et al. (2020) found that pairing a Tetris (1985) style game with therapy could help relieve combat-related PTSD symptoms. Similarly, Colder-Carras et al. (2018) found that playing video games could help veterans who were suffering from PTSD and drug problems by facilitating adaptive coping (e.g., distraction, control, symptom substitution); eudaimonic well-being (e.g., confidence, insight, role functioning); and socializing (e.g., participation, support, brotherhood) (p. 124).

Playing an engrossing game has effects beyond distraction and can lead to periods of flow/fascination (Csikszentmihalyi, 1975; Jin, 2012) which, in turn, can provide mental health benefits (Riva et al., 2016). For instance, Ley et al. (2017) worked with torture and war survivors who were experiencing PTSD symptoms. The authors treated patients with sport, dance, and movement therapy and found that providing periods of intense concentration (flow) in recreation could reduce some of the symptoms of PTSD, provide a distraction from illness-related thoughts, facilitate the feeling of being in the present *here and now*, and increase the experience of mastery/achievement.

Reframe Tragedy

Many health professionals use humor to relieve tension in a crisis (Kim et al., 2024). Dark humor is a specific kind of humor that mixes tragic and comic elements (McCreaddie & Wiggins, 2008). People in frontline and first responder jobs use dark humor to distance themselves from immediate threats and reduce feelings of anxiety and helplessness (Martin & Lefcourt, 1983). Dark humor also has a social identity function as the humor is shared within the group of people who experience tragedy. For example, crime scene technicians are exposed to disturbing sights every day. Over time, most technicians become accustomed to the work, but they often have trouble adjusting to novel or particularly gruesome crime scenes. In an effort to help technicians deal with the stress, one police department created a crime scene Bingo game. The game included squares corresponding to the various ways a technician might find a body. To an outsider, the game might seem callous, but technicians reported that one of the most disturbing elements of a call to a death scene is not knowing how they will find the body. The bingo game helped reduce dread by making light of it.

Set Reasonable Expectations

Simulations can provide a form of realistic job preview. That is, simulations can give job applicants realistic expectations for the nature and difficulties inherent in a job. Employees who have realistic expectations can more effectively use proactive coping strategies (Ślebarska & Soucek, 2020), which in turn, can increase well-being (Saks et al., 2011). Proactive coping strategies are actions taken to avoid or prepare for future stressors and include seeking social support as well as planning for difficulties and anticipating frustration (Aspinwall & Taylor, 1997).

One example of a game used to set reasonable expectations was America's Army (2002). This video game was developed as a recruiting tool for the U.S. armed forces. It allows players to explore various aspects of Army life such as working as a medic, firing weapons, driving a Humvee, etc. One goal of the game is to help prospective recruits decide whether the Army is a good match for the player's interests and abilities. Similarly, the public can sample the job of dispatcher by downloading 911 Operator (2017) or 911 Emergency Dispatcher (2024) games through the Google Play app. Players assume the role of an emergency communications operator and then dispatch police officers, paramedics, and firefighters to various emergencies. There are similar games for firefighters (e.g., Mission Chief (2022), Hazmat Response Training Simulator (2024)), emergency room technicians (e.g., Vital Signs (2020), Medical Shift (2024)), EMTs (e.g., Emergency Ambulance Simulator (2018), Ambulance 911 Simulator (2024)), and police officers (e.g., Police Simulator: Patrol Officer (2022)). Simulations are not perfect. Real soldiers, police, and firefighters do not respawn. Further, some games focus on the most exciting parts of a job rather than the most tedious. But simulations provide a partial preview of jobs and may help set realistic expectations.

Increase Perceived Competence

For those who are currently working in a job, games and simulators can increase employee competence. According to Deci and Ryan's Self-determination theory (Ryan & Deci, 2000), this has benefits for wellness. For example, several companies offer 911 simulators that can be used to train employees (e.g., 911Trainer.com (2024), 911 Simulators.com (2024)). These simulations involve live or simulated instructors calling the trainee with realistic emergencies. Trainees then direct calls to police, fire, and EMS. The simulations are run on desktop computers and include background noise, mapping, caller ID, multi-tasking, and multiple information channels (split-ear).

For EMTs, there are simulations of car accidents (Chodos et al., 2012) where participants rescue and transport victims to an emergency room. The *Realistic and Adaptive Interactive Learning System* (RAILS) (2024) is another simulation created to help first responders deal with radioactive materials (Winso et al., 2010). *Triage Trainer* (Knight et al., 2010), a card sorting game, helped trainees practice how they would sort victims in a mass casualty event. *MediSim* (Stansfield et al., 1998), was created to provide training for medics on the battlefield. The simulation includes sensors placed on the participant's body to provide input for a virtual avatar. BioSimvr (2019) (Stansfield et al., 2000) is a game in which participants deal with a hostage situation and biological weapons. Virtual reality (VR) technology is also being used to prepare first responders for mass casualty emergencies. Researchers at The Ohio State University, Wexner Medical Center (2023) have developed an immersive VR game where first responders can practice working in a subway bombing scenario. Participants can move around, interact with victims, and make life-saving decisions.

One of the most common purposes of using simulation and games in employment settings is for increasing job competence. There are many more examples of games that increase knowledge and skills for first responders. Lindquist et al. (2021) created a phone-based, trivia game to train 212 emergency medical technicians on prehospital procedures. The game was comprised of 12 weekly challenges, with each challenge containing 10 questions. The authors report that even though only about 12% of the EMTs stayed with the game all 12 weeks, most participants enjoyed the game and reported that it made them feel better prepared for their jobs.

Some universities have created realistic simulations of hospital settings to train nurses and physicians. For instance, Minnesota State University, Mankato has a floor in a campus classroom building that, for all practical purposes, looks like a hospital floor. The Nursing Simulation Center includes a reception desk, hospital beds, simulated patients (including some that can give birth), a surgery center, and many monitors. The center is used for one-on-one coaching to full-scale emergency response training simulations with police, ambulance drivers, nurses, and actors playing the role of patients.

As is evidenced by the popularity of the television show *CSI* (Bruckheimer et al., 2000–2015), the public is fascinated by the idea of crime scene investigations. A number of companies have created computer games around this concept including

Scene Investigators (2024) and CSI: Crime Scene (2003). These games give amateur investigators the chance to explore detailed scenarios. Traditionally, educators have created mock crime scenes to teach students the fundamentals of investigation. Over the last few years, researchers have been experimenting with the use of virtual reality technology to teach students such skills. Mayne and Green (2020) equipped learners with Oculus Quest headsets and asked them to investigate a living room crime scene. The authors found that participants enjoyed the simulation. They also found that after initial investment, VR is a cost-effective way to teach CSI. The use of VR has expanded quickly since this study.

Desensitize to Stressors

Simulations and games have also been developed with specific components to help individuals cope with stress. The United States Air Force used a virtual reality simulator to help returning veterans who were experiencing PTSD reacclimate to life at home. Airmen were placed in a virtual simulation of a traumatic experience they experienced in Iraq. Wearing VR headset and hand carrying a mock M16 rifle, Airmen would take a virtual walk through an Iraqi village. The participants stood on a platform equipped with a vibration pad that could create the feeling of passing vehicles and distant explosions. One of the more innovative aspects of the simulation was the use of a scent machine that would release common smells of villages (garbage burning, diesel exhaust, body odor). Once the simulation started, the Airman would talk through the experience with a psychologist in the lab. The hope was that over repeated sessions, the Airman's arousal response would become less intense and feel more controllable. This would desensitize the Airmen to unpleasant, even horrific memories (Hillman, 2009).

Similarly, virtual-reality exposure therapy (VRET) has been used to help people with claustrophobia, fear of driving, agoraphobia, and social anxiety. There are many other examples of virtual reality and augmented reality training solutions that can help with PTSD. One creative use of gamification is the *T2 Virtual PTSD Experience* (Holloway & Reger, 2013). The game is set in a virtual world (Second Life, 2003) and provides military personnel and their families with a chance to understand the causes, symptoms, and treatment of PTSD. Information about PTSD is embedded in the environment as players explore the virtual world.

Facilitate Peer Support

Peer support is help (advice, listening, and empathy) offered among people who share similar backgrounds, experiences, or disorders. Peer support has been shown to moderate the relationships between occupational stress and burnout among first responders (Foley & Ricciardelli, 2023). There are several examples of peer support apps that are appropriate for first responders. PeerConnect (2019) was designed to connect first responders with a peer supporter, anonymously and confidentially. Users can reach out to others in the peer support network when stressed. They receive regular peer support check-ins, including check-ins on important dates such as anniversaries of traumatic events. Foley and Ricciardelli (2023) found the app helped police, correctional workers, firefighters, paramedics, and public safety communications reduce the stigma around peer support use and to help raise awareness of wellness. Other apps, like CrewCare (2024), a mental health app for first responders, do not focus on peer support specifically but include a list of support team member contacts. Finding peer support is particularly a problem for those whose jobs involve working with the deceased. In response, one woman in the UK created a website called "Dead Meet" to help death professionals' find dates (Dead Meet, 2024).

Facilitate Mindfulness/Meditation

A literature review on the application of mindfulness interventions for police officers (Vadvilavičius et al., 2023) shows that these interventions can reduce police officers' stress and sleep problems, post-traumatic stress disorder (PTSD), negative affect, and burnout. For instance, Headspace (2024) (includes daily activities, lessons, meditations, and group sessions. Similar apps include Healthy Minds (2022) and Calm (2024).

Provide Biofeedback

Heart rate variability (HRV) is the change in the time intervals between heartbeats. There are now biofeedback techniques and apps that allow a person to watch his/her heart rate and variability on a computer monitor or mobile device. HRV therapy involves encouraging patients who are experiencing stress to visualize positive settings and synchronize their breathing to their heart rate. A meta-analysis of 24 studies demonstrated that HRV feedback appears to be an effective treatment for anxiety and stress (Goessel et al., 2017)

Military and law enforcement agencies are using the Stress Resilience Training System (SRTS) (2024) program that runs on an iPad and includes training about stress and resilience, training in a series of self-regulation techniques, and the use of heart rate variability (HRV) biofeedback. Users complete a series of progressively more challenging games that use stress resistance skills. Weltman et al. (2014) found the program helped police officers lower stress responses.

Rewire Neural Pathways

There has been a recent push to look more closely at the neural mechanisms behind learning to take advantage of how the brain learns best. *Neuroplasticity* is a broad term that describes the brain's ability to reorganize structurally and functionally. Regarding training, neuroplasticity refers to a methodology to build neural connections that prioritize perceptual patterns and drive habitual behaviors. As an example of neuroplasticity-based training, Preflex First (2024) was developed for law enforcement to help officers process information more efficiently and respond more appropriately, especially when under stress. This company developed short, two- to four-minute micro training exercises delivered to officers on portable devices like smartphones, tablets, and laptops. The micro training sessions did not just tell officers what to do but *showed* them what to do and had them practice repeatedly to build patterns and habits. The training improved officers' threat detection, critical thinking, problem-solving, use of force, emotional intelligence, resilience, and self-control.

Support Exercise

Exercise is good for mental health. Some police departments are using Garmin watches to help officers track exercise. Other departments use Nike Training Club (2024), a phone app that plans fitness workouts for 15, 30, and 45 minutes. Runkeeper (2024) is a phone app that utilizes GPS to track pace, distance, route, and time for running and walking. There are specialized apps to help recruits train to academy fitness standards. Volt (2024) is an app designed for police that personalizes training programs.

It is difficult to summarize all the possibilities of fitness application because as of 2024, there were 97,000 fitness and health apps for tablets and mobile devices (HealthWorks Collective, 2024). The apps can help people set goals, they provide fitness information, track performance, and reward goal attainment.

Track Sleep

Many jobs in emergency settings involve shift work and inconsistent schedules which disrupt sleep. A recent meta-analysis shows that 31% of first responders suffer from a sleep disorder (Huang et al., 2022). There is a growing number of apps to track sleep. For instance, Fitbit (2007) monitors heart rate and allows wearers to track how many hours and minutes they have slept. It also provides a sleep quality score. Sleep Cycle (2024) uses a phone's microphone to listen to sleep patterns (e.g., snoring, moving). Its alarm clock function wakes the user when they are in their lightest sleep cycle. Other useful sleep apps include *Medito* (2024), *Sleep Tracker* (2024), and *Sleep Watch* (2024).

Manage Depression

Literature reviews on using games and gamification for treating depression (Dewhirst et al., 2022; Fleming et al., 2014; 2017) are promising. In addition, meta-analyses show that mental health apps like *SuperBetter* (2024), *Space from Depression* (2024), and *Mood Gym* (2024), are effective in reducing depression symptoms (Firth et al., 2017; Six et al., 2021; Wahle et al., 2017). Across apps, it is difficult to tell which elements (e.g., points, leveling up.) contributed to the therapeutic effects. Some apps focus on mediation, some involve AI chatbots, and still others provide social connections with others who are facing depression. More research is needed to identify the specific elements of games that have the greatest effect on depression.

Manage Anxiety/Panic Attacks

There are a variety of apps that use distraction games, mood tracking, breathing exercises, and educational materials to help people manage anxiety. For instance, *ACTing Minds* (2022) is a game based on acceptance and commitment therapy (ACT) which focuses on building psychological processes such as acceptance, values identification, and recognizing thought patterns through cognitive defusion (Hayes & Pierson, 2005).

Limit Alcohol Use

Alcohol is both the cause and the effect of many mental health problems. *Sober Time* (2024) is an app to track sobriety goals and there are other apps designed to track sobriety streaks (number of days without a drink). Tracking the streak can help people maintain sobriety (Wray, 2022) and is an aspect of gamification that can help motivate individuals toward behavior change. Flaudias et al. (2020) found that a gamified training procedure on a touchpad could reduce attentional bias to alcohol for patients being treated for alcohol dependence.

We have presented an overview of how simulations, games, and apps have been used and are being used to support the mental health and well-being for individuals in highly stressful work environments. In the next section, we provide a psychologist's reflections on using gamification, simulations, and apps in military and law enforcement settings.

Reflections from the Field—David Englert

Very early in my journey as a psychologist, I attended a month-long training that combined small group discussions with a few large auditorium lectures each day. My small group was about a dozen of us, with several hundred in attendance for the lectures. To be honest, it was tedious and, frankly, boring. The very worst part was the few people who sought attention though asking what my group believed were silly or irrelevant questions. To our frustration, that usually extended our time in the lecture hall by 10 to 15 minutes each session as each of them felt the need to raise their hand.

To be clear, I was getting paid to be there. The physical environment was comfortable and my time there was limited to about eight hours each day. To say the worst part of this entire experience was a few attention seekers is to say I really did not have much to complain about. But we did. We dreaded the lectures. We knew they would be there, and it was almost physically painful as we awaited the inevitable. That is until one of my groupmates suggested a Bingo game—we each drew up our cards with the list of offenders, and eagerly attended the next lecture. It was nothing short of gleeful. The lectures were still boring and uninformative, but the last 10 to 15 minutes was delightfully entertaining. Very quietly, we cheered or groaned, depending on our card arrangement, as each of them stood to ask their questions. As the days went by, we adjusted their names strategically on our cards and found it to be a wonderful distraction.

Years later, while with a military law enforcement team in Iraq, the commander and I talked about complacency and boredom. When the team left the base, the biggest concerns were improvised explosive devices (IED) and ambushes. Both of which have telltale signs for which the team must constantly search. However, it is boring driving through the desert looking for random pieces of garbage, dirt that may be freshly dug, etc. Certainly, one would expect that a threat to your life is a big incentive to be on guard, but that increased anxiety persists for only so long.

Thinking back to my frustrating Bingo game, we drew up a list of all the indicators of danger along with a few other things one might commonly see, such as random lone goats, etc. The goal was to complete the entire list first, or to have the most possible that trip. Prizes were small but the bragging was incredible. As competitive as they all were, it turned a necessary but tedious burden into a competition that we were each desperate to win.

In the course of my career, I have found myself doing the same training session with many of the same people. As readers have likely found for themselves, it can be hard to maintain the same energy and enthusiasm once you have taught the same course over and over. In particular, a few of us were traveling to present a two-day long training. The travel, along with the repetition, meant it was getting harder and harder to be consistently energetic and enthused. Then I remembered an old Steve Martin movie, *Leap of Faith (*Pearce, 1992*)*. Like his character in the movie, I challenged each of my co-presenters to insert a random phrase that I gave them into their presentation, and they did the same for me. The goal was that it had to "make sense" so they could not just randomly say the phrase but had to build this unique, and always silly sentence, seamlessly into their talk—"death by shaved carrot" was a difficult one, but I am proud to say I pulled it off. Participant feedback was consistent that we were upbeat, we seemed to enjoy the topics, and we interacted well with each other.

After I retired from the military, I went to work as the first psychologist at a large metropolitan police department. As I went to the various units, I heard what almost all of us hear—the frustrations of their job. As I listened, it became apparent to me that what frustrated officers the most were also the things most likely to negatively impact their emotional health. It was not their boss or the dangers of the occupation as much as the various misery and sorrow that they encountered. Sometimes it was the small nuisances that just added up. I created a game for one group that addressed the nuisances and, for a second group, that addressed some of the grislier aspects of their job. My goal was the cognitive reframe to something more stress relieving and, if not "fun," then at least distracting. I found that it led to them coming back and talking more with their colleagues about their standing in our "game."

All mental health providers who work with first responders know their jobs entail encountering frequent gruesome scenes, sometimes daily. They also realize they are hesitant to talk about what they see. First, because they do not want to expose their family and friends to the ugly side of what they do, and second, because most in these occupations do not want to be seen as emotionally weak or unable to handle the realities of the job. The various games gave them the permission to share their experiences with coworkers in an acceptable format.

Over the course of the next year, I helped several different units in the police department create games to address both frustration and ease discomfort with disturbing scenes. The best part of this endeavor was when it grew beyond me as I found various units started their own competitions without me. While I don't work with that department any longer, I still regularly receive texts from some officers letting me know about their latest "win."

It's Not all Fun and Games

Simulation and gamification are not without their critics. One criticism is that not all employees find simulations and games enjoyable (Bogost, 2011, 2015). We imagine this is particularly true for introverts with social games, overloaded employees with long simulations, cynics with cutesy games, and the technologically-challenged with high-tech games. Of course, there is no way to please everyone.

Another criticism is that simulations and games have only modest effects on employee learning and engagement, especially when they are not implemented well. Gamification efforts have less profound effects than simulations, partly because gamified activities are not full games. When Pelling (2011) coined the term *gamification*, he made it "deliberately ugly" because he was not a fan of partial or incomplete application of game elements to an activity.

There are various ethical questions related to gamification which have not been fully answered. Should employees be encouraged to have fun when their clients are clearly not having fun? Crime Scene Bingo and Turkey Tally Sheets come to mind. Certainly, the games involve dark humor and may be therapeutic, but these games might not be well received by the public.

Another ethical question is, should first-person shooter games be used to treat patients? Etter et al. (2017) found many (41%) former and current military members play first-person shooter games. These games include realistic weapons, simulated injuries/deaths, and detailed combat scenes. There is evidence that the games might contribute to aggression (Colman & Gnanayutham, 2010). Further, although first-person shooter games can provide distraction, there is a chance that they might trigger PTSD for some individuals (Elliott et al., 2015). The net effect of playing the games has not yet been determined.

Conclusion

Simulations, gamification, and apps are evolving rapidly and show promise in strengthening the mental health of frontline employees, first responders, and military personnel. The success of these programs is supported by individual studies, meta-analyses, literature reviews, and the experiences of mental health professionals. Keeping up with the changes is difficult and it is hard to guess what Artificial Intelligence technology will bring. It should be noted that very few games or simulations are an effective substitute for therapy (Hoffmann et al., 2017); instead, these methodologies should augment therapy or therapeutic advice from trained professionals.

References

911 emergency dispatcher [Computer game]. (2024). Supersonic Studios.
911 operator [Computer game]. (2017). Games Operators.
911 simulators.com [Computer simulation]. (2024). 9–1-1 Simulators.com.
911trainer.com [Computer simulation]. (2024). 9–1-1 Trainer.
Abt, C. C. (1970). *Serious games*. Viking.
ACTing minds [Mobile application]. (2022). Google Play.
Ambulance 911 simulator [Computer game]. (2024). Grizzly Games.
America's army [Computer game]. (2002). U.S. Army.
Armstrong, M. B., & Landers, R. N. (2017). An evaluation of gamified training: Using narrative to improve reactions and learning. *Simulation & Gaming, 48*(4), 513–538. https://doi.org/10.1177/1046878117703749
Aspinwall, L. G., & Taylor, S. E. (1997). A stitch in time: Self-regulation and proactive coping. *Psychological Bulletin, 121*, 417–436. https://doi.org/10.1037/0033-2909.121.3.417

Becker, F. W., & Tews, M. J. (2016). Fun activities at work: Do they matter to hospitality employees? *Journal of Human Resources in Hospitality and Tourism, 15*(3), 279–296. https://doi.org/10.1080/15332845.2016.1147938

Biosimvr [Virtual reality simulator]. (2019). MedisimVR.

Bogost, I. (2011, August 8–9). *Gamification is bullshit* [Conference presentation]. For the Win: Serious Gamification.

Bogost, I. (2015). Why gamification is bullshit. In S. P. Walz & S. Deterding (Eds.), *The gameful world* (pp. 65–80). The MIT Press.

Bradley trainer [Computer game]. (1981). Atari.

Bruckheimer, J., Zuiker, A. E., & Peters, C. E. (Executive Producers). (2000–2015). *CSI: Crime Scene Investigation* [TV series}. CBS Productions; Jerry Bruckheimer Television.

Buildfire. (2024). *Mobile app download statistics & usage statistics.* https://buildfire.com/app-statistics/

Butler, O., Herr, K., Willmund, G., Gallinat, J., Kühn, S., & Zimmermann, P. (2020). Trauma, treatment and Tetris: Video gaming increases hippocampal volume in male patients with combat-related posttraumatic stress disorder. *Journal of Psychiatry Neuroscience, 45*, 279–287. https://doi.org/10.1503/jpn.1900274

Calm [Mobile application]. (2024). Calm.

Captain Novolin [Computer game]. (1992). Raya Systems.

Chan, S. C. H. (2010). Does workplace fun matter? Developing a usable typology of workplace fun in a qualitative study. *International Journal of Hospitality Management, 29*(4), 720–728. https://doi.org/10.1016/j.ijhm.2010.03.001

Chan, S. C. H., & Mak, W. (2016). Have you experienced fun in the workplace?: An empirical study of workplace fun, trust-in-management, and job satisfaction. *Journal of Chinese Human Resource Management, 7*(1), 27–38. https://doi.org/10.1108/JCHRM-03-2016-0002

Chen, Y., Zhang, J., & Pu, P. (2014). Exploring social accountability for pervasive fitness apps. In *Proceedings of the eighth international conference on Mobile ubiquitous computing, systems, services and technologies* (pp. 221–226).

Chernikova, O., Heitzmann, N., Stadler, M., Holzberger, D., Seidel, T., & Fischer, F. (2020). Simulation-based learning in higher education: A meta-analysis. *Review of Educational Research, 90*(4), 499–541.

Chodos, D., Gutierrez, L., & Stroulia, E. (2012). Creating healthcare training simulations in virtual worlds. *Proceedings of 2012 4th international workshop on software engineering in health care* (58–64). IEEE. https://doi.org/10.1109/SEHC.2012.6227008

Choi, Y. G., Kwon, J., & Kim, W. (2013). Effects of attitudes vs. experience of workplace fun on employee behaviors: Focused on generation Y in the hospitality industry. *International Journal of Contemporary Hospitality Management, 25*(3), 410–427.

Civilization [Computer game]. (1991). MicroProse.

Colder-Carras, M., Kalbarczyk, A., Wells, K., Banks, J., Kowert, R., Gillespie, C., & Latkin, C. (2018). Connection, meaning, and distraction: A qualitative study of video game play and mental health recovery in veterans treated for mental and/or behavioral health problems. *Social Science & Medicine, 216*, 124–132. https://doi.org/10.1016/j.socscimed.2018.08.044

Colman, J., & Gnanayutham, P. (2010). Ethical considerations when using video games as therapeutic tools. In P. Gnanayutham, H. Paredes, & I. Rekanos (Eds.), Proceedings of the 3rd international conference on software development for enhancing accessibility and fighting info-exclusion (pp. 69–76). (9789726699941). University of Trás-os-Montes and Alto Douro.

Cook, D. A. (2014). How much evidence does it take? A cumulative meta-analysis of outcomes of simulation-based education. *Medical Education, 48*(8), 750–760.

CrewCare [Mobile application]. (2024). Imagetrend.

CSI: Crime scene [Computer game]. (2003). Radical Entertainment, Ubi Soft.

Csikszentmihalyi, M. (1975). *Beyond boredom and anxiety: Experiencing flow in work and play.* Jossey-Bass.

Dead meet [Website]. (2024). www.dead-meet.com.

Deci, E. L., & Ryan, R. M. (1985). *Intrinsic motivation and self-determination in human behavior*. Plenum Press.
Dewhirst, A., Laugharne, R., & Shankar, R. (2022). Therapeutic use of serious games in mental health: Scoping review. *BJPsych Open, 8*(2), e37. https://doi.org/10.1192/bjo.2022.4
DietBet [Mobile application]. (2017). Burch Creative Capital.
Elliott, L., Golub, A., Price, M., & Bennett, A. (2015). More than just a game? Combat-themed gaming among recent veterans with posttraumatic stress disorder. *Games Health Journal, 4*(4), 271–277. https://doi.org/10.1089/g4h.2014.0104
Emergency ambulance simulator [Computer game]. (2018). SkisoSoft.
Etter, D., Kamen, C., Etter, K., & Gore-Felton, C. (2017). Modern warfare: Video game playing and posttraumatic symptoms in veterans. *Journal of Traumatic Stress, 30*, 182–185. https://doi.org/10.1002/jts.22172
Firth, J., Torous, J., Nicholas, J., Carney, R., Rosenbaum, S., & Sarris, J. (2017). Can smartphone mental health interventions reduce symptoms of anxiety? A meta-analysis of randomized controlled trials. *Journal of Affective Disorders, 218*, 15–22. https://doi.org/10.1016/j.jad.2017.04.046
Fitbit [Watch]. (2007). Apple.
Flaudias, V., Zerhouni, O., Chakroun-Baggioni, N., Pires, S., Schmitt, A., De Chazeron, I., Llorca, P. M., & Brousse, G. (2020). Reducing attentional bias in individuals with alcohol use disorders with a tablet application: A randomized controlled trial pilot study. *Alcohol and Alcoholism, 55*(1), 51–55. https://doi.org/10.1093/alcalc/agz080
Fleming, T. M., Bavin, L., Stasiak, K., Hermansson-Webb, E., Merry, S. N., Cheek, C., Lucassen, M., Lau, H. M., Pollmuller, B., & Hetrick, S. (2017). Serious games and gamification for mental health: Current status and promising directions. *Frontiers in Psychiatry, 7*, 215. https://doi.org/10.3389/fpsyt.2016.00215
Fleming, T. M., Cheek, C., Merry, S., Thabrew, H., Bridgman, H., Stasiak, K., Shepherd, M., Perry, Y., & Hetrick, S. (2014). Serious games for the treatment or prevention of depression: A systematic review. *Revista de Psicopatología y Psicología Clínica, 19*(3), 227–242. https://doi.org/10.5944/rppc.vol.19.num.3.2014.13904
Foley, G., & Ricciardelli, R. (2023). Views on the functionality and use of the PeerConnect app among public safety personnel: Qualitative analysis. *Journal of Medical Internet Research Formative Research, 7*, e46968. https://doi.org/10.2196/46968
Ford, R. C., Newstrom, J. W., & McLaughlin, F. S. (2004). Making workplace fun more functional. *Industrial and Commercial Training, 36*(3), 117–120. https://doi.org/10.1108/00197850410532131
Georganta, K., & Montgomery, A. (2016). Exploring fun as a job resource: The enhancing and protecting role of a key modern workplace factor. *International Journal of Applied Positive Psychology, 1*, 107–131. https://doi.org/10.1007/s41042-016-0002-7
Goessl, V. C., Curtiss, J. E., & Hofmann, S. G. (2017). The effect of heart rate variability biofeedback training on stress and anxiety: A meta-analysis. *Psychological Medicine, 47*, 2578–2586.
Hamari, J., Koivisto, J., & Sarsa, H. (2014, January 6–9). *Does gamification work?—A literature review of empirical studies on gamification* [Conference presentation]. 2014 47th Hawaii International Conference on System Sciences, Waikoloa, HI, United States.
Hammedi, W., Leclercq, T., Poncin, I., & Alkire (Née Nasr), L. (2021). Uncovering the dark side of gamification at work: Impacts on engagement and Well-being. *Journal of Business Research, 122*, 256–269. https://doi.org/10.1016/j.jbusres.2020.08.032
Harackiewicz, J. M., & Sansone, C. (1991). Goals and intrinsic motivation: You can get there from here. In M. L. Maehr & P. R. Pintrich (Eds.), *Advances in motivation and achievement: Goals and self-regulatory processes* (Vol. 7, pp. 21–49). JAI Press.
Hayes, S. C., & Pierson, H. (2005). Acceptance and commitment therapy. In A. Freeman, S. H. Felgoise, C. M. Nezu, A. M. Nezu, & M. A. Reinecke (Eds.), *Encyclopedia of cognitive behavior therapy*. Springer. https://doi.org/10.1007/0-306-48581-8_1

Hays, R., Jacobs, J., Prince, C., & Salas, E. (1992). Flight simulator training effectiveness: A meta-analysis. *Military Psychology, 4*, 63–74.

Hazmat response training simulator [Computer Simulation]. (2024). SimsUShare.

Headspace [Mobile application]. (2024). Headspace Health.

HealthWorks collective [Website]. (2024). https://www.healthworkscollective.com/mobile-medical-apps-a-game-changing-healthcare-innovation/

Healthy minds [Mobile application]. (2022). Healthy Minds Innovations.

Healthy together [Mobile application]. (2024). Healthy Together.

Hillman, V. (2009). *Virtual reality treatment speeds recovery from PTSD Air Mobility Command.* https://www.amc.af.mil/News/Article-Display/Article/147349/virtual-reality-treatment-speeds-recovery-from-ptsd/

Hoffmann, A., Christmann, C. A., & Bleser, G. (2017). Gamification in stress management apps: A critical app review. *Journal of Medical Internet Research Serious Games, 5*(2). https://doi.org/10.2196/games.7216

Holloway, K. M., & Reger, G. M. (2013). T2 virtual PTSD experience: A virtual worlds environment to educate service members and veterans about combat-related posttraumatic stress disorder. *International Journal of Human-Computer Interaction, 29*(9), 594–603. https://doi.org/10.1007/978-1-4899-2271-7

Huang, G., Lee, T. Y., Banda, K. J., Pien, L. C., Jen, H. J., Chen, R., Liu, D., Hsiao, S. T. S., & Chou, K. R. (2022). Prevalence of sleep disorders among first responders for medical emergencies: A meta-analysis. *Journal of Global Health, 12*, 04092. https://doi.org/10.7189/jogh.12.04092

Jacobellis v. Ohio. (1964). Jacobellis v. Ohio378 U.S. 184.

Jin, S.-A. A. (2012). Toward integrative models of flow: Effects of performance, skill, challenge, playfulness, and presence on flow in video games. *Journal of Broadcasting & Electronic Media, 56*(2), 169–186. https://doi.org/10.1080/08838151.2012.678516

Karl, K. A., & Peluchette, J. (2006a). Does workplace fun buffer the impact of emotional exhaustion on job dissatisfaction? A study of health care workers. *Journal of Behavioral and Applied Management, 7*(2), 128–141. https://doi.org/10.21818/001c.16553

Karl, K., & Peluchette, J. (2006b). How does workplace fun impact employee perceptions of customer service quality? *Journal of Leadership & Organizational Studies, 13*(2), 2–13. https://doi.org/10.1177/107179190701300202 01

Karl, K. A., Peluchette, J. V., & Hall, L. M. (2008). Give them something to smile about: A marketing strategy for recruiting and retaining volunteers. *Journal of Nonprofit & Public Sector Marketing, 20*(1), 71–96. https://doi.org/10.1080/10495140802165360

Karl, K., Peluchette, J., Hall, L. M., & Harland, L. (2005). Attitudes toward workplace fun: A three sector comparison. *Journal of Leadership & Organizational Studies, 12*(2), 1–17. https://doi.org/10.1177/107179190501200201

Kim, A., Luo, R., & Ng, L. (2024). A bite of dark chocolate? Black humour in mental health services. *Australasian Psychiatry, 32*(1), 68–73. https://doi.org/10.1177/10398562231222815

Knight, J. F., Carley, S., Tregunna, B., Jarvis, S., Smithies, R., de Freitas, S., Dunwell, I., & Mackway-Jones, K. (2010). Serious gaming technology in major incident triage training: A pragmatic controlled trial. *Resuscitation, 1175–1179.* https://doi.org/10.1016/j.resuscitation.2010.03.042

Lamm, E., & Meeks, M. D. (2009). Workplace fun: The moderating effects of generational differences. *Employee Relations, 31*(6), 613–631. https://doi.org/10.1108/01425450910991767

Latham, G. P., & Locke, E. A. (2007). New developments in and directions for goal-setting research. *European Psychologist, 12*(4), 290–300. https://doi.org/10.1027/1016-9040.12.4.290

Ley, C., Krammer, J., Lippert, D., & Barrio, M. R. (2017). Exploring flow in sport and exercise therapy with war and torture survivors. *Mental Health and Physical Activity, 12*, 83–932. https://doi.org/10.1016/j.mhpa.2017.03.002

Lindquist, B., Gaiha, S. M., Vasudevan, A., Dooher, S., Leggio, W., Mulkerin, W., Zozula, A., Strehlow, M., Sebok-Syer, S. S., & Mahadevan, S. V. (2021). Development and implementation of a novel web-based gaming application to enhance emergency medical technician knowledge

in low- and middle-income countries. *AEM Education and Training, 5*(3), e10602. https://doi.org/10.1002/aet2.10602
Mango health [Mobile application]. (2020). Mango Health.
Martin, R. A., & Lefcourt, H. M. (1983). Sense of humor as a moderator of the relation between stressors and moods. *Journal of Personality and Social Psychology, 45*, 1313–1324. https://doi.org/10.1037/0022-3514.45.6.1313
Martín-delosReyes, L. M., Jiménez-Mejías, E., Martínez-Ruiz, V., Moreno-Roldán, E., Molina-Soberanes, D., & Lardelli-Claret, P. (2019). Efficacy of training with driving simulators in improving safety in young novice or learner drivers: A systematic review. *Transportation Research Part F, Traffic Psychology and Behavior, 62*, 58–65. https://doi.org/10.1016/j.trf.2018.12.006
Mayne, R., & Green, H. (2020). Virtual reality for teaching and learning in crime scene investigation. *Science & Justice, 60*, 466–472. https://doi.org/10.1016/j.scijus.2020.07.006
Mazeas, A., Duclos, M., Pereira, B., & Chalabaev, A. (2022). Evaluating the effectiveness of gamification on physical activity: A systematic review and meta-analysis of randomized controlled trials. *Journal of Medical Internet Research, 24*(1), e26779. https://doi.org/10.2196/26779
McCreaddie, M., & Wiggins, S. (2008). The purpose and function of humour in health, health care and nursing: A narrative review. *Journal of Advanced Nursing, 61*(6), 584–595. https://doi.org/10.1111/j.1365-2648.2007.04548.x
McDonald's monopoly [Boardgame]. (1987). McDonald's/Parker Brothers.
Medical shift-Emergency room simulator [Computer game]. (2024). Aerosoft.
Medito: Meditation and wellness [Mobile application]. (2024). The Medito Foundation.
Mission chief [Mobile application]. (2022). SHPlay GmbH.
Mitchell, A. A., & Ivimey-Cook, E. R. (2023). Technology-enhanced simulation for healthcare professionals: A meta-analysis. *Frontiers in Medicine, 10*, 1149048. https://doi.org/10.3389/fmed.2023.1149048
Mood gym [Online therapy tool]. (2024). EhubHealth.
Mourtzis, D., Doukas, M., & Bernidaki, D. (2014). Simulation in manufacturing: Review and challenges. *Procedia CIRP, 25*, 213–229. https://doi.org/10.1016/j.procir.2014.10.032
Mousa, M. (2021). How workplace fun is experienced in the banking sector? A qualitative study. *Employee Relations, 43*(3), 687–703. https://doi.org/10.1108/ER-04-2020-0156
National Research Council. (1998). *Modeling human and organizational behavior: Application to military simulations*. The National Academies Press.
Nike training club [Mobile application]. (2024). Nike.
NordicTrack [Exercise Equipment]. (2024). NordicTrack Inc.
Oregon trail [Computer game]. (1971). Minnesota Educational Consortium.
Pearce, R. (Director). (1992). Leap of faith [Film]. Paramount Pictures.
PeerConnect [Mobile application]. (2019). First Response Mental Health.
Pelling, N. (2011). *The (short) prehistory of gamification*. https://nanodome.wordpress.com/2011/08/09/the-short-prehistory-of-gamification
Piot, M. A., Dechartres, A., Attoe, C., Jollant, F., Lemogne, C., Layat Burn, C., Rethans, J. J., Michelet, D., Cross, S., Billon, G., Guerrier, G., Tesniere, A., & Falissard, B. (2020). Simulation in psychiatry for medical doctors: A systematic review and meta-analysis. *Medical Education, 54*, 696–708. https://doi.org/10.1111/medu.14166
Pokémon go [Mobile application]. (2016). Niantic Nintendo.
Police simulator: Patrol officer [Computer game]. (2022). Aesir Interactive, Astragon Entertainment.
Preflex first training [Mobile application]. (2024). Cognitive Command Group, LLC.
Reader rabbit [Computer game]. (1984). Learning Company.
Realistic and adaptive interactive learning system (RAILS) [Computer simulation]. (2024). Spectral Labs.
Rees, T., Alexander Haslam, S., Coffee, P., & Lavallee, D. (2015). A social identity approach to sport psychology: Principles, practice, and prospects. *Sports Medicine, 45*(8), 1083–1096. https://doi.org/10.1007/s40279-015-0345-4

Riva, E., Freire, T., & Bassi, M. (2016). The flow experience in clinical settings: Applications in psychotherapy and mental health rehabilitation. In L. Harmat, F. Ø. Andersen, F. Ullén, J. Wright, & G. Sadlo (Eds.), *Flow experience: Empirical research and applications* (pp. 309–326). Springer International Publishing/Springer Nature. https://doi.org/10.1007/978-3-319-28634-1_19

Ruangkanjanases, A., & Chen, C. (2019). Attitude, job satisfaction, and task performance of Thai millennial employees toward workplace fun. *International Journal of Research in Business and Social Science, 8*(5), 113–122. https://doi.org/10.20525/ijrbs.v8i5.305

Runkeeper [Mobile application]. (2024). ASICS.

Ryan, R. M., & Deci, E. L. (2000). Self-determination theory and the facilitation of intrinsic motivation, social development, and Well-being. *American Psychologist, 55*(1), 68–78. https://doi.org/10.1037/0003-066X.55.1.68

Sailer, M., & Homner, L. (2020). The gamification of learning: A meta-analysis. *Educational Psychology Review, 32*(1), 77–112. https://doi.org/10.1007/s10648-019-09498-w

Saks, A. M., Gruman, J. A., & Cooper-Thomas, H. (2011). The neglected role of proactive behavior and outcomes in newcomer socialization. *Journal of Vocational Behavior, 79*(1), 36–46. https://doi.org/10.1016/j.jvb.2010.12.007

Sansone, C., & Harackiewicz, J. M. (2000). *Intrinsic and extrinsic motivation: The search for optimal motivation and performance*. Academic Press.

Scene investigators [Computer game]. (2024). EQ Studios.

Second life [Computer game]. (2003). Linden Lab.

SFS1 flight simulator [Computer game]. (1979). Sublogic.

Sherif, M. (1956). Experiments in group conflict. *Scientific American, 195*(5), 54–59. https://doi.org/10.1038/scientificamerican1156-54

Six, S. G., Byrne, K. A., Tibbett, T. P., & Pericot-Valverde, I. (2021). Examining the effectiveness of gamification in mental health apps for depression: Systematic review and meta-analysis. *JMIR Mental Health, 8*(11), e32199. https://doi.org/10.2196/32199

Ślebarska, K., & Soucek, R. (2020). Change of organizational newcomers' unmet expectations: Does proactive coping matter? *PLoS One, 15*(12), e02432343. https://doi.org/10.1371/journal.pone.0243234

Sleep cycle [Mobile application]. (2024). Sleep Cycle Inc.

Sleep tracker [Mobile application]. (2024). Leap Fitness Group.

Sleep watch [Mobile application]. (2024). Bodymatter Inc.

Snake [Arcade game]. (1976). Gremlin Industries.

Sober time—sobriety counter [Mobile application]. (2024). Sociosoftware LLC.

Space from depression [Online therapy tool]. (2024). Center for technology and behavioral health, Geisel school of medicine at Dartmouth college.

Stansfield, S., Shawver, D., & Sobel, A. (1998). MediSim: A prototype VR system for training medical first responders. In *IEEE 1998 virtual reality annual international symposium* (pp. 198–205). IEEE. https://doi.org/10.1109/VRAIS.1998.658490

Stansfield, S., Shawver, D., Sobel, A., Prasad, M., & Tapia, L. (2000). Design and implementation of a virtual reality system and its application to training medical first responders. *Presence: Teleoperators & Virtual Environments, 9*(6), 524–556. https://doi.org/10.1162/105474600300040376

Stornaway software. (2020). Stornaway.io.

Stress resilience training system (SRTS) [Mobile application]. (2024). Perceptronics Solutions.

SuperBetter [Mobile application]. (2024). SuperBetter LLC.

Tetris [Computer game]. (1985). Tetris Company.

Tetteh, S., Dei Mensah, R., Opata, C. N., & Mensah, C. N. (2022). Service employees' workplace fun and turnover intention: The influence of psychological capital and work engagement. *Management Research News, 45*(3), 363–380. https://doi.org/10.1108/MRR-12-2020-0768

Tews, M. J., Michel, J. W., & Allen, D. G. (2014). Fun and friends: The impact of workplace fun and constituent attachment on turnover in a hospitality context. *Human Relations, 67*(8), 923–946. https://doi.org/10.1177/0018726713508143

Tews, M. J., Michel, J. W., & Bartlett, A. (2012). The fundamental role of workplace fun in applicant attraction. *Journal of Leadership & Organizational Studies, 19*(1), 105–114. https://doi.org/10.1177/1548051811431828

Tews, M. J., Michel, J. W., & Stafford, K. (2013). Does fun pay? The impact of workplace fun on employee turnover and performance. *Cornell Hospitality Quarterly, 54*(4), 370–382. https://doi.org/10.1177/1938965513505355

The Ohio State University Wexner Medical Center. (2023). *Ohio State virtual reality technology prepares first responders for mass casualty events.* https://wexnermedical.osu.edu/mediaroom/pressreleaselisting/vr-disaster-response-training

Vadvilavičius, T., Varnagirytė, E., & Jarašiūnaitė-Fedosejeva, G. (2023). The effectiveness of mindfulness-based interventions for police officers' stress reduction: A systematic review. *Journal of Police and Criminal Psychology, 38*(2), 223–239. https://doi.org/10.1007/s11896-022-09570-2

Vahdatikhaki, F., Langroodi, A. K., Makarov, D., & Miller, S. R. (2019). Context-Realistic virtual reality-based training simulators for asphalt operations. *Proceedings of the 36th International Symposium on Automation and Robotics in Construction (ISARC).* https://doi.org/10.22260/ISARC2019/0010

Vital signs [Computer game]. (2020). Breakaway Games.

Volt [Mobile application]. (2024). Volt.

Wahle, F., Bollhalder, L., Kowatsch, T., & Fleisch, E. (2017). Toward the design of evidence-based mental health information systems for people with depression: A systematic literature review and meta-analysis. *Journal of Medical Internet Research, 9*(5), e191–e101. https://doi.org/10.2196/JMIR.7381

Weltman, G., Lamon, J., Freedy, E., & Chartrand, D. (2014). Police department personnel stress resilience training: An institutional case study. *Global Advances in Health and Medicine, 3*(2), 72–79. https://doi.org/10.7453/gahmj.2014.015

Where in the world is Carmen Sandiego? [Computer game]. (1985). Pharo Books.

Winso, J. H., Rolando, J. B., Knight, W. H., Ackermann, E. S., Wijekumar, V. J., & Yu, H. (2010). Integration of radiation transport models in an interactive video game to train law enforcement and first responders on preventative RAD/NUC detection (PRND) methods. *IEEE nuclear science symposium & medical imaging conference* (560–565). IEEE. https://doi.org/10.1109/NSSMIC.2010.5873823

Wray, T. B. (2022). Exploring whether addictions counselors recommend that their patients use websites, smartphone apps, or other digital health tools to help them in their recovery: Web-based survey. *JMIR Formative Research, 6*(6), e37008–e30078. https://doi.org/10.2196/37008

Yildirim, I., & Sen, S. (2021). The effects of gamification on students' academic achievement: A meta-analysis study. *Interactive Learning Environments, 29*(8), 1301–1318. https://doi.org/10.1080/10494820.2019.1636089

Chapter 17
The Right Stuff: How Clinicians Can Offer What First Responders Need

Colby Mills

This chapter is aimed at practitioners, and its focus is on how to provide therapy and other supportive services in an ethical, appropriate, and successful manner. The target audience is clinicians with solid therapeutic skills who are interested in working with first responders, or who are new to such work. Other resources exist for how to provide high-quality assessment services; this chapter is specific to providing supportive intervention[1] services because there is relatively less guidance on this topic. I make no pretense that this chapter is an authoritative guide on the subject: literal books have been written on the topic, albeit relatively few. This chapter is intended to complement, not compete with, those works. I hope that you will take away from this chapter facts and concepts that will help you think about whether this work is a good fit for you and, if so, how to succeed in it from both a clinical and practical standpoint.

A caveat for research-minded readers: this chapter is unique in that it leans somewhat more heavily on my professional experience and opinions than on the available research evidence. One important reason for this is the troubling lack of available research evidence! Another (possibly related) reason is the difficulty in quantifying certain aspects of this topic. I was unable to find research data quantifying the crucial importance of cultural competence, for example, and perhaps it is prohibitively difficult to quantify. I will do my best to clarify when my opinions have empirical support and when they are simply my opinions, in which case the reader is encouraged to take them with a grain or even an entire shaker of salt.

[1] The International Association of Chiefs of Police (IACP) has designated four domains of police psychology: the intervention domain includes psychotherapy and related clinical supportive services.

C. Mills (✉)
Mind Balance, LLC, Apex, USA
e-mail: colbymillsphd@gmail.com

V. B. Van Hasselt and M. L. Bourke (eds.), *Advances in First Responder Mental Health*, Advances in First Responder Mental Health 1,
https://doi.org/10.1007/978-3-032-27978-1_17

Clinicians are a unique supportive resource for first responders. There is some evidence that first responders seek out clinicians slightly more often than other supportive resources (Blalock et al., 2024). As health providers, clinicians can offer confidentiality protections not available to Peer Support and chaplains (e.g., HIPAA and 42 CFR). Among the supportive resources, clinicians are unique in their ability to diagnose and treat psychological injuries and mental illnesses when those arise. Clinicians also face unique drawbacks, including the stigma of going to see a "shrink" and the perception (often accurate) that we have not directly experienced their world, versus a Peer Support member who they know has firsthand experience.

Just as we do not necessarily know their world, first responders often make assumptions about "the doc" born of a lack of knowledge about our methods and our limits. Our expertise in the poorly understood field of psychology sometimes creates false impressions that we are also clairvoyants, psychics, and human lie detectors.[2] We are also often assumed to have expertise regarding psychiatric medications and other related medical knowledge, an assumption we must be careful not to feed. Public safety clinicians are sometimes described as unilaterally taking actions that in reality are in the sole power of commanders, such as removing someone from duty. Somewhat like the Wizard of Oz, a public safety clinician is a fallible expert who is assumed to be "great and powerful" by those who cannot see behind the curtain.

To avoid an Oz-like pretense, we must provide ongoing education to our public safety clients about both our competence and its limits. I would argue that, because we are in a position of power and trust (however un-magical), we carry certain responsibilities as well. Communities depend on first responders, and they carry the responsibility to remain worthy of that trust. Because those first responders sometimes depend on us, it is likewise incumbent on us to be forthright and trustworthy. What follows is a list of some of the qualities and skills clinicians need to have, or develop, to remain worthy of first responders' trust.

Cultural Competence

Cultural competence is crucial: clinicians cannot succeed in this specialty field without it. The American Psychological Association (APA) defines cultural competence as "the ability to understand, appreciate and interact with people from cultures or belief systems different from one's own" (DeAngelis, 2015). Cultural competence is a necessary, but not sufficient, component of being a high-quality public safety clinician: A clinician with an intimate knowledge of police culture, but limited crisis intervention skills, would not be in a good position to help a suicidal officer, for example.

Cultural competence is also a multifaceted concept. The domains of knowledge range from general knowledge of public safety culture, to the more specific and more

[2] Military personnel take it a step further, referring to mental health professionals as "wizards."

crucial knowledge of the subcultures within public safety (police culture, fire culture, etc.), to granular knowledge of the specific agency you serve or intend to serve.

Acquiring such knowledge is not a "one and done" achievement, but an ongoing process throughout the career. Agency cultures, public safety culture in general, and ethical guidelines all change over time, and our continuing education must go beyond acquiring enough CEs to satisfy our licensure boards. The gradual trend toward greater acceptance of behavioral health services within public safety is another example of change: that trend is unfolding differently in each branch of public safety and from one agency to the next.

Achieving and demonstrating cultural competence with any public safety population involves a combination of formal training, self-study, and practical experience. Formal training programs are becoming more popular in the United States, including curricula or specialty tracks within graduate programs, and an increasing number of stand-alone training programs. Many of the latter offer certification after completing the study program and passing an exam. Some of those, like the Cordico Clinician Certification (formerly the National Emergency Responder and Public Safety Certification), also require a ride-along or other experiential component.

Two professional organizations offer board certification or a diplomate in police psychology, though they are not easily or quickly attained. The Society for Police and Criminal Psychology (SPCP) offers a diplomate in police psychology that requires five years of postgraduate work in police psychology. The American Board of Professional Psychology (ABPP) offers board certification in Public Safety Psychology for candidates who can demonstrate at least 3,000 h of postgraduate work. In both cases, applicants must also submit written work samples and pass an examination.

Knowledge, Skills, and Abilities (KSAs) for a First Responder Clinician

There are several sets of guiding principles for police psychologists and other public safety clinicians. Among them are guidelines from the International Association of Chiefs of Police (IACP), the Fire Service Psychology Association (FSPA), and (for those conducting pre-employment evaluations) the California Commission on Peace Officer Standards and Training (POST). As the existing guidelines make clear, general competence as a clinician is necessary, but not sufficient, to serve public safety populations. Clinicians must possess unique knowledge, skills, and abilities as well. Below is a list of qualities, some obvious and some less so, that clinicians must have. Foremost among them is the ability to navigate ethical dilemmas, which often arise in a subtle or complex manner with this population.

Ethics: Principles and Pitfalls

Public safety work presents unique challenges to ethical principles, especially regarding confidentiality, professional boundaries, and multiple roles. To successfully navigate the challenges, clinicians must be clear both on their ethical requirements and on how to think through new, unanticipated situations as they arise. Below are some of the most common ethical issues clinicians must navigate.

Confidentiality

Confidentiality, while always paramount in clinical work, has perhaps even greater importance to the first responder population. Trust is an all-or-nothing issue to them: they can shift without warning from initial wariness to "the doc knows best" once you are considered trustworthy. Because they are fairly open with each other, it is not uncommon for them to breach their own confidentiality. When I worked in-house for a police department, I felt quietly horrified when officers left my office after a confidential session… and then loudly announced that to the major down the hall! The burden of confidentiality is on the clinician, and we must take precautions even beyond the laws (HIPAA, 42 CFR, state laws) and ethical principles that govern clinical work.

Confidentiality may present greater challenges to clinicians who work in-house (employed by or contracted full-time to a department). First responders, especially those who are referred or "voluntold" to see you by their commander, may offer to give you *carte blanche* to provide information within the agency. Our responsibility is to carefully educate them about their rights as well as the consequences of releasing (or declining to release) protected health information.

For example, clinicians are sometimes called out to check on first responders following a critical incident. This most often happens inside a station or other department building. Unless there are clear procedures in place, and knowledgeable commanders to enforce them, this can be a fairly chaotic environment and one in which confidentiality is easily breached. Unlike most clinical situations, your client list will be common knowledge, and supervisors and commanders may approach you in public spaces to ask you about the mental state of their personnel, albeit out of a keen interest in whether their people are doing okay. Practical considerations include: reserving a private office or room in which to meet with the officers, discussing confidentiality as part of gaining informed consent, and identifying one point of contact to whom to provide feedback (which needs to be as limited as possible).

Challenges to confidentiality can come from inside and outside a public safety agency. Internal challenges include administrative investigations,[3] concerned commanders, and curious peers. These are often informal and unexpected: your patient's colleague or supervisor might ask, "I know you see Bob, is he doing okay?" First responders often think nothing of sharing personal information with each other

[3] Commonly called Internal Affairs, Office of Professional Responsibility, etc.

in the break room or around the breakfast table (or to the major down the hall), and this can even include seeking therapy despite the remaining stigma around mental health "issues." Even when they breach their own confidentiality, of course, we must still preserve it.

Given the public scrutiny of first responders and the potential damage to their careers from a confidentiality breach, securing our records is a crucial aspect of confidentiality. Physical records need to be double-locked and stored offsite from the public safety agency. Protecting electronic records is no less important, of course, and public safety clinicians must use electronic health record systems with encryption that matches or exceeds HIPAA standards. The U.S. Department of Health and Human Services offers guidance concerning how to meet those standards, as well as how to address an electronic breach (U.S. Department of Health and Human Services, 2024). We must also be mindful of the Freedom of Information Act (FOIA) and how text messages, unsecured emails, and even the department printer might be subject to future FOIA requests. This is another area in which, even when our patients are cavalier about the risks, we must remain vigilant.

Professional Boundaries

This refers to two issues: boundaries of competence and interpersonal boundaries. The American Psychological Association has this to say regarding boundaries of competence:

> 2.01(a) Psychologists provide services, teach, and conduct research with populations and in areas only within the boundaries of their competence, based on their education, training, supervised experience, consultation, study, or professional experience (American Psychological Association, 2017)

The ethical codes governing social workers and other clinicians also address this issue. Whether you are an independent clinician in private practice or working for the public safety agency, you will often be on your own to determine where your competence starts and stops. As noted earlier, first responders and their commanders typically assume we can do anything related to mental health. We hold the responsibility to make thoughtful judgments and to provide plain-English education about what we can and cannot do. This is especially challenging when you are the only acceptable and qualified clinician who is readily available. Their trust in us, combined with our own compassionate desire to help them, can pull us beyond our boundaries; the best defense is continued self-assessment.

Interpersonal boundaries can also prove quite challenging. As discussed below, many first responders want to have a sense of the clinician as a person before they decide to extend trust. Therapists working with first responders feel pulled for a certain amount of self-disclosure in a way that is not present in other clinical settings. Professional codes of ethics are silent on the issue of self-disclosure, and many clinicians' only guiding principles are black-and-white assumptions that were drilled into us ("no self-disclosure!") as students and trainees. Two critical ethical principles to guide decisions about self-disclosure are beneficence (the good of the patient) and non-maleficence ("do no harm") (Gutheil, 2010). Once we have made a disclosure, we must assess its impact on the therapeutic relationship. If it appears that the disclosure has damaged the relationship, we take steps to address that with the patient and repair the damage.

Examples of self-disclosure go beyond intentional decisions to share information to include accidental and assumed self-disclosure. Accidental self-disclosure occurs when your patient, a highly trained observer, gleans information from your comments, your non-verbal signals, or even your office decor. I use the term *assumed self-disclosure* to refer to impressions first responders make about clinicians, whether or not there is evidence to support the assumption. Many first responders (particularly officers and firefighters) make assumptions about therapists' political beliefs, for example, even if we are careful to remain neutral on the subject. Even when self-disclosure was not intentional, we still carry the responsibility to assess the impact on the therapeutic relationship and discuss it with the patient as needed.

In my experience (time for that grain of salt), another potential ethical pitfall is more insidious and less clearly delineated by professional guidelines. As clinicians work more and more with first responders, we can start to overidentify with their culture. For a variety of reasons, we can gradually shift from being *alongside* them to thinking and speaking as if we are one *of* them. It takes patience and diligence to be accepted by first responders, and to finally be welcomed wholeheartedly into the public safety family can feel somewhat intoxicating for a clinician who has never served in uniform. Managing this ethical challenge depends on self-awareness and on finding other ways to meet our needs for connectedness and belonging. Failing to stay in our professional lane leads to a host of bad outcomes, including lost credibility and diminished clinical effectiveness.

Multiple Relationships

When working with or within public safety agencies, the issue of multiple relationships is one that must be navigated because it cannot practically be avoided. The APA Code of Ethics defines multiple relationships as taking place:

> …when a psychologist is in a professional role with a person and (1) at the same time is in another role with the same person, (2) at the same time is in a relationship with a person closely associated with or related to the person with whom the psychologist has the professional relationship, or (3) promises to enter into another relationship in the future with the person or a person closely associated with or related to the person.[4]

Clinicians who operate in small towns or rural areas are very familiar with both the unavoidable nature and the potential ethical dilemmas of multiple relationships. Public safety clinicians know that first responder communities are much like small towns, both regarding the sharing of information and the limited options for professional help. Examples of multiple relationships include:

---

[4] APA Code of Ethics, 3.05 (a).

- Intervening with an existing therapy patient after a critical incident (or vice versa)
- Serving on a committee or working on a project to which a therapy patient is assigned
- Being referred to a first responder for therapy whom you had screened as an applicant
- Consulting with a former therapy patient, now promoted to commander

To completely avoid multiple relationships, we would have to actually possess the clairvoyant and psychic powers sometimes attributed to us. Not only can they not be completely avoided, situations involving multiple relationships may actually establish or enhance your credibility with your client population. Consider the clinician who begins to get therapy referrals from a police department because she successfully intervened with its officers after a critical incident.

One of the best ways to navigate multiple relationships is to proactively discuss the possibilities with patients, both in our written informed consent forms and in conversation in the therapy room. When one relationship or role creates potential harm for a patient, we must address it with the patient as soon as possible. Dr. Jeni McCutcheon, an experienced police psychologist, has written an exceptionally helpful chapter on multiple relationships in police psychology, and one whose concepts can easily be adapted to other public safety cultures (McCutcheon, 2016).

Client and Payor

Sometimes referred to as the "who's the client" dilemma, this ethical issue arises from the multiple meanings of the word "client." We refer to the individuals we serve as clients, but we use the same word to refer to the agencies to whom we provide contracted services. This overlap can blur crucial distinctions between the obligations we have to our therapy patients and those we have to the public safety agencies for which we work. Regarding interventions, it may be more helpful to refer to individuals who are using our services as clients or patients, and refer to other entities as "payors" or "contracted agencies." The term payor refers to the person or entity paying for your services, which might be a public safety agency, an insurance company, or the patient himself.

Conflicts Between Ethics and Department Requests

In various forms, this ethical issue comes up very often in peer supervision groups and informal consultations among public safety clinicians. Agency commanders and directors (who employ you, either as a contractor or an employee) may ask you to:

- Release protected health information
- Provide clinical services outside your areas of competence
- Render psychological opinions about someone you have not examined
- Advise on operational situations (e.g., use of force) that conflict with your ethics

The APA Code of Ethics offers specific guidance about how to handle such situations when they arise:

> …psychologists clarify the nature of the conflict, make known their commitment to the Ethics Code, and take reasonable steps to resolve the conflict consistent with the General Principles and Ethical Standards of the Ethics Code. Under no circumstances may this standard be used to justify or defend violating human rights.[5]

An especially thorny variant of this issue regards requests for assessments or interventions that, while informal or called by other names, closely resemble fitness for duty evaluations (FFDEs). For the uninitiated, IACP defines a fitness for duty evaluation thus:

> A psychological FFDE is a formal, specialized examination of an incumbent employee that results from (1) objective evidence that the employee may be unable to safely or effectively perform a defined job and (2) a reasonable basis for believing that the cause may be attributable to a psychological condition or impairment (International Association of Chiefs of Police, 2018).

Like any formal evaluation, an FFDE must conform to the individual's rights under the Americans with Disabilities Act (ADA). IACP and other professional organizations, including the APA, offer detailed guidance about the parameters and process of an FFDE. Far less clear are the many instances in which you may be asked to evaluate someone's fitness in a more informal or less comprehensive manner. Some examples include:

- Being asked whether a first responder is ready to return to duty after a critical incident
- Being asked whether a police officer should be issued a replacement weapon after an officer-involved shooting[6]
- Mandatory annual evaluations for specialty personnel (e.g., SWAT, negotiators, or child exploitation investigators)

The theoretical distinctions between these assessments and an FFDE are, in practice, both small and subjective. They can become even smaller in hindsight, such as when a first responder alleges bias or malpractice or in the intense scrutiny and potential court involvement following the use of lethal force or in-custody death.

Here are two questions that may help in navigating any such request. First, *What is the purpose of the evaluation?* A wellness check, even when mandated, is typically focused on the first responder's well being, versus an intervention to assess his or her work performance. The second question is, *Who receives your conclusions?* If your professional opinions or feedback are to be disclosed to the agency, proceed with caution (and thorough informed consent). If your intervention is solely focused on the individual's well being, there is no need or reason to breach confidentiality. When conducting mandatory wellness checks, some agencies choose to monitor

[5] APA Code of Ethics, 1.03.

[6] The officer's firearm is taken as evidence; for both practical and psychological reasons, the department typically issues a replacement weapon.

attendance but nothing about the content of the appointment, including your conclusions or recommendations. These questions will also help sort through the ethics of interventions such as department-mandated treatment or disciplinary diversion.

Resolving Ethical Dilemmas

The first (and easily overlooked) step in resolving a dilemma is recognizing that one exists, and for this reason I recommend *slowing down* every time a new request is made of you, especially any request related to protected health information. Taking time to think it over and ask questions may be frustrating to first responders, for whom making quick decisions is a cultural norm, but will almost always be worthwhile. Once you have identified a dilemma, the 17-step decision making model from Pope and Vasquez (2016) is a good, comprehensive framework to translate what may be an intuitive "bad feeling" into a solution that can be articulated (and documented!). Seek consultation from peers and mentors as well; other experienced public safety clinicians are an invaluable resource. Finally, some professional liability insurance companies offer free ethical and legal consultations, albeit not specific to first responder culture.

Knowledge and Proficiency

Evidence Based Therapies

First responders often have to overcome significant individual and cultural obstacles to seek help; when they do, we bear a responsibility to offer them the most effective forms of treatment available. There is clear expert consensus for many mental illnesses on which psychotherapies have the best research support. Although there is relatively little research on treatment efficacy in first responder populations, military treatment guidelines are a close comparison. Joint consensus guidelines from the U.S. Department of Veterans Affairs and the U.S. Department of Defense offer clear recommendations to guide treatment for Major Depression, Posttraumatic Stress Disorder, and other conditions (U.S. Department of Veterans Affairs, 2024).

Risk Assessment and Intervention

Evidence strongly suggests that first responders are at more risk from themselves than from any other person, and that their suicide rate is higher than in the average population (Nissim et al., 2022; Violanti, 2010; Violanti et al., 2012). Most first responders have easy access to lethal means: police carry firearms on their hips, and EMS personnel ride with lethal drugs in the ambulance. First responders also may have a greater capability for suicide owing to a decreased fear of death (Chu et al., 2016). To properly serve this population, we must be able to continuously ask about risk issues in a calm, direct manner... and do our best to maintain that same demeanor when a patient endorses risk issues. Should a first responder endorse an imminent risk issue, effective safety planning involves a collaborative discussion between client and clinician, as well as the clinician's knowledge of culturally competent resources for the correct level of care (see next section). On the other hand, overreacting to passive suicidal ideation by pursuing an inpatient hospital admission may needlessly damage the therapeutic alliance (and your credibility).

Culturally Competent Levels of Care

Imagine that, despite your good clinical care, one of your first responder patients develops acute suicidal intent. The first question, of course, is: *Where do you send him or her?* First responders are more restricted in terms of acceptable options for inpatient treatment, intensive outpatient programs, etc. They are understandably unwilling to present at an emergency room that they frequent in their professional lives, for example. There are also few inpatient (or residential, IOP, etc.) programs that truly demonstrate cultural competence for first responders. Thus the second question is: *Where is your patient willing to go?* A successful clinician will cultivate a list of culturally competent programs so that, when crisis strikes, there are viable options to consider. For levels of care less intensive than inpatient, geography is less of an obstacle: many IOP and residential programs for first responders will arrange transportation from as far as several hundred miles away and across state lines.

Legal Knowledge

Public safety clinicians must maintain awareness of both relevant state and federal statutes, and also trends in case law, in order to stay ahead of potential pitfalls for themselves and their patients. A good place to start is the American Board of Professional Psychology, which maintains a "core legal knowledge" document with citations for important federal statutes and summaries of key legal cases such as *Garrity v. New Jersey* and *Brady v. Maryland* (Corey, 2012)

Important Abilities

Emotional Suppression and the Ability to "Hear It"

Sadly, most first responders have at least one "bad therapy" story to tell. Anecdotally, the most common bad experience they have is watching their new therapist become visibly upset while they are telling a trauma story (or simply describing a graphic event that is for them run-of-the-mill). When they "make the therapist cry," first responders shut down and withdraw. They rely on us to practice good emotional containment for them as they explore a distressing event: When we lapse, the trust that was tentative to begin with will quickly vanish. As lifelong rescuers and helpers, they also tend to be extremely vigilant for any sign that their "toxic material" might be doing emotional harm to someone else, including their therapist.

Again, the best defense is ongoing self-awareness. Squeamish clinicians may not be well suited for working with first responders. Those without a natural tolerance for graphic or morally disturbing material will ultimately serve themselves and first responders better by choosing a different specialty. Even experienced practitioners need to remain vigilant: There is a parallel process between first responders who suddenly struggle more with child-related calls when they become new parents... and clinicians who can have a corresponding vicarious reaction to hearing about those calls in session.

Public safety clinicians must be able to reliably maintain a "poker face" and temporarily suppress reactions of horror, disgust, and fear as their patients talk about disturbing calls or scenes. By doing so, we create a safe environment for them to process traumatic events, and we suggest by example that even the worst past events are now only memories, creating distress but not danger (we also mirror the first responders' struggle to maintain a calm demeanor in every operational situation). Finally, the potential for vicarious trauma requires us to practice aggressive self-care in order to remain healthy and effective.

Genuineness and Demeanor

First responder cultures place an extremely high value on being forthright,[7] and law enforcement officers in particular are highly attuned to any mismatch between one's words and demeanor. It is, therefore, no surprise that first responders expect us to be genuine and straightforward. And while we need not (indeed should not) abandon our professional demeanor, it is also helpful to be a bit more spontaneous and informal with them.

A sense of humor is another important intangible quality. The ability to "hear it" also extends to off-color or gallows humor, which for many first responders is a way to distance themselves from the darkness they absorb every shift. It is less important to initiate jokes and banter than it is to be able to receive them, ideally with a polite chuckle rather than pronounced disgust or horror. This has its limits, of course, and first responders usually react well to being redirected or gently called out for using humor to avoid or deflect.

[7] In North Carolina, honesty and "good moral character" are hiring requirements for law enforcement applicants (12 NCAC 09B).

Adaptability

I refer to "adaptability" as something of a catch-all term to include several important therapist behaviors. The distraction-filled, unpredictable world of a first responder can play havoc with our expectations about what a therapy session should be, especially when they have to see you while on shift or on call. They also sometimes must cancel appointments on short notice and cannot always notify us in advance. During the session, they will sometimes need to monitor their phone, radio, or work computer. Working with this population means accepting these distractions and interruptions—and being thoughtful about office policies regarding late cancellations and missed-appointment fees (first responders are generally also not independently wealthy). Finally, therapists must be comfortable with first responders carrying their "tools of the trade" into the therapy room: an officer in uniform needs his firearm with him as much as you need your notepad or laptop, and for the same basic reason.

Conclusion

Treating first responders offers rewards and challenges in equal measure; it is not work to which every clinician is suited. Strong clinical skills are necessary, but not sufficient, to properly serve this population that needs and deserves the best we can offer. The responsibility falls to us to make sure we have the necessary cultural competence, personal qualities, and ethical reasoning to both take the correct actions and explain our reasoning to clients and agency leaders who often understand little of our world. Acceptance and trust are hard-won from first responders; when they do invite us into the "family," we cannot lean in so far that we lose our objectivity or our professional identities.

References

American Psychological Association. (2017). Ethical principles of psychologists and code of conduct (2002, amended effective June 1, 2010, and January 1, 2017). https://www.apa.org/ethics/code

Blalock, J. R., Black, R. A., Bourke, M. L., & Van Hasselt, V. B. (2024). Emergency communication operators: Findings from the national wellness survey for public safety personnel. *Journal of Police and Criminal Psychology, 39*, 34–43.

Chu, C., Buchman-Schmitt, J. M., Hom, M. A., Stanley, I. H., & Joiner, T. E., Jr. (2016). A test of the interpersonal theory of suicide in a large sample of current firefighters. *Psychiatry Research, 240*, 26–33.

Corey, D. (2012, July 11). Core legal knowledge for the practice of police & public safety psychology. *American Board of Police and Public Safety Psychology.* https://abpp.org/wp-content/uploads/2022/07/Core-Legal-Knowledge-in-PPSP-050915.pdf

DeAngelis, T. (2015, March). *In search of cultural competence.* Monitor on Psychology. https://www.apa.org/monitor/2015/03/cultural-competence

Gutheil, T. G. (2010, May 18). Ethical aspects of self-disclosure in psychotherapy. *Psychiatric Times, 27*(5). https://www.psychiatrictimes.com/view/ethical-aspects-self-disclosure-psychotherapy

International Association of Chiefs of Police. (2018). *Fitness for duty evaluation guidelines*. https://www.theiacp.org/sites/default/files/Fitness%20for%20Duty%20Evaluation%20Guidelines%202018.pdf

McCutcheon, J. L. (2016). Multiple relationships in police psychology: Common, unavoidable, and navigable occurrences. In O. Zur (Ed.), *Multiple relationships in psychotherapy and counseling* (pp. 73–83). Routledge.

Nissim, H. S. B., Dill, J., Douglas, R., Johnson, O., & Folino, C. (2022, May). *The Ruderman White paper update on mental health of first responders*. Ruderman Family Foundation. https://rudermanfoundation.org/white_papers/the-ruderman-white-paper-update-on-mental-health-and-suicide-of-first-responders/.

Pope, K. S., & Vasquez, M. J. T. (2016). *Ethics in psychotherapy and counseling: A practical guide* (5th ed.). Wiley. (as cited in Pope, K. S., n.d.). https://kspope.com/memory/ethics.php

U.S. Department of Health and Human Services. (2024, October 24). *Cyber security guidance material*. https://www.hhs.gov/hipaa/for-professionals/security/guidance/cybersecurity/index.html

U. S. Department of Veterans Affairs. (2024, September 24). *VA/DOD clinical practice guidelines*. https://www.healthquality.va.gov/index.asp

Violanti, J. M. (2010). Police suicide: A national comparison with fire-fighter and military personnel. *Policing: An International Journal of Police Strategies & Management, 33*(2), 270–286.

Violanti, J. M., Mnatsakanova, A., Hartley, T. A., Andrew, M. E., & Burchfiel, C. M. (2012). Police suicide in small departments: A comparative analysis. *International Journal of Emergency Mental Health, 14*(3), 157.

Index

V. B. Van Hasselt and M. L. Bourke (eds.), *Advances in First Responder Mental Health*, Advances in First Responder Mental Health 1,
https://doi.org/10.1007/978-3-032-27978-1

S

T

V

GPSR Compliance

The European Union's (EU) General Product Safety Regulation (GPSR) is a set of rules that requires consumer products to be safe and our obligations to ensure this.

If you have any concerns about our products, you can contact us on ProductSafety@springernature.com

In case Publisher is established outside the EU, the EU authorized representative is:

Springer Nature Customer Service Center GmbH
Europaplatz 3
69115 Heidelberg, Germany

Batch number: 10732218

Printed by Printforce, the Netherlands